The mind and art of Calderón

Don Pedro Calderón de la Barca (1600–81) was, with Lope de Vega, the greatest exponent of the Spanish Golden Age drama. Professor Parker's essays, nine of them previously unpublished and the remaining sixteen substantially revised, are the fruits of a highly distinguished career spanning forty-five years. They provide a wide-ranging survey of Calderón's secular, three-act plays (*comedias*) through detailed analyses of individual works. The themes found in the plays are studied in relation to the background of ideas in seventeenth-century Spain and to the development of Calderón's own view of the intellectual life and the social, ethical and moral problems of this age.

From the tensions of Calderón's early family life and his intellectual struggle with the associated problems, the book passes to the wider tensions in the social and political life of his time, and concludes with a demonstration of how Calderón raises all these human problems onto a wide 'philosophical' level through his use of myths and symbols.

D PETRVS
CALDERON
DE
LABARCA.
Ætat.ſuæ.

QVID RETRIBVAM DOMINO. PRO OMNIBVS. QVÆRETRIBVIT MIHI?
Pſalm.115.

P. Villafranca, Sculptor Regius.
ſculpſit Matriti. 1676.

Portrait of Calderón from the 1677 edition of the Autos sacramentales, *reproduced by permission of the Syndics of Cambridge University Library*

The mind and art of Calderón

Essays on the *Comedias*

ALEXANDER A. PARKER

Professor Emeritus of the University of Texas at Austin and
Honorary Fellow of the Gonville and Caius College, Cambridge

Edited by Deborah Kong

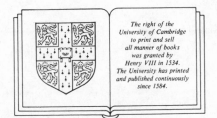

The right of the
University of Cambridge
to print and sell
all manner of books
was granted by
Henry VIII in 1534.
The University has printed
and published continuously
since 1584.

Cambridge University Press

Cambridge

New York   New Rochelle   Melbourne   Sydney

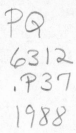

Published by the Press Syndicate of the University of Cambridge
The Pitt Building, Trumpington Street, Cambridge CB2 1RP
32 East 57th Street, New York, NY 10022, USA
10 Stamford Road, Oakleigh, Melbourne 3166, Australia

First published 1988

Printed in Great Britain at the University Press, Cambridge

British Library cataloguing in publication data

Parker, Alexander A. (Alexander Augustine)
The mind and art of Calderón: collected essays.
1. Drama in Spanish. Calderón de la Barca,
Pedro, 1600–1681. Critical studies
I. Title   II. Kong, Deborah
862′.3

Library of Congress cataloguing in publication data

Parker, Alexander Augustine.
The mind and art of Calderón.
Includes index.
1. Calderón de la Barca, Pedro, 1600–1681 –
Criticism and interpretation. I. Kong, Deborah.
II. Title.
PQ6312.P37 1988   862′.3   88–11851

ISBN 0 521 32334 7

O degli altri poeti onore e lume,
vagliami il lungo studio e'l grande amore
che m'ha fatto cercar lo tuo volume.

Divina Commedia, I, 82-4

Contents

Author's preface		*page* ix
Editor's preface		xiii
Introduction	Plays and playhouses	1
	Biographical outline	7

I   Stylistic and dramatic craftsmanship

1	Principles of interpretation	13
2	From metaphor to symbol	25
3	The dramatic structure of *El alcalde de Zalamea*	42
4	'Poetic truth' in the shaping of plots	51
5	The Coriolanus theme: *Las armas de la hermosura*	57

II   From experience to myth

6	The father–son conflict	69
7	Segismundo's tower: a Calderonian myth	86
8	Horoscopes and their fulfilment	96
9	Fate and human responsibility (1): the problem	107
10	Fate and human responsibility (2): a dramatic presentation – *El mayor monstruo los celos*	114

III   The tensions of social life

11	The functions of comedy	133
12	The vicissitudes of secrecy (1): *La dama duende, El galán fantasma*	143
13	The vicissitudes of secrecy (2): *El astrólogo fingido*	153
14	Secret betrothals and secret marriages: *El postrer duelo de España*	169
15	From comedy to tragedy: *No hay cosa como callar*	181
16	A Calderonian conception of tragedy: *El pintor de su deshonra*	196
17	The tragedy of honour: *El médico de su honra*	213

IV   **The tensions of public life**

18   The king as centre of political life   241
19   Religion and the state: *La cisma de Ingalaterra*   250
20   The issue of religious freedom   283
21   Religion and war: *El príncipe constante*   288
22   The drama as commentary on public affairs   312
    Las armas de la hermosura and the Catalan Rebellion
    (1640–52)   312
    Amar después de la muerte and the Morisco problem   315
    Historical allusions in *El alcalde de Zalamea*   320

V   **From symbol to myth**

23   The court drama   329
24   Mythology and humanism   340
25   The destiny of man   348

Epilogue   360

Notes   367
Index   410

Author's preface

My professional activity as a teacher covered the literature of the Spanish Golden Age and was spread over forty-five years from 1933 until my retirement in 1978. Calderón figured more prominently than any other Golden Age writer in my publications, beginning with my first book in 1943. Never my exclusive interest, he always remained the dominant one. It was my intention to dedicate the leisure that retirement would bring me to rounding off my critical interpretation of his drama by completing my study of his *comedias*, or plays for the public and palace theatres.

Rapidly deteriorating eyesight, however, left me within three years unable to read or write. Shortly before my retirement I announced my intention of writing a book with the title that the present one bears, and was granted a fellowship by the John Simon Guggenheim Memorial Foundation of New York for the furtherance of this project. Overtaken by partial blindness, I thought this could never be fulfilled, but when I found that I could complete another unfinished book that I had on the stocks by means of dictation and the help of readers, I realised that I had perhaps been too pessimistic. Nonetheless, the project I had had in mind seemed too vast to attempt in that way.

I saw a possible way out of my difficulty when the Cambridge University Press offered to publish my collected papers on Calderón, if I could find a suitable editor. I proposed adding to these some unpublished papers, working up some new topics from lecture notes, and rearranging the whole of this material in such a way as to cover a general survey of Calderón's development as a dramatist from first to last. The present book republishes all my Calderonian papers except two (on *El mágico prodigioso*, to be republished soon). They have been revised, in some cases with extensive additions, and with the new material have been placed in a consistent and, I hope, coherent context. The new material can be distinguished by the absence of a note referring to previous publication. Not all the plays here studied are those I would have selected had circumstances permitted, but I hope the selection is sufficiently representative of the dramatist's work.

This book has a further and more serious limitation in that my acquaintance with the work done on Calderón stops virtually around the centenary year of 1981, which saw so many new publications. It would have been impossible to attempt to keep abreast of developments. I therefore decided to make this book one man's view of Calderón evolved over a lifetime of teaching. The new material that has been added is based for the most part on notes that have been re-read to me. In order to fill in some gaps in the general survey I had some plays put on tapes and have incorporated my thoughts on these. I hope that those who have written on Calderón in recent years will not take my silence about their judgements on him to mean that I would not respect or value these judgements could I read them. This limitation also means that I have for the most part not tried to become familiar with new critical methods or new approaches to literature in general. Such development as there may be in my general approach to literature and my particular approach to Calderón will be development of the principles formed when I began to write, expanded as my experience of literature grew. To one man more than any other I owe my 'training'. He was never formally my teacher, nor was he even a Hispanist. Primarily a specialist in English literature, he was, when I first knew him, loosely attached to the *Scrutiny* group of English scholars and critics. He became Professor of English at the University of Fribourg and later worked for the British Council. He was the most brilliant linguist and had the widest literary culture and the finest critical mind that I have ever come into contact with. He was James Smith, and at the end of my career as a literary historian and critic I wish to place on record this tribute to his memory.

I am indebted to a number of people for help in the preparation of this book. First and foremost, I must express my gratitude to Michael Black and the Cambridge University Press for their interest in my work, it never having occurred to me that my Calderonian essays might be reprinted.

Very special thanks are also due to my editor, Deborah Kong, who after completing her Doctorate willingly agreed to undertake this task despite having in the meantime assumed the duties of wife and mother. My thanks must include her husband Leslie, who uncomplainingly looked after two small children while his wife came to help me at hours when all work is normally completed. Her work has consisted not only in rearranging and adding to published material but also in taking down new chapters from dictation. I have constantly strained her forbearance by demanding changes in work already done, insertions here, and deletions there, through all of which she not only found her way, but kept me on the right lines. I owe much also to her comments and suggestions.

From the moment I became unable to read and write my greatest support has been my friend and neighbour Denis Aliaga Kelly. He has read to me in English and Spanish, of which he has an excellent knowledge, and I dictated to him and he took down my notes on what he read. Another friend of long standing, William Cunningham, has read to me in French and German and also helped me to formulate notes on these readings. Frances Dorward gave me invaluable help by recording some of Calderón's plays on tape.

Francisco García Sarriá of Edinburgh University has also given invaluable help by obtaining books for me from libraries, as well as photostat copies of articles in periodicals.

Very special gratitude is due to Don Cruickshank of University College, Dublin. His Calderonian erudition has been freely placed at my disposal. No enquiry was ever too much trouble to be answered by return of post, often at length. James S. Cummins of University College London, is someone who also freely answered all my requests for help. Jennifer Lowe, of Edinburgh University, has done the same; all three of these friends willingly supplied me with photostat copies of research material. Where I have received help on a particular point this is acknowledged in the text.

A special debt of gratitude is due to Elaine Edgar, who uncomplainingly undertook the task of typing and carried it out so skilfully.

Though this book has serious limitations the help I have received from all these friends has been unlimited. I am more grateful to them than I can say.

January 1987   A. A. Parker

Editor's preface

In the writing and editing of this book we have acted upon certain suggestions made to us by Mr Michael Black of the Cambridge University Press. These suggestions were made in order that the book could appeal to a wider audience than a specialist one; so that anyone (for example, a student of European literature) with an interest in Calderón but with little or no knowledge of the Spanish language may read the book without being handicapped in any way.

The guidelines are as follows. Articles which were originally in Spanish have been translated into English. A note at the beginning of the relevant chapter notes indicates where this has been done. All quotations from secondary sources other than English ones have been translated without the original but with the reference given so that the reader may go to the source if he wishes. All titles of plays when first mentioned and citations of Calderón himself have been given first in Spanish and then paraphrased in English. The Spanish spelling, for the sake of consistency in the book, has been modernised where necessary; where this has been done, reference has been made to it.

A similar approach has been adopted with regard to the plays themselves and their context, so that people who did not have a chance to acquire this background knowledge should not be at a disadvantage. Therefore, the Introduction deals not only with a biographical outline of Calderón, but also with information about the types of play to be found in seventeenth-century Spain and their staging. In the body of the book the background to historical plays has often been outlined and a previous knowledge of history – of Henry VIII's break with the Church of Rome, and the Portuguese wars in North Africa, to take two examples – has not been taken for granted. This knowledge of history, as becomes clear in the book, is necessary to the interpretation of Calderón's historical plays. Similarly, the plots of some plays have been outlined where a knowledge of the plot is essential to the understanding of the arguments put forward in this book.

Finally, a note on the editions of Calderón's plays used here. It was obviously advisable that references to a single edition of Calderón's complete works should be given after each quotation in the text. The Aguilar edition in three volumes, edited by Ángel Valbuena Briones (vol. I, *Dramas*, vol. II, *Comedias*) and Ángel Valbuena Prat (vol. III, *Autos sacramentales*) is the one most widely used; but a problem arises here, which is that each new printing of this edition brings about a change in pagination. It was therefore decided to go back to the complete works in the *Biblioteca de autores españoles* (*BAE*) series, edited by Juan Hartzenbusch, 4 volumes, Madrid, and this is the edition referred to second after each quotation in square brackets. The reference given first in round brackets is, in most cases, to the edition used in the original article. References to the *autos sacramentales*, which are not included in the BAE edition, are to the Aguilar edition. There are occasional textual differences between the two references; where the differences are great, the reader's attention is drawn to them.

We have tried to implement these guidelines in such a way as to be truly useful to the non-Hispanist reader, feeling that we are justified in doing so for the sake both of widening the book's appeal and of introducing consistency in the form of the book. We trust that the expert will not find the additions too intrusive.

March 1987   D. A. Kong

Introduction

Plays and playhouses

The Spanish Drama of the Golden Age (sixteenth and seventeenth centuries) is one of the most important in world literature. In most respects it differs from other contemporary dramas, being most like the Elizabethan and most unlike the French. It grew out of the demand for popular entertainment in the streets and squares of the towns, and never became entertainment directed exclusively at an educated upper-class audience.

The plays are divided into three classes. The *auto sacramental* derived from the oldest tradition, representing the Liturgical, Miracle and Morality plays of the Middle Ages, a tradition which in Spain alone survived the classicising culture of the Renaissance and the religious turmoils of the Reformation. As in the rest of Europe these plays were open-air performances on the Feast of Corpus Christi. Around the middle of the sixteenth century they had become directly associated with the celebration of the Feast in the sense that they became connected with the theology of the Eucharist in the desire to bring the plays into direct relation to the purpose of the celebrations. Their connection with sacramental theology, which can be made in a variety of ways and through many different themes, made them 'Eucharistic Drama'. They were allegorical and symbolical plays performed on a fixed stage in a main square, round which were grouped carts on which were placed two-storey tower-like structures, containing painted scenery and symbolical figures. Each storey could open and close during performances, and the actors emerged from them and could re-enter them. This was a dramatic tradition and a religious festival that survived until 1765, when they were prohibited by government decree as being unsuitable in the Age of Enlightenment. This book will not deal with the *auto sacramental*, except in the last two chapters, when this tradition and the last stage of the Calderonian secular drama coincide in symbolical technique and a certain type of theme.[1]

There were two types of plays written for the public theatres: a three-act play, called *comedia*, and a one-act play, or interlude, called an *entremés*. The latter was a comedy or farce, written in prose and performed between the acts of *comedias*. In modern Spanish, the latter term means 'comedy', but in the Golden Age it meant any kind of stage-play more than one act in length. So characteristic is the structure and metrical form of Golden Age plays that *comedia* has become a technical term and is invariably used when referring to the drama of the late sixteenth and seventeenth centuries. There was no special term for comedy as such; comedies were distinguished descriptively, as will be explained in chapter 11. In addition to *tragedias*, there were *tragicomedias*, the last-named plays being at first tragedies with more than the average amount of comic relief; later the term was used of tragedies that did not fulfil the conventional requirements, by having middle-class persons or even peasants as protagonists, in other words with a social milieu not limited to the 'heroic'.

When its form was once established from about 1580, the *comedia* retained its essential structure and conventions until the emergence of neo-classicism in the middle of the eighteenth century. The formal structure was established by Lope Félix de Vega Carpio (1562–1635), called Lope de Vega, or simply Lope for short. A phenomenally prolific dramatist, he had a flair for sensing what the still unformed public taste would want the stage to offer. He rejected the various attempts that had been made to approximate Spanish plays to the dramas of Greece and Rome and refused to follow the neo-Aristotelian Italian dramatic theorists. He deliberately set out not to follow alien traditions but to write plays that reflected the impulsive temperament of his countrymen and that would so engage their interest as to keep them rooted to their places for the two-and-a-half hours of a theatrical entertainment. The five classical acts were replaced by three, on the straightforward principle of a Beginning, Middle, and End. Thus the first act would, so to speak, place all the cards on the table by introducing the characters, with their aims and intentions, their sympathies and antipathies, indicating the potential clashes between them. Act II would develop the conflicts arising from the clash of temperaments and intentions. Act III would bring the conflict to a crisis and provide the solution (the Spanish word *desenlace* has the same literal meaning as *dénouement*, an 'untying').

A feature of the *comedia* was its polymetrical structure. Nearly every metre (and by this is meant not only scansion but also stanza forms with blank verse, rhyme or assonance) made its appearance in a *comedia* on the general principle that the metres should convey the particular tone required by the action and the dominant emotion of particular scenes. This polymetrical structure is unique to the Spanish *comedia*. Lope suggested the metres that would be most appropriate to particular scenes, but did not conform his practice to any consistent patterns. Variety and flexibility characterised his poetic diction as much as they did the structure of his plots. There was thus no fixed dramatic metre; all the verse forms of literary tradition could be utilised – epic, ballad and folk-song with their assonance, as well as the more 'cultured' verse-forms adopted from Italy at the Renaissance, with their sometimes complicated rhyme-schemes. Even the Petrarchan sonnet could be employed (regularly used as Lope recommended, for a soliloquy representing a break between scenes). In the Lope period plots tended to be crowded. There was no unity of plot; a sub-plot was frequent, sometimes even two. As the *comedia* developed to maturity, sub-plots became closely connected with the main plot in theme, this being particularly characteristic of Calderón, in whose plays unity of theme instead of plot is a universal feature. The unity of action was thus not observed; neither were the unities of time and place. In *Don Quixote*, Part I, chapter 48, Cervantes delivers an attack on Lope de Vega for failing to uphold the principles of literary art and pandering to uneducated taste, the non-observance of the unities being the main grounds for condemnation. Cerventes' own plays, however, did not hold the stage, and before the end of his life he was breaking the unities himself, recognising that times had changed and that fashions had changed with them.

For plots, Lope turned to practically every form of prose literature, ancient or modern: histories, chronicles, pastoral romances, the Italian *novella*; and his fertile imagination could invent any number of plots that mirrored the preoccupations, the ideals and the problems of contemporary social life. One feature was universally followed: no matter what period of time or what country was being represented, the costumes and the customs were all made contemporary. This applied to Assyria, to Old Testament times etc.; ancient Romans fought duels, and ancient Greeks could fire pistols. The principle behind this was that no illiterate member of the audience should be alienated by an unfamiliar world, and that every dramatic conflict should be a human situation that could be as contemporary as it was ancient. By accepting these conventions and anachronisms and the reasons for them, the modern reader should have no difficulty in feeling at home in this dramatic world.

Plots were full of movement; the characters tended to be types rather than 'rounded', falling into groups that became conventional. The characters representing young men were called *galanes* (gallants), the young ladies were called *damas*, and older men were called *barbas* (beards). Every gallant has to have a servant (*criado*), and one of these servants generally provided the comic relief (and was then called the *gracioso*); similarly every lady had to have her servant (*criada*), and one of these *criadas* supplemented the comic relief of her male counterpart. The servants received the confidence of their masters and mistresses and thus fulfilled an essential dramatic function beyond their status. Women's parts were played by women. Plots in which young women, dressed as men, went in search of lovers who had betrayed them were very popular; this was probably because male attire showed off the shape of a leg and because the faces of the actresses were uncovered, which they otherwise never were in public in the streets.

This structure and these conventions endured in essentials until the eighteenth century. There are very great differences between the early plays of Lope and the late plays of Calderón, but they have the same recognisable framework. Much greater is the difference between Lope's plays and those of his immediate predecessors. Because of this difference, his type of drama was called *la comedia nueva*, 'the New Drama'.

The public theatres in which the *comedias* were performed grew out of the early practice of erecting fixed stages in suitable open spaces. The most convenient of these were courtyards between buildings. If a yard was specially suitable, it could be adapted into a permanent playhouse by alterations to the surrounding buildings or by new constructions. Such playhouses were called *corrales* ('yards') and had the general type of a large Spanish house with an internal patio. There were two entrances into the 'yard' or quadrangle from the street. At the far end was a fixed apron stage. The buildings at the back and on each side became part of the playhouse. The windows at the back and sides of the stage were used in performances as part of the stage for conversations between the inmates of a house and persons in the street. At the back of the stage, on an upper floor, there ran a gallery connected to the stage by stairs, and this gallery also formed part of the setting, not only to represent upper floors, but also, if the setting was in the country, the top of a hill or the slopes of a mountain. Calderón's play *La vida es sueño* (Life is a Dream) opens with the heroine supposedly riding on horseback dressed as a man through rugged mountainous country. She is presumed to be thrown by her horse, which plunges to its death, leaving her to tumble down the mountainside. This would have been represented by her stumbling onto the gallery, and then down the stairs. There were two doors at the back of the stage, leading into the building, which provided exit and entrance for the actors. They could also be used to indicate change of place. Thus in Tirso de Molina's *El burlador de Sevilla* (The Libertine of Seville), the first version of the Don Juan theme, a stage direction reads 'they leave by one door and enter by the other'. In between these two doors there was a covered area that was curtained off. The drawing of the curtains provided the space for what were called 'discoveries'. For instance, in Calderón's *El médico de su honra* (The Surgeon of his Honour) a servant has rushed to tell the king that his mistress has been bled at the order of her husband, who is allowing her to bleed to death, and that there may still be time to save her. They rush into the house, the curtain is drawn, and Doña Mencía is 'discovered' lying dead on her bed, with the bandage loosened from her arm.

The stage area was covered, but the *corral* floor itself was not. The parts of it adjacent to the stage could be brought in to supplement the stage space, steps or ramps being used to join the two levels. The open quadrangle provided space for the audience. Men were separated from women, and the upper classes from the lower (the effective division resulting, of course, from the price of the tickets). The floor of the quadrangle was the cheapest area for men, who stood throughout the performance, there being no seats. At the front of the quadrangle, above the entrances, was the gallery reserved for women; along each side were benches arranged in tiers. The windows in the buildings at each side of the quadrangle had chairs for the well-to-do auditors, and here men and women could mix. These seats were the equivalent of our 'boxes'. The 'boxes' on the upper floor at each side were reserved for the clergy. As regards the public theatres 'cultural' distinctions thus occurred in the distribution of the auditors and not in the type of play. It is a striking feature of the sociological history of Spain that throughout the long life of the *comedia* this form of entertainment had a vast popularity embracing all social classes, with the exception of king and courtiers, who came to have their own theatres. Madrid had two public theatres, and each city had its own.

A special room was reconstructed in the Madrid Alcázar for the performances of plays. This was in use before 1623. Later the Palacio del Retiro was constructed for Philip IV just outside Madrid, in what is now the Park of that name. This was opened in 1634. The Palace complex contained a special building for a theatre, known as the Coliseo, which was inaugurated in 1640. This was a theatre of our modern type, with a proscenium arch separating the stage from the auditorium. At first, there was no differentiation between plays for the people and plays for the court, those written for the *corrales* were repeated in the Alcázar; but with the opening of the Coliseo, there arose distinctive palace plays, requiring sumptuous productions such as the public theatres could never provide. But nonetheless the distinctive feature of the Spanish drama as a form of entertainment uniting the whole population of Madrid from the king downwards survived because after the first performances of a palace play to the court and state officials, the general public was admitted to the Coliseo for later performances. These distinctive court plays are the *comedias palaciegas*, which constitute another species within the genus of *comedia*. They led to the development of opera in Spain.

The separation of the *comedia* from the *auto sacramental* did not mean that religious themes were excluded from the former. They were distinguished by different staging requiring a different dramatic technique that came to make the themes of the *autos* more abstractly theological. Representational religious subjects, however, such as themes from the Old Testament and episodes from the lives of saints formed part of the *comedia*; hagiography provided plays known as *comedias de santos*.

Performances were of course by daylight. The programme consisted of a short *Loa* or Prologue; Act I; an *entremés*; Act II; dancing, clowning or singing in the second interval; then Act III, followed by more dancing or singing. The whole performance would last about three hours, and was continuous, the auditors being allowed no time to get bored. The theatrical season lasted from Easter to the beginning of Lent, and was broken only by periods of national mourning. Although stern clerics would inveigh against the 'immorality' of plays and against the allegedly scandalous lives of actors and actresses, they never managed to have the *corrales* permanently closed. This was because the *corrales* were hired by the municipality to professional actors' companies, and the money thus obtained was used for the support of hospitals and other charitable institutions.

The enormous popularity of the stage meant that a constant supply of plays was needed, especially since the most successful play lasted barely a week, the average play lasting perhaps three performances. The fact that necessity was the mother of invention explains the extraordinary productivity of the dramatists. Lope de Vega claimed to have written over 1,000 plays, but 800 would be nearer the mark. Tirso de Molina (alias Fray Gabriel Téllez) (1580?–1648) said that he had written between 300 and 400, Calderón wrote just over 100 *comedias* and about 80 *autos*. Exact figures are difficult to determine because many plays did not survive and those printed were not always attributed to their rightful authors. Also, dramatists could collaborate by each writing one act of a play. As the seventeenth century advanced, the inventiveness of dramatists flagged. Old plays that few might perhaps remember were reworked (*refundiciones*) in the newer, more regular and tighter structures, and thereby improved. Agustín Moreto (1618–69) was a dramatist of considerable distinction whose output consisted almost exclusively of *refundiciones* of old plays. Generally the titles were altered, but this was not always the case; two of Calderón's most famous plays, *El alcalde de Zalamea* (The Mayor of Zalamea) and *El médico de su honra* were *refundiciones* of plays attributed to Lope de Vega.

Biographical outline

Calderón has struck most of his readers as a quite impersonal dramatic poet. Not only do his plays seem remote from real life, but they do not seem to disclose their author's character, experience and feelings. His work appears abstract, or at least too intellectual. This book will suggest that such a reaction, while valid in part, is far from being a true judgement of the man and his works. The support for this statement will be found in different sections of this book, but the main outline of his life may serve as a preliminary introduction.

Don Pedro Calderón de la Barca was the leading dramatist in the second period of the Golden Age drama. He was born in 1600, when Lope de Vega, the 'founder' of this drama, had begun his phenomenal success in the Madrid theatres. The two periods have sometimes been called 'the school of Lope de Vega' and 'the school of Calderón'. The term 'school' can be applied to Lope more properly than to Calderón, for Lope was an innovator who carried all before him; and his immediate success as a playwright made it inevitable that other would-be dramatists followed in his footsteps immediately or adapted themselves quickly to the new theatrical style. Calderón began to write plays around 1623 and inevitably followed the patterns and conventions of Lope's *comedia nueva*. In the ten years or so that passed between Calderón's first compositions and the death of Lope in 1635, Calderón had already written or was engaged in writing some of his most famous plays, such as *El príncipe constante* (The Steadfast Prince), *La vida es sueño*, and *El médico de su honra*. In these he had developed a style and a technique distinctively his own, and such plays cannot be confused with the productions of other dramatists. The technical framework of these plays, however, is that of the theatre of Lope. From then onwards his distinctive style developed into a distinctive structure and form that, while preserving conventions established by Lope, moves away from the Lope drama into a more disciplined, tightly knit and mannered art. The characteristics of this dramatic art are further developed until his death in 1681. In fact, with the court plays of the 1650s onwards, Calderón merges his art into what is essentially a new type of play. Though he tends in the last period of his life to repeat details of plots, stage devices, imagery, and even copy long passages of verse from an earlier play, he never really ceases to develop.

The changes he effects in the structure of Lope's *comedia nueva* are naturally determined by his social position and his education, which were very different from those of his famous predecessor. Lope came from the lower middle class, a man of the people who never reached the University. He acquired a wide education in his reading, but without an academic training. As the title 'Don' indicates, Calderón was an *hidalgo* or nobleman, although of low rank. His father, Don Diego, had an important position as an official (or civil servant) in a government office. Pedro's secondary schooling was the highest that Spain could offer, the Colegio Imperial, or Jesuit College, in Madrid. The Jesuit scholastic training left a profound mark in his disciplined manner of thinking and writing. He was destined for the Church, in order to qualify for a living in the gift of a grandmother. To prepare for this, he underwent academic training in a two-year Arts course at the University of Alcalá, followed by four years of Logic, Philosophy and Theology at Salamanca, which formed his mind in the scholastic mould, probing definitions and making distinctions. In short he had an intellectual formation, of which his own personal gifts were able to make full use. When he finally abandoned an ecclesiastical career, he had to seek, like all the younger sons of *hidalgos*, the support of a noble of higher position. He entered the service of the Constable of Castile, one of the great offices of State. But his heart was in poetry and the stage.

As a later chapter will describe, his boyhood witnessed domestic scenes of stress, strain, and even violence, which had moulded his temperament away from academic intellectualism into the emotions and passions of drama. There is evidence that he mixed in the rowdy life of actors, that he was involved in a duel, and on one occasion he allegedly profaned the sanctuary of a convent in which an actor who had stabbed one of his brothers had taken refuge. The whole affair created a scandal and was denounced from the pulpit by the famous court preacher, Fray Hortensio Paravicino. The young Calderón retorted by making a satirical reference to the preacher in *El príncipe constante*. The outraged preacher accused Calderón of blasphemy and *lèse-majesté*, and it needed the tact of the President of the Council of Castile to restore peace. The offending passage in the play was removed and Calderón and his brother escaped severe punishment. There were two sides, then, to Calderón's character; the intellectual, philosophical and religious, and the passionate and potentially violent. Together these qualities, at times separated, at times juxtaposed, gave him his distinctive mark as a dramatist.

One last difference from Lope was the fact that Calderón's standing as a young *hidalgo* and his connection with the Constable of Castile gave him an entry into the Court. Philip IV, who came to the throne in 1621, was an ardent devotee of the theatre. The king attracted young dramatists to his palace theatre, and of these Calderón soon became the leader. He never lost his position as court dramatist, and this became, in the last fifty years of his life, the major element in the development of his art. Lope de Vega had always wanted to be accepted as a court poet but never achieved this position.

Calderón's connection with palace performances made him the principal writer of *libretti* for music dramas, a new fashion imported from Italy. Calderón's first production of this kind was in 1648 or 1649; a two-act opera entitled *El jardín de Falerina* (The Garden of Falerina) with music possibly composed by the court composer, Juan Hidalgo. In 1660 he wrote the text for *La púrpura de la rosa* (The Crimson of the Rose), a music drama in which the two acts were reduced to one. At the end of the same year there was performed the first full-length opera in three acts, with words by Calderón. *Celos aun del aire matan* (Jealousy, even of the Wind, can Kill) was the title, and it was in fact a normal *comedia* with sung parts. This was later thought too long, and one-act operas became the norm. Calderón's association with music dramas gives an added stylisation to his court plays from this year onwards. In these three-act plays only certain choruses are sung, with some main speeches in recitative. This makes Calderón develop balanced metrical schemes with the numbers of the stanzas balanced from chorus to chorus or from speaker to speaker.

Two other events in Calderón's life after the death of Lope de Vega are important. After the opening of the Palacio del Retiro and a spectacular performance out of doors and on a lake in the park of *El mayor encanto, Amor* (Love, the Greatest Enchantment) in 1635, followed the next year by a performance of *Los tres mayores prodigios* (The Three Greatest Marvels), the king decorated Calderón in 1636 with the Commandership of the Military Order of Santiago. As a member of this Order Calderón was required to fight in any war. The occasion came with the Revolt of Catalonia in 1640 and its attempt to break away from the Union with Castile. Calderón fought in part of this campaign until illness caused him to be invalided out of service. The second incident was a liaison he contracted with a lady whose name he never disclosed, and who bore him a son. This was no ordinary love-affair but obviously a *matrimonio clandestino*, or 'secret marriage', to which custom attached no moral stigma, despite its illegality in the eyes of the State, and its invalidity in the eyes of the Church. This lady died and Calderón publicly recognised the boy as his son, thus removing his illegitimacy. Shortly afterwards he announced his intention of taking orders, thus belatedly fulfilling his father's wishes and making provision for the care of his son. He was ordained in 1651; the boy died shortly afterwards, aged about twelve. 'Secret marriages' will be described below (chapter 14). The reasons for the secrecy in this particular case are not known. Calderón was careful not to reveal the identity of the lady, and only referred to her when legitimising his son. His treatment of love, marriage and women in his plays is based on experience. It has been assumed, and there is no reason to doubt this, that the lady's death was the reason for his decision to take orders. The genuineness of his religious faith cannot be doubted in any period of his life. The concept of *desengaño* or 'disillusionment', which is so important in the moral philosophy reflected in his plays, is intimately bound up with his religious feeling. This is almost certainly a real experience and not just an abstract doctrine. It denotes that when faced with the loss through death of what one holds most dear there must come the realisation that enduring happiness cannot be found in this life.

After his ordination he announced his intention of writing no more for the theatre, but was prevailed upon by royal command to continue to write plays for the palace. The period of his ascendancy as a writer of *autos sacramentales* had now begun. Earlier, when presenting *autos* for the competition to select the plays for Madrid, he had had to compete with dramatists of established reputation, some of whom were clerics, but now he was commanded to write the two *autos* for Madrid each year, and did so until his death. The feast of Corpus Christi and the *fiestas palaciegas* thus directed his dramatic activity during the last thirty years of his life. After his ordination he was given a benefice in the Cathedral of Toledo, but later at his own request he transferred his residence to Madrid, where he lived until his death, enjoying universal respect. He died on 25 May 1681. In his will, drawn up five days previously, he stipulated that in the funeral procession to the church he should be carried with his face uncovered, 'in case it be possible to atone in part for the public vanities of my misspent life with the public disillusionment of my death'.

It can be said that from the first duels and scandals to the final clerical seclusion Calderón's life presented every aspect of the society of his age, including ones that are not normally to be found in the life of a popular dramatist; the religious, ecclesiastical aspect and the intellectual, almost academic aspect, not to speak of the sophisticated minority entertainment of opera.

I Stylistic and dramatic craftsmanship

1 Principles of interpretation

The revaluation of 'baroque' poetry in Spain started shortly before the tricentenary of Góngora's death in 1627 and proceeded rapidly thereafter. Round about the same time Ángel Valbuena Prat attempted to associate a 'Vuelta a Calderón' (Return to Calderón) with the fashionable 'Vuelta a Góngora', but though a new interest in Calderón can be said to date from this time, he lagged far behind the new interest in Góngora. *Culterano*, or 'Gongoristic', vocabulary and metaphors in the dramatist were evidence of the extensive influence of Góngora in Spain towards the end of his life, but they did not serve as tools for *dramatic* criticism, especially since the interest in Góngora's poetry scarcely carried, at that time, an interest in his subject-matter. Dramatic poetry, being written for an audience, must have something to say. The 'intentional fallacy' theory, which maintains that we cannot and must not attempt to extract from a poetic work what the authors had in mind when writing it, cannot possibly apply to writing for the stage. A stage play had to communicate ideas through poetic dialogue and action, and those ideas had to give the action unity and purpose. Unless the poetry of drama expresses these ideas, in the way proper to drama, it will only give rhetorical colour, a range of intensified emotions, and excitement. This will not represent human life in action in a way that can lead the audience to pass judgements on it.

Students and readers of Spanish literature in the 1930s had to realise that Calderonian plays could, through the ideas they developed, pass human life in review in a way not only historically important for understanding their age, but also universally significant (i.e. acceptable but not necessarily accepted) beyond the time and the place of their composition. This had been obscured by the strict interpretation of 'verisimilitude' in the neo-classical period, and of 'realism' in the nineteenth century. The adverse judgements passed on Calderón because his dramatic actions were not true to life and because his characters were not recognisably beings of flesh and blood failed to make the distinction between art and nature. These judgements did not realise that art could, or even should, be selective, stylised, and therefore unrealistic in order to convey the significance of human life more effectively than was possible by a 'photographic reproduction'.

These departures from the natural and the realistic must be a means of conveying a range or depth of meaning that could not be adequately expressed in other ways. Instead of condemning such departures without more ado, as even critics of the stature of Menéndez Pelayo did, they should have speculated on what their purpose could have been. It is hoped that the pages that follow will give ample examples of this first principle of interpretation.[1] In any one play the meanings of unrealistic techniques and devices must be in harmony with each other, and consonant with the general theme that the reader is extracting. Every writer of the past has a 'language', derived from his own education and experience and from the sensibility and culture of his age. Nowadays the tendency is to disregard the special 'languages' of the past, and to interpret its literature for the most part in terms of our own lives, giving approval or disapproval according to the extent to which we are making the work mirror our own views and feelings. This book will not proceed along those lines; instead, it will try, to the degree that this is possible, to interpret the life and ideas of the Spanish seventeenth century in the mould given them by Calderón, in their own terms as valid preoccupations and judgements for their own age and thus with a potential universality for humanity as a whole. Nothing human should be foreign to us, however separated from us today in space and time. If we come to understand the literature of the past as significantly valid for the time when it was written (provided it was significant and valid), we are then in a position to find the universality that every student of human thought and culture should be seeking. The principle of 'suspension of disbelief' rather than instant rejection should apply. We suspend our disbelief in a writer's views, making our own ideas and views irrelevant to the task of criticism and accepting the particular views we are assessing *as if* they are true, as indeed they will be for artistic purposes. We can only make other views our own if we can recognise that these views are intelligent and mature instead of worthless and trivial. This necessitates establishing a sympathetic accord with what we try to understand.[2]

This book will therefore not dismiss Calderón as outdated or as too 'irrational' and 'unscientific' to deserve attention; nor will it dismiss his poetic art as too formalised and mannered to be able to appeal to us today. Instead, it will be looking for the purpose that such 'artificial' constructions serve within the artistic framework as a whole, and this will include the communication of thought as well as of feeling. Calderón should therefore be praised, when he is praised, for his success in achieving his artistic ends, and this will not necessarily mean that those ends are those that a modern critic should accept for his own day, or that the 'philosophy' that Calderón's poetic drama is communicating should be accepted as right for all his present-day readers. The understanding of Calderón during the last fifty or sixty years has indeed been helped by some of the changes in intellectual life of our own times. We have become intellectually more tolerant than we used to be, and we are no longer confined within a narrow rationalism. Instead of being constricted within our dogmatic school, we are open to all that Comparative Religion has to offer. In particular, the new understanding of the human mind and sensibility that anthropology and psychology have given us make it possible for us to see sense in Calderón where previously it was easier to see nonsense. For instance, in considering what must still be held to be his most famous play, *La vida es sueño*, Gerald Brenan said of it that the reason given by Segismundo for his conversion, namely that life is a dream, does not make sense, for if life is a dream nothing can have permanent meaning or value; yet the play goes on to assert the responsibility of all men for their own actions; there can be no responsibility in a dream-world. 'As an allegorical drama it [*La vida es sueño*] is a muddle'.[3] *La vida es sueño* is not an allegory, and Brenan is not in tune with its mode of thought. A present-day anthropologist gives us the right perspective. In discussing 'Indian symbolisms of Time and Eternity', Mircea Eliade gives us exactly the right kind of mental context for Segismundo's conclusion for rejecting, in the dream-world of life, all thoughts of revenge, of victory in war, and of political power:

> in reciting or listening to a myth, one resumes contact with the sacred and with reality, and in so doing one transcends the profane condition, the 'historical situation'. In other words, one goes beyond the temporal conditions and the dull self-sufficiency which is the lot of every human being simply because every human being is 'ignorant' – in the sense that he is identifying himself, and Reality, with his own particular situation. And ignorance is, first of all, this false identification of Reality with what each one of us *appears to be or to possess*. A politician thinks that the only true Reality is a political power, a millionaire is convinced that wealth alone is real, a man of learning thinks the same about his studies, his books, laboratories and so forth. The same tendency is equally in evidence among the less civilised, in primitive peoples and savages, but with this difference, that the myths are still alive amongst them, which prevents them from identifying themselves wholly and completely with non-reality. The periodic recitation of the myths breaks through the barriers built up by profane existence.[4]

On the plane of myth in which Eliade is placing the universal concept, Segismundo's problem and its solution is fully intelligible and entirely comprehensible. Eliade comments that 'myth . . . raises the listener to a superhuman and supra-historical plane; which, among other things, enables him to approach a Reality that is inaccessible at the level of profane, individual existence.'[5] Within the framework of literary criticism, Northrop Frye identified one of its modes as 'Mythical Phase: Symbol as Archetype'.[6] A sympathetic awareness of this will be a great help in the understanding of Calderón. It is not that by applying these insights the literary critic is employing the findings of modern psychological and sociological science anachronistically where they cannot possibly apply, for symbols, archetypes and myths have been uncovering what have been aspects of the human psyche and sensibility throughout the centuries and across all frontiers.

This new understanding of literature has illuminated Calderón's manner of thinking and the nature of his dramatic incidents in a way entirely closed to the positivist literary critics of the last century.

A point that no longer needs stressing is that unreality in Calderón's thought is coupled with unrealism in his characterisation, which used to be even more of a stumbling-block to his understanding. The commonest criticism that was made of Calderón was that his characters were too unlifelike to engage our sympathies. Presumably readers of poetic plays will always prefer 'rounded' characters, whose personality appears to be complete and entirely real, to 'type' characters, who are restricted to displaying only the single trait that their part in the play requires, e.g. a miser, a hypocrite, a hypochondriac, and so on. These and similar psychological qualities are just as human as those of the rounded characters but, since these are only what the characters are required to represent in the plot, 'roundness' is unnecessary. T. S. Eliot, when discussing dramatic poetry, made an important distinction that is very relevant to Calderón. He said that 'whereas in Shakespeare the effect is due to the way in which the characters *act upon* one another, in Jonson it is given by the way in which the characters *fit in* with each other.'[7] In other words, in a Calderonian play, each character is, so to speak, a piece in a jigsaw puzzle: he has only the shape required by the theme. Restriction of characterisation to narrow limits can provide a dramatic sharpness and an effective economy of technique. One alleged defect of characterisation in the Spanish Golden Age drama used to be stressed in a rather derisory manner. It has often been noted that Spanish plays present numerous examples of husbands, fathers and brothers, and of wives and sisters, but never any mothers. This is an exaggeration, but a pardonable one. The explanation used to be that mothers in Spanish life are so revered that it was demeaning to their dignity to expose them to contact with passions and vices. The reason for the scarcity of mothers is that the Spanish society of the seventeenth century was essentially more male-dominated than possibly any other country in Western Europe, more akin in this respect to Muslim countries, with which Spain had been of course in very close contact for centuries. In this society mothers had no governing rôle and made no decisions; they therefore had no part to play in the dramatic plots that presented domestic and social problems. Their presence on the stage would therefore have been uneconomical, since the fewer actors there were on the stage, the more effective the action would be. In Calderón there is one remarkable exception to the principle of absent mothers. In *Las tres justicias en una* (Threefold Justice in One Sentence), which will be mentioned later, there is a tragically moving mother who has to experience the unruly behaviour of her son and his execution by the law, all because in an attempt to win the love of a stern husband she had unwittingly created an impossible situation in which the boy became the victim. A mother here was needed by the plot, and so she appeared. If the theme requires a mother, then she is put there on the stage. There are other examples of mothers in Calderón's mythological plays, notably the tragic Climene in *El hijo del sol Faetón* (Phaethon, son of the Sun).

This means that characters, whether 'rounded' or 'type', are not on the stage for their own sake, but for the sake of the theme. In interpreting a Calderón play, the critic should seek to understand why aspects of characterisation are put in when they appear unnecessary or why others are omitted when one would expect them. A disciplined economy of technique and the subservience of all details to the overriding demands of the theme are the hallmark of Calderón's technique as he moves into his maturity. This discipline may not always be welcome to the modern reader, but once its purpose is realised, it is easier to accept it.

The removal of superfluity in plot and action is as important to Calderón as the pruning of characterisation. Once again, the criterion to apply is whether sparseness and rapidity of incident help or hinder us in grasping the theme. The following terms would here be used in these senses. 'Plot' is the story that is being dramatised, expressed through the characters and their acts. The 'actions' of the play are the characters communicating the plot in speech and movements. Again, no part of the dialogue and no incident should be disregarded as apparently pointless. The 'action' is what the eyes see and the ears hear; the 'theme' is what the audience should understand by it. It is, in short, the meaning of the play as it gradually unfolds before the enquiring minds of the audience. Since the play is a work of art, its meaning cannot be paraphrased, for it is conveyed by the dialogue, by its poetic imagery, by the poetic tone, by the characters as they reveal the human qualities they represent, and by the nature of the incidents within their particular contexts. The response of audience or readers is conditioned by all these elements interacting on each other; the reader, in particular, should be made aware by the end that the separate parts of the play have been interwoven into a unity. The discovery of the resulting artistic unity is perhaps the main satisfaction to be derived from the study of Calderón's better plays. For the unity of the total construction is the hallmark of Calderón's special genius as a dramatist. Not, of course, that he always achieves it, for some of his plays are repetitive and conventional; but when the reader has met a play that he feels and knows to be great, then analysis will reveal the unity of its close-knit texture.

Unity of action depends on unity of theme, and does not exclude two or more plots. A plot is a story in which one incident leads into another: there should be a causal connection, not of course directly in the actual incidents on the stage, but in the time scheme that the story is representing. Events that do not occur in the action, if narrated in the dialogue, will be causes or effects of what is enacted on the stage. Double or multiple plots are generally considered defective dramatic art, and they are indeed so if there is no relevant connection between the plots. In Calderón the main plot and the sub-plot generally follow their separate courses until they are linked and produce a single chain of cause and effect which brings the *dénouement*. In Calderón the ending of a play will have its first cause in what was the start of the main plot and what was the cause of the sub-plot. As the two plots are unfolded, interlaced, but causally separate, there will be points in which they impinge briefly on each other. Take, for instance, *La vida es sueño* (1635), so well known to every reader of Calderón.[8] The starting-point of the main plot is the decision of the King Basilio to cast the horoscope of his new-born baby son and his determination to foil the calamities it presages. The starting-point of the sub-plot is Rosaura's determination to fight for her honour when Astolfo abandons her after seducing her with a promise of marriage. The main plot follows the wrong done to Segismundo and his fight for freedom. The sub-plot follows Rosaura's efforts to vindicate her honour. Although the characters of one plot take part in the other, the series of events are quite separate, until the two plots converge in Act III when Rosaura sees no other course open to her than to ask Segismundo to be her champion. When he realises that his duty lies precisely there, and not in seducing her for his own ends, the last act constitutes a single plot and the end of the play, which is Segismundo's pardon of the king; his compelling Astolfo to marry Rosaura is the result of the starting-point of the main plot and the starting-point of the sub-plot. It is possible to follow the causal sequence of events from main plot to the end of the sub-plot and vice versa; that is to say, Segismundo wins his freedom and acts with responsibility *because* Rosaura determined not to take Astolfo's betrayal of her as final, as well as *because* he lived through the trauma of his dream world. Before converging at the beginning of Act III, the two plots meet momentarily in Act II, when Segismundo and Rosaura meet in the palace and when Segismundo attempts to rape her. Calderón is a past-master of the art of causal plot construction and, of course, the fact that Act I starts with these two young people, so soon to be so closely linked in each other's destiny, meeting in a rocky wilderness, neither having the slightest idea who the other is – this, in retrospect, makes the plot structure so very impressive. These two plots are unified in what becomes a single story with two separate strands, but their unification depends upon the relevance of one life-history to the other. This relevance itself depends entirely upon the theme of the play. The destiny of Segismundo and that of Rosaura illustrate two different facets of a single theme. This, and not the fact that the two plots converge in the course of the action, is what gives unity to the dramatic structure. Much more complex examples of a double plot-structure will be found later, for example in *El médico de su honra*.

Calderón, therefore, follows the principle already exemplified in the best plays of Lope de Vega; that unity, which is essential to all art, is found in drama not in unity of plot and action, as the neo-classicists were later to insist, but in unity of theme. A play's theme can have many facets, and several can be illustrated in the single theme, illustrated by comparison or by contrast. Every character in *La vida es sueño*, with possibly the single exception of Estrella, either dreams his life until his rude awakening, or strives steadfastly not to dream, but to stay awake. The fact that Gerald Brenan could still fail in 1950 to grasp the theme of *La vida es sueño* shows that Calderón must not be read like a straightforward realist. It was left to E. M. Wilson to disclose the single theme interconnecting all the characters.[9]

An example of a seemingly extraneous episode unconnected with either plot or theme is the opening of *La devoción de la cruz* (Devotion to the Cross) (probably between 1623 and 1625). It is a scene only with rustics, to be followed by a scene between two young men connected with the social world of the gentry. If this were a play by Tirso de Molina, one could be certain that the contrast between rustics and gentry would be intended to show the superiority, in natural virtue, of the rustics to the gentry. There is perhaps something of such a contrast here in Calderón, but there is much more. Two rustics are present; a woman riding a she-donkey and a man leading it. Without noticing where he is going, the man realises that the donkey is stuck in the mud. Both try to move it, but it will not budge. The man then tells a story: a coach is being driven not through a country lane, but through the streets of the capital city; it gets stuck in the mud, and no amount of assistance can help it, until nosebags with barley are dangled before the horses, when they move forward to reach it. The woman rustic, who had gone back to the village for help, returns with companions. At first they cannot find the one who had stayed behind with the donkey, but find him later in a state of shock, and there is no further mention of the donkey. In between, Lisardo and Eusebio have fought a duel (without knowing that they are brothers). Eusebio, who is a young man of unknown parentage, has met Lisardo's sister (and his), and they have fallen in love. Curcio, the father of Lisardo and Julia, is outraged at Eusebio, a man of no social standing whatever, daring to promise to marry his daughter. Lisardo goes to put an end to what threatens to be the family dishonour. Eusebio argues with Lisardo, explaining who he is and what he knows of his life, but Lisardo furiously insists that he is a man without social honour, totally unfit to have dealings with a nobleman's family. Stung by this insult, Eusebio draws his sword, they fight, Lisardo is mortally wounded, and Eusebio carries him to a priest for him to make his last confession. The rest of the play discloses that Curcio, the proud nobleman who is the father of Lisardo and Julia (and of Eusebio, without knowing it) was so fanatical about his honour that when his wife became pregnant while he was journeying away from home, he became convinced that she must have been unfaithful to him, and took his pregnant wife into a desolate mountain spot to kill her. Accused of adultery, she pleaded her innocence so movingly that Curcio realised she was indeed innocent, but the fact that he had thought her an adulteress was an impossible burden for a man of honour to bear, and so she had to be killed, though innocent.

Returning to the donkey and the coach, we remember that the rustic who has stayed behind with the she-donkey says to her that she is in this sorry state because she has been walking with them along the road; up till then she has been a very honourable donkey, in fact 'the most honourable of the whole village';[10] she had never left home, she had never gazed out of the windows, leading the demure life that custom demanded of all Spanish women. Does she not foreshadow Curcio's wife? She becomes stuck in the mud of 'dishonour' (and disappears) because nothing could make Curcio waver in the very slightest from his obstinate belief in her guilt. The second victim of the mud is the coach, which is called 'vergonzante', as distinct from 'vergonzoso'; both words can mean shameful, but the first means 'causing shame', while the other means 'being ashamed'. It is an unexpected epithet to apply to a coach, but the satirical literature of the time, like Quevedo's *Sueños*, indicates its first or overt meaning. Private coaches for use in towns were a relatively new phenomenon. They enabled ladies of fashion to move around without having to walk through the mud of the streets. But it was suspected that a lover could be hidden in a coach before it left the coachyard, and the lady could have her tryst with him while the driver drove it slowly around the city. The meaning, then, would be that all coaches are by nature places that produce shame for their owners. But a second meaning cannot be excluded, especially at a time when conceited metaphors were at their height. 'Coche vergonzante' can retrospectively bring Curcio to mind, for he had caused his own shame, and saw no reason to be ashamed. But the main point is that nothing moved Curcio from his terrible need to avenge himself, stuck in the quagmire of honour. This quagmire holds Lisardo also. Nothing whatever will move him from the desire for vengeance on the 'unworthy' Eusebio, who will immediately appear on the stage to fight the duel on which Lisardo blindly insists. If he had listened to Eusebio and talked rationally with his wife, his 'coach' could easily have been freed.

This interpretation may not seem immediately convincing, but what else could be the point of the scene, preceding as it does the duel that forms the first episode in the terrifying story of the unrelenting obstinacy of honour?[11]

This is an example of apparently irrelevant episodes contributing to the unity of a play through its theme. The same principle applies, in many cases, to the imagery. A striking example is in the speech by Rosaura that opens *La vida es sueño*.

Rosaura, in search of the treacherous Astolfo, arrives in Poland, dressed as a man. Galloping on a rocky mountainside, the horse throws Rosaura from the saddle. She apostrophises her horse in the following lines:

> Hipogrifo violento,
> que corriste parejas con el viento,
> ¿dónde rayo sin llama,
> pájaro sin matiz, pez sin escama,
> y bruto sin instinto
> natural, al confuso laberinto
> de esas desnudas peñas
> te desbocas, te arrastras y despeñas?
> Quédate en este monte,
> donde tengan los brutos su Faetonte;
> que yo, sin más camino
> que el que me dan las leyes del destino,
> ciega y desesperada,
> bajaré la cabeza enmarañada
> deste monte . . .

('Violent hippogryph, you who did vie with the wind, where – lightning without flame, bird without colour, fish without scales and brute without natural instinct – where into the confusing labyrinth of those bare rocks have you bolted, where did you fling and hurl yourself? Stay in that wilderness, so that brutes may have their Phaethon; for I, in desperation, with no other path than the one that the laws of destiny have mapped out for me, shall blindly descend the tangled head of this lofty mountain . . .')

La vida es sueño, ed. Albert E. Sloman (Manchester, 1961),

ll.1–15 [*BAE*, i, p. 1a]

The key images here are 'without natural instinct', 'confusing labyrinth', 'with no other path than the one that the laws of destiny have mapped out for me'. The rocky wilderness that houses Segismundo in his prison has been difficult for horse and rider to negotiate; it has been a labyrinth from which Rosaura could find no exit. But so also is life. Clotaldo will later use the same image of 'confuso laberinto' to refer to the dilemmas that beset him. The play will show that all life is a labyrinthine confusion, in which it is essential to keep awake. Rosaura will keep awake and find her way out of the labyrinth by faithfully following the path mapped by 'the laws of her destiny', which means facing up to events as they come, without trying to mould them. This she will do by keeping her eyes steadily on the single aim of regaining her moral dignity as a woman and not surrendering to the treacheries of life. To do otherwise is to do what her horse did; it rejected 'its natural instinct' when it sought to gallop along and climb over the mountain boulders at breakneck speed. It was a hippogryph, a fabulous creature, mixing features of eagle, horse and lion. So it has tried to be a ray of lightning but without its fire; a bird but without coloured plumage; a fish but without scales – in short, a beast that has forsaken the path allotted it by nature. This distortion of nature is the result of its ambition to be more than it was intended to be, so that finally the horse becomes Phaethon for all other animals; the man, namely, who tried to drive the chariot of the Sun and crashed into the sea. The play will show that if men do not follow the path of their individual destinies, they will be led to failure or disaster by an overweening ambition, the desire to be more than they should be. This at first sight disorderly jumble of unrealistic metaphors used to be cited as a good example of Calderón's baroque 'bad taste'. It is, on the other hand, a fine piece of dramatic construction in which poetic imagery is pointing to the theme of the whole play.[12]

Extravagant metaphors do not necessarily exist, so to speak, in their own right, but in terms of the total theme of a play. This, however, does not always apply. When it does, the extravagant metaphors, or conceits, are organic. Inorganic metaphors of this kind are a feature of Calderón's earliest plays, especially those that have a larger-than-life or 'heroic' action. In such cases, they are more likely to be rhetorical set-pieces, to be savoured as an oratorical display. An example of this would be the long speech in Act I of *El príncipe constante*, where Muley reports to the king of Fez the arrival of the Portuguese fleet off Tangier and the first battle that has ensued. The dawn is described as when the sun shakes back its golden locks over roses and jasmine; the sun's locks are a golden cloth drying the fiery and frozen tears of the dawn, which the sun was changing into pearls. As the fleet is sighted on the horizon, the uncertain first light makes the ships appear clouds or cities at a distance. Their masts pierce the clouds, appearing to make the rain that the clouds conceive as crystal, sapphire to which the sea gives birth. There is a certain splendour to this riotous imagery; but one feels that it would be a misguided ingenuity that linked it with the theme of the play. The actual concepts on which the metaphors are based are conventional in the high style of literary composition. They are found in a less elaborate form in the pastoral novel. At the beginning of a chapter that refers to the morning having come, Cervantes satirises this florid writing in the chapter recording Don Quijote's first sally.

> Apenas había el rubicundo Apolo tendido por la faz de la ancha y espaciosa tierra las doradas hebras de sus hermosos cabellos, y apenas los pequeños y pintados pajarillos con sus harpadas lenguas habían saludado con dulce y melíflua armonía la venida de la rosada aurora, que, dejando la blanda cama del celoso marido, por las puertas y balcones del manchego horizonte a los mortales se mostraba . . .

> (No sooner had the rubicund Apollo spread over the face of the broad and spacious Earth the gilded filaments of his beauteous locks, and no sooner had the little singing birds of painted plumage greeted with their sweet and mellifluous harmony the coming of the Dawn, who, leaving the soft couch of her jealous spouse, now showed herself to mortals at all the doors and balconies of the horizon . . .)[13]

Muley's speech would lend itself to sarcastic treatment, but it is of course intended seriously as poetry in the high style. Such poetry is much more common in Calderón's early period: it is rare in his maturity for conceits to have no special point. The growth of organic metaphors marks the commencement of his maturity.

Calderón achieves artistic unity through the conventions of the *comedia nueva*, which he adopted, which he expanded and to which he added. How this unity exists will be indicated in the studies that follow of individual plays. The particular principles of interpretation that have been indicated will be recognisable in these studies; others will emerge as his technique is analysed in more detail.

In general it may be said that literary criticism in this book will aim at disclosing the total meaning of a play by analysing its structure – the way in which the structural elements, plots, characters, and poetic imagery are moulded to fit in with each other. Thus it will do in full what has been done in miniature in the analysis of the opening scenes of *La devoción de la cruz* and *La vida es sueño*, where analysis of the imagery, through the action of the plays, has served as a pointer to the theme, which will be the plays' ultimate meaning.

2 From metaphor to symbol

In the centenary year of 1881 the young Marcelino Menéndez Pelayo brought his course of lectures on Calderón to a close by enumerating the defects of his art. They were: 'Verbosity, the empty pomp of his diction, attention paid more to intrigues and to the movement on the stage than to the painstaking and careful dissection and analysis of a character.'[1] Since then, the third centenary of Calderón's death has been celebrated, and a very different picture emerged from most of the commemorative addresses. It has become more usual, in fact, to look for his artistic merits precisely in his 'language', in the 'intrigues' of his plots, and in the 'movement on stage'. One aspect of his style and technique which is fundamental for the study of his art forms the subject of this chapter.

A characteristic example of my preoccupation is the relatively early play, *La cisma de Ingalaterra*, whose metaphors and symbols will be dealt with in general terms here, while the fuller study of its theme and its dramatic significance will be taken up again in a later chapter. The play was performed in the *salón de teatro*, the small private theatre in the Madrid palace before the *Coliseo* was constructed. At the beginning of this play, King Henry VIII receives two letters, one from the Pope and one from Luther; he mistakenly throws the Pope's letter at his feet and puts Luther's on his head. Later, Anne Boleyn enters; so arrogant is she that she dislikes kneeling even before the king, but as she approaches him, she stumbles and falls. This action foreshadows her later repudiation and beheading by the king. All these are stage actions because the metaphors denote movement: that of lifting or rising and that of lowering or falling. In the dialogue of this drama there are numerous metaphors connoting ascent or descent: the former are connected, naturally, with the desire to better one's position, with vainglorious ambition, while the metaphors of descent are connected with disillusion, failure and disaster. Moreover, since an obvious image for success and self-glory is the Sun, which rises, and an obvious metaphor for disaster is Night, which falls, we find related to the paired metaphors of ascent and descent other paired metaphors of light and darkness. To express their ambitions, ideals and aspirations the characters in *La cisma de Ingalaterra* use metaphors like these: 'the light is burning', 'the flame rises with spreading rays', 'to rise up to the Sun', 'it is as if I am in the Sun', 'the Sun's rays are encircling my brow', 'to touch the Sun's holy light', 'to behold the white dawn'. To express their fears and misfortunes they use metaphors like these: 'to dim the light', 'to extinguish the light', 'to live in sad night', 'to touch darkness and shadows', 'to tread on the shadows of death'. Finally, to express hesitation and uncertainty, they say 'to see the mingling of night and day', '[groping] in the shadows', 'to brighten with darkness', etc.

These images are related to the tragic sense of the play; but what needs emphasising now is that by means of a completely natural linguistic and poetic process, Calderón has passed from the metaphors 'to raise onto one's head' and 'to lower to one's feet' to two symbols, the Sun and Night. In the following pages the dramatic function of these symbols will be discussed in connection with other plays of Calderón. At present we need only note their existence as symbols.

Although the first of these actions was a ceremonial gesture, in real life putting one letter on one's head and throwing the other at one's feet have no literal meaning; letters are not worn instead of hats or shoes. The significance of these actions is to be found only in their metaphorical meanings. Consequently, the actions of raising or lowering the letters are symbolical actions. Symbolism is the opposite of realism.[2] Generally, though not always, Calderón's art is not realistic. It does not represent reality as perceived by the eyes of the audience: the visible action demands to be interpreted, and the interpretation should be consonant with the key images.[3]

It can be said, as a broad generalisation, that there are three main types of symbols in Calderón. The first, and the most transparent, is a place in which, or an object around which the action of the play unfolds; this place or this object will have a special significance in the theme. A simple example is offered by the two pairs of doors in *Casa con dos puertas mala es de guardar* (A House with Two Doors is Difficult to Guard), where each of the two houses has two doors: in the first place, they represent furtive secrecy, emerging unseen from where one had not entered; in the second place, the two-edged blade of love: love which is wooed with secretive cunning easily founders in jealousy. A more profound symbol of this type is the wayside cross in *La devoción de la cruz*: it does not function dramatically as an object of a more or less superstitious devotion, but as a symbol of *clemencia*, or mercy: once this is realised, the whole meaning of the play is transformed, as will become apparent in a later chapter.

The second type of symbol is constituted by an abnormal or fantastic situation in which a character finds himself; such a situation, if it is repeated from one play to others, comes to acquire a meaning that is not restricted to one of the occasions on which it occurs. The prison of Segismundo is the typical example; the tower or cave in which a human being, man or woman, has been confined from birth. This is found repeated on several occasions in Calderón's drama. Blanca de los Ríos was the first to note this repetition, but she was not interested in the imprisonment as such, but in the prison as a representation of the dramatist's main idea, the dream character of life. The reader of Calderón, however, should be interested in it as imprisonment and see this as a symbol; and as such it will be interpreted in these pages.[4] Here it will be called the symbol of the Prison: but it must be borne in mind that this is not imprisonment as punishment of a crime, since in no single case has there been a crime, which is what increases the metaphorical character of this prison. This symbol is accompanied by a prophecy, a divination, an omen, or a horoscope. Prison and prophecy form a single symbol, but the prophecy alone, without the Prison, is very frequently found in Calderón: in such cases it will scarcely have a symbolical meaning; it will serve to focus on a moral problem.

The third type of symbol occurs when a metaphor takes, so to speak, a tangible shape on the stage. This can happen in two ways: first, when the metaphor comes to form part of the action, or when it is created by the action; secondly, when the metaphor gives rise to a series of metaphors, all of them being variations on the theme of the dominant image. Examples of metaphors becoming actions are the letters raised to the head or dropped at the feet in *La cisma de Ingalaterra*, which give rise to symbolical actions. How a metaphor can produce an action can be found in *La vida es sueño*: the action represents an event, Basilio invents a metaphor to explain it and, when this metaphor is accepted by Segismundo as the explanation, it influences his future conduct, and the symbol to which the action gives rise is the 'drama'. The 'Sun' and 'Night' and the variations to which they give rise in *La cisma de Ingalaterra* are examples of the series of metaphorical variations upon one predominant concept.[5]

In addition to *La vida es sueño* there are two plays that have as their titles metaphors closely relating to the themes of the plays, namely *El médico de su honra* and *El pintor de su deshonra*. Neither of these phrases denotes a realistic concept; one is a surgeon of the body, not of honour, and what one paints is a picture, not an abstract idea. The first metaphor gives rise to the symbol of healing, given concrete expression in the blood-letting administered to Mencía, this bleeding being her subsequent murder. The second metaphor gives rise to the symbol of painting, which is twice made visible, at the beginning of Act II when the painter, at work on the portrait of his wife, despairs at the impossibility of capturing her likeness, and at the end when, ready to paint her again, he kills her instead. On the metaphor of the dream life, nothing now can usefully be said. The simplest explanation, that of Edward Wilson, is still acceptable, despite so many later elaborations.[6] The explanation of painting as a symbolical act will be discussed later (pp. 206–7). There remains *El médico de su honra*. A great deal has been written about this famous play, but something still remains to be said within this present context. This drama will serve to illustrate the way in which metaphor and dramatic action are fused together, and how this fusion pinpoints the interpretation that one should give the play. Further symbols, to be explained later, are Night, Prison and Sun.

Bruce Wardropper was the first to emphasise the importance of the metaphor of the 'Surgeon of his Honour'. He held that the whole play was a long and elaborate metaphor in which Don Gutierre is the surgeon, Doña Mencía the patient, and marital dishonour the illness. The diagnosis is mistaken, as sometimes happens in real life; the operation kills the patient, which also can sometimes happen in real life. But here, said Wardropper, the metaphor does not apply; real surgeons kill only by accident, while Gutierre prescribes death and heals the illness but not the patient. Wardropper maintained that this false analogy did not affect the poetic and dramatic value of the metaphor.[7] All this is very true; nonetheless, it is possible to go further and to hold that the poetic and dramatic value of the metaphor lies precisely in the false analogy, which is what makes the metaphor a metaphysical conceit. Only by seeing how the metaphor appears and how it is developed within the action can one discover whether the false analogy is accidental or intentional.

The metaphor 'surgeon of his honour' was not, of course, invented by Calderón. It is the title and the plot of the play that Calderón refashioned. In the source-play, the metaphor appears only twice: on the first occasion the barber quotes these words while reporting the death of Doña Mayor to the king:

Mi honor adolece,
y así, yo soy de mi honra
médico, y para curarla
importa que hagas agora
a esa enferma una sangría.

(My honour is sick/and I am therefore the surgeon of my honour, and to cure it, it is necessary for you to administer a bleeding to the patient.)

The second occasion is in the closing lines of the play:

> Se da fin a aquesta historia
> del honor en la sangría
> y *médico de su honra*

(Here ends the story of honour in blood-letting, and *the surgeon of his honour.*)[8]

That is all. The metaphor is produced by the way in which the strict vengeance is carried out: it does no more than describe the *dénouement* and it never appears, nor is it even suggested, in the course of the play. That is to say, it fulfils no *dramatic* purpose. In contrast, Calderón, having accepted the *dénouement*, and thus the metaphor, for his title, uses his extraordinary feeling for dramatic unity and makes the idea of curing central to the action from the beginning of the dramatic conflict.

The first character to use a metaphor of curing is not Don Gutierre, but Doña Mencía. When Gutierre comes home unexpectedly, she has to hide Enrique; but she then does just the opposite of what one would have expected her to do: she herself raises the alarm and ensures that Gutierre discovers Enrique, and in this way makes it seem as if Enrique has been hiding there without her knowledge. It is here that the medical metaphor appears for the first time; Mencía says, when she decides upon this course of action: 'En salud me he de curar' ('although healthy, I must cure myself').[9] This is, of course, an idiom. Taken literally, it is nonsensical, because if one is healthy, there is no need for a cure; metaphorically speaking, however, the phrase means two things: to guard against trouble before it happens and to vindicate oneself before one is accused. For Calderón, both these courses of action denote imprudent and rash behaviour. In *La vida es sueño*, Basilio, in trying to forestall trouble, brings it upon himself; and this self-defeating aspect of prevention is a constant element in the Calderonian symbol of the Prison. In the same way Mencía, in attempting to ward off an accusation against her, causes Gutierre to find the dagger and to think, for the first time, about accusing her. Later, when Mencía decides to write to Enrique and ask him not to leave Seville, she does so acting upon the advice of her maid, who says

> El remedio mejor será, señora,
> prevenir este daño

(The best remedy, my lady, lies in forestalling trouble)
                                                    (III, ll. 344–5) [*BAE*, I, p. 362a]

This is again *curarse en salud* ('curing in health' – preventive medicine), and, in fact, the letter does cause the very harm it thought to prevent. Calderón, whenever he uses the metaphor of 'curing oneself while in health', does so in a reproving fashion. The most succinct mention is found in *Los hijos de la fortuna* (The Children of Fortune):

> Curar en salud es medio
> muchas veces de enfermar
>
> (Curing oneself, while in health, is often a means of falling ill)[10]

This is precisely what Mencía does, within the metaphor; from a state of good health, she produces the symptoms of a mortal disease. This is intimately bound up with the contradiction which the phrase 'to cure oneself while in health' contains when it is taken literally. Thus, the first example of a medical metaphor establishes a tension, or an ambiguity, between its literal and its metaphorical meaning; and this tension or ambiguity with regard to the metaphors of curing is sustained until the end of the play.

In the same way, when Gutierre first uses a 'curing' metaphor, saying 'y os he de curar, honor' (and I must cure you, honour), (II, l. 645 [*BAE*, I, p. 357c] curing is used in the sense of prevention. He says

> sea
> la primera medicina
> cerrar al daño las puertas,
> atajar al mal los pasos;
> y así os receta y ordena
> el médico de su honra
> primeramente la dieta
> del silencio, que es guardar
> la boca, tener paciencia
>
> (let the treatment begin by closing the doors against harm, and cutting short the advance of illness; therefore the surgeon of his honour is going to prescribe and order for you first of all the diet of silence, which means holding your tongue and being patient)
>
> (II, ll. 648–56) [*BAE*, I, p. 357c]

It is important to notice the contrast between these two methods of preventive medicine. Mencía aims to cure by means of shouting, Gutierre by keeping silent; and, while the former action is imprudent, the latter action would have been prudent, were it not for the fact that the spectre of jealousy came between Gutierre and his reason: in believing that he has good cause to be jealous, he turns, from a rational man into a passionate fury. It is now that he begins to talk about 'curing his dishonour' ('curar su deshonra'). (II, ll. 852–3) [*BAE*, I, p. 358c]. The metaphor changes in the third act to 'dar vida a la honra', that is 'giving life to honour'. This still has, at first, the purpose of prevention. Gutierre asks the king to forbid Enrique to see Mencía again, saying

La vida de vos espero
de mi honra; así la curo
con prevención, y procuro
que ésta la sane primero

(I hope to gain from you life for my honour; in this way I will cure it by being
on my guard and so preventing it, and hope that this method will make it
healthy)

(III, ll. 41–4) [*BAE*, i, p. 360b]

Notice how the metaphor is changing: 'prescribing a regimen of silence'
is to do nothing; that is a negative method which could never give rise to
a wrong diagnosis; 'curing dishonour' is a little more positive, although
this method only implies the wiping away of a defect; while 'giving life to
honour', in other words encouraging it, is much more positive. The
introduction of the word 'life' is very significant. 'To hope that honour
will live', which is what Gutierre says to the king, means to hope that
Mencía will live, that she will not have to die; when, however, the
evidence of dishonour appears to be incontrovertible, Gutierre, instead of
changing the metaphor, changes its meaning, so that, on the metaphorical plane, it becomes a non-sense comparable with the non-sense
contained in the literal meaning of the phrase 'curing oneself while in
health'. So he says

Médico soy de mi honor,
la vida pretendo darle
con una sangría

(I am the surgeon of my honour; I intend to bleed it into life)

(III, ll. 582–4) [*BAE*, i, p. 363c]

It is here, with this contradiction, that the metaphor falls down
completely. 'Bleed it into life.' Into life for whom or what? For honour.
But there is contradiction between the figurative plane and the real
plane: Mencía can be bled, but honour cannot; and bleeding her will not
preserve her life but rather cause her death. Gutierre has reached a state
of confusion wherein positives are identified with negatives, where one
thing means another, and where giving life means giving death, and vice
versa. The terrible irony caused by the confusing of the metaphor
culminates in the horrifying dialogue which closes the play. See, says
Gutierre to Leonor when the king obliges him to take her hand in
marriage:

Mira que médico he sido
de mi honra: no está olvidada
la ciencia

(See how I have been the surgeon of my honour: I have not forgotten this science [of healing])

To which she replies:

> Cura con ella
> mi vida, en estando mala

(Use it to cure my life, after I have fallen ill)

(III, ll. 898–901) [*BAE*, ɪ, p. 365c]

Here, then, is the final phase in the development of the medical metaphor: 'curing life'. This phrase in itself is, of course, perfectly rational: life becomes sick when it is threatened by death. The difference is that life is cured by being saved, while Leonor, in accepting Gutierre's medical knowledge, also accepts the fact that life is saved through death. In this context, the metaphor of 'curing life' which she so proudly uses is monstrous.[11] This is not a breakdown in metaphorical meaning caused by carelessness on Calderón's part; but rather the effect which his art has deliberately produced. Let us review the metaphor's different stages. 'To cure oneself, being healthy'; 'curing dishonour'; 'giving life to honour'; 'curing life'. This is a consistent progression, passing from a phrase which is nonsensical on the real plane but significant on the metaphorical plane, to a phrase which is acceptable on the level of reality but nonsensical on the level of metaphor. In other words, the action's progress is marked by a metaphor which has been inverted or put back-to-front; similarly, in the theme, the proper meanings of truth and justice are turned upside down.

Another symbol used by Caldéron demonstrates how this progressive inversion of the metaphor is not done by chance. Wardropper, Sloman and Dunn all point out that Night is an important symbol in *El médico de su honra*.[12] The symbol is bound up in the action, since the episodes showing the growth of jealousy and of the desire for vengeance take place at night, and the phrase 'matar la luz' (put out – literally kill – the light) has both literal and metaphorical significance in the play. Images of darkness dominate Gutierre's speeches, and reach their peak during his account of Mencía's death. Dunn explains how this imagery of darkness shows what a negative action Mencía's sacrifice is: Gutierre merely thereby creates shadows in the spiritual order.[13] The analysis of the metaphor of curing has also led us to this negative concept of *non-being*: to a senseless contradiction.

For the purposes of this chapter, it only remains for me to dwell here on two of the images presenting the symbol of Night. These both occur in Gutierre's monologue at the end of Act II, and are spoken as he jumps over his own garden wall, at night, in order to spy on his wife. She is lying asleep with a lighted candle beside her. The monologue ends when he wakes her up. He first douses the light, saying

> Mato la luz, y llego
> sin luz y sin razón, dos veces ciego

> (I kill the light, and arrive twice blind; without light and without reason)
> (II. ll. 890–1) [*BAE*, I, p. 359a]

Night, then, signifies the blindness of passion; it is the extinction of the light of reason. At the beginning of this monologue, night is linked with the rejection of reason in a striking image:

> En el mudo silencio
> de la noche, que adoro y reverencio,
> por sombra aborrecida
> como sepulcro de la humana vida,
> de secreto he venido
> hasta mi casa

> (In the dumb silence of night, night which I adore and reverence, for being the hated shades of life's tomb, I have come with stealth to my house)
> (II. ll. 841–6) [*BAE*, I, p. 358c]

Hartzenbusch, stating that it is impossible to adore something which is hated, wanted to emend the text.[14] He did not pay proper attention to the work. Gutierre, when he sentences Mencía to death, writes: 'El amor te adora, el honor te aborrece' (Love adores you, honour loathes you). Things which are impossible seen in the light of reason are possible in the shadowy code of honour. Night in its rôle as the shadow of death is loathsome; Gutierre loves it because it gives him a chance to spy dishonourably on his wife, because, without light and without reason, he comes to love that which he loathes – death, in other words. Now we can understand precisely how blood-curdling Leonor's final words are: 'cure my life'. Life is the greatest of God's gifts, the one which embraces and gives rise to all the rest. To cure life with death is not only to overturn reason, but also by the same token is to commit a monstrous blasphemy; just as it is blasphemous to loathe something which one loves, and to love and loathe life simultaneously because it is the tomb of life. 'Adoring night', 'curing life': symbol and metaphor are joined on the stage in the visible action of the putting out of the light, the light of reason.

That the metaphor of Don Gutierre as the surgeon of his honour breaks down at the end cannot be accidental, then, but rather a deliberate and desired effect. The analysis of Calderón's poetic language, or rather the realisation of the far-reaching importance of his dramatic metaphors and symbols, can only confirm that interpretation of this masterpiece which clears Calderón of wanting to support the casuistry of vengeance. Metaphor and symbol add another critical dimension to the interpretation of Calderón, and support this revaluation.

Calderón's symbolism reaches a peak in his mythological plays, which were mostly written in his later period. For a long time, commentators had been turning the world of classical mythology into a collection of moral and didactic allegories. Calderón had to follow this tradition, although this does not mean that he had to accept its allegorical interpretations. The unreal atmosphere of these stories naturally lent itself to a symbolical type of poetry, and Calderón made the most of this. As a result, these plays may appear absurd to some people, while to others they are vague and enigmatic. In his useful editions of two of these plays, Aubrun has emphasised their special interest and has shown how unjust it was that they should have been forgotten.[15] It is in these plays that we find the culmination of the two symbols which are to be examined now: that of the Prison and that of the Sun.

The symbol of the Prison contains an element which is more or less constant: a prophetic prediction that a certain individual will cause harm in the world. To prevent this individual from having the freedom to fulfil what is forseen for him, he (or she) is kept imprisoned from infancy, but is freed at the beginning of the drama and faces his (or her) fate. The symbol is variable, and there are many variations.[16] One thing, however, is constant: that the prophecies are always fulfilled; if they appear not to be, this is because they are either incomplete, or so phrased as to be inconclusive (like so many of the prophecies given by the oracles of antiquity). Fate, or an irreversible destiny, is a dominant factor in much of Calderón's work. As such it will be discussed in later chapters. For the present the symbol that must here be considered is that of the Prison, bearing in mind that the prisoner (as *La vida es sueño* and the 'Prophecy plays' which followed it make clear) is a prisoner because that has been willed by the 'fate' that governs human life.

The exact significance of this symbol must now be determined. It is a concept which is analogous, to a certain extent, to the theological concept of original sin. Original sin, as an inseparable part of human nature, is an imperfection or weakness of the human will, which produces a tendency towards evil, thus making sin appear natural without being in any way inevitable or invincible. The Calderonian symbol of the Prison does not mean a tendency towards evil in this sense, but rather a propensity either to suffer or to cause unhappiness: this concept has nothing fatalistic about it, nor is it directly concerned with morality, because it is almost always the pain which is underlined rather than the 'sin', which can be almost non-existent. This tendency towards suffering can arise from a number of causes: the environment, temperament, a physical gift, such as beauty in a woman; or it may be a defect inherent in human nature itself. Finally, while the symbol is only embodied in one or two characters in any single play, this does not prevent it from being a universal symbol: Calderón conceives it as an innate feature of human life: humanity as a whole is condemned to a life of pain, or is a prisoner in the Prison.

Before giving an example of this, it is necessary to examine the symbol of the Sun. This was first mentioned with reference to *La cisma de Ingalaterra*, where it denoted the characters' aspirations, ideals or ambitions. Another example, of a later date, may be found in *La hija del aire* (The Daughter of the Air) (before 1643), where metaphors like 'to oppose the Sun' and 'to wish for the light' are frequently found, and where the protagonist, Semíramis, is called 'Queen of the Sun', metaphors which denote the ambitious pride which leads her on to perform her masculine deeds.[17] She herself likens humility to living 'hidden from the Sun'.[18] The Sun, then, stands for the pursuit of happiness, whether it be for fame, for power or, as shall be seen, for love. It is the opposite of the symbol of the Prison.

Mythology, in the character of Apollo and his chariot of fire, provides us with an excellent concrete example of the symbol of the Sun. The Sun, that is to say the star itself, appears on-stage in the play *El hijo del sol, Faetón* (Phaethon, Son of the Sun). One can tell from the title that this is one of Calderón's most spectacular plays. Only in analysing the symbol can we find out whether it contains more than mere spectacle. The play forms the sequel to another play, *Apolo y Climene* (Apollo and Clymene). The two plays, which were probably written around 1660, reveal their writer at his most mature.

As the reader will be aware, Ovid is the principal source for the Phaethon myth.[19] Calderón retains all the essential points of Ovid's account, but he adds a quantity of new material which he has invented himself. Traditionally, Phaethon has become the epitome of an ambitious, but heroic man. Ovid says how, although his downfall was great, yet his daring was greater; Villamediana says of him: 'a sobrando valor faltó ventura' (he had excessive courage, and insufficiency of luck),[20] and Lope de Vega says,

> Dirá que ciego y ambicioso fuiste,
> pero no negará que confirmaste,
> muerto en el cielo, que del Sol naciste

(They say that you were blinded by ambition, but they can't deny what you confirmed; killed in the heavens, you were the child of the Sun)²¹

Calderón's Faetón, naturally enough, is also blind and ambitious; the comic servant, at the close of the play, says that

> los discretos
> sacarán cuán peligroso
> es desvanecerse

> (sensible people will learn from this how dangerous it is to overreach oneself)
> (Aguilar, i, p. 1951b) [*BAE*, iv, p. 198c]

Most of the characters in the play are in agreement with this verdict. Calderón, however, gives it the lie by presenting his protagonist in a way which is almost totally sympathetic. The youth is neither violent nor arrogant, but rather unlucky through no fault of his own, a man for whom nothing goes right. The rivalry between Phaethon and Epaphus, which in Ovid merely consists of the latter making fun of the former for his belief in being Apollo's son, comes to mean much more in Calderón: Faetón performs noble and heroic deeds and everybody thinks that they were performed by Epafo; when Faetón tries to take the credit for what he has done, he is thought to be arrogant; when Epafo says that he does not deserve any praise, he is thought to say this out of modesty, and is praised all the more. Finally, to fill Faetón's cup of bitterness to the full, Epafo turns out to be the king's long-lost son, while Faetón remains a foundling, without honour. Driven by this misfortune, he tries to win fame for himself, in order to have his merits recognised and to ingratiate himself with the lady whom he is courting. When he finds out that he may be Apolo's son, and enthusiastically announces the fact, he is rejected as a madman. He is, nevertheless, Apolo's son; but proof of his birth only serves to cause his downfall, since, in order to appear in public as the god's son, he has to drive the Sun's chariot across the heavens. Thanks to this excessive ambition, the world almost catches fire, and to save it Júpiter has to hurl a thunderbolt at Faetón. He has all our sympathy; he is the almost innocent victim of an unlucky star: in trying to ascertain the truth, he rebels against that star, and brings about his own downfall.

Faetón, son of the Sun, is thus brought down by the very thing which should have exalted him. What does the symbol of the Sun mean here? The answer to this question is found in the first part of this double drama, *Apolo y Climene*, where the mystery of Faetón's birth is explained. Here we have the most important change which Calderón has introduced in his mythological material. While mythology records that Clymene is

Phaethon's mother, neither Ovid nor any other source gives any details of her love-affair with Apollo. Calderón, on the other hand, devotes an entire play to this subject, and his imagination embellishes the story and presents the symbol of the Tower in an extremely interesting form.

At the beginning of this first part, Climene laments the seclusion in which she is forced to live and, in terms which bring Segismundo to mind, longs for her liberty. The daughter of a king, she is imprisoned in the temple of Diana, placed there by her father, Admeto, because when she was born it was predicted that she would give birth to a son so arrogant and proud that he would set the kingdom of Ethiopia on fire. So that she cannot have a child, then, her father keeps her in seclusion and dedicated, as a priestess, to the service of Diana; dedicated, in other words, to chastity. As time goes on, however, Admeto can no longer resist her pleas, and allows her to come and go as she wishes, on condition that she always remains a priestess; if she breaks her vow, he will sacrifice her on Diana's altar himself. Thus a moral imprisonment takes the place of a physical one. But through a series of accidents, which are not her fault, she appears to be compromised with Apolo (who, in the guise of one of Admeto's shepherds, is an exile on earth). He rescues her when her father tries to sacrifice her to Diana; she experiences love, and gives birth to a son, who is separated from his mother and who grows up without knowing who his parents are.

The symbol of the Tower can be interpreted only within the context of the play's action: in other words, in the light of what happens to Climene. The interesting thing here is that at no point in either the first or the second play is Climene a free individual. As soon as her father has freed her from the seclusion of the temple of Diana, Apolo and Fitón hide her from her father's wrath in the Palace of Venus, which she calls her 'new prison' (Aguilar, I, p. 1900b) [*BAE*, IV, p. 170b]. When Apolo ascends again to the heavens, and when Climene's father discovers her to be still alive, Fitón hides her again, and she remains a recluse in this cave until Faetón reaches manhood, only leaving it to hunt for food. Thus she becomes, in the second part, the mysterious wild beast who is feared by everybody until her own son captures her and she is found to be a woman. Climene, then, lives all her life in seclusion. This means that, throughout her existence, she is under some form of constraint. The only thing that happens to her, as she passes from one prison to another, is that she experiences love. She does not cease to fear the prophecy, but she is deceived by Fitón, who tells her that he has the power to prevent its fulfilment; only with this promise does Climene accept Apolo's love; that is, she accepts love believing, deceived as she is, that it will save her from impending sorrow: she is a victim even in this. The fact that she learns about love under constraints means, then, that the emergence from the first prison signifies the attainment of adolescence; the step from innocence to the experience of passion, which is nature's compulsion. When her father extracted from her a promise of chastity, he had not actually realised that her companions, the other priestesses of Diana, were already indulging in secret love-affairs. Humanity, generally speaking, is not free to dedicate itself to Diana's service; the law of passion is one which must be obeyed. In this play, *Apolo y Climene*, the Sun is thus a symbol of love. As the symbol develops, we encounter a very curious paradox. This propulsion towards loving, which is exemplified when Climene ceases to resist Apolo's advances, is the work of the magician Fitón. This character is the mythical Python, the serpent who is enemy to Apollo's mother Latona (Leto).[22] Calderón states explicitly that he represents the Devil.[23] The compulsion towards love which Climene experiences is, therefore, a compulsion towards 'evil'; however, she loves a god, that is, she loves something which is good. The object of her love is good; the force which inclines her towards that object is an 'evil' one.

This paradox leads us into the realms of philosophy. It is that paradox which, implicitly or explicitly, is diffused through all of literature's idealisation of human love, from courtly love, especially from the middle of the fifteenth century, through Neoplatonism until Quevedo's love poetry. The paradox is that man is made up of body and soul; although his origins are divine, he is subject to ontological evil in that, according to Platonic concepts, all matter is evil because it is a defect of the spirit; because of this inherent defect, man has a proclivity towards moral sin, because the sensual part of his nature can confuse and blind the rational part. Love's paradox lies (or lay, in Calderón's time) in the fact that the human spirit cannot accept as perfect any type of love which is not completely spiritual, while the body demands that love should exist on a sensual and therefore imperfect plane.[24] As a result of this paradox, Climene, compelled by her nature to love, loves a god; but she cannot keep him. He has to abandon her in order to return to the heavens, while she has to remain in the seclusion which Fitón has prepared for her, deprived of her liberty by the chains of the flesh. The love between Apolo and Climene, as presented to us by Calderón, could not be more chaste; but it is the sensuality inherent in human love which makes Climene Fitón's prisoner and, in the second part, a beast to be feared.[25] In addition to being the Sun, Apolo is the god of reason; in order to be made human, he has to be exiled from his divinity, because reason can only operate imperfectly in a human body. Apolo makes constant mention of his exile and always lays stress on the confusion of good and evil in the world of mankind.[26] For this reason, Apolo and Climene's union cannot last. At the end the *gracioso* talks about the play in these terms:

Si a esta perdonéis los yerros,
por la novedad siquiera,
dama y galán dividiendo,
de acabar ella en divorcio,
cuando otras en casamiento

(Please excuse the play's faults, even if only because of its novelty, since it ends in divorce, by separating hero from heroine, where other plays end in their marriage)

(p. 1908b) [p. 174c]

When Calderón mentions dramatic conventions, he usually does so in a humorous way: here, the humour masks a serious concept. Humanity and divinity are forcibly divorced, because physical substance is placed between them; it is Fitón who persuades Apolo, who is loth to abandon Climene, that he must return to the heavens. In love, the human and the divine can touch, but not unite. Or, to put it in the poetic terms of Calderón's symbolism, man strives for the Sun; in love, he most feels the heat of its rays, but the Sun sets and Night takes its place. When Apolo goes, Climene hides in the darkness of her cave, a prisoner, that is to say, a victim of the imperfections of life.

Her son, Faetón, is similarly life's victim, but in a different way: he is a victim of circumstance, of the fortuitous nature of events. Everything turns out badly for him, and he is not to blame. His freedom of action is similarly circumscribed, since none of his actions produce the expected result: he cannot do what he wants to, nor can he succeed. This restriction of his liberty is symbolised in the prophecy which condemns him to set the world on fire. This, of course, is also an indication of which way his temperament inclines: if he had not been too spirited to humble himself, he could have accepted misfortune with humility. But he must prove his worth. The ambition which goads him on and ruins him stems, then, from the nature of life itself on the one hand, and from his own natural goodness on the other. The world cheats him constantly; for this reason he aspires towards the Sun, and brings about his own downfall. He is also an example of the paradox of the human condition. The son of a god, his spirited behaviour and the knowledge of his own worth are the divine spark which fires his desire to break the chains restricting his liberty. In Faetón, as with Climene, the paradox of the human condition is a tragic one: it is, in both of them, the divine element which holds out a promise of consummation which life itself makes impossible. Man cannot prevent himself from longing to perfect his being; but neither the world, nor love, can be perfect.

It is necessary now to sum up the meaning of the sun-symbol in these two works. When Climene and Faetón, climbing up the rainbow, arrive before the dawning Sun, they sing these alternate lines:

Climene: Sagrado dios de Delo . . .	(Sacred god of Delos . . .)
Faetón: Alma del mundo . . .	(Soul of the world . . .)
Climene: Corazón del cielo . . .	(Heart of the heavens . . .)
Faetón: Vida de las humanas monarquías	(Life of the human monarchies . . .)
Climene: Arbitro de las noches y los días	(Arbiter of night and day . . .)
Faetón: Espíritu admirable . . .	(Admirable spirit . . .)
Climene: De racional, sensible y vegetable . . .	(Rational, sensitive and vegetable)
Faetón: Esplendor de esplendores . . .	(Splendour of splendours . . .)
Climene: Alimento de los frutos y las flores . . .	(Nourishment of fruits and flowers . . .)
Faetón: Anhélito suave . . .	(Gentle breath . . .)
Climene: Del bruto, de la fiera, el pez y el ave . . .	(Of brute, wild beast, fish and bird . . .)
Faetón: Padre común del hombre . . .	(Common father of all men . . .)

(p. 1945 a-b) [*BAE*, iv, p. 195 a-b]

The Sun, then is the creative source of life, of all beauty, and life's energy: it indicates the divinity which lies behind the universe. Because he is Apollo, the Sun is also the impulse behind art, the sciences, and civilisation: it is the longing felt by humanity to perfect itself, the longing which every man feels for freedom and for fulfilment. But the Sun burns anyone who gets too close; man must not try to rule it, he must not become proud and make himself out to be God; he has to accept the lowliness and disillusionments of life; that is, he has to accept that which deprives him of total freedom, he has to accept his imprisonment in the defects which the flesh imposes on the perfect operation of the spirit.[27] He has to resign himself to suffering.

The purpose of this chapter has been to call attention to one aspect of the development of Calderón's technique; a development which leads from metaphors full of ideas which shed light on the themes, to metaphors which turn into symbols, then to symbols which become visible in the action, and finally to symbols which are brought to life in the actual characters themselves. Symbols are an important key to the interpretation of Calderón's work, in that they take us away from material reality and lead us towards artistic reality, where we can only fully comprehend the poetic vision which Calderón offers of human destiny. His mythological plays may never become popular with the majority of readers of Spanish drama; there is no doubt, however, that symbolism is one of the most powerful methods used by art to convey universality. Climene and Faetón, as representatives of classical antiquity, were nonsensical characters to Pierre Paris;[28] to a discerning reader, this mother, perpetually imprisoned and kept away from the god she loves, and this son, who tries to prove his divine relationship by proudly hurling himself into cosmic flight, and who not only is annihilated but also threatens to annihilate the world in a fire (which, thanks to the progress of science, we now see to be prophetic); these two characters are universal symbols, and as such invite our sympathy.

3 The dramatic structure of *El Alcalde de Zalamea*

The claim that Calderón's method of constructing a plot was a disciplined and orderly one, where symmetry and regularity seem to follow self-imposed rules to the detriment of inspiration (as has been generally held) can be very clearly exemplified from *El Alcalde de Zalamea*, generally thought to have been written between 1642 and 1644. The first date marks the end of Calderón's military service in the Revolt of Catalonia, which would have given him experience of military life on campaign; the second date was 1644, when it became apparent that the war with Portugal was already lost. The play is set during an earlier campaign against Portugal, when in 1580 Philip II supported his claim to the Portuguese accession with an invading army. The episode dramatised in the play is said to have taken place on the march of one regiment to Lisbon. This play is not a record of an actual event, nor are the details of the march or of the military command accurate. There is no reason why the plot should have been connected with Portugal other than Portugal's expulsion of the Spanish garrisons in December 1640 and the declaration of a state of war, although no campaign followed.

Calderón's fondness for symmetry has been noted in connection with his versification, especially when his plays are libretti. This symmetry can become elaborate in the court plays of his middle period and old age, as also in his *autos sacramentales*. Whole scenes are constructed in a fixed metrical pattern, often built up round a leitmotif which is developed and repeated at regular intervals. The pattern is invariably symmetrical, the different parts balancing and contrasting with each other. Such symmetry, however, is not confined to versification; it also exists where one would not normally expect it – in the way the advancing action in the plot-construction follows, in a logical and disciplined manner, how the theme is conceived and worked out. Here there is symmetry, of comparison or contrast, between episodes within an act and between the acts themselves.

'An art constructed with rigorous strictness and precision'; this is how Casalduero characterised Calderón's workmanship. 'In *La vida es sueño*, as in any work of the baroque period, nothing is there by chance or by accident. The last period of that age (Calderón, Zurbarán, Velázquez) made great demands on artists' technique. Our author came to compose his plays with an extraordinary rigour. His art has something mathematical about it; its pomp, and its sensuousness are transferred to a mental plane'.[1] The novelty of this statement did not lie in the fact, which was already known, but in the numerous examples of this rigorous method of composition, examples with which Casalduero succeeded in illuminating a play so well known and so much discussed as *La vida es sueño*, in the same way as he has shed new light upon so many other works of Spanish literature.

He noted how this play 'is markedly divided by its centre (in lines 1532–47; the play has 3,315) at the precise moment when Segismundo discovers his identity'.[2] A centre, namely, which is almost exactly mathematical. Casalduero also noted that the scene between Rosaura and Segismundo at the beginning of the play (ll. 103–272) consists of seventeen *décimas*, and that the scene in the same metre which brings the third Act to a close (ll. 2019–88) also consists of seventeen *décimas*.[3] These balanced correspondences are extended also to the theatrical 'space':

> When he was born, Segismundo was placed in a Tower. That is what the Tower is: to enter the world is to enter its prison; the prison of the body. The commonplace is familiar, but its representation is not. The play closes with the Rebel Soldier being confined to the Tower: instincts, the lower part of human nature, are necessary, which is why they exist, but they exist only to be imprisoned.

They are extended also to the characters:

> two pairs of young people and two old men support the action; Rosaura–Segismundo, Basilio (Segismundo's father), Clotaldo (Rosaura's father) and Astolfo–Estrella . . . Basilio (the learned man) governs life in the Palace, Clotaldo (the sinner) governs life on the Mountain. The pairs are equally balanced and, like the old men, correspond to particular places. For Rosaura–Segismundo the Mountain, for Estrella–Astolfo the Palace.[4]

To the best of my knowledge, nobody, before Casalduero, had noticed this balanced construction. One further example to show his perspicacity:

> the servant had been thrown out of the window. Clarín dies. The same end to the lives of these two characters, which preserve so well the character of the baroque, are warnings for the king: the first to avoid the arms of his son, the second to seek them.[5]

These balances serve to indicate what Casalduero calls 'an action of opposing poles': 'symbolical places: mountain–palace; a building: tower of Segismundo, tower of the rebel. The polarised action: to sleep – to wake, chained – free. The struggle between the men and the beast'.[6] When plot and theme are attractive by themselves, as in the case of *La vida es sueño*, the structural rigour and precision in the theatre of Calderón generally pass unnoticed. But in the majority of cases they convey, for the general reader, an absence of naturalness, which is why his art appeals less than that of Lope de Vega and Tirso de Molina. Since *El alcalde de Zalamea* seems to be a notable exception, it is the only play by Calderón which has received practically no adverse criticism; it has been considered an almost perfect play precisely because of its vigorous realism.

Studying the 'plurimembración correlativa' in Calderón's dramatic poetry, Dámaso Alonso came to see that 'the Calderonian correlation is profoundly structural'; *Amigo, amante y leal* (Friend, Loving and Loyal), for instance, is 'a clear example of a work planned with a three-part correlation'. That is why Alonso said that Calderón's thinking is 'that of a constructional mathematician'. This is evident even in those plays that relate to contemporary life. In connection with *El alcalde de Zalamea*, constructed on the duality soldier–peasant which gives the two-part correlation Don Lope–Pedro Crespo, Alonso exclaimed: 'What vitality, what expressive strength and what strong realism can be enclosed by art in the most rigid forms!' In concluding that 'the Calderonian play least divorced from reality thus presents a stylised duality of the world', he made us see that this 'realism', so much praised because so 'exceptional', was in fact a very relative realism.[7]

Going beyond these correlations, Peter Dunn distinguished others of the type pointed out by Casalduero in *La vida es sueño*. His indispensable analysis begins by stating that there are 'balances and symmetries in the layout which may seem surprising in a play which is held to be a model of realistic action' and which concludes: 'These underlying symmetries, counterbalances and so on also show how careful we must be in talking about the "realism" or "simplicity" of a stage action.'[8]

The purpose of this present essay is to demonstrate that, in addition to the stylistic correlation and the symmetries and counterweights so well studied by Alonso and Dunn, the dramatic structure of the stage scenes in *El alcalde de Zalamea* can also show that exceptional realism is neither exceptional nor realistic.

By 'scenes' one does not mean the division of an act according to the particular number of characters who are on the stage at a particular moment. This is the French system, and has nothing to do with the structure of Golden Age plays. In general, the division by change of place had also no structural function; such a system, because of the supposed changes of time implied, often violates the actual dialogue, as Sloman has shown, precisely in the Acts of *El alcalde de Zalamea*.[9] Act I of this play is usually divided into eighteen 'scenes', with four changes of place: 'Countryside near Zalamea', 'Street', 'Courtyard or porch in the house of Pedro Crespo', and 'Upper room in the same house'.[10] In the *comedia*, the only scene-changes that occur are those where the stage direction 'Exeunt all' is followed immediately by the entry on to the stage of one or more characters other than those that have left. Here, presumably, the stage would remain empty for a few moments, which would have indicated lapse of time or change of place, or both together. But the fact that this division does not exist does not mean that the scene does not change. The whole of the first Act of *El alcalde de Zalamea* constitutes one single scene, namely, an uninterrupted performance during which the imagination of the audience, following the indications in the dialogue, can pass from a place so far away from Zalamea that the town cannot be seen, until it mounts the stairs leading to Isabel's room in Pedro Crespo's house. The dialogue takes us through all the intermediate places without the time taken by this 'journey' (three-quarters of an hour, more or less) bearing any relation to the time needed for the actual journey (which would take several hours).

In analysing the structure of this play we cannot pay attention to any 'scenes' which can split up the action and be numbered. Nonetheless, there do exist decisive moments marking the development of the plot. If Act I is examined from this angle, one notices that the plot is developed through the successive entrance on to the stage of the principal characters, thus dividing itself into the following six 'important episodes', namely

(1) I, ll. 1–137: *The Soldiers, with Rebolledo and La Chispa*. This serves as the Introduction. They are subordinate characters in the action, but they serve to present the tone and the setting of military life, with its disorderly conduct, carefree and unruly, which is to be the background against which a dramatic conflict will unfold. La Chispa is a cheerful woman of loose life, who is to serve as the contrast with the modest and demure Isabel. Against this background, the principal characters appear one by one, this being a structure that completes the thematic exposition by the continuous addition of new elements. *La vida es sueño*, for example, follows a different pattern: one in which the first Act, which in the structure of the Spanish *comedia* comprises the whole exposition, presents two mysteries, the identity of Segismundo and that of Rosaura; later, in the second Act, there appear the characters who disclose this information. The disclosure is given in two narrations which are equivalent to two 'flashbacks'. This means that two problems have come

to a head; they must then be explained and lastly resolved. In *El alcalde de Zalamea* the problem will emerge before the eyes of the audience, and one must first of all present all the factors that will explain the genesis and the nature of the problem. The presentation will follow the ordered process of reasoning, and not the fluctuations of real life.

(2) I, 137–224: *The Captain*. He is a nobleman and an officer. His conversation with the sergeant reveals that, since he is part of the disorderly life of the army, he is a cynical seducer of women. As a nobleman, he despises the common people; however beautiful a peasant girl may be, she is not worthy to become his wife.

(3) I, 225–422: *Don Mendo*. From the cynicism of the military nobleman, we pass to the decadence of the idle nobleman, which completes the picture of aristocratic pride. Don Mendo is a grotesque 'figure',[11] because anyone is ridiculous who believes that nobility is based only on an *ejecutoria*, or 'patent of gentility', and who prefers to die of hunger rather than demean himself by working.

(4) I, 423–556: *Pedro Crespo and his family*. Pedro Crespo and his son Juan now enter the stage so that two commoners should present the contrast with the two noblemen. Don Mendo is impoverished; Crespo is wealthy because he works. Don Mendo is an aristocrat and therefore 'honourable' because of his *ejecutoria*; Crespo refuses to buy a patent of nobility, because this would be 'honor postizo', artificial and deceptive honour, equivalent to placing a wig on a bald man's head. The contrast establishes the fact that honour depends on what one is, and that commoners and peasants have every right to self-respect.

(5) I, 557–776: The conflict is foreshadowed. This develops around two focal points: the respect in which noblemen should hold peasants, and the respect in which all men should hold women.

(6) I, 777–end: *Don Lope de Figueroa*. The conflict ceases with the arrival of the General, who stands for authority and therefore social order. He arrives last of all for two reasons. First, because authority and social order are to be the most important aspects of the theme. They prevent disorder, or they incarnate Law, which punishes disorder if it has not been prevented. Secondly, because it presents a double contrast, as much with the Captain as with Crespo. He is an aristocrat like the former, but he is a just and honourable man, and he can recognise that the common people also have the prerogative of honour. As the representative of authority he defends protocol and law: however criminally the Captain may have behaved, the right to punish him does not belong to Crespo. Where Don Lope upholds the letter of the law, Crespo upholds the inner spirit of justice.

This conflict, thus announced at the end of Act I, will break out at the end of Act III. Having solved one problem, Crespo will have to face another much more serious one. Crespo came onto the stage in the middle of Act I. The Captain had come on earlier, and Don Lope comes on later: Crespo in between the two opponents of the peasant class, the contempt of the aristocrats and the military code. The structure of this Act follows the logical exposition of the theme step by step. Each character appears when what he will contribute to the theme has to be explained, and the exposition develops in ascending order of importance. After indicating that Crespo will come into conflict with the Captain, the climax is made clear, namely that after the conflict with the Captain, Crespo will not be able to avoid a conflict with the law, that is to say, with the authority of the Army and the State.

Consequently, Act I divides logically and dramatically into six sections. And there is something still more surprising: not only is there this symmetry between Acts I and II, but there is also a perfect symmetry within Act II itself, as the diagram makes clear.[12]

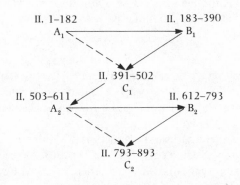

A = Disorder and the characters who stand for it
(Don Mendo, the Captain and the Soldiers)

B = Order (Crespo, Don Lope, Juan, Isabel)

After Group A has come onto the stage and withdrawn, Group B comes on. C represents a fight, which takes place when A returns and meets B. The first fight (C) takes place when the serenaders return and when Crespo and Don Lope go out of the house to chase the soldiers away.

In the second half of the Act the series A–B–C is repeated. The second fight, C_2, is the kidnapping of Isabel; Juan hears her cries, and follows them. Before Juan had departed with Don Lope, Crespo had given him some words of advice which Juan now puts into practice when he hears the cries of Crespo and Isabel without knowing who they are:

> Dos necesidades son
> las que apellidan a gritos
> mi valor; y pues iguales
> a mi parecer han sido,
> y uno es hombre, otro mujer,
> a seguir ésta me animo;
> que así obedezco a mi padre
> en dos cosas que me dijo:
> 'Reñir con buena ocasión,
> y honrar la mujer', pues miro
> que así honro a la mujer,
> y con buena ocasión riño.

Two cries for help are summoning me; since the two seemed equal in urgency and one is a man and the other a woman, I resolve to follow the latter; in this way I shall obey the two commands my father gave me: 'Fight only in a good cause and respect women', in this way I both respect a woman and fight in a good cause.

(II, 882–93) [*BAE*, III, p. 80a]

The close of this Act, structured with remarkable symmetry, thus points forward to Act III, since the struggle of the peasant commoner against the contempt that the nobleman has for his class, and against the law of the land, will be 'the fight in a good cause'.

We will now not be surprised to find that Act III is also divided into six sections. We return to the structure of Act I in the sense that the six main characters appear again one after the other. Crespo, however, remains on stage almost the whole time, and the successive emergence of each character onto the stage means that the action advances by making Crespo face the problem that each character presents to him in turn.

(1) III, 1–78: *Isabel* – the Act is introduced by the dramatic climax. Isabel's dishonour is made known: she does not know what to do. This is the general problem that awaits Crespo. Now he faces it.

(2) III, 79–348: *Crespo and Isabel*. The solution to the problem is completely altered when Crespo is informed that he has been elected Mayor and therefore chief Magistrate.

(3) III, 349–634:[13] *Crespo and the Captain.*

(4) III, 635–714: *Crespo and Juan.* This adds a new facet to Crespo's dishonour, since Juan seeks to restore the family honour by killing Isabel, and also since he is in danger through having wounded the Captain.

(5) III, 714–851: *Crespo and Don Lope.* Since Crespo refuses to obey the authority of the Army, Don Lope orders his men to attack the town.

(6) III, 851 to the end of the Act: *Crespo and the King*. The arrival of the King prevents the battle and proves that right was on Crespo's side.

It is not only that the structural plan of Act III is the same as that of Act I, it is also the case that the ending of Act III repeats the ending of Act I: in Act I the conflict ceases with the arrival of authority (Don Lope); in Act III the conflict, which enveloped not just a single family but the whole town of Zalamea, is brought to an end by the arrival of the supreme authority of the State. There is a perfect symmetry in the whole play: the last Act repeats the plan of the first, and the second half of Act II repeats the plan of the first half. That is to say, that the whole play has a kind of circular structure.

Such a structure cannot, *qua* structure, be called realistic. In the real world, more is the pity, the events of human life are not ordered in logical and symmetrical series. It is an extremely artificial structure, governed by the rigidity of a sexpartite formula. This cannot possibly be accidental. It may be possible that the construction was not conscious in all its symmetry, but in this case it would have been due to a habit not only of composition, but also of thought. The sexpartite formula follows from the tripartite division imposed by the theme: Crespo between the Captain and Don Lope at the beginning; Crespo between Don Lope and the King at the end. On this basis it would have been natural for Calderón to make three the basis both of Crespo's family (Crespo, Juan and Isabel) and of the world outside it (Don Mendo, the Captain, Don Lope). It is unquestionable that the logical system of classifying concepts, which was characteristic of Scholastic philosophy, which divided and subdivided a whole into its parts, opposing to each part its contrary, and classifying on the bases of analogical and contrary qualities, etc., came to constitute a habit of mind in Calderón, a definite mode of thinking and therefore of writing.

What has this to do with Art? Nobody could maintain that the dramatic value of *El alcalde de Zalamea* is due to its symmetrical and perfectly balanced construction. Would it not be rash, however, to hold that the dramatic vitality exists *in spite of* its structural symmetry? The orderliness and coherence of the plot have always aroused universal admiration; but these qualities do not exist, nor could we imagine them, apart from this structure. The consistent development of the theme, the march of events with such sure and rapid strides, exist in the form Calderón has given them to us, and in no other. No doubt he would have found this type of structure especially satisfying.

Although the structural elements here analysed are different from the Calderonian 'correlations' studied by Dámaso Alonso, they belong to the same artistic world, and it is necessary to give emphasis to the words of this distinguished critic:

Thus, for very different reasons, in dozens and dozens of plays, the Calderonian stage separates into parallel branches (in two, in three, in four, in five . . .) adjoined only by some neutral element. The reasons for this are many: an economy in time which achieves a plastic spatial presentation of the philosophical and theological pluralities in the *autos*; the possibility of filling attractively and harmoniously the stage space in the court plays with their scenic effects; or a variety of human relationships (here preferably two-part relationships) which are what alone enable the audience to follow the thread of the highly intricate intrigues in the Cloak and Sword Plays. *And always, always an artistic liking for a precise plan and for a complex symmetry; a need to impose order and to unravel in a stylised fashion the entanglements of real life and to dispel the fogs of thought.*[14]

This artistic taste controls the composition of the most 'realistic' plays as well as the most stylised ones. What is aesthetic taste in the dramatist can be aesthetic pleasure in the reader or, dependent on a sensitive producer, in the audience. Those of us who are unable to penetrate the technique of musical composition can feel aesthetic pleasure when we hear a Bach fugue, but the pleasure must be greatly enhanced in those who can appreciate the mathematical subtleties of the composition. In order to appreciate the essential values of the dramatic world that Calderón presents to us, it is not necessary to follow all the ramifications of 'the mathematical construction of his thought'; moreover, there is always the risk that the essential values may be placed on a lower level than the technical skill. Nonetheless, in the majority of such cases the ability to discern how the 'mathematical' technician works at his material gives the reader an added pleasure. In the particular case of *El alcalde de Zalamea* the human values it enshrines are not subordinated to anything; we are here impressed aesthetically by the triumph of an art able to express so much life and so much reality by means of such an artificial stylisation.

4 'Poetic truth' in the shaping of plots

The preceding chapters have demonstrated how 'reality' is moulded to fit the poetic and dramatic ends that Calderón had in mind. 'Reality' is moulded through metaphors into symbols, and a 'real-life' plot is given a structure that has a unity imposed by a logical plan. The action of *El alcalde de Zalamea*, however, does not distort or pervert 'reality'; on the contrary, it serves to highlight it. Frequently, however, Calderón takes vast liberties with plots that come straight from historical sources, or from well-known literary sources, such as mythological fables. This freedom aroused the scorn of neo-classicists and of all later critics who considered, naturally enough, that historical plays should be true in essentials to the events they were re-imagining. Marcelino Menéndez Pelayo, in his centenary study of Calderón in 1881, could not impute ignorance of history to the dramatist, and had to fall back on the charge that his failure to be 'historical' was due to negligence or total disregard of the nature of historical drama.[1] This charge was, on the face of it, unlikely to be true, and in fact when he made it he was himself guilty of disregard of the fact that the literary theorists of the Golden Age expressly repudiated fidelity to historical sources as a strict requirement in drama; either because he thought that Calderón went much further than they would have been allowed, or because he could not condone any departure from truth even on the part of reputable Renaissance theorists. This dramatic licence goes back, of course, to Aristotle, and since Calderón frequently avails himself of it, he must have thought that it was very important for his art. Aristotle makes a fundamental distinction that retained its validity until the eighteenth century. In the literary theory of Calderón's age, this distinction was bound up with the principle of 'decorum' and the principle of what has become known, in English, at least, as poetic justice. In accordance with these two principles, Calderón reconstructs already existing stories and plots in order to give what he considered an artistic shape to the theme he wished to extract from the story or plot. 'History', said Aristotle, recorded events as they actually happened, but 'poetry' recorded them as they ought to have happened;

in this respect 'poetry' was more 'philosophical' than 'history'. Poetic justice is implicit in his conception of tragedy, though not given a name:

> A good man must not be seen passing from happiness to misery, or a bad man from misery to happiness. The first situation is . . . simply odious to us. The second . . . does not appeal either to the human feeling in us [i.e. our sense of 'poetic justice'] or to our pity, or to our fears.[2]

Part of the principle that 'history' must be made 'poetic' is the conception of poetic justice in its basic form. It is so natural that it occurs, however crudely, throughout folk or popular literature. Thus when King Roderick lost Spain to the Moors, legend (and so epic and ballad poetry) had to invent both a crime (the seduction of La Cava) to explain this national disaster and an expiation (Roderick's penance and death by being sealed in his tomb).

Poetic justice in literature is thus part of the universal concept of guilt and retribution, which is given a simple form in primitive cultures and a profound one in the Christian doctrine of the Atonement. In the Spanish drama, in accordance with this concept, it was considered fitting that wrongdoing should not go 'unpunished' and that virtue should not remain 'unrewarded'. The converse of the necessary 'punishment' of the evildoer is also implicitly asserted, though not so invariably: namely that nobody should suffer disaster without deserving it (unless, of course, he is the innocent victim of the wrongdoing that the play sets out to 'punish').[3] The different types of 'punishment' meted out to the characters range from consigning them to hell to thwarting their purposes. Damnation is rare, but it is implied in Calderón's treatment of Cardinal Wolsey in *La cisma de Ingalaterra*. It indicates, of course, that the evil in question has been so great and so deliberate that there are no extenuating circumstances to redeem it. Below damnation comes death,[4] and below this there are various degrees of frustration, which consist in the shattering of a character's plans. A common form of frustration is the non-attainment of a marriage on which a character had set his hopes, but there are many others, some of which are not generally recognised as such. It is important to realise that death is not the only form of expiation in the Spanish drama, and that its absence does not necessarily imply a 'happy ending' in the usual sense. The frustration which a character meets with at the end of a play is a sign of the dramatist's condemnation of his actions, and therefore a pointer to the interpretation of the theme. 'Punishment' of this kind is nearly always present to some degree, although it can be mitigated by forgiveness: in *La vida es sueño*, for instance, Basilio is restored to the throne by the generosity of Segismundo, but his pride is humbled beforehand and he is compelled to admit his error.

The operation of poetic justice is simple, even crude, when the theme of a play is a straightforward contrast between black and white; but there are many subtle plays in which poetic justice is very far from crude. It can, for instance, be implicit in the situation with which the play closes. In Calderón's wife-murder tragedies the fact that the avenging husbands appear to go scot-free is ironical. It must be realised that their cases are not parallel to Othello's, for in *A secreto agravio, secreta venganza* (Secret Vengeance for a Secret Dishonour) the wife is guilty of adultery in intention, and in *El médico de su honra* she has made herself appear so, and her murder means that her innocence can never be made known to her husband. Both husbands therefore sincerely believe they have acted rightly according to the 'justice' upheld by the standards of their society, and cannot, in consequence, become aware of any need to expiate guilt. Nonetheless, if they and their society do indeed remain 'unpunished' then this will be a 'justice' that Calderón himself upholds. But this is not the case: in the first of these plays the King is Sebastian of Portugal who from the very start is preparing the ill-fated expedition to Morocco from which, as Calderón's audience knew, he and the flower of his nobility would not return. At the end, after killing his wife and her would-be lover, Don Lope de Almeida says to the King that he can now accompany him to Africa since he has nothing more to live for. This does not make the interpretation of the play depend upon a future event beyond the stage action, for it is the action itself that indicates that Don Lope will shortly die.[5] The case of *El médico de su honra* will be discussed in a later chapter.

There are certain types of themes where poetic justice cannot be overt, not because of irony but for 'reasons of state'. These are themes in which kings are the wrongdoers. Only if the themes came from ancient history could such kings be killed or deposed or commit suicide. This was not only for fear of political repercussions: it was due in the first place to the literary principle of 'decorum'. It was a question of tone and propriety. Language and imagery should be appropriate to the particular subject (hence the theory of the Three Styles); the tone should fit the social standing of the characters. So should the actions and the passions imputed to the characters; the more exalted a character, the more impossible it was to make him guilty of violent actions governed by base motives.

The principle of decorum can be exemplified by the striking departure from history (as Spaniards then knew it) in the treatment of Queen

Elizabeth in *El conde de Sex* by Antonio Coello; a play in which Philip IV himself was reputed to have had a hand, and which was performed in 1633 and published in 1638.[6] Francisco Bances Candamo, referring to this play in 1690, states that no queen was more wanton than Elizabeth, yet despite this and the fact that she had no descendants whose feelings needed to be taken into account, she is presented as a woman of honour and of such delicate feelings that she cannot reveal her love to Essex, although historically she had been his mistress. This he explains as follows:

> It is an inviolable principle of the stage that none of the characters should act in any way that would insult what he stands for or fail to correspond to it, that none should commit a vile or unfitting act. For how can a princess be presented in an unworthy light, especially when poetry alters history; since the latter presents events as they occurred, while the former portrays them as they should have happened?[7]

This principle of literary fitness merged into the sense of moral fitness ('that none of the characters should act in any way that would insult what he stands for or fail to correspond to it') that lay behind the conception of poetic justice. This merging of the two, together with the fact that considerations of this kind could necessitate a departure from 'truthfulness to life', has been demonstrated by Casalduero in his acute analysis of the two endings to *El celoso extremeño*,[8] where without mentioning it he disposes of Américo Castro's explanation[9] of Cervantes' change of mind. The comparison he draws between the ending of the first version of this story and that of *El curioso impertinente* reveals conclusively that Cervantes 'has carefully weighed up the end that each one of his characters deserved'. Cervantes does this, in fact, with a subtlety of nuance and a delicate precision for which there is no parallel even in the drama of Calderón.[10] None the less this first ending did not satisfy him, for while adultery is artistically appropriate in the case of Camila, whose situation is unfolded on the level of tragedy, it is inappropriate in the case of Leonora who is pathetic in her innocence; adultery is a degradation her character does not deserve:[11] in the second version it is therefore not consummated, and verisimilitude is sacrificed to artistic truth, which for Cervantes is inseparable from moral truth.

It is on this plane of artistic principle, and not on that of a moralising didacticism, that poetic justice must be placed, and this is the answer to the misguided criticism that (despite the authority of Aristotle) it has received in modern times. Allardyce Nicoll has called poetic justice 'trivial' because of 'the narrowness of that conception of tragedy which makes death a punishment and life a reward'. Death, he says, is no punishment for Macbeth; his punishment had already come when, realising the uselessness of all he had done, he understood the sadness of life.[12] This, of course, is true; but the real point is surely a technical one of plot invention. What would happen to the play and to our feelings as spectators of the action if Macbeth instead of meeting with death were to succeed in making good his escape? Such an ending would jar on our feelings by its incompatibility with the way they had been worked upon prior to the climax: it would be an artistically inappropriate conclusion. It is a question not of rewards and punishments, but of artistic propriety. Far from disclosing the triviality of poetic justice *Macbeth* demonstrates the technical necessity for it in practice.

Where this kind of artistic fitness is concerned historical verisimilitude was no more sacrosanct for Calderón than naturalistic verisimilitude was for Cervantes. There are numerous examples in the Spanish drama of plays that avoid the tragic ending related in the source. The 'happy ending' given to the story of Romeo and Juliet as dramatised by both Lope de Vega and Rojas Zorrilla is to be explained by the principle of poetic justice; since passionate love of itself did not merit a tragic end, much less so when it was making for the reconciliation of feuding families. This alteration jars on us nowadays, and both Lope and Rojas possessed the sense of tragedy that would have made better plays. The point, however, is not whether we like it or not, but that the principle of poetic justice was an important factor in determining the structure or shape of Spanish dramatic plots in the Golden Age.

The principle of decorum where royalty is concerned links up with poetic justice where this is not made to operate because of the difficulty of punishing kings on the stages of a strongly monarchical country. As already stated, this punishment is possible if the play is set in remote times or in distant countries. In more modern times, such punishments could have suggested that political sedition was legitimate and perhaps needed.[13] *El alcalde de Zalamea* is diverted from being a tragedy of a particularly pitiable kind, when the village magistrate having sentenced and executed the army captain who raped his daughter is not himself sentenced to death by the King for exceeding his authority by not handing his prisoner over to a military tribunal. He would certainly have been executed in real life, as will be seen below (p.322). Pedro Crespo would have been a real tragic hero in that event; upright, with a true sense of honour, and determined that justice be done; but with the hubris of excessive self-confident zeal, making true justice violate the laws of the State. Calderón would not have conceived the plot in this way, for he could not allow that Pedro Crespo committed any act of injustice or sinned from pride. In this respect his treatment has been questioned by some modern critics who find Crespo too devious and sly to be a worthy hero meriting the praise given to him by the King at the end. Since this was a village magistrate of peasant stock going counter to the laws governing the privileges of the army and of the aristocracy Calderón had to give him a certain cunning. Purely as drama it might have been a more impressive ending if the King had hanged Crespo for violating the laws of the State while letting the Captain go free; but as a drama mirroring the social life of the time the ending, with its pardon of Crespo and the honour given him by the King is unquestionably more impressive. This is an instance where Calderón makes poetic justice go counter to the prevailing socio-political ethos of his age.

Particularly important in Calderón are historical plots where Calderón deviates from history by rescuing his hero from the punishment that was in fact inflicted on him, or by making his protagonist suffer a disaster that goes directly counter to history. Such changes used to be laughed at. It will be shown that such deviations from history can be explained only by the ways in which poetic justice operated on the Spanish stage. When Calderón changes his source in any way the reader must accept that he does this for a conscious purpose and investigate what that purpose would have been. One such example is Calderón's dramatisation of the Coriolanus story.

5   The Coriolanus theme: *Las armas de la hermosura*

Coriolanus, a Roman military leader, had been given this name after capturing the Volscian city of Corioli, when he restored his liberty to the leader of the enemy. Despite many later services to Rome, he was refused the consulship by the people, and this caused a resentment which rankled, with the result that the antagonism of the people to him grew more violent. Brought to trial by the Senate, he was banished, and defected to the Volscians, Rome's former enemies. He was warmly received and advised by them to make war against Rome, and he marched against his native city at the head of a Volscian army. Various embassies were sent to him by his frightened countrymen, but he was deaf to all pleas to save Rome until finally his mother Veturia and wife Volumnia came out to plead with him. He greeted them tenderly, but he remained for long relentless in his desire for vengeance. At last the entreaties of the two women caused him to withdraw his army. The women had saved Rome, and a temple to 'Female Fortune' was erected in thanksgiving. The Volscians, however, turned in anger against Coriolanus for his betrayal, and he was murdered in 488 BC before his trial could be held. The Roman matrons put on mourning for his loss.

Calderón's version of this theme is *Las armas de la hermosura* (Beauty's Weapons) (1652). This was based on the play, *El privilegio de las mujeres* (Women's Privilege) (published 1636), in which Calderón collaborated with Pérez de Montalbán and Antonio Coello. A comparison of Calderón's play with the earlier one was made by A. E. Sloman.[1] The further discussion of the reasons that led Calderón to reshape the story will corroborate, from another angle, Sloman's interpretation.

The three main sources for the story that would have been known to Calderón all give substantially the same facts, but they differ in their treatment of the protagonist. Livy[2] is the most objective, dispassionately recording the events without praise or blame of Coriolanus's actions. Dionysius of Halicarnassus[3] presents Coriolanus in the most heroic light; his attitude is sympathetic and on the whole approving. Plutarch,[4] while doing justice to Coriolanus's personal integrity, can find nothing but severe censure for all his political and military actions: even his one good deed – the pardon of Rome – was reprehensible in that it was done for the wrong reasons, since by first refusing clemency to the ambassadors and the priests and then granting it to his mother, Coriolanus was not honouring his mother but insulting Rome, for he was making its ransom rest on the grief of one woman as if the city were not of itself worthy of pardon.

Calderón's treatment of Coriolanus becomes slightly less unhistorical if we take it to derive from Livy's impartial account rather than from Plutarch's condemnatory one. That Livy and not Plutarch was Calderón's main source (direct or indirect) is borne out by the fact that in the former (as also in Dionysius) the mother of Coriolanus is called Veturia, while in the latter she is called Volumnia; in Calderón the woman who intercedes for Rome is called Veturia. But certain aspects of Calderón's handling of the theme suggest that he also knew Plutarch.

The story, especially as related by Plutarch, offers a ready-made plot for a dramatic tragedy. Shakespeare was able to utilise it without introducing any basic modification, but not so Calderón. If we approach the story from the standpoint of poetic justice we can see that it contains what for Calderón would have been a fundamental inconsistency that made it impossible for him to dramatise it as a tragedy.[5]

The difficulty is this. Coriolanus's march against Rome was an act of treason and vindictiveness, and as such reprehensible; but he did not actually capture and sack the city, instead he pardoned it, and this was not an evil act but a good act, and therefore not one that in itself deserves the punishment of death. Though Coriolanus had treasonable intentions, he repented and never actually carried them out. The fact of his repentance would thus turn his death into something like the death of a martyr, for Coriolanus, knowing that to do the right thing will mean death, does not shirk doing it.[6] Apart from the fact that Calderón would scarcely have considered a martyr's death as a fitting consequence of a thirst for revenge, this way out of the difficulty merely shifts the moral problem further back. Coriolanus, through his own free actions, has placed himself in the dilemma of having to choose between doing the right thing or meeting death. Can the punishment for his wrongdoing consist primarily in his being placed in this dilemma? If so, what wrong has he done that places him in it?

This leads us back to the initial situation from which everything else starts – the political conflict between the patrician Coriolanus and the plebeian class. To oppose the representation of the people in the Senate may have been, as Plutarch states, political imprudence, but no seventeenth-century Spaniard – least of all the court dramatist of Philip IV – could have looked upon it as a crime that, on the level of poetic drama, deserved death. It is, of course, true that where a dramatic conflict in the Golden Age drama (in plays of the type of *Peribáñez* and *El alcalde de Zalamea*) results from the contempt of the aristocrat for the plebeian, the sympathies of the dramatists are with the common people; but the crime of the aristocrat is always a moral offence against the *villano*, an outrage against his personal honour.[7] It is only on this level that class conflict was a live issue on the Spanish seventeenth-century stage. The tragic death of Coriolanus could not be 'justified poetically' by the mere fact of his hostility to popular representation in the Senate.

Taking all these considerations into account, we see how impossible it was for Calderón to view the Coriolanus story as tragic drama. The death of a protagonist on the stage could only be punishment for a moral crime, but Coriolanus never at any stage actually commits one. A sacrificial death was impossible on the Spanish stage, except in the context of specifically religious plays like *El príncipe constante*.

If, then, Calderón could not dramatise the Coriolanus story as he found it in Roman history, and if its political background had no special interest for him or his times, why did he turn to the story at all? Ultimately for the same reason as Shakespeare, because its central episode, the crisis of the story, attracted and gripped his imagination. The peripeteia whereby the avenging warrior renounces vengeance because of his mother's pleading is of course highly dramatic. For Calderón it had the special attraction of illustrating in a striking way the vengeance–forgiveness motif that runs through so many of his plays up to 1652. *Las armas de la hermosura* appears as the culmination of this motif in his drama, as the final development in a series of plays dealing with vengeance. His free transformation of the Coriolanus story is made intelligible by the traditionally close association in the Spanish drama of vengeance and honour. Through the subservience of women to the dictatorial rule of their husbands, the theme of honour was bound up with the question of the position of women in society. It was because the Coriolanus story offered Calderón the opportunity of dealing with vengeance and forgiveness in this particular setting that he turned to it. In the honour plays women had pleaded in vain for mercy from their revengeful husbands; in the Coriolanus story a woman pleads for mercy from a revengeful man and obtains it.

Faithful to this central episode, Calderón reconstructs all the rest around it. Sloman refers to the departures from history, which are substantially the same in both plays; my own purpose here is to account for the particular reconstruction that the story undergoes. The first major change is that the story must cease to be a tragedy, and Coriolanus does not therefore die.[8] The second major change is that the conflict from which the action flows is not the oppression of the plebeians by the Roman patricians, but their oppression of women. This follows not only from the fact that the political conflict would have had little interest for his audience, but primarily from the special significance Calderón sees in the central episode of the pardoning of Rome. The change suggests that Calderón knew the story from Plutarch as well as from Livy, for whereas the latter merely refers in passing to the fame the women earned in Rome because of their success in making Coriolanus abandon his vengeance,[9] Plutarch lays considerable emphasis on the fact that it was to the women that Rome owed her salvation. He makes Volumnia, Coriolanus's mother, say that the fortunes of Rome have sunk desperately low if women are now her only hope. And after the success of their mission, he stresses the fact that the joy of the Senate and citizens found expression in the honours they showered upon the women, to whom they recognised that their escape and security from danger were alone due.[10]

The third major change Calderón introduces is to turn the women of Rome into the abducted Sabines, and to make the rape of the Sabine women the background to his theme. This, of course, is a telescoping of chronology, for the legend of the rape is associated with the reign of Romulus, therefore three centuries before Coriolanus. This is not an arbitrary change but is essential for the special significance Calderón is giving to his theme, for throughout his play Rome is presented as the oppressor of women, and the reason for this lies in the fact that Rome was built upon an injustice done to women, a crime that Livy makes the Sabines call a violation of religion and honour.[11]

Again, the suggestion for this change could well have come from Plutarch, for when the women of Rome ask Coriolanus's mother to intercede for the city, Plutarch makes their spokesman say that this action will 'lift you who consent to do it to a more conspicuous fame than that which the daughters of the Sabines won, when they brought their fathers and husbands out of war into friendship and peace'[12] – a reference to the outcome of the rape of the Sabines, when the women threw themselves between the two armies and stopped the battle that their kinsfolk were fighting in order to free them. This first occasion when women rescued Rome from danger is thus associated by Plutarch with the second occasion under Coriolanus. That was all Calderón needed to round off his conception of the theme. Since the women of Rome become the abducted Sabine women, the Volscians disappear and are replaced by the Sabines.

From these three major changes in the story numerous minor changes follow in Calderón's play. The effect of them all is to rebuild something quite new round the central episode of the pardon of Rome. The changes are so sweeping that, in effect, all the characters except Coriolanus are new. Livy's name for Coriolanus's mother, Veturia, is retained by Calderón for the woman who breaks down the hero's vindictiveness, but he turns her from his mother into his betrothed. What Calderón makes of the story and the special significance he extracts from its reconstruction is as follows.

Las armas de la hermosura opens with the contrast between war and love. The Sabines are attacking Rome in order to free their women and avenge the dishonour done to them. In Rome itself the elder senators whose spokesman is Aurelio, the father of Coriolano, fear that the presence of the women has made the men effeminate. The women are dominating the social life of the city and have introduced a new element of elegance and refinement; the pleasure of their company, so it is alleged, has enticed the young men into soft living and the stern martial virtues of Roman men are being forgotten: throughout the play the patricians are associated with war and the hardness that goes with it.[13] Coriolano is at a banquet with his betrothed, the Sabine Veturia, when they are interrupted by the appearance of Aurelio with the news of the Sabine attack. Angry at what he considers his son's effeminate decadence, he orders the banquet tables to be removed and calls the men to the hard task of war. Coriolano accepts the challenge and is made the general of the army, which he leads to victory. But during the battle the Roman Senate withdraw all the privileges and freedom of the women. Fine dresses are forbidden and they must remain indoors, confined to their houses as virtual slaves so that men may remain warriors. That is what, for the patricians, women are: creatures to be abducted and slaves to be kept to menial tasks. On Coriolano's triumphal return to Rome Veturia braves the Senate's ban and emerges to complain in public against this alienation of women's rights. Coriolano, angered by this development, refuses to accept the Senate's law and makes himself the public champion of women's freedom. For this he is imprisoned and tried. His father, fearful of losing his honour by failing in his public duty to the state, casts his vote for his son's death as a rebel, but the Senate passes sentence of banishment after public degradation. Aurelio himself publicly strips his son of all his honours.

The exiled Coriolano is welcomed by the Sabines, who place their army under his leadership so that he can exact his revenge against Rome. The city, besieged and threatened with famine, decides to surrender. Aurelio is sent to negotiate terms, but Coriolano will hear of none: he is determined that the city must be destroyed. The position of father and son is now reversed – a typical Calderonian touch to which

Sloman has given due emphasis. The father appeals to his son's sense of honour but the son pays the father back in his own coin: the father had sacrificed his son to his sense of public honour; the son will sacrifice his mother, the city, in order to avenge the degradation he has suffered. Coriolano angrily asserts that he has no honour; Rome has taken it away, and the vengeance he demands is the only thing that can restore it. His personal honour, not the fate of the city or his father, is his only consideration.

Another appeal on behalf of Rome is made by his closest friend, but Coriolano is deaf to the appeal of friendship; friend as well as father must be sacrificed to the rehabilitation of his honour. Lastly Veturia, his betrothed, pleads with him, not on behalf of the patricians who had wronged both him and her, but on behalf of the common people who had no share in his degradation and sentence. But Coriolano is adamant. She then pleads that forgiveness is nobler than vengeance, but this also has no effect. She then refuses to do what he asks, to remain with him while Rome perishes: she will share the city's fate. Then she begins to weep and asks for one last embrace. This and the sight of her tears soften Coriolano's heart and he relents. He pardons Rome, but only on condition that women are given back their freedom and that those of them who wish to return to the Sabines should be permitted to do so. This freedom of the Sabine women includes their right to engage in any profession; the play thus claims for women equality of social status with men. But Coriolano also lays down another condition which by conferring a still greater privilege on women discloses the full significance of the play. Sloman claims that this condition constitutes a clear indictment of the *pundonor* (the code of honour) of Calderón's day. The point is so important that it needs elaboration.

Honour is presented as something that fosters a purely selfish placing of one's own reputation and social dignity above everything else. Honour makes Aurelio publicly degrade his own son and vote for his sentence to death; honour makes Coriolano prepared to destroy his native city. Honour conceived in this way destroys all human ties because it makes love and friendship impossible, since it can demand a vengeance that overrides all human affection and all pity. Veturia inveighs against this conception of honour when she claims that forgiveness is nobler than vengeance. It is a woman who makes this plea because it is women, not men, who feel and show tenderness. A tender love, bringing with it the readiness to forgive, is the prerogative of the gentleness of woman's nature.

The theme of *Las armas de la hermosura* is therefore ultimately this. The virtues peculiar to men are the military virtues of courage, endurance and a strict obedience to a sense of duty. The stern, warrior-like patricians of Rome symbolise these virtues, which have their necessary place in war. But war is not the whole of human life and, when transferred to another sphere, the virtues that make men warriors make them arrogant, unfeeling, unforgiving, capable of sacrificing the closest of human ties; they make of each man a tyrant jealously guarding his own selfish honour. Whereas, on the other hand, women bring gentleness into the world, and with gentleness love and forgiveness. They alone can soften the harshness of man's nature, and they should therefore be given the social and moral freedom that will enable them to make of the world a human place instead of a military camp, that will enable them to turn proud, revengeful and tyrannical man into a civilised human being. The dominance of men in society produces the cruelty of the code of honour; by contrast it is women who, according to this play, produce the civilising, because humanising, influence. *Las armas de la hermosura* must therefore be placed in the context of the traditional Spanish honour plays, where husbands, in certain circumstances, conceive it their duty to kill the wives they profess to love because honour so demands, in the same way as Coriolanus conceived it his duty to destroy Rome. That is why Calderón, in order to drive home his point, changed his hero's mother into his betrothed and future wife.

The reason for Calderón's introduction of the Sabine women is now obvious. Rome has committed a crime against womanhood, and because of this crime she is brought to the brink of destruction; but she is saved through the intercession of the very women she had wronged – for Veturia stands for all the Sabine women. What she demands is not the vengeance on Rome to which she has a right, but the city's pardon.

It is natural to bring the theme of this play and its treatment into association with the position of women in Spain at the time the play was written. They were placed in a position of subjection to men, very far from being the arbiters of men's honour. On the contrary, the Spanish drama gave men the right to judge the honour of women exclusively in the light of their own honour, they alone having the right to judge whether their wives had violated this honour. The theme of vengeance and pardon within the framework of the social relationships of men and women to each other must be the reason why the Sabine women are brought into the Coriolanus story, and this rape must constitute a symbolic judgement on the contemporary position of women in Spain. If we take the words of the play literally, we would be tempted to conclude that Calderón goes, within the standards of his age, as far in the direction of feminism as it is possible to go; because Coriolano's final condition for the pardon of Rome is that as the greatest of the privileges to be conferred on women they and they alone are to be the arbiters of the honour of men:

> Y por mayor privilegio,
> más grave y más eminente,
> pues por las mujeres yo
> sin honra me vi, se entregue
> todo el honor de los hombres
> a arbitrio de las mujeres.

> (And as their greatest privilege, the most solemn and most eminent, since for the sake of women I found myself deprived of honour, let all men's honour be placed under the jurisdiction of women.)[14]

Only if women could reign in the domain of honour will there be the possibility of love, reasonableness and forgiveness ruling in the relations of human beings to each other.

Is it possible, however, to take literally such a sweeping reversal of the accepted standards? Even if we allow for the fact that the dramatic treatment of a wife's suspected adultery is 'larger than life', there is plenty of evidence to make us concede that a husband's right to punish his wife with death was acceptable in principle. It is true that a growing feeling for the moral rights of women can be detected within the Spanish literature of the last seventy years or so of the seventeenth century, but there is nothing to show that such a statement as the above could have been acceptable at any time to public opinion, although it possibly would have been to moral theologians. Can we imagine these words in championship of women's social and moral rights being recited on the stage without being whistled off by the often vociferous groundlings?

In the *corrales*, or public theatres, the answer would be 'no'. To see the effective, and not merely theoretical, purpose of these lines, we must realise that *Las armas de la hermosura* was not written for the people's stage, but for the court theatre. Court plays were addressed to royalty and marked the respect in which the royal family was held. The Court comprised the queen, princesses, and also ladies-in-waiting. These had to be shown as much respect as the king and his male courtiers. The exaggeration in the conclusion to which Calderón brings his play must have been a refined example of *courtoisie*, of that chivalrous gallantry towards women that this term denotes. Calderón is paying the royal ladies and their entourage the most graceful compliment he could devise. Actually, the compliment paid women in the source play, *El privilegio de las mujeres*, was even more extreme. One of the privileges conferred on women (in the Act written by Coello) is this: 'y que podáis, si ofendidas/ de vuestros maridos fuereis,/ castigar, como los hombres,/ su adulterio con la muerte' (and that, if you are dishonoured by your husbands, you may punish, just as men do, their adultery with their death).[15] The source play was also a court play, and Coello was one of the regular court dramatists. These lines are not preserved by Calderón in his reworking of this play, probably because he did not wish to make women capable of the cruelty of any kind of vengeance.

There is a curious paradox in the reputation Calderón has enjoyed. The term 'honor calderoniano' was long used by Spaniards (and perhaps still may be by many) to denote the most cruel and unrelenting vengeance of a husband on his supposedly adulterous wife. A truer reading of his wife-murder plays in the light of his dramatic technique, now much better understood, proved how unjust it was to hang this term round his neck. The pendulum went full swing, and Calderón came to be called a 'feminist'. It is suggested here that one has to consider the social contexts of the performances of plays used as proof before supporting the assertion. 'Feminism' is an emotive word at the time of writing (1985) in English-speaking countries, and to call Calderón a 'feminist' is to make too vast a leap across the centuries from culture to culture. What is quite certain, however, is that Calderón's plays show a deep sympathy for women and a special understanding of the difficulties and hardships which the social standards of the seventeenth century inflicted on them. This will become evident from most of the chapters that follow.

Calderón's version of the Coriolanus theme is one of the many expressions of this sympathy and respect for women. As such, it has a significance for him that entirely justifies his free adaptation of it. The changes he introduces into the story are not capricious and arbitrary but are an entirely logical expansion (and one relevant to his own times) of its central episode – the victory over vengeance of a woman's pleading. The facts of the original story largely disappear, but this central episode remains with a heightened significance. It could never have occurred to Calderón that anybody would ever expect from his drama lessons in ancient history; for the requirements of drama, which *pace* Menéndez Pelayo he never neglected or forgot, were summed up in the Aristotelian precept that poetic drama should be 'more philosophical than history'.

While the above arguments remain valid there is another probable reason for Calderón refashioning the plot of *El privilegio de les mujeres* published in 1636. There would seem to be a very clear connection between the play's vindication of Coriolano and contemporary Spanish history, a connection that will be fully explained in chapter 22. This will give an added justification for Calderón's departure from history.

II From experience to myth

6 The father–son conflict

In a dramatist who by any ordinary standards wrote so much (though not by the phenomenal standards of Lope de Vega or even of Tirso de Molina) it is not easy to speak of sources of inspiration. The ultimate source of inspiration must, however, be his own experience of life, transmuted into dramatic poetry. In the case of Calderón we can detect a group of plays that can be plausibly connected with his early life on the basis of documentary evidence, and these contain plots for which he draws on his direct experience. These form the first division of his output. The second division is formed by plays that most reflect his involvement in his society, but still more reflect or are directed towards his audience's involvement in their common society. A further heading would cover religious themes. Although Calderón has some striking religious *comedias*, his attempt to find dramatic form for the problems of faith and religious experience lies mainly in the corpus of his *autos sacramentales*; though these derive from the medieval drama, they are so far advanced in conception and execution that they really form a whole dramatic genre in themselves, which is excluded from this book. Calderón's religious *comedias*, as befits the secular stage, bring religion into closer contact with the life of society. They deal more with the impact of religious faith on public life, such as crusading wars, and various problems covered by religion and politics, which include the question of conformity or non-conformity to religious beliefs imposed by political means. Lastly there are plays whose plots derive more from the vicarious experience of life provided by history and legend and also by literature in the widest sense. In the latter case a main fund of stories was provided in the post-Renaissance period by classical mythology. Such stories were commonly used as libretti for operas in the seventeenth century and for much of the eighteenth, but libretti are generally so telescoped and stylised to fit the expansive demands of singing that they can rarely serve as dramatic plays in their own right, although Wagner later made them do so by extending the time of the performances. Calderón's mythology plays are vehicles, to a varying extent, for recitative and solo singing but not to the same extent as libretti as we normally understand the term.

They are plays in their own right, although showing an extra degree of stylisation and a further remoteness from real life than the rest of his *comedias*.

These divisions, established by the examination of his dramatic plots, will be explored in this book, commencing with plays which must have been connected with his own personal experience, passing to values and conflicts of social living, then to stories deriving from education and reading (history, legend), then plays that can be covered by the terms religion and politics, and lastly the world of classical fable. The movement will be from direct experience of life 'realistically' conveyed, through progressive imaginative developments, until we arrive at plays that are connected with the world of real life only through the presentation of abstract concepts in imaginative forms. I start with plays in which Calderón's personal experience seems directly and deeply involved.

Among the plays of Calderón's first period there is a group that dramatised a recurring theme, that of a stern, authoritarian father in conflict with a wild and rebellious son, who is sometimes not acknowledged to be an actual son until the end of a play, having appeared until then to be a youth of unknown parentage. These plays contain the most impassioned scenes in all Calderón's output. This alone would suggest that Calderón was emotionally more involved in these plays than in others, and the recurring theme within a period of some ten years points to a connection between them that needs explanation. From the will of the dramatist's father, we can plausibly reconstruct some of the early life of the Calderón family.

The dramatist was born into a respectable, well-to-do family, his father being a government official, Secretary of the Council of the Treasury of the Kingdom of Castile, a post that, together with another in the Accountancy office of the Council, had belonged to his own father, Don Pedro, who had acquired the right to hold a double office and bequeath it to his heirs. In order to have the social status commensurate with the dignity of these appointments, Don Pedro had obtained an *ejecutoria de hidalguía*, or patent of nobility, which passed to his descendants. All of them had the right to use the title 'Don' or 'Doña'.

The dramatist's father, Don Diego Calderón de la Barca, had married Doña Ana María de Henao y Riaño. They had seven children, of whom two died in infancy. The dramatist, born in 1600, had an elder brother Diego (born 1596) and a younger, José (born 1602) and two sisters, of whom one, Dorotea (born 1598) had entered a convent, and the other had died before the father's death, which took place on 21 November

1615. The dramatist Pedro was therefore fifteen when his father died. The father's will, drawn up three days before his death, reveals a very strained family life. The largest share of his estate he left to the eldest son, Diego, but with the following stipulation:

> I expressly command my son Diego Calderón not to marry or dispose of his person without the permission and consent of my executors or most of them, and in particular I forbid him to marry a person with whom I was told he was negotiating marriage, or any of his cousins. He and my executors have knowledge of this 'prohibition' because I have so informed them, and if nonetheless he should do this, or marry any other woman, without the said permission, I herewith declare null and void everything that I have bequeathed to him in this will, and I forthwith disinherit him, for being a disobedient son, in every way that the laws of the kingdom permit, and I forthwith increase by a third and a fifth the legacies of the said Pedro and José Calderón. [His brothers Pedro and José] I order to have no communication nor intercourse with him, because with open defiance he has dishonoured his grandparents and parents. This must be scrupulously carried out in either of those two eventualities.[1]

There is nothing in the will to indicate that Diego, who was then nineteen, was not living at home; but when his grandmother had made her will in January 1612, she had stated that he was residing in Mexico; at that time he was only sixteen. Cotarelo presumed that his father must have sent the boy overseas, where he probably had relatives, because of some serious misdemeanour.[2] It is difficult to imagine any other reason why a youth of good family should have gone so far from home for such a relatively short time; if this is so, on the evidence of the father's will, the misdemeanour is not likely to have been anything more than association with a girl his father disapproved of, perhaps even the one referred to in the will.

This clause of the will presents us with a clear picture of a strict, authoritarian father determined to control the life of his son even beyond his own death, and determined also to impose the harshest sanctions on him that the law permitted. There could have been little affection, if any, between them; so far as the father was concerned their relationship would seem to have meant unlimited authority on his part and unquestioning obedience on the boy's. The other brothers, being only fifteen and thirteen years old, were too young to have worried the father by showing any wills of their own; but it is symptomatic that the father, having already decided that Pedro should enter the Church and having sent him to the University, stipulates on his deathbed that he must on no account abandon his studies or his ecclesiastical career.[3]

One would normally attach no particular importance to all this, since it was not uncommon for fathers in the seventeenth century to be strict disciplinarians. But there is a codicil added to the dying man's will two days later which puts a different complexion on the matter:

> I state and declare that I have a natural son who is called Francisco González, son of a very well-born lady, whose name I do not here give because she is dead. He has been so unruly and of such bad [illegible word] that he compelled me to throw him out of my house, and he is lost somewhere in the world (*anda perdido por el mundo*). If he should appear at any time, I wish each of my sons, from their share of my estate and legacies that fall to them, to give him his fair share according to the laws of the land, without the said Francisco Calderón needing to prove that he is my son; and I expressly command him not to marry that woman whom he sought to marry; if he should do so, and if the laws of the land permit me to disinherit him entirely, I do so.[4]

This young man had been living with the family, he and they being ignorant of their kinship.

This illegitimate son did in fact reappear. There is a document of four years later in which his brothers arrange for the legacy he claims; in this document he is called Francisco González Calderón.[5] The only other mention of him occurs forty years later, in 1655, when, in the will of Diego's son, José Calderón, he is referred to as 'a former servant of my parents'.[6] After his reappearance it would seem that he had become a retainer in the household of the eldest of his half-brothers.

The will of Calderón's father is thus a revealing document. It discloses a family life that must have been full of tension and strain. The existence of this illegitimate lost son, abandoned by the father for his bad conduct, also to be disinherited if he ceased to obey his father's wishes after the latter's death, completes the background for the way in which the father–son relationship is presented in Calderón's drama. Clearly the dramatist's early youth was overshadowed by the authoritarian father, by the brothers not being allowed to have wills of their own, by one of them being illegitimate, abandoned by his father for unruly and disobedient behaviour and by the fact that 'andaba perdido por el mundo'. The first thing that Pedro did when he left the university was to disobey his father's wishes by abandoning his ecclesiastical career, choosing instead to write plays and living a life not devoid in some respects of scandal and notoriety – a natural reaction against his authoritarian upbringing. The psychological obsession produced by this strained family life produced in its turn the recurring father–son theme of his early period in which the memory of the bastard Francisco clearly plays the biggest part, making it something more significant than a poeticised Oedipus complex.

At the same time – apparently – that Francisco was turned out of the home, Diego had been sent to Mexico, but he was back in Madrid when his father died. The surviving sister, Dorotea, had been placed in a convent at the age of thirteen; even at that period this was an exceptionally early age, too early to make it a freely chosen vocation; the girl must have been put there without her consent. We cannot fail to recall Julia in *La devoción de la cruz*, who is forced by her father to enter a convent against her will, the reason being that she and Eusebio are in love, both being ignorant of the fact that they are brother and sister. This parallel brings out other striking parallels in these early plays. Chronology helped me in earlier studies to conjecture a possible connection between these recurring dramatic incidents and the will of the dramatist's father, but a document that was brought to my notice after the publication of the earlier studies casts doubt on the reliability of these conjectures. So striking are the coincidences, however, that they are repeated here while leaving open any question of historical interpretation. The family history and dramatic plots coincide in a way that does appear remarkable. The repetition of these coincidences is not intended to determine the interpretation of the plays. The understanding and evaluation of each play must stand and fall on each individual text. My own interpretation and evaluation of these plays are the same as when I first expounded them before ever seeing their possible connection with the dramatist's life.

When Doña Inés Riaño y Peralta, grandmother to the children in question, made her will on 5 January 1612, she refers to Diego as being at that time in Mexico, and refers to Dorotea as being a novice in the convent of Santa Clara la Real in Toledo. On 21 October 1610 the dramatist's mother, Doña Ana María de Henao, signed a will in which she made her five children her heirs.[7] There is no mention here of Diego being in Mexico. One could assume, therefore, that he went there in 1611, the year in which Dorotea was put in the convent. We do not know when Francisco, the illegitimate son, was expelled, but the Eusebio–Julia situation in *La devoción de la cruz* could point to its being the same year. In 1611 Diego was fifteen. Since this was an unusually early age for a boy to be sent to Mexico, as unusual as thirteen for entry into a convent, it is probable that he was sent there, as Cotarelo conjectured, because of a serious misdemeanour.[8] It seemed to me possible to presume that this was an incident of a sexual kind between Francisco and Dorotea, aided and abetted by Diego, all three being ignorant of their kinship: in fact one may be more explicit. What the misdemeanour might have been is suggested by *La devoción de la cruz*. Eusebio and Julia love each other unaware that they are brother and sister. Her seduction and the act of involuntary incest is prevented by the birthmark of the cross on her breast. Another brother, Lisardo, is involved in the courtship, though as antagonist, not accomplice. In *Las tres justicias* the young Don Lope and Violante are in love: he is her brother, but neither knows it: a second young man, Guillén, is involved in an attempted mediation. In *Los cabellos de Absalón* (The Hair of Absalom) incest is consummated through Amón's rape of Tamar; their brother Absalón is involved in the consequences of the affair and this leads to a rebellious quarrel with his father. One of the suggested explanations for Calderón's adoption of Tirso's Act II for his version of this biblical story was a moral scruple that prevented him from dealing himself with this scandalous theme: this hypothetical family situation could point to a deep psychological or emotional inhibition.

One other detail seemed to add further plausibility to the hypothesis of incest in the Calderón family. Only Dorotea's early age makes her entry into the convent unusual (she was not professed until sixteen, which was the canonical age of consent). She was enclosed in a convent in Toledo, not in her home town, Madrid, and was taken there by her godparents and not by her father. This might show the need for secrecy, to remove the girl from the curiosity of neighbours, as if to avoid a scandal.[9] On the supposition that incest might have been attempted or could in fact have occurred, the harsh punishment of the children is explicable according to the standards of the age. Even if Dorotea had been the innocent victim of a rape, she would still have had to spend the rest of her life enclosed in a convent; as was the case with Isabel, in *El alcalde de Zalamea*, whose rape made her life-long enclosure in a convent inevitable.

The fact that Calderón seemed to have an obsession with incest in these early plays was of course noted by early critics, such as Ángel Valbuena Prat. It was in fact conjectured by Constandse that Calderón must have felt a sexual attraction for his sister Dorotea. Proceeding on the hypothesis of an attempted incestuous act in the Calderón family, due to ignorance of the brother–sister relationship, one might see a possible explanation for the otherwise inexplicable command in the father's will that neither his legitimate son, Diego, nor his illegitimate son, Francisco, should ever court or marry one of their cousins. Might there not have been in the wider family circle a female cousin who was not in fact a legitimate offspring of an uncle or aunt, and therefore a half-sister of Diego and Francisco? Marriages between first cousins generally required a special dispensation, but did not infringe the law against consanguinity, being, in fact, common enough. Another illegitimate member of the family could have produced an actual incestuous marriage.

Calderón was eleven at the time of such hypothetically reconstructed events and fifteen when he learned that the vanished Francisco had been his brother. The emotional shock would have been intense, otherwise the father–son conflict would not have become a dominant motif in his theatre. As these pages will reveal, another dominant motif in his plays, not this time confined to the early ones, is rape, either threatened or perpetrated. Both themes reveal a constant preoccupation in his mind, especially when, for his plays, he sought to unravel the tangled skeins of human motives, above all the guilt and responsibility, with the wider problem of free will.

La devoción de la cruz and *Las tres justicias en una* both present a hard, unloving father; both also present an unruly anarchical son who commits crimes for which he suffers death; in each the plot is so constructed that the son's anarchy is presented as the effect of the father's harsh character and actions.

In *La devoción de la cruz* the father, Curcio, is a fanatical man of honour who, obsessed with the unjust thought that his wife had been unfaithful to him, had tried to kill her as she was about to give birth to twins. He did not succeed in killing her, but his action led to the disappearance of one of the babies, the boy Eusebio, who grows to manhood without knowing who his father is. As a result, when the action of the play begins, he has fallen in love with his own sister and she with him. The prospective marriage horrifies Curcio, who is of course ignorant, like everybody else, that Eusebio is in fact his son; it horrifies him because Eusebio is poor, of ostensibly low birth, and does not know who his father was. (As has already been suggested, there may be echoes here of the opposition of Calderón's father to the marriages of both Diego and Francisco.) Curcio's tyranny takes the form of attempting to force his daughter into a convent to prevent her from marrying the man she loves, angrily threatening to kill her if she disobeys. His other son, Lisardo, to abet his father in preventing the marriage, taunts Eusebio with his low birth and challenges him to a duel. Eusebio, stung by the taunts and in defence of his self-respect, accepts the challenge and kills Lisardo. Curcio therefore has him hunted as a murderer, and Eusebio, a fugitive from justice, becomes a rebel against the world that has stigmatised him as unworthy of the woman he loves. Among his crimes he heaps further dishonour on Curcio by causing Julia, the daughter, to flee from her convent and become a public criminal. Curcio, seeking revenge, leads the soldiers who track Eusebio down and wound him. Before he dies, Curcio discovers Eusebio is his own son, whom, by seeking to murder Eusebio's mother, he had sought to murder at birth.

The conflict between father and son revealed by this play could not be more violent or more terrible. Looked at as a purely human situation the action is terrifying in its relentless ferocity. But the tone of the play is not; it is imbued with a sympathy and compassion for Eusebio that lead Calderón, by means of a subsidiary religious action, to emphasise that the abandoned son, the outlawed criminal, who is deprived of the mercy of men, receives the mercy of God. In other words the sympathy of the dramatist is with the son and not with the father. This is also indicated by the structure of the plot, which links all the actions of Eusebio to Curcio as to their first cause. Eusebio becomes a criminal and dies a criminal's death because Curcio considered him unworthy, through his unknown parentage, to marry his daughter; but Eusebio was of unknown parentage and fell in love with Julia precisely because he had been abandoned as a baby by Curcio, his own father, when the latter had tried to kill his innocent wife on the mere suspicion that she had tainted his honour. In other words, the fanatical sense of honour and the harsh cruelty of the father are what, directly and indirectly, lead the son into vicious and criminal behaviour. The intention of killing the innocent wife leads to the disowning in practice of the son who, if he had grown up in his father's home, would never have fallen in love with his own sister. There is an evident connection here with Francisco González Calderón, who had grown to manhood unacknowledged by his own father, who had tried to marry a woman of whom the father disapproved, who had been abandoned by the father because of his bad behaviour, and had disappeared. When Francisco reappeared our poet was nineteen years old: he must have been deeply moved by the tragedy of his illegitimate half-brother.

Las tres justicias en una repeats this father–son conflict in a less violent, more subtle way. We again have a harsh father, and we again have an unruly young man who does not know who his real father is. The young man who is the centre of the tragedy (Don Lope *hijo*) has an impetuous character which leads him into a criminal life, for which he is finally executed. At the beginning of the play he appears as a bandit; gradually the circumstances surrounding his conduct are disclosed until they are fully revealed at his execution. He himself attributes his disorderly impulses to an antagonism he feels towards his father (Don Lope *padre*) because of his cold and unloving character. The coldness of Don Lope *padre* is not really genuine; he is fond in his own way of his wife and son, but he has been brought up and confirmed in the belief that it is unmanly to demonstrate outwardly any tenderness or affection, sternness and discipline being the hallmark of the man of honour. This sternness and this assumed coldness have not only brought an unhappiness to his wife Doña Blanca, which the son cannot bear to witness, but have created an atmosphere of strained hostility between father and son for which the latter seeks an outlet in anarchical behaviour, and which culminates in the son's striking the father in public. This personal dishonour impels Don Lope *padre* to denounce his son to the law. This strained family situation follows from its being an unnatural home in more senses than one. Unknown to himself and to Don Lope *padre*, the young man is not the son of either of his reputed parents. Doña Blanca, made miserable by her unhappy marriage, had set her hopes on having a child who would create a bond of affection between her husband and herself. Frustrated in this hope, but clinging to it, she had deceived her husband by successfully passing off her sister's baby as her own. In this she aimed not only at her own good, but at that of mother and child, for the latter was the illegitimate offspring of dishonour. The real father is the King's Chief Justice, and as such he is directly involved in the tragic fate of someone he does not know to have been his son until after the execution.

We have again, in this very fine and moving play, the two factors in the strained situation of the Calderón family. Don Lope *hijo* becomes a criminal and meets with a tragic end because his rebelliousness was a reaction against the cold and stern character of the man who passed as his father, and because he was exposed to this unhappy relationship by his real father, who by begetting him illegitimately had deprived him of his real home.

The parallels between the plots of so many Calderonian plays and known facts in the lives of Dorotea and Francisco González Calderón need to be fully emphasised; nonetheless, to push them as far as to conjecture a very close analogy with the Eusebio–Julia relationship in *La devoción de la cruz* has been proved too rash by a document that was unknown to me and to others who had mentioned this subject.[10] It is a document from the Archivo de Indias, dated 30 April 1608, which states that Diego Calderón de la Barca (the dramatist's father) wishes to send his son Diego to Mexico City. He requests permission for this, and for him to be accompanied by four servants. The request was granted with the stipulation that he should go with *one* servant. On the verso of the document the boy Diego is described as twelve years old, of pale complexion, with a birthmark on his forehead, and light brown hair. His servant is called Francisco and is described as eighteen years old, dark haired and with a long face.

This document clearly indicates that it was the father's intention to send Diego to Mexico in 1608. It is possible, even probable, that the single servant allowed him by the immigration authorities was his illegitimate half brother. This document does not of course prove that the two boys did actually sail to Mexico; but the nature and tone of the document make it unlikely that this was the occasion when Francisco was summarily ejected from his house, to remain 'lost somewhere in the world'. If the document removes one mystery, it creates another, and a more tantalising one. We do not know why Diego was to have been sent to Mexico at such an early age; if he indeed went we do not know if his servant was Francisco. If Francisco did go, we do not know when he returned. Neither do we know why he was turned out of his father's home, nor can we take it for granted that this was *not* connected with Dorotea's enclosure in a Toledo convent. The actual affair must remain open, but the dramatic situations are unaffected.

In both these plays, therefore, we have an anarchical son who is not to blame, or only partially to blame, for his criminal deeds; in both plays the ultimate blame rests with the father, real or reputed. Fathers drive their sons to rebellion, to anti-social behaviour, by tyranny or a cold lack of affection, or by giving them the stigma of illegitimacy. It is unnecessary to insist how much more significant this is than a straightforward Oedipus complex as defined by Constandse.[11] Rather than the mere clash between the instinctive urge to resist authority and the instinctive fear of disobeying it, Calderón gives us a pattern of human relationships that lies at the very heart of moral responsibility. In this particular pattern, whereby one human being unwittingly causes another human being to sin, we have the characteristic Calderonian conception of tragedy, which will be studied later when these plays are analysed from that point of view. In both these plays this inner family conflict, which must reflect what Calderón had witnessed in his own home, leads to tragedy. The two sons are doomed by their fathers to rebellion and death with the terrible inevitability of tragic drama. In these two plays Calderón certainly did not deprive his audience of the catharsis necessitated by the tragic emotions aroused by his human situation.

But precisely because he allowed his dramatic material to unfold to its artistically natural end, he posed for himself a grave human problem. If one man leads another indirectly but inevitably to sin, how far is the latter man predetermined to sin and so deprived of free will and responsibility for his own actions? How far is a son necessarily forced into rebellion if his father unnaturally deprives him of his right to affection and to freedom? Modern psychology has made us familiar with the problem which had long ago been posed by St Augustine (see postscript below). It was axiomatic for Catholic theology that all human beings, provided they are not insane, can contribute to the saving of their souls by their own free efforts, and are not driven to sin by an inherited tendency. But is there no hope *in this world* for the wronged sons of the Calderonian drama? Is there no other answer than hatred and vengeance to the quarrels and conflicts between men?

Calderón, for his own peace of mind, for his own spiritual tranquillity, must have needed to find a human and not just a spiritual solution to the problem of the tyrannical father. He finds it, of course, in *La vida es sueño*, in Segismundo's magnanimous forgiveness of Basilio; but only after he has strongly condemned his father for the cruel injustice inflicted on him. Basilio, the only father in the Calderonian drama who is pardoned is, and for that very reason, the only one who is openly and explicitly condemned. Calderón has to continue to emphasise the primary guilt of the father. But the son's forgiveness of the father is only one aspect – the practical aspect – of the human problem that posed itself. Is there no escape from the harm a father can do his son? Is there no limit set to a father's capacity to injure him?

The play explicitly denies predetermination. Segismundo's rejection of vengeance is made the assertion of a free will that the stars cannot inhibit, yet the action, as regards Basilio, seems to demonstrate it.

The horoscope motif introduces a new dimension into the general theme of the father–son conflict. It is Calderón's way, as he is wrestling with the last problem posed by the tyrannical father and the rebellious son, of emphasising the efficacy of a man's free will in establishing his responsibility for his own actions. The device of the horoscope and its apparent influence on events opens up the problem of tyranny, rebellion, guilt and punishment in a way that departs from a real-life situation and leads directly into a universalism that will finally require symbols and myths to express it. The human situation of the son wronged by his father and seeking conscious, as well as unconscious, redress by his rebelliousness links *La vida es sueño* with *La devoción de la cruz* and *Las tres justicias en una*; but the expansion of the conflict that the horoscope introduces points away from Calderón's own personal experience towards a wider 'philosophy of life'. This new conception with the resulting change of 'mode' will be covered in the following chapter. The theme, however, has introduced us to the reflection in dramatic art of the real-life figure of the dramatist's illegitimate half-brother, Francisco González Calderón. He will not, as a dramatic character, specifically form part of the human problems into which the horoscope motif leads; but since he does recur in recognisable forms throughout Calderón's work, it will be appropriate to summarise here the ways in which the memory of this painful situation kept coming to the fore.

In that form the problem does not recur in his drama. A conflict between father and son does not again constitute the central issue of a play; it recurs only as a secondary motif, sometimes suggested by the source on which he draws, sometimes imposed upon a plot against the source. For *Los dos amantes del cielo* (The Two Lovers of Heaven) (probably written during the decade 1640–50) Calderón found in the legend of St Chrysanthus and St Daria[12] a father who persecutes and imprisons his son for wishing to become a Christian; but Calderón goes further than this by making the son (Crisanto) repudiate his human father (Polemio) in favour of the fatherhood of God, and by making the father be the first to consign the son to a cruel death:

Crisanto   Padre, aunque la muerte pido . . .
Polemio   Ese nombre no me des.
Crisanto   No hablaba contigo, pues
               aunque tú a mi vida diste
               el ser, de padre perdiste
               el dulce nombre después
               que otro, con más alta palma,
               el ser del alma me dio;
               y así, en cuanto al ser venció
               de la vida el ser del alma,
               tanto el vencer está en calma;
               y pues que tu mano ingrata
               vierte el humor que desata,
               más de padre el nombre adquiere
               el padre que por mí muere
               que el padre que por mí mata.

(*Crisanto*   Father, although I ask for death . . .
Polemio   Do not call me by that name.
Crisanto   I was not addressing you; although it was you who brought my life into being, you forfeited the loving name of father after another, of much higher authority, brought my soul into being. Therefore, since the life of the soul is superior to physical life, by the same token, it is certain that I can claim Christ as my father. And since your harsh hand pours out the blood it causes to flow, the name of father is deserved by him who for me dies and not by him who on my account kills.)[13]

Polemio   a la cárcel le llevad
               pública, y en ella no
               sea en nada preferido
               al más torpe delincuente.
               Entre la mísera gente
               desnudo esté y abatido:
               allí de hierro herido
               su cuerpo, morir se vea.

(*Polemio*   Off with him to the public dungeon, and let him have no better treatment than the commonest criminal. Among the wretched prisoners let him be stripped and humiliated: and there with his body wounded by his irons let his dying be visible to all.)

                                (801b) [*BAE*, iii, p.252 a–b]

Polemio   Aquí, soldados, están
           y yo he de ser el primero
           que les dé muerte, porque
           no piensen de mí que tengo
           a mi hijo más amor
           que a mis dioses.
(*Polemio*   Soldiers, here they are, and I shall be the first to kill them, so that
            no-one may think that I love my son more than I love my gods.)
                                              (805b) [*BAE* III, p. 254b]

In *Las armas de la hermosura*, Calderón adds several innovations to the Coriolanus story, one of which is to centre the conflict between Coriolano and Rome in a conflict between him and his father. The father casts his vote for his son's death as a rebel; when the Senate passes sentence of banishment instead of death, it is the father who publicly strips his son of all his honours. Later, after Coriolano's victory, the position of father and son is reversed. The father pleads for mercy and the son refuses to show it. This is made a particular illustration of the wider theme of honour, vengeance and forgiveness. These additions to these two plays do not by themselves represent anything dramatically unusual, but within the context of the three earlier plays they can be seen as echoes of what had once been a leading theme.

Though, after *La vida es sueño*, conflicts between fathers and sons are relegated to a subordinate position, the same is not true of the figure of the fatherless son. He recurs several times and in ways that are always central to the particular themes. The basic symbolism of *La vida es sueño* – seclusion, freedom granted on trial, the 'dream' – reappears in *En la vida, todo es verdad y todo mentira* (1659) (In Life, Everything is True and Everything False). This complicated version of the Heraclius story does not seem to me a particularly successful play, but it is directly connected with the theme of this chapter. There are two sons who do not know their parentage till the play ends: Heraclio (son of the Emperor Mauricio, killed by Focas) and Leonido (son of Focas who has usurped the throne). It is necessary for Focas to know which is which in order, by killing the son of Mauricio, to ensure his continued possession of the throne and his succession by his own son. He believes that since the one has a natural reason for hating him and the other a natural reason for loving him, each will reveal his identity in his instinctive reaction to him (Focas). But this is not what happens; when put to the test, it is Heraclio who is benevolent towards him and Leonido who is hostile; only when they learn their identities are these reactions reversed. Calderón does not deny an instinctive affinity between a son and his father (Leonido feels it with Focas) but the play emphasises that this is not strong enough to influence action. In other words, no son is impelled by nature to show good will to his father. Benevolence and hostility are instinctively influenced not by the tie of blood but by character or temperament. Heraclio is benevolent towards Focas (whom he ought instinctively to hate) because he (Heraclio) is wise and prudent; he is this because his father was a good man. On the other hand Leonido is hostile to Focas (whom he ought to love) because he (Leonido) is arrogant and aggressive; he is this because his father is an evil man. Love between father and son is not instinctive, but temperament is inherited. This is a further, a more detached and 'scientific', way in which Calderón continues to emphasise a father's share in his son's wrongdoing. Since a son is not compelled by nature to love his father, he can rebel against him; if he does so, it will be because he has inherited his father's cruel temperament. This kind of inheritance is, in general terms, the 'stars' or the 'fate' a son may have to conquer within himself.

The fatherless son is detectable in *El hijo del Sol Faetón* (mentioned in chapter 2). Phaethon, son of the Sun god Apollo, who by driving his father's chariot hurls himself to his own death, repeats on a higher dramatic level the tragic situation of Eusebio in *La devoción de la cruz*. Eusebio is conscious of the stigma of his birth when he is mocked at by Lisardo for being of inferior social standing; he rebels against the imputation of unworthiness in order to assert his sense of pride and self-respect; for a similar purpose, Phaethon, in the myth, needs to know who his father is, since he is laughed at, misunderstood, mocked, dismissed as worthless. To satisfy himself and others of his own worth, Calderón's Faetón must prove an illustrious descent – in his pride he imagines himself to be the child of a god, of Apolo. When he finds that this is true, his ambition impels him to demonstrate his divine sonship by driving his father's chariot of fire; in the same way Eusebio is impelled by pride to possess the woman of whom his social inferiority deprives him. Eusebio is driven by this ambition to the death his father has sought for him, in the same way as Faetón's ambition leads his father to sentence him to death. If the mythical figure of Phaethon is seen in association with Eusebio, Don Lope *hijo* and Segismundo, we see how freedom, self-respect, self-assertion, self-realisation, self-justification, honour, ambition, pride are all motives contained for Calderón in the symbol of the fatherless and rebellious son.

Calderón's illegitimate half-brother appears transposed into the allegorical mode of the *autos sacramentales* (allegorical theological plays), where the symbol of the fatherless son reaches its culmination, especially in *Los alimentos del hombre* (Man's Maintenance),[14] written in 1676, more than forty years after *La devoción de la cruz* and *La vida es sueño*. This remarkable *auto* reveals that the psychological strains of Calderón's boyhood were still in his old age inspiring poetic drama, and that he found in the Christian interpretation of existence an ultimate meaning for the sufferings of human life and the quarrels between men.

The protagonist of this play is Adam. He is the son of Paterfamilias, the great Husbandman of the World. Adam is an ill-behaved and rebellious son, who is turned out of the home and disinherited by his father in favour of Emmanuel, the younger son. Abandoned and destitute, Adam must beg for alms, and finding no other hope begs of his brother Emmanuel the right of maintenance on the grounds that the Law of Nature forbids any father to deny his son the subsistence he requires. Even a son who is disinherited should not be exposed to starvation and death, for he is still the son of his father, and this is a relationship that can never be severed. Emmanuel, the younger brother, hears the plea for forgiveness and compassion, and gives Adam the sustenance of the Sacraments.

We recall the codicil to the will of Calderón's father: his confession that he has a lost natural son whom he had disowned because of his bad conduct, and his request that the younger brothers should give him his share of the estate should he reappear. By acknowledging his fatherhood, Don Diego Calderón acknowledged his natural son's right to maintenance.

If *Los alimentos del hombre* is looked at purely as theology, its allegory must be condemned as inaccurate, since man has no 'legal' claim on God for salvation. But ultimately the allegory does not stem from theology but from Calderón's experience of his own boyhood, which offered him the conception of Man as the disowned and disinherited son of God, claiming maintenance from his father and receiving mercy from Christ, his brother, who is God's obedient son. In the great central mystery of the Christian faith, Calderón found the principle of reconciliation between men which overcomes the sources of division whereby father can persecute son and son rebel against father.

It has often been said that Calderón is a detached and remote dramatist, that the conflicts on his stage tend to represent abstract questions of casuistry and that his plays have therefore little contact with real life. Against this view it can be shown that one of the leading themes of his drama, running through it from beginning to end, is based unmistakably upon a real experience that had left a profound impression on the poet's mind as a boy. It is a very moving thought that Francisco González Calderón, an obscure and insignificant Spaniard of the early seventeenth century, who suffered in his youth the unhappiness of illegitimacy and the stern authority of an outraged father, should, by the accident of having had a great poet as a half-brother, have found a new and an immortal life in the dramatic literature of the world, until he became allegorised as Adam and thus as the symbol of the whole human race.

The significance and the moving quality of the relevant plays in this chapter do not require the historical accuracy of the hypothetical relationship of Francisco Calderón to Dorotea. If, however, the hypothesis is seen to be plausible and therefore possible, we become aware through the conceptual transmutations of Francisco, through Segismundo, into Adam, how a poetic dramatist can fashion his earliest experience into expanding art forms. The horoscope of *La vida es sueño* is not a necessarily logical part of this particular conceptual development, but it is a necessary part of the artistic form that it helps to fashion. Horoscope and the associated motif of the Prison are expanded into a series of dramatic transmutations that come to acquire, as the next chapter will endeavour to explain, an archetypal and mythical significance in the artistic forms with which Calderón's imagination gave life to his memories and concepts.

Postscript: Sins of the fathers

The belief that men suffer calamities as a result of their own wrongdoing or that of their forbears was universally held in antiquity. In Ode vi of Book III, Horace apostrophises the Romans, telling them that they will have to suffer for the crimes of their fathers as long as they do not rebuild the crumbling temples of the gods or restore their statues, and as long as they do not direct the beginning and the end of all things towards the supremacy of the Immortal. They will have to expiate the crimes of their ancestors by suffering continued military disasters.

'The sins of fathers are visited on their children' is a proverbial saying that paraphrases Numbers, chapter 14, verse 18: 'The Lord is slow to anger . . . but he will by no means clear the guilty, visiting the iniquity of fathers upon children, upon the third and upon the fourth generation' (Revised Standard Version). 'Visiting' here means 'inflicting punishment for (wrongdoing) *on* or *upon* a person' (The Shorter Oxford English Dictionary).

The prevalence of this belief in the Old Testament caused it to pass into Christianity. A proverb expressed it among the Jews: 'The fathers have eaten sour grapes and the children's teeth are set on edge' (Ezekiel xviii, 2). Ezekiel emphatically rejects this belief, affirming: 'The soul that sins shall die. The son shall not suffer for the iniquity of the father, nor the father suffer for the iniquity of the son: the righteousness of the righteous shall be upon himself, and the wickedness of the wicked shall be upon himself' (Ezekiel xviii, 20).

Nonetheless, the historical books of the Old Testament offer many examples of the sins of fathers being visited on a second and later generations. When Noah was lying naked and drunk, Ham summoned his two brothers to see and laugh at the spectacle, but they, without directly looking, covered their father. When Noah awoke and realised what had happened, he prophesied to Canaan, Ham's son, that on account of this he would become the slave of his brothers. When Solomon was guilty of impiety and of breaking the Law, God announced that punishment would fall on Israel, that through the revolt of Jeroboam the House of David would lose the territories of eight of the ten tribes. Thus Rehoboam, Solomon's son and heir, was punished, yet because of the merits of King David, the whole of Israel's kingdom was not lost.

St Augustine, discussing the contradiction between such punishments as these, which are directly attributed to God, and the categorical repudiation by Ezekiel, denied that there was any failure of justice, since the punishments belonged to the temporal order and did not affect salvation within the spiritual order (*Opus Imperfectum contra Julianum*, Lib. iii, l–liv).

All this became part of Christian theology, but it is not on this level that the problem is presented or implied by Calderón. In his dramatic situations the question left in the mind of the spectator or reader is whether a young man inherits an *inclination* to wrongdoing, inherits, that is, a disposition or predetermination.

St Thomas's discussion of freedom of the will is not strictly relevant to the question whether sins of fathers are visited on their children. The latter problem seems to be more directly connected to the Greek idea of Fate. A man has inherited a temperament which disposes him in certain circumstances to act in a way that is detrimental to his freedom and well-being. Every man is under a Nemesis which his father contributed to form, but, as Calderón suggests, other men who have had contact with and influence on him have contributed to cause the circumstances that operate the Nemesis.

This difficult but very important problem will recur later in this book, especially when Calderón's most characteristic type of tragedy is discussed. The following chapter is not relevant to the expansion of this theme in the Calderonian theatre.

7 Segismundo's tower: a Calderonian myth

La vida es sueño (1635) clearly marks a new pattern of play in the Calderonian drama, one that can be associated with what Northrop Frye called the 'mythical mode' in literature. It is a curious fact, not previously explained satisfactorily, that Segismundo, a fatherless son brought up in a prison and alternating between imprisonment and freedom, becomes not so much a 'type character' for Calderón as a 'type figure', even an 'archetypal' one. This change is effected when a young man or woman, brought up in prison from birth for reasons that he or she cannot fathom, and yearning for the freedom of which he or she, alone in the world of nature, seems to be deprived, is suddenly given freedom and proceeds to exercise it. In calling this a 'Calderonian Myth' the intention is not to stress its associations in classical mythology, although it has these; rather is it intended to denote a personal myth, one that Calderón invents for a purpose that has become, with *La vida es sueño*, very significant for him.

The change of 'dramatic mode' is indicated by the fact that while the type figure of the fatherless son is presented in the plays previously under review within a 'real-life' situation, and therefore capable of being imagined by the reader, *qua* action, as 'realistic', *La vida es sueño* presents a non-real situation, in fact a humanly impossible one. No human baby can be put into a prison immediately after birth, placed under the care of a jailer who visits him from time to time and who raises him to manhood, instructing him about the world and its organisation, educating him to speak eloquently and to reason cogently, and so on. This impossible unrealism brings the plot of *La vida es sueño* into line with the symbolic mode as defined by Auerbach, namely something that clearly means more than it says. This symbolical quality, though on occasion becoming rather conventional, will continue throughout the derivations of the Segismundo situation.

Attention was first called to this particular subject by Blanca de los Ríos in a lecture delivered in Madrid and published in 1926, with the title '*La vida es sueño* y los diez Segismundos de Calderón'.[1] She pointed out that Segismundo's experience, that of being brought up in captivity and yearning for freedom, is found ten times in Calderón's drama, with girls as well as with boys. Segismundo, she said, has a tenfold projection. But her lecture failed to ask why this should be so. She saw no problem of interpretation here: Calderón was a repetitive writer, and poverty of imagination was the explanation given. She thought Calderón had been so pleased with Segismundo that he repeated the basic situation as often as he could for no apparent reason, and with no apparent improvement. The idea of imprisonment from infancy within the concept of Life as a Dream places us, she maintained, before the mystery of Being and Non-Being, Time and Eternity. This was potentially of profound significance, but it was a dramatic failure because Calderón was incapable of giving it a human dimension: Segismundo is not a man of flesh and blood whose experience we can feel and share. The other nine Segismundos, she continued, merely repeat the failure, and thus do no more than demonstrate a conventional and mechanical art.

Doña Blanca was not quite right about the ten Segismundos. She omitted two *comedias* but included the *auto sacramental* version of *La vida es sueño*. If the *autos* where Man is created by being brought out of the prison of non-being are to be included, then there would be nearer twenty Segismundos than ten. But these are transpositions, not repetitions, of the theme. Keeping to the *comedias*, and adding the two missing from Doña Blanca's list, we have eleven rather than ten.[2] It will here be contended that the repetition of the Prison–Horoscope motif had a deep emotional and intellectual significance for Calderón, and that this is conveyed to us in a non-realistic form because it is universalised. It will be evident that this theme and its variations are uniquely central to Calderón's whole work. They may be considered to constitute what Henry James called 'The Figure in the Carpet', a necessary clue to his mind and his art.

In chapter 2, I offered a general interpretation of the symbol of the prison which, in its simplest terms, means that humanity as a whole is condemned to a life of pain, suffering being a prison into which all men are born. I treated the first Segismundo's imprisonment in his tower within the wider context of Calderón's developing use of metaphors and symbols. Now it will be treated by itself, and within a context of another kind, that of myth.

Symbols and myths are related and embody archetypes, and are closely connected with allegory. All these terms can overlap; they refer to a manner of writing that is not precise statement: in other words, not realistic but a mode that is, as it were, 'double'. Symbols and myths contain both a literal reference and a much greater range of unwritten meaning, implication and emotion. Archetypes are the expression of universal motifs or patterns of human experience and beliefs that are rooted in human instinct and that come charged with primary emotional force. Thus Segismundo's tower is archetypal: it conveys the concept of an imprisonment that goes beyond simple punishment for the breaking of an ordinary social law. It communicates the idea and emotion of guilt in a much deeper way than that of a courtroom case. When Segismundo explains his otherwise inexplicable confinement by saying:

> pues el delito mayor
> del hombre es haber nacido

> (since man's greatest crime is the fact that he was born)[3]

we are in a realm of instincts and emotion beyond the reach of realistic statement. The sense of indefinable guilt is at the root of human experience as disclosed by anthropology and psychology; it is at the heart of religion. Segismundo's tower is thus an archetype; given a concrete literal expression as part of a dramatic action, it becomes a symbol. Myths, whether traditional or created by a writer, are the narrative forms of the specifically archetypal symbols which together present a coherent but indirect revelation of what lies deepest in the well-springs of human feelings and perception.[4]

The placing and function of Segismundo's tower in the action of *La vida es sueño* are important. Its spacing in the play should be noted: it is there at the very beginning and for half of Act I; it is there at the end of Act II; again at the beginning of Act III, and finally there at the end of the play. By 'there', one means, of course, that we see it in our imagination, and that the original audience saw it, as the curtained recess at the back of the stage.[5] It is symmetrically spaced in the action of the play. It begins and ends it. At the beginning a young man *emerges*, longing for freedom; at the end another man *enters* it, losing his freedom. This symmetrical spacing of the tower, with the circular pattern of action whereby the ending inverts the beginning, cannot be an accident. The tower obviously means much more than a device for presenting a mysterious hero. We are impelled to ask what it means. The poetic imagery surrounding it, calling it the *cuna y sepulcro* (the cradle and the grave) of the inmate, takes us away from an ordinary prison, to the mystery of life and death, of fate and human destiny. The tower means more than it is; it has a significance far wider than that of a building on a mountainside. It is a symbol of something that must refer beyond the primary concept of imprisonment. Its association with birth- and death-imagery makes it a symbol of mankind's subjection to death: we are, each of us, imprisoned in a tower. That, however, is the symbol's secondary reference. The primary reference is wider, more elusive, more challenging.

The tower is inseparable from the horoscope, which is Basilio's pretext for condemning his son to it from birth. Tower and horoscope together have a universal reference beyond the personal experience of an individual prince. It is as if at the birth of mankind the Fates prophesied that men would bring dissension, violence and strife into the world. All of us live today under the horoscope of terrorism, assassinations, bombings, civil war; all of us share, by the mere fact of being human, in the cosmic guilt incurred by mankind for making the world a battlefield instead of a beautiful and peaceful place. Segismundo, when he clamours for freedom, does not yet know of his personal horoscope, but he knows intuitively why he has grown up in his tower. Addressing the heavens, he says:

> Bastante causa ha tenido
> vuestra justicia y rigor;
> pues el delito mayor
> del hombre es haber nacido.

> (Your rigorous justice has been well justified; since man's greatest crime is the fact that he was born.)

> (109–12) [*BAE*, i, p. 1c]

More than anything else in the play, these devastating words reveal the universal mythical element of the plot.

The reason for the plot's circular structure, with the end inverting the beginning, is of course this. Segismundo has been deprived of freedom in order to prevent him from becoming a rebel and the cause of civil war. But this cannot be prevented. Segismundo leads the army against his father, defeats him and holds him at his mercy. The horoscope is thus fulfilled. He then vindicates his right to freedom when his reason convinces him of the need to renounce personal advantage and submit to the rule of law. But the archetypal tower of human guilt is never empty. The soldier who has chosen to lead the rebellion and to cause civil war for the sake of personal gain has to enter the tower. Rebellion or submission; false freedom or true freedom: the soldier chooses the imprisonment of seditious self-interest rather than the freedom of loyalty to the body politic.

Tower and horoscope, with this wide range of reference and a suggestiveness that give them universality, thus introduce a 'mythical' narrative. Since Calderón proceeds to repeat this through the rest of his life, we must conclude that this was a permanent preoccupation of his mind.

In the particular case of *La vida es sueño*, where this new development begins, we are primarily still facing the problem of a father's power to coerce the son into rebellion against him. Horoscope and tower are the dramatic device whereby the limits of coercion and freedom are suggested.

A common mistake made by critics is to assert that Segismundo's conversion prevents the horoscope from being fulfilled;[6] by this they mean that he never deposes and kills his father. Though he does not actually say so, Basilio would indeed seem to expect to be deposed and killed,[7] but this fate is actually not predicted. The horoscope, as Basilio casts it, is fulfilled to the letter, and it is essential for the full understanding of the play that this be realised. What the horoscope predicted is this:

> Yo, acudiendo a mis estudios,
> en ellos y en todo miro
> que Segismundo sería
> el hombre más atrevido,
> el príncipe más cruel
> y el monarca más impío,
> por quien su reino vendría
> a ser parcial y diviso,
> escuela de las traiciones
> y academia de los vicios;
> y él, de su furor llevado,
> entre asombros y delitos,
> había de poner en mí
> las plantas, y yo rendido
> a sus pies me había de ver
> (¡con qué congoja lo digo!),
> siendo alfombra de sus plantas
> las canas del rostro mío.

(Having recourse to my studies, I see in them and in all other indications that Segismundo would be the most impetuous man, the cruellest prince and the most heartless monarch, one through whom his kingdom would be divided into warring factions, a school for treason and vice; and I see also that he, driven by fury, in the midst of all this criminal upheaval, would trample on me; and that I would be prostrate at his feet and (oh, what agony it costs me to say this) the white hairs of my head and beard would be a carpet for his feet.)
(ll. 708–25) [*BAE*, I, p.4c]

This (allowing for poetic hyperbole) is exactly what happens. It was natural for Basilio to expect his own death, but his death does not happen, precisely because he did not foresee it. What he did not foresee is what depends on Segismundo's free choice; and this makes us realise that what Basilio foresees is only the result of *his own* free act – the result, that is to say, of the imprisonment he chooses to inflict on his son. As Segismundo emphasises to him, it was precisely this deprivation of freedom that turned him into a rebel; but it did not force him to vengeance through parricide, because between the stirring up of the passion of rebellious anger and the act of murder Segismundo's reason and free will interpose themselves. The influence of a father's cruelty can predispose his son to rebellion, but it cannot force him to consummate it in the ultimate criminal act. That is as far as the limit of a father's capacity to harm his son through a tyrannical upbringing can extend. The son cannot avoid the unruliness of passion which will be the result of this; but he can avoid the irrevocable succumbing to it. Great though the suffering and effort may be, a son is ultimately free to counter the influence of a father's tyranny. Basilio can foresee in the stars that Segismundo will be stirred to anger and rebellion against him because this is precisely what the treatment he will choose to give his son must inevitably produce; he cannot, however, foresee in the stars that Segismundo will pardon him, because the free act that this presupposes is beyond the reach of a father's influence.[8]

By isolating the horoscope–tower motif from the wider theme of the father–son conflict, it can be brought into association with myth in order to account for one of its permanent features. The horoscope–tower motif is associated with the awakening of sexual passion and its disorderly consequences. This is evident in the symbol's first appearance in *La vida es sueño*: Segismundo's violence is tempered by tenderness at the sight of Rosaura, the first woman he has ever seen. Later, in the palace, tenderness gives way to lust, as he attempts to rape her. At their next encounter the temptation to assault her recurs. Clearly, rape was part of the violence that the horoscope had foreseen, although in *La vida es sueño* it remains secondary to the violence of rebellion and revenge.

In *La devoción de la cruz* and *Les tres justicias* there is no horoscope or prophecy. Its appearance in *La vida es sueño* marks the widening of the theme away from a more or less recognisable world into a mythical framework. The fact that father and son are now a king and a prince is part of this, for classical mythology is full of prophecies at the birth of princes. In the myth of Oedipus the prophecy that a son would kill his father, the King of Thebes, led the father to reject the son. But Segismundo's horoscope and imprisonment are closer to another type of Greek myth, of which Danaë is the best-known example. The daughter of Acrisius, king of Argos, she was confined in a tower by her father, who had been told by an oracle that his daughter's son would put him to death. Her imprisonment to keep her away from men proved ineffectual, for Jupiter, who was enamoured of her, introduced himself into her bed by changing himself into a shower of gold. Danae gave birth to Perseus. Mother and baby were set adrift on the sea, but were saved. Perseus grew to manhood and inadvertently did kill King Acrisius, his grandfather.

Segismundo is followed by ten further dramatic characters, who reintroduce the horoscope-tower myth. In only one of these is the myth found in Calderón's source; in all others he introduces it of his own accord. In eight of these cases he associates it with sexual passion or fear of it. In six of these cases the prisoner is a woman, in four a man. Not all the plays are good, but at least three of them (in addition to *La vida es sueño*) are masterpieces in the mythical mode of Calderón's late period. These are *La hija del aire*, *Eco y Narciso* (1661) and *Apolo y Climene*.

It is obvious that, with Segismundo, one of the references of the tower myth is to the onset of adolescence, the awakening of erotic instinct and passions, and the need to discipline them in a proper direction. Part of the reference to the horoscope, which is always fulfilled, is that it is hopeless to try to prevent the dominance of passion by a repressive education, by seclusion from society, or by an insistence on virginity and chastity as very special virtues. Adolescence is, so to speak, a 'horoscope' that portends possible disorder in every human being. Basilio makes the terrible mistake of thinking his son can be prevented from violent behaviour if he is deprived of freedom to exercise his passions. By seeking to prevent it, he brings it to pass. In the past, and especially so in Calderón's time, everything possible was done to deprive boys, girls and young people through a repressive education and upbringing, of the chances to do wrong. In particular this was the case with girls, who were kept secluded until brought out into society to be married. In his beautiful treatment of the Narcissus myth, Calderón adds the motif of horoscope and confinement. A prophecy has foretold that disaster will overtake Narciso if he should fall in love. Liríope, his terrified mother, tries to keep him secluded from all women, and she brings him up in the wilderness in a cave. Her fear of sex derives from her having experienced it herself in its most savage form. She had been raped (this, too, is Calderón's addition to the myth), and Narciso is the offspring of this violence. So that it should not be repeated, the mother keeps the son secluded from women, with the result that his erotic instinct has nothing to fix on except the reflection of his own face in the river. He can only fall in love with himself, and he drowns in the river as he seeks to reach the loved one. This disordered, perverted affection would never have happened, if his mother had not been violently raped. Among the plays containing the 'prison myth' *Eco y Narciso* is the one that most clearly makes puberty and adolescence its central theme.

In *La hija del aire* and *Apolo y Climene* the prisoner in the tower or cave is a girl. This gives the Calderonian myth its fullest development, for it is woman, not man, who becomes the type of tragic humanity, both the begetter and the victim of the passions that rend the human world. Though it must be repeated that there is no proof for this conjecture, it is hard not to think of Calderón's sister Dorotea, immured in a convent at the age of thirteen for something done to her by one of her brothers.

La hija del aire deals with the legend of Semíramis, the warrior-queen of ancient Assyria, who, as Calderón presents her, murdered her husband the king and usurped the throne of their son, leading her armies to victory until she was finally vanquished on the field of battle.[9] To explain the abnormality of such qualities and such behaviour in a woman, Calderón adds to the legend his own myth, placing her in a prison from her birth. He makes her the daughter of a mother who was a priestess of Diana and therefore vowed to chastity, and of a father who was a votary of Venus. The father raped the mother, and after the act the mother stabbed and killed him. She died herself as she gave birth to the baby who, lying beside her dead mother, is tended and kept alive by birds sent by Venus. Semíramis was thus born of strife and violence, but under the star of Venus; she is therefore marked with her beauty. She is discovered by a shepherd, to whom it is prophesied that the baby will grow into a woman who will beget strife and violence in the world. Paying no heed to the prophecy, Semíramis makes it come to pass and, as she dies in the battle, she cries out that Diana has been victorious.

Semíramis deliberately disregards the prophecy because she is conscious of the power that her beauty gives her over men. Her first victim describes her in what is in effect a rapturous hymn to woman's beauty. But in the light of the disasters that follow, what must we make of this hymn? Is the rapture an illusion to be shunned Narcissus-like, or condemned with puritanical horror?

A later mythological play, *Apolo y Climene*, develops the tower motif further. In Greek mythology Clymene was the mother of Phaethon, whose father was Apollo. Mythology does not recount how the god Apollo came to love a human woman, though it does present him as at one stage exiled on earth as the shepherd of the flocks of King Admetus. What interested Calderón was the significance of a god in love with a woman and producing offspring. A woman in love with a god means that there is in human love a spiritual orientation, an expression of the human soul: love can be noble and pure. But if the sensual element takes exclusive control, then the orientation of love is not spiritual, but the opposite. Calderón's imagination, channelled into these mythological terms, elaborated the Clymene story in this way. She is a woman imprisoned in the temple of Diana by order of her father, the king, because of a prophecy that she would bear a son so proud and arrogant that he would set the kingdom of Ethiopia on fire. (This will be Faetón, who will drive the sun chariot of his father, Apolo, and crash to earth; this second play (1661) is the sequel to the Climene drama.) In order to prevent her bearing any child, Climene is secluded in the temple of Diana, in other words compelled to chastity, her father exacting from her a solemn vow. What King Admeto does not know, however, is that the priestesses of Diana have one and all broken their vows in furtive liaisons with men. This signifies that humanity is not free to serve the cult of Diana in what of course is equivalent to the ideal of Platonic love that had dominated sixteenth-century literature: erotic passion is the law of life, which must be obeyed, whatever disorders and calamities it presages. Climene in due course must obey it secretly, like all the other priestesses. She breaks her vow to Diana by loving Apolo, who is already on earth in the service of her father, and who finds an entry into the guarded precincts of Diana's temple through a hidden tunnel, an obvious sexual symbol.

Calderón's primary interest in this myth centres on the fact that a god loves a human woman, and the development of the prison symbol conveys the power of sexuality to overcome the spiritual love that should be the human ideal. This theme is not germane to our present purpose. It is an essential feature of Calderón's 'Philosophy of Love', which has been treated elsewhere.[10] The impossibility of totally fulfilling the spiritual nature of human love within sexuality, while remaining orientated towards the divine, which should be the law of human nature, means that the god can unite with Climene, but that she cannot keep him. When Apolo leaves her, she has to enter another prison, in which she is deprived of freedom through the fetters of the flesh; a victim, that is to say, of the imperfection and imperfectibility of human nature.

This is what Calderón develops out of the archetypal tower of Segismundo. All men are born prisoners of the imperfectibility of life: all men are doomed to suffer or to cause suffering and violence of some kind or another, for men make of the world a place of discord and chaos. Yet, as the horoscope symbol indicates, it is fatal by repression of any kind to try to prevent individual men from doing wrong: each man and woman must have with adolescence the freedom to face their destinies, although that may be their doom.

These concepts and the dramatic and poetic images that gave them life on the stage have grown out of the poet's early experience of life in his family circle. This represents experience refined and distilled over the years through the techniques that art offers the imagination. Though the reconstruction of the events of 1611 in the life of Calderón's family is conjectural only, and though the genesis of the tower symbol and the father–son conflict in his plays is also conjectural and cannot be proved, it can be argued that the plays themselves make the conjectures possible. But even if the conjectures are rejected as unfounded, the interpretation here offered of the dramatic theme and its variations would still hold good and would be arrived at from Calderón's plays themselves, even if his father's will had not survived. The expanding horoscope–tower symbol would still demand explanatory analysis instead of the virtual dismissal that Blanca de los Ríos thought it deserved.

If, however, these conjectures can appear well-founded, what they add to the interpretation of the Calderonian myth is an insight into how the imagination of a poetic genius can transmute the raw material offered by reality into the universal terms of drama. The elements of the myth form a consistent and constant thread through Calderón's work from 1628, or perhaps earlier, down to 1680. This ceaseless revival of motifs and expansion of the basic themes reveals a mind permanently meditating on the problems of life. Experience becomes drama; it is deepened by symbolism, by an education through literature, by the reading of Greek mythology and by the study of philosophy, until all the elements of the myth take poetic shape. In reality, the development of the horoscope–prison symbol was taken further than the point reached in this chapter; with philosophy expanded into theology, it became for Calderón the fundamental existentialist problem, as the final chapter of this book will try to show. May the myth here analysed not be considered the 'Figure in the Carpet' of Calderón's work through which we can share his meditation on the human condition?

Before we reach 'the fundamental existentialist problem' ('to be or not to be'; would it not have been better if man had never been created?), we must continue to follow the development of the horoscope–prison symbol in another direction. What connection does Calderón make between his dramatic use of prophecies and the contradictory concepts of fate and human freedom?

8 Horoscopes and their fulfilment

La vida es sueño has been shown to be a seminal work. Horoscopes had been introduced into earlier plays, but apart from the doubtfully authentic *Las cadenas del demonio* (The Devil's Fetters), they had not been associated with imprisonment from birth. This association gives form and content to the 'myth' of the prison and starts it on its long career. *La vida es sueño* is also seminal in that it gives a clear analysis, in dramatic terms, of actions that aim to control events and make them conform to one's own plans ('dreaming') and those that follow from an acceptance of events as they are, aiming at following a course of action in accord with events as they unfold and not against them ('being awake'). Making decisions and planning courses of action in accord with events without seeking to control or counter them is at the heart of the dramatic function of horoscopes and prophecies as Calderón presents them, and is therefore bound up with the problem of Fate.

The basic quotations adduced as evidence of Calderón's concept of Fate and Destiny come, naturally enough, from *La vida es sueño*. On the one hand there is the clear assertion that it is impossible to escape one's fate; on the other hand it is also asserted that prudence can overcome Fate. Before he dies, Clarín says:

> que no hay seguro camino
> a la fuerza del destino
> y a la inclemencia del hado.

> (There is no sure escape from the force of destiny and the inclemency of fate.)

This compels Basilio to conclude

> que son diligencias vanas
> del hombre cuantas dispone
> contra mayor fuerza y causa

> (that all those efforts are fruitless that a man makes to counteract a more powerful force)

And this lesson is confirmed by Segismundo when he says

Lo que está determinado
del cielo, y en azul tabla
Dios con el dedo escribió,
de quien son cifras y estampas
tantos papeles azules
que adornan letras doradas,
nunca mienten, nunca engañan.

(What has been determined by Heaven, written by God's finger on the tablet of the sky, of which all those documents written on blue with gilded letters are abridged copies, never lie, never deceive.)

The contrary thesis is propounded by Clotaldo:

no es cristiana
determinación decir
que no hay reparo a su saña.
Sí hay, que el prudente varón
vitoria del hado alcanza

(no Christian may determine that there is no protection from its fury. Yes, there is, for the prudent man can emerge victorious over fate)[1]

This last statement is repeated several times throughout the *comedias.* For example, in *Los tres afectos de amor* (The Three Emotional Effects of Love) (1658), Seleuco, the astrologer-king who casts the horoscope of his daughter Rosarda, says

es verdad
que no siempre su palabra
cumple el hado, y que el prudente
sobre las estrellas manda

(it is true that fate does not always fulfil what it predicts, and that the prudent man can influence the stars)[2]

A little later in the play, the same character states

puede el entendimiento
predominar en los astros

([human] intelligence can predominate over the stars)

(I, 1328a) [*BAE,* III, p. 338c]

Hence there arose what is virtually a commonplace of criticism, that Calderón's plays hold the traditional orthodox doctrine, which he frequently quotes, that 'the stars can predispose the will but cannot compel it'. It is generally said that Calderón's theatre upholds the freedom of the will (which is true), even against Fate and the force of Destiny (which is doubtfully true).

As pointed out in the previous chapter, the belief has prevailed that Segismundo's free will triumphs over the stars when he proves the horoscope to be untrue; but in reality what he triumphs over is his violent temperament, and the horoscope is fulfilled exactly as forecast by Basilio. He did not foresee in the stars the death he comes to expect when forced to kneel before his victorious son; he thought this would be the natural consequence of his lying prostrate in defeat before him. This was because the edict of fate reached thus far and no farther, and this has been fulfilled, despite all the efforts Basilio made to prevent it.

The most obvious case of the fallibility of Fate is the very last *comedia* that Calderón wrote, *Hado y divisa de Leonido y Marfisa* (The Fate, Emblem and Motto of Leonido and Marfisa) (1680). Peter Berens, in his study of tragic fatality in Calderón, says of this play that the tragic calamity does not occur because the fate that was foreseen is not fulfilled.[3] Casimiro does indeed put a stop to the duel which is to fulfil the fate that was forecast, saying

> que pues revoca el decreto
> de que mates o que mueras,
> con sus piedades el cielo

(since Heaven in its mercy revokes the decree that you should kill or die)

later adding that

> el hado fiero
> ha mejorado la suerte

(cruel fate has bettered your lot)[4]

So that Marfisa neither kills nor is killed as the horoscope had forecast. This contradiction can be seen as no more than apparent only if all the circumstances attendant on the horoscope are considered. It is always necessary to do this in a Calderón play rather than give exclusive attention to the words spoken by one character alone. In this particular instance the astrologer Argante had told Marfisa that the horoscope that threatened her had disclosed this:

> sabe que el hombre, que más
> te quiera y tú quieres . . .
> te pondrá en tan gran desgracia
> que o tú has de matarle a él
> o él a ti.

(You must know that the man who will love you and whom you will love will bring you face to face with so great a disaster that either he will have to kill you or you will have to kill him.)

(II, 2114a) [*BAE*, IV, p. 371a]

He does not say that the one will definitely kill the other, but that she will be placed in a predicament in which this alternative is to be expected. In fact, the horoscope is actually fulfilled when Marfisa, disguised as a knight, engages in a life-or-death duel with Leonido. Casimiro stops this duel when he realises who they are. There is a very clear indication that the horoscope was indecisive, when Argante states that he does not know what end Leonido will have, because being unable to penetrate his free will, he does not yet know what wishes and intentions will guide him.

It can be maintained, therefore, that the horoscope in *Hado y divisa* is fulfilled, and not revoked as Casimiro was later to state. It is one of several prophecies that are inconclusive: they predict the threat without disclosing the ending. The classical example is *La vida es sueño*, where Basilio cannot complete the horoscope because (although he does not know this) he cannot penetrate Segismundo's free will.

It is clear from the plays themselves that Calderón's prophecies and horoscopes (except the demonic ones) are always fulfilled, but it also would seem clear that this had to be so from what was the orthodox doctrine in his day. Juan de Horozco y Covarrubias wrote a work on horoscopes and prophecies entitled *Tratado de la verdadera y falsa prophecía* (Treatise on False and True Prophecy) (1588). Apart from hoaxes and deliberate deceptions, all prophecies, he said, were either used or permitted by God or else were the work of the Devil. This does not, of course, apply to divinations, where wishful thinking took effect. God's aim in using prophecies was first of all to further Revelation and make clear the truths of Faith, and secondly, to serve as warnings of possible punishment to come. All prophecies inspired or permitted by God must be fulfilled. The only ones that are never fulfilled are those that are the work of the Devil or represent human wish-fulfilment. Prophecies that are demonic or obviously malevolent are very rare in Calderón. His interest in prophecies is always in connection with fate or destiny. Covarrubias states that 'good' prophecies may sometimes not be fulfilled; this will be because the outcome was dependent upon certain circumstances prevailing at the time of utterance, and if these conditions no longer hold good then the outcome no longer applies.[5] The primary purpose of Covarrubias's work was to disseminate the condemnation of judicial astrology by Pope Sixtus V. It is possible, he says, that movements of the planets may influence the bodily make-up of human beings and therefore their temperaments, but since God created human beings with free will, it is impossible for the motions of the planets to determine human destinies (fo. 132v–133r).

Calderón does not write as a theologian when he presents horoscopes that are fulfilled; he is writing as a dramatic poet within a classical culture and using horoscopes for special theatrical effects. When he makes his Semíramis die on the battlefield, crying out that Diana has been victorious, he has followed a horoscope that had to be fulfilled, because the fate forecast was quite unambiguous and because he showed that Semíramis had herself chosen of her own accord to forge each link in the chain of causality. This does not of course remove the problem of a predetermined series of events (to be discussed later), but it does show her will acting within a determined series of events. In other words, her horoscope *had to be fulfilled*. One must, in fact, maintain that all astrological prophecies are infallibly fulfilled in Calderón's plays *in the manner forecast*; and that Calderón never presents a single instance of a 'learned and prudent man overcoming the decrees of the stars' insofar as these decrees refer to prophecies which the heavens have actually revealed in the play concerned. This assertion is based on eleven plays in which Fate or Destiny constitute the axes round which the plays revolve. These do not include the numerous plays in which there are fatal omens (such as *La Cisma de Ingalaterra*), nor do they include prophecies which serve to indicate the psychological orientation of a particular character (like the cases of the Emperor Aureliano in *La gran Cenobia* (The Great Zenobia), or of Fénix in *El príncipe constante* (The Steadfast Prince)). In these cases, the prophecies do not determine the course of the action or influence it.

It is possible that some play with an unfulfilled secondary prophecy has slipped from one's mind; but with this reservation the general statement may stand that Calderonian fate is always upheld in the manner foreseen and that this forms the basis of his conception of Destiny. This statement conflicts with what has so often been stated about Calderón's dramatic world, that it firmly upholds belief in the freedom of the human Will against the Calvinist theology that upheld the doctrine of Predestination, whereby no man can alter the events of his unfolding life, which have been pre-ordained in the mind of God from all eternity. This belief is based on misconceptions which will be removed, it is hoped, in the following chapter. For the moment the statement must be re-emphasised that Calderón presents no prophecy that remains unfulfilled. Before examining the problem of fate and free will in any detail, this statement must be substantiated through an examination of the function of horoscopes in Calderón's drama.

The eleven 'fate plays' mentioned above can be classified in the following way:

1 The prophecies predict a disaster unambiguously. This class is divisible into two types:

(a) The victim attempts to prevent the fulfilment of the prediction, but fails because he does not clearly understand the warning it contains. This is the type in *El mayor monstruo los celos* (Jealousy, the Greatest Monster).

(b) The victim hopes that the prophecy will not be fulfilled, but does nothing, directly or indirectly, to prevent it. Examples are *La hija del aire, Apolo y Climene, El hijo del Sol, Faetón*.

2 A calamity is forecast, but in an enigmatic fashion:

(a) The victim can understand the prediction wrongly by interpreting it in a form favourable to himself: the example of this is *Los cabellos de Absalón*.

(b) The victim does not understand the prophecy and does not understand where the threat lies: *Eco y Narciso*.

These first two types contain complete prophecies: they are all tragedies.

3 There is a third class of play in which disasters are prophesied but in a vague way: the characters try to forestall the events, but the outcome is inconclusive, and because the actual ending had not been predicted, the threatened disasters do not take place. These are plays with a 'happy ending'.

Examples: *Las cadenas del demonio* (if authentic), *La vida es sueño, Los tres afectos de amor, Hado y divisa de Leonido y Marfisa*.

4 Finally, there is one play which does not fit into any of these categories, although it might be considered a variant of Class 1, without a tragic *dénouement*. In this play a prophecy predicts a calamity: the victim begins by struggling against this fate, striving to prevent it, but later he accepts it and collaborates with it, with the result remaining inconclusive. This is *El monstruo de los jardines* (The Monster of the Gardens) (written by 1667), which may well be considered a fourth type in the classification of the fate plays. The concept of destiny which it presents differs from the fate that prevails in the other plays, and this is because the character facing the horoscope comes to accept it as a destiny that it is his duty to fulfil. He freely accepts it and rejects the 'destiny' which he had planned for himself and which represented his view of future happiness. To be true to his own nature he must accept his horoscope and face the calamity it portends.

This conception of a destiny that must be fulfilled because it is in accord with one's own nature gives 'destiny' thus allied with 'duty' the sense of 'vocation'. A 'vocation' is an aim in life that is implanted within one. Whether it brings happiness or not is immaterial.

For this reason, the concept of destiny as vocation exemplified in *El monstruo de los jardines* can serve to lead into the whole question of fate, which is basically unwilled and undesired as an impelling force that is felt to be unjust and therefore malign. This play dramatises legends connected with the childhood of Achilles, legends which are recorded by Homer, Ovid and Apollodorus, among others.[6] This famous Greek hero becomes one of the 'prisoners' who exemplify the archetype of Segismundo in his tower. This version of Calderón's myth stresses all its constituent elements, namely the rape of the mother and the emergence from the prison as the onset of sexuality. Achilles was the son of Peleus and the sea-deity Thetis. In mythology Peleus, angered by Thetis's refusal to accede to his demands, captured her while asleep and tied her up so tightly that she could not escape. She thus consented to marry him against her inclination. Calderón, as we have come to expect, transforms this into the violation that remained in the forefront of his mind. She puts it thus to Aquiles:

> Basta, pues (¡ay infelice!),
> que embrión de una violencia
> fuiste, porque no te quejas
> de mi sino de tu estrella;
> pues eres tan desdichado,
> que cuando todos se precian
> que nacieron de un amor,
> naciste tú de una fuerza.

> (Suffice it to say (unhappy youth!) that you were conceived in violence, so that you should blame not me but your star; for you are so unfortunate that, while all others take pride in being born of an act of love, you were born of an act of violence.)

> (I, 1791b) [*BAE*, IV, p. 220c]

The violence from which Tetis suffered is in the sources; not so the vengeance she exacts on Peleo, for she slays him. Calderón also makes Aquiles her first son, when he was in fact the seventh. These radical changes indicate the importance that this erotic inheritance had for the dramatist.

The classical sources state that the oracle of Calchas decrees that Troy can never be conquered without the help of Achilles; fearing his early death in the war, Thetis seeks to circumvent the oracle by dressing the boy as a girl, placing him among the palace maidens in order to save his life. Serving the Princess Deidamia, Achilles falls in love with her and she, though hostile to men, is attracted to him in his woman's clothes. Calderón converts the oracle and the decision reached by Tetis into two distinct prophecies: the horoscope that Tetis casts as her child is born, and the oracle in the temple of Mars, uttered at the beginning of the play, when Aquiles is to emerge from his seclusion. The horoscope states that in the fifteenth year of his life he will be threatened by

> la más fiera
> lid, la más dura batalla,
> la campaña más sangrienta
> de cuantas en sus teatros
> la fortuna representa

> (the fiercest fight, the harshest battle, the bloodiest campaign among all those performed by fortune on her stage)
>
> (I, 1792a) [*BAE*, IV, p. 221a]

That is why, she explains to Aquiles, she has hitherto guarded him from harm; now he must guard himself, until the period of danger has passed. The oracle of Mars announces its prediction at the moment when Aquiles is about to rebel against the tutelage of his mother. Mars declares:

> Troya será destruida
> y abrasada por los griegos,
> si va a su conquista Aquiles,
> a ser homicida de Héctor.
> Aquiles, humano monstruo
> de aquestos montes, en ellos
> un risco . . .

> (Troy will be set on fire and destroyed by the Greeks, if Achilles is in the conquering army as the slayer of Hector. Achilles, the human monster of these mountains, in which a steep and rugged ridge . . .)
>
> (I, 1783a) [*BAE*, IV, p. 215a]

The oracle could not complete the description of Aquiles' 'prison' because of an earthquake caused by Venus in order to prevent the Greeks from finding Aquiles. In consequence, they know whom to look for but not where to find him. This prophecy is inconclusive because it fails to state whether Aquiles will or will not to go the war: this could thus be a free decision on his part, not one imposed by fate. The horoscope is likewise inconclusive, since it presents only a threat, and does not predict the death of Aquiles in the war. If the two prophecies are placed side by side, it becomes clear that 'the bloodiest campaign' of the horoscope must be the destruction of Troy predicted by the oracle. Since the oracle is addressed to the Greeks when they are already preparing their expedition, it must differ from the horoscope, cast fifteen years earlier. There is no special significance, therefore, in there being two separate prophecies on the same subject.

Nonetheless, the division of a prophecy into two constitutes a new variant in Calderón's presentation of fate. Prophecies of doom are all threats, either clear or vague, and the horoscope of Aquiles conforms to the general type. The second prophecy, however, is not a threat; on the contrary, it is the promise of victory in a heroic enterprise: Aquiles will be the victor in single combat with the Trojan champion, from which there will follow the destruction of the city. This is the type of prophecy found in *La gran Cenobia*, where it is foretold that Aureliano will become emperor, but in that case there is no threat. On the other hand, in *El monstruo de los jardines* there is a threat. In addition to a threat which the protagonist must fear and which he ought to seek to evade, there is also something positive, the promise of fame; but the promise and the threat go hand in hand. For what may be the only time in a major Calderonian play the threat presented by fate is not solely negative: the man to whom it refers has to accept it and face up to it actively and positively. There is no question here of fate persecuting or oppressing its victim, as in other fate plays; it is no longer a question of what *Hado y divisa de Leonido y Marfisa* called 'the merciless anger of destiny'.

There can be no doubt about this distinction, because the whole of the dramatic conflict rests upon it. The dramatic conflict is whether to reject or to accept the destiny presented by the oracle. This is the actual choice that lies before Aquiles, but the theme of the play is wider and more significant than this. It deals with man's restless search for happiness and how happiness is to be sought and found by men and by women.[7] Here the theme of the horoscope and oracle and their fulfilment is isolated from the main conflict of the drama. Ulises is entrusted by the Greeks to find Aquiles, and concludes that since the oracle has given him a hero's rôle, his nature must respond to the call to arms. He therefore has drums and trumpets played continuously.

Aquiles does indeed respond to the call of destiny, and placed in the conflict between love and duty he feels for the first time the shameful dishonour of his woman's clothes, and eventually accepts the destiny that enables him to 'cumplir con su natural' (fulfil his own nature). Deidamia, for her part, feels the same agonising conflict and must in the end accept the cruel sacrifice of letting Aquiles go to war. As so often in Calderón, it is woman who is the main sufferer in life, suffering here, like Climene, because she must let go what makes life most worth living. To love and to suffer is woman's 'vocation'.

A tragic outcome threatens both the lovers. They are about to be slain by the representatives of the society they have dishonoured, but when the secret love of Aquiles and Deidamia is made public, and when Tetis calms the tumult, peace is restored. Calamity for Aquiles is postponed. The fact that he knew he would lose his life in the bloodiest of all campaigns did not make him flinch from his destiny. This actual prophecy is inconclusive, because the play does not tell us whether it was fulfilled or not; but of course the audience, when they first heard it, knew that it would be, for the bloodiest of all campaigns could only be the Trojan War, in which the audience knew that Aquiles' end is already 'predestined'.

The concept of a personal vocation or calling as a personal destiny necessitates its recognition as such and the willing collaboration with the workings of fate that will bring it about. Aquiles co-operates while Semíramis did not, the difference being that his call was to heroism, while she had stultified her vocation as a woman by the ambitious desire for self-aggrandisement; she was fighting against Nature.

To co-operate with Destiny as vocation or to struggle against it as a malevolent threat is the duality that for Calderón lies at the heart of the problem of fate and free will. Technically, *El monstruo de los jardines* is not a tragedy, neither is *La vida es sueño*; yet both plays would doubtless have been 'better' if each had marched straight to the tragic ending that seemed its proper and inevitable destination. This is tantamount to saying that the calamities of tragedies are more profoundly moving than the 'happy endings' of comedy or tragicomedy. Aesthetic considerations are not the only ones to be applied here. Calderón had become conscious in his boyhood of the agonising problems of human suffering in connection with Good and Evil, and he had to work out for his own sake and that of his audience some sort of reconciliation between suffering and happiness. The reconciliation in the Achilles play is weaker than it is in the remote 'prototype' of *La vida es sueño*, but the play must not be denied an important place in the Calderonian treatment of fate and freedom. There are tragedies enough in his drama, though this was long denied. The problem of fate in human life dominates this theory and practice of tragedy, which itself has dominated dramatic art. No-one put the harrowing problem of fate and suffering more profoundly than Shakespeare when he made King Lear cry out:

> as flies to wanton boys are we to the gods, –
> they kill us for their sport.

> (IV, i, 36–7)

It has often been stated that tragedy is incompatible with Christianity and its belief in an overruling Providence. This is why it has been assumed that the Spanish Golden Age drama as a whole, thus including

Calderón, shunned tragedy. Whether this is the case with Calderón needs to be more closely examined than it has been, and this necessitates a survey of the problem of fate in the literary and philosophical traditions which formed his mind and sensibility.

9 Fate and human responsibility (1): the problem

Fate is a dominant strand in the overall pattern of Calderón's dramatic world; and not only in the *comedias*, because the struggle against the fulfilling of prophecies has its counterpart in the *autos sacramentales*, where the Devil and his confederates, perpetually disturbed by the Messianic promises, conjure up the enactment of future events in order to try to prevent their implementation, only to find no hope of escape from the fate in which they are trapped. Fateful predictions are not absent from Lope's plays, but they would seem to be part of the machinery to set the action in motion rather than its inner motivation. They represent no problematic element in life for the plays' themes to explore.[1] For Calderón, on the other hand, *el hado* is clearly something that men must come to terms with, both for their general understanding of existence and for the practical task of ethical living. Fate and what is bound up with it (principally *la fortuna* and *el desengaño*) may therefore be considered the most problematical element in Calderón's world.

Peter Berens attempted to analyse the meaning of Calderonian fate sixty years ago,[2] but his laudable effort suffers today from the general inadequacy of Calderonian criticism at that time, in particular from the failure to see how important are all the details in the structure of individual plots, and how varied these are because of these details. A later study by Charles Aubrun has the general title 'Natural determinism and supernatural causality in Calderón' but is in effect a study only of *El mayor monstruo los celos* (Jealousy, the Greatest Monster of All).[3] Even in this limited respect it is based on the assumption that in *La vida es sueño* Calderón had said his last word on determinism and free will.

Closer analysis, however, reveals that the prophecies in these two plays are not the same in kind or in function. There is, in consequence, still room for an investigation of the motif of prediction in all its ramifications. It is right that *La vida es sueño* and *El mayor monstruo los celos* should be paired: they both belong to the same relatively early period, and the entire action is dominated in both by prophecies. But they should be paired as contrasts, not as parallels. The latter play has been given only a fraction of the attention devoted to the former. By lessening the imbalance it will be easier to point the contrast.

Life in classical times was ruled by divinations, recourse to oracles and sibyls, and interpretations of omens, prodigies and portents. Roman historians record countless instances of this kind, and it would have been from their writings that Calderón learned how life could be lived in constant apprehension of the future and with the restless anxiety to probe its secrets. The fact that the practice of astrology flourished more strongly in the sixteenth century, despite the continuing hostility of the Church, than it had in the Middle Ages, is to be attributed to the revival of classical learning.[4] In Covarrubias's work on true and false prophecy in which he intended to disseminate Pope Sixtus V's condemnation of judicial astrology, ten times more space was devoted to classical antiquity than to the Biblical and Christian times. It is not surprising, therefore, that Calderón's first play from Roman history, *La gran Cenobia*, should be filled with dreams, predictions and oracular utterances; nor is it surprising that he should have projected this same pagan atmosphere into the Christian world, especially in plays with a tragic tone. To predictions and dreams he added omens. Don Enrique stumbles and falls when he lands on the shore of Africa, which for him portends the defeat of the Portuguese expedition, and he is quickly proved right (*El príncipe constante*). Anne Boleyn stumbles and falls when she first meets Henry VIII (*La cisma de Ingalaterra*). Rosaura falls off her horse just before meeting Segismundo (*La vida es sueño*); the Infante Enrique falls off his just before meeting Doña Mencía again (*El médico de su honra*). These are omens from Roman history.[5] They indicate encounters that are fateful because they will have tragic consequences, but not fatal in the sense of being foreordained. None of these characters is being impelled towards a foreseen disaster. Nor are the characters in *La gran Cenobia*. Not till *La vida es sueño* (with Basilio and Segismundo) and *El mayor monstruo los celos* is it possible to talk of Fate as a force shaping a dramatic plot because it can shape a human life.

In the case of Calderón one should not avoid the term 'fate' in favour of 'predestination' or 'predetermination'. Nor is it at all helpful to associate Calderón with the controversy between Báñez and Molina, so often mentioned in this connection, which had no direct impact on Spanish literature (except perhaps on *El condenado por desconfiado* (Damned through Despair), where the connection is not a necessary one). This controversy had been the latest (and most subtle) discussion of a problem that is as old as Western literature and that did not need the advent of Christianity to be formulated and debated. Much more relevant for *El mayor monstruo* than the controversy between Bánez and Molina is the background in classical antiquity, which will be discussed first.

Divination came into existence as a form of prayer in that it sought to effect a modification of human destiny in a particular direction by means of divine intervention.[6] The foreknowledge attained by divination gave men the means either of escaping from disasters or of transforming hope into certitude. In the former case the desired result would be the modification of the future by the gods, which meant that their knowledge of it had been conditional only, able to be altered in answer to human petitions. This concept of a future formed of still undecided possibilities, dependent on human free will, could not be harmonised with the idea of fixed laws necessitated by the spectacle of an ordered universe. Popular instinct was irresistibly led to the conviction that the future, because foreknown to the gods, was unalterable, untouchable even by them. This conviction was expressed by the creation of an abstract being, Destiny (Moira) or Necessity (Ananke). If the future is foreseen, it must be immutable; it can only be revealed because it is so. Therefore, the human being seeking foreknowledge is deluded if he thinks he has the freedom to avoid it. There was thus introduced into philosophy the perennial conflict between divine foreknowledge and human freedom, in which neither can be pressed to its natural conclusion without suppressing the other. Báñez and Molina no more succeeded in solving the problem than had the Greek thinkers. In consequence, through divination and prophecy, men sought in most cases to find out what had to be done so that human actions might conform to the will of the gods. In this way man entered spontaneously into the ways of Providence, without seeking to impose his will, as a rival force, on destiny.[7]

If human freedom existed and a man had the power to shape his own destiny, the future would consist of an infinite number of possibilities; the world would thus be ruled by chance, not order. To safeguard Providence and the dignity of Zeus, the Greek poets of the fifth century BC suppressed human freedom, and fatality dominated the tragic drama. The problem thus posed for Aeschylus by the denial of human freedom was analogous to the one that the horoscope forced Calderón to face in *La vida es sueño*: how to affirm human responsibility in the face of destiny.[8] His solution was to assert that every man who is unfortunate has deserved to be so. At the source of all misfortune there was a sin – ordinarily the fount of presumption and pride. The gods could force a man who deserved punishment to commit this formal sin so as to have reason for punishing him; the guilty man was pursued by divine vengeance, and his sufferings produced a long chain of further suffering that often continued into his posterity.[9] These, of course, are the remote *literary* roots of the 'poetic justice' that guides the structure of Spanish dramatic plots, and which cannot be absent from Calderón's dramatic handling of Fate; the Christian theology of guilt and expiation, with its

Judaic foundation, was ultimately rooted in the same universal religious sense of mankind as the drama of Greece.

The tragedies of Aeschylus are permeated by absolute faith in the infallible efficacy of oracles: the gods keep their word. Nevertheless, they are removed from the earlier concept of an irrational fate, blindly enchaining human freedom; Sophocles completes the replacement of this concept by a Divine Rationality, in which the immutability of destiny is combined, not with blindness, but with Intelligence. In this religious climate the place of divination lay in the fact that the future could be revealed to men by Zeus, or by Apollo his prophet, in order to place human will on guard against the presumptuous blindness that provokes the curse of the gods.[10]

In later philosophy, the Stoic doctrine on fatality and freedom has a close relevance to Calderón. The Stoics believed in Providence. They also believed in divination on the grounds that the gods were too good to deprive men of so valuable a benefit. If, they argued, the gods exist and yet do not announce to men what is going to happen, this would be for one of five reasons: they do not love men; they do not know the future themselves; they think that men are unconcerned about it; it is beneath their dignity to announce it; or, lastly, they are incapable of announcing it. Each of these hypotheses is inadmissible; therefore, divination exists.[11] So does fatality. The theory of a universal sympathy uniting all created things means that everything is interlinked: a man cannot lift a finger without the effects of this action spreading throughout the universe. Fatalism is a necessary corollary of this. Virtue therefore consists in the orientation of the will, which is either free to conform of man's own accord to the divine plan, or compelled to follow it despite itself. When their opponents asked what was the use of divination if everything was ruled by Fate, the Stoics replied that its utility lay in enabling man to co-operate with the divine plan. This self-identification with the Divine Will is the act of the wise man. In the midst of an absolute fatalism, free will exists only in the wise man's unforced conformity to Fate.[12]

With the coming of Christianity, divination and oracles were condemned as the work of evil spirits, and omens were dismissed as superstition. All revelation of the future was considered either divine or diabolic. Only that prediction was good which could be known or shown to come from God. Astrology was reduced, in principle, to the discovery of a man's 'complexion'. The revival of the classical world in the philosophers' habits of thought and in the 'fictions' of the poets, made it possible for Calderón to resurrect belief in prophecies and omens, and to use them as significant dramatic devices.[13] But in any case a new dynamism was given to the concepts of Fate and freedom by the

Protestant Reformation, which opened up all Christian doctrines for renewed examination. The generation before Calderón had been plunged into acute controversy by the emphasis given first of all by Luther and then much more profoundly by Calvin to the rigid belief in Fate as Predestination.

The main point at issue concerned Predestination. Since God is omnipotent and omniscient, with an unchanging and timeless existence, he must know as he created each individual man whether he is destined for Heaven or for Hell. What God knows out of Time must infallibly come to pass within Time, so that when God wills to create an individual man, he wills the end to which that man is destined through Divine foreknowledge. He has willed all things from all eternity.

It had been traditional Christian teaching from the time of Paul that men cannot be saved by their own efforts or on their own merits, but are saved by the Grace God grants them through the redemptive merits of Christ. If a soul is damned, that saving Grace must be withheld. Calvin established with strict logic the doctrine of Absolute Predestination, whereby God has decided prior to each man's birth that he will be saved in Heaven or damned in Hell, and nothing that he can do during his life can change his destiny. No matter how devout and pious a life he might lead, no amount of devotional practice could work for his salvation: he could be justified only by faith. This doctrine conflicted with the hitherto universally accepted belief that a man's salvation or damnation was due not only to his faith but to some extent to the moral quality of his life (his 'Good Works'). In consequence, traditional Catholic theology, reaffirmed by the Council of Trent, held that every man was free to co-operate with or reject Grace in determining his spiritual destiny; free, that is, to accept or reject the saving Grace that would infallibly be offered him. But Catholic theologians had now to defend by argument this doctrine against the belief in Absolute Predestination.

The famous theological debate on Predestination, Grace and Free Will between the Dominican Domingo Báñez and the Jesuit Luis de Molina lasted from 1598 to 1607. Literary critics who are Hispanists have quoted this controversy more often than they have understood it. It is generally believed by laymen that Báñez, following St Augustine, upheld the doctrine of Predestination, while Molina upheld the contrary doctrine of Freedom of the Will. This is not the case. Both theologians, together with all their Catholic colleagues, believed both in Predestination and Free Will.

In 1588 Molina published a book on the reconciliation of Free Will with Grace, Divine foreknowledge, Providence, Predestination and Damnation. From 1584 onwards Domingo Báñez published in seven volumes his commentary on the *Summa Theologica* of Thomas Aquinas, which represented what Báñez had taught at the University of Salamanca. He impugned the new ideas propounded by Molina, and there followed a public debate in Valladolid between these two theologians. Since the matters in dispute could not be settled, the arguments were sent for adjudication to the 'Congregation *De Auxiliis*' in Rome, which was itself unable to pronounce between the two sides. The Pope ultimately silenced the debate, and both doctrines have since then been accepted as orthodox.

Given the respective premises that each man's faith is already determined by God's foreknowledge and that human beings know from their own experience that they are free to choose or not to choose, the solution to this dilemma could only be found in some logical sleight of hand, in which scholastically trained minds were adept. Báñez, following Aquinas, held that God's foreknowledge moved men to act or not to act, but He moved them according to the nature He had given them; since it was their nature to act freely, He moved them in such a way that they did act freely. For Molina, this was in effect to deny Free Will; he solved the dilemma by positing a special 'middle knowledge', or *scientia media*, in the Divine Mind, whereby God knew the future contingent actions of men as contingent.[14] For Báñez, this was to deny God's omniscience. The dilemma has remained insoluble. Error has, however, crept into the interpretation of the debate. It is not true that Báñez denied Free Will, or that Molina denied Predestination. Both were, and are, orthodox Catholic doctrines, and each theologian believed in both. Faith and Hope can reconcile them within the spiritual life, but Logic can effect a 'reconciliation' by in effect emphasising one to the apparent weakening of the other. Another popular error is to make either Predestination or Free Will apply to the whole of human conduct. The debate was not about that, but about Grace, Salvation or Damnation, and the Freedom under discussion was the freedom to accept or reject the Grace that can bring Salvation.

It is a mistake, therefore, to maintain that Calderón was a Molinist. The concept of *scientia media* could scarcely have been performable on the stage, even the stage of the *auto sacramental*. It is true that in all the moral conflicts presented in Calderón's plays, freedom of choice occurs, but it is also true that all non-malevolent prophecies are fulfilled and that, while some of his characters do control their lives, others do not, and succumb to a fate that lies outside their control.

The foregoing discussion has demonstrated that Calderón does present Fate or Destiny as a force beyond human control, fulfilling decrees that are fore-ordained at the birth of individual human beings.

The horoscope (or similar prediction) is the familiar device he adopts for presenting this concept. The human being, by being 'true to his or her own nature', can implicitly accept fate and so co-operate with his destiny. He can also disregard his threatened fate and go down to defeat by battling against it. This is the case of Semíramis in *La hija del aire* who, by fighting against her fate, does in effect co-operate with it and fulfils it. But Calderón also presents fate as an external force, apparently totally separate from its victim's volition. Here he suggests a different dramatic relationship between fate and free will by emphasising the workings of Chance. A character can seek to forestall a doom he fears, but though he acts freely and deliberately his actions seem to unfold in a different dimension. Such a dimension is presented in *El mayor monstruo los celos*.

10 Fate and human responsibility (2): a dramatic presentation – *El mayor monstruo los celos*

Tirso de Molina preceded Calderón in dramatising the story of Herod and Mariamne. Despite the great differences between the two plays, Blanca de los Ríos affirmed that Calderón owed much to *La vida y muerte de Herodes*.[1] Since the plays have absolutely nothing in common, all that can be affirmed is that Tirso's play may have been the stimulus that made Calderón's mind turn to the Herod story. That he read Tirso's play is certain, for it was published in the latter's *Quinta Parte de comedias* (1636) for which Calderón wrote a respectful *aprobación*[2] (censor's official approval). The composition of *El mayor monstruo los celos* could have followed this, for it was published in his *Segunda Parte* in 1637, though this does not leave much time for the play to have been performed, and for the text to have become corrupted before it reached the printer. Calderón later revised it and the revision was licensed for performance in 1667, and again in 1672; at the end it is stated that the play is

> Como la escribió su autor;
> no como la inprimió el urto,
> de quien es su estudio echar
> a perder otros estudios

> (as the author wrote it; and not as it was printed by piracy, whose purpose is to spoil another's production)[3]

There is nothing in the texts of the two plays to indicate that they are in any way dependent. *La vida y muerte de Herodes* has a type of structure that Tirso frequently favoured, one that is tantamount to a tripartite play. The first section deals with the wooing and winning of Mariadnes (as Tirso calls Mariamne) by Herod, who abducts her from his brother, Faselo, her officially chosen husband. The second section deals with the jealousy of Herod, aroused by his sister's slanders, and with his conviction that Mariadnes has betrayed him. The third section deals with the Massacre of the Innocents (preceded by scenes that constitute a fine Christmas play in the tradition of the *officium pastorum*), Herod's madness and his death in a fit of raving. There is much splendid poetry and a few impressive scenes, but no matter how one tries to find a unified theme, this strange play remains unsatisfactory. The first two sections are connected by the violence of Herod, but this plot is unfinished, for the introduction of the Innocents prevents the death of Mariadnes and the remorse of Herod. Acts I and II might be seen as actions bringing into existence the madness that can order the Massacre, but this is top-heavy. If the play had been about the Massacre, it should have begun with, and developed, the theme of lust for power: to gain the throne Herod murders his brother; to retain it, in face of the report of a new King's birth, he murders the infants. But for this theme the Mariadnes motif is extraneous.

Calderón is much closer to Josephus. There are two accounts, with some discrepancy in the details, a short one in *The Jewish War* and a long one in *Antiquities of the Jews*.[4] The portrait occurs in the former: Herod's mother and sister falsely accuse Mariamne of adultery and allege that she had sent her portrait to Mark Antony in order deliberately to show herself, 'though she was absent, to a man that ran mad after women'. This is the reason, in this version, for Herod's secret instructions to have his wife killed should he himself be executed by Antony. In the longer version the alleged portrait is replaced by Herod's fear that Antony has fallen in love with Mariamne on hearing reports of her beauty. Here the instruction to kill her is given twice: when Herod journeys to Rhodes to make his peace with Octavian after the battle of Actium, and later when Herod goes to join Octavian in Egypt after Antony's death. On both occasions Mariamne learns of the secret instructions, and each time her resentment leads her to scorn Herod and to refuse cohabitation. Convinced, after the second time, that Sohemus would never have discovered the secret to Mariamne had he not enjoyed her favours, Herod has her brought to trial and condemned to death. For this he is later bitterly repentant, but lives for many years into old age. Under the pain of his last disease he attempts suicide but is prevented; Calderón anticipates this act of despair by making it follow Mariamne's death.

Another major change he introduces is also an elaboration of suggestions in Josephus. Octavian, not Antony, sees an actual portrait of Mariene (as Calderón calls Mariamne) and becomes enamoured of the sitter. The consequences are Calderón's invention: Octavian visits Herod in Jerusalem and tries to save Mariene from what he believes to be the danger of Herod's fury; in the fight between the two men Mariene is accidentally killed. A further change is important for the presentation of Herod's jealousy: in Josephus Herod has no difficulty in convincing Octavian of his loyalty, who heaps favours on him; in Calderón, Herod's intentions are traitorous and it is Octavian's love for Mariene that prevents him from receiving a traitor's punishment. Lastly, Calderón is the sole inventor of the double prophecy concerning Mariene's death, and of the fateful dagger; by these means Herod's jealousy is raised above the level of passion on to that of Fate.

For most critics it is precisely this that mars the play. Menéndez Pelayo thought it 'an admirably planned drama, but very unevenly carried out and written'. The two omens with the dagger he found 'casi cómicos' (almost comic). 'All those theatrical effects are somewhat puerile within so fine a subject, and this double fatality which runs through the whole work is unnecessary, it does not serve to heighten the sense of tragedy, since the interest of the play lies in the Tetrarch's character, which, unlike other Calderonian characters, is in every respect a true character, although a little outside the bounds of reality.' Lastly, the ending is a serious defect: 'The Tetrarch should kill Mariene deliberately and through jealousy; but he kills her only by mistake and through the putting out of the lights. So that what begins as a tragic drama finishes as a comedy of intrigue; with a purely accidental act unwilled by the character.'[5] These strictures are here resurrected because they all point to the purpose of this chapter, which is to explain devices that can, at their face value, appear trivial and unnecessary.

Berens, searching for this explanation, could come to no satisfying conclusion. He found an unresolved dualism in the play, deriving from the dual prediction. Mariene will be killed by the 'greatest monster', which is the Tetrarch's jealousy; but the instrument of her death will be the dagger. The latter prediction is enigmatic, not stating who will wield the dagger, because it must be Fate that strikes with it. The two predictions produce two plots – jealousy and fear of the dagger – which are never fused together; thus it is not an act of jealousy when the Tetrarch throws the dagger out of the window. The dagger is thus required only by Fate ('fatales Requisit'), not by Character. Whether Calderón postulates a third and higher destiny between and above these two (Providence?) remains an open question. Character and Fate work side by side or successively, never together. Berens found that the dualism continues into the ending, because the death of Mariene, which is the work of Fate, is offset by the suicide of the Tetrarch, which is an act of free will. While her death had stressed the helplessness of human freedom, that of the Tetrarch makes human freedom trespass into God's domain. Thereby an unwilled irony enters into the play's theme. By the suicide Calderón intended to make the Tetrarch still more repellent; in effect he causes a 'destiny' ('Schicksal'), nourished within a human breast, to rise up beside an 'hado' (fate) brought in from outside, and such was not his intention.[6] Berens correctly saw a dramatic problem but seemed to be looking for a non-dramatic, metaphysical solution; the explanation is to be found in the causal nexus of the action itself.

Aubrun went still further and discussed the whole play in metaphysical, even theological, terms. He saw it as presenting all the problems posed by natural predetermination, and as giving the 'Catholic and Spanish' doctrine. The Tetrarch faced up rationally to the threat of the double prediction, but when things began to go wrong (the double omen of the dagger) he gave up the struggle and abandoned himself to his misery. Aubrun held that the Tetrarch remains obstinate in his error to the end, imputing to the stars the responsibility for a crime that was the result of his own free choice, having freely rejected various opportunities for avoiding it. He abdicated the control over nature which God has entrusted to men, and so allowed physical forces free scope to determine destiny. '*El mayor monstruo* is a protest against a tragic conception of life and Calderón is the anti-tragic poet *par excellence*'.[7] Aubrun maintained that the doctrine by which Calderón condemns his Tetrarch is that, despite the natural laws to which we are subject, we are entirely responsible for each and every one of our actions. We are not acted upon; we act of our own free choice. Mariene and the Tetrarch are punished for having turned their backs on Grace. She died because of the very passivity with which she apprehensively awaited her destiny; he died because he too did not go against his destiny, did not transcend it.[8]

What should they have done instead? In order to explain their errors Aubrun gave the following exposition of Calderón's views on destiny. Man is entirely subject to the absolute determinism that exists in the physical and psychical orders. Calderón seems to make a distinction between *sucesos* (events) and *casos* (accidents). The former are the links in the chain in the expected sequence; the latter are the unforeseen links in the chain of events: the *casos* offer men the possibility of breaking the first chain and starting a second. Without the fact of determinism being in any way altered, the human will can utilise a fortuitous *caso* to orient determinism in a new direction. Aubrun contended that we are endowed with free will and can use it to modify the succession of events in our lives, but we are being determined physically and psychically even when we exercise our authority over the things of this world.[9]

From this it followed that the function of the understanding is to enable us to know our destiny, and by foreseeing it to give a turn to the wheel ourselves, thereby 'precipitating' the events of our lives. Error lies in refusing, like Herod, the destiny which the mind discloses. Divine Grace intervenes when we question the stars; it is what enables us to accept our destiny unconcerned with the pursuit of happiness or the shrinking from unhappiness. By despising the world and ceasing to struggle against misfortune, we attain to the *desengaño* (disillusionment) that gives a meaning to life. Human dignity is exercised when men refuse to submit totally to physical and psychical determinism, which they do when they go counter to their passions by controlling all impulses that come from the natural order. Bewitched by the horoscope, the Tetrarch and Mariene become its prisoners. If we take up the burden of our destiny, if we look at it from above, and not from below or from within, then we see it from God's viewpoint and can harmonise what we want to make of our destiny with what he wants to do with it. Our free will, thus enlightened by Grace, is fused with God's will.[10]

This is what Aubrun called Calderón's 'Catholic and Spanish doctrine'.[11] Its resemblance to the Stoic doctrine outlined in the previous chapter will be obvious. If it is 'Spanish', it is so because it is part of the general neo-stoicism of the age; this does not of course prevent it from also being Catholic, and in essentials as much a doctrine for today as for post-tridentine times.[12]

One recognises in this account the wisdom that both Basilio and Segismundo (in *La vida es sueño*) learn through *desengaño*. The former had endeavoured to prevent the fulfilment of the horoscope; the latter had sought to fulfil it:

Contra mi padre pretendo
tomar armas y sacar
verdaderos a los cielos.

(I aim to take up arms against my father, and to prove the heavens true.)
(2379–81) [*BAE*, i, p.14a]

But each comes to repudiate the intention to prevent or cause events, and each eventually accepts with resignation what fate has in store for him – Basilio, when he kneels at his son's feet expecting death; Segismundo, when he in his turn kneels at his father's feet and exposes himself to his vengeance. But each can only do this because at that particular moment neither knows what his next fate is to be. The horoscope has been fulfilled to the letter, but it went only as far as Basilio's kneeling in defeat before his seditious son. Only because the fulfilment of the prediction has taught him that it is error to resist, can Basilio now learn to co-operate with Fate (or with Grace, if one wills, though there is no suggestion in the play of anything supernatural). Segismundo thus states the 'doctrine':

No antes de venir el daño
se reserva ni se guarda
quien le previene; que aunque

puede humilde (cosa es clara)
reservarse dél, no es
sino después que se halla
en la ocasión, porque aquesta
no hay camino de estorbarla.

(He who forestalls harm is not holding back or safeguarding himself before the harm comes; for although it is clear that he can, with humility, hold himself back, this can only be when he finds himself in the actual situation, for there is no way of preventing the situation from happening.)

(3220–7) [*BAE*, I, p. 18b–c]

The case of the Tetrarch and Mariene is in no way parallel. For them there can be no 'después' (afterwards) to the event predicted; since this is Mariene's death, it is final, with no possible undetermined course of action to follow. For them, therefore, 'no hay camino de estorbarla' (there is no way of preventing the situation from happening). There is nothing Mariene can do but await her death; nor is it very helpful to the Tetrarch to say that his will ought to be fused with God's will in encompassing the slaying of his own wife. There is no proper understanding of the play along these lines.

Aubrun deduced his 'Spanish and Catholic doctrine' from *La vida es sueño*, where it is presented positively in the change of mind and heart of both son and father. The doctrine is not, however, presented positively in *El mayor monstruo*; Aubrun applies it from *La vida es sueño* by a contrasting analogy, and it is in consequence, strictly speaking, irrelevant. This play presents fate as the active force and human free will as its helpless victim. We must reject *La vida es sueño* as irrelevant, and realise that *El mayor monstruo* deals with a prediction of a different type. It is different also in another respect, for while in the former the prediction is essential to the plot, in the latter it could be removed and a satisfactory plot would remain. If one considers only the action by itself with the conflict of human passions, there is no doubt that Menéndez Pelayo's criticism is tenable, for the action and its motivation are as follows.

The Tetrarch is a proud and ambitious man. There is a certain splendour in his arrogance, as there is in the passionate possessiveness of his love for his wife. He already sees her enshrined as a fixed star in heaven's firmament:

Hermosa Mariene,
a quien el orbe de zafir prebiene
ya soberano asiento,
como estrella añadida al firmamento.

(Beautiful Mariene, for whom the sapphire orb is already preparing a sovereign place, as for a new star added to the firmament.)

(25–8) [*BAE*, I, p. 481a]

Meanwhile she deserves the highest acclaim that men can give her, nothing less than to have the world at her feet with a Roman triumph as she stands by his side when he is crowned Emperor. To this end his political activity is directed, and in the rivalry between Mark Antony and Octavian he plays a double game:

Y yo, pues, ¿con falso trato y doble estilo
de Antonio no defiendo
la parte? Porque así turbar pretendo
la paz, y que la guerra
dure a fin que después, quando la tierra
de sus güestes padezca atormentada,
y el mar cansado de vna y otra armada,
pueda, desechos ambos, declararme
y en Roma, tú a mi lado, coronarme.

(Do I not defend Antony's cause with false words and double dealing? Because in that way I aim at disturbing the peace in order to prolong the war so that afterwards, when the earth suffers the burden of their armies, and the sea is weary with the burden of both fleets, with the destruction of both forces, I may be declared emperor and crowned in Rome with you at my side.)

(46–54) [*BAE*, I, p. 481a]

His passion for Mariene is part of this ambition; it is not, therefore, an unselfish devotion but an element in this self-aggrandisement: he alone deserves to possess such beauty, and he must parade it before the whole world. But just as his political ambition is served through treachery, so is he capable of betraying his love for Mariene by allowing jealousy (the self-seeking inversion of love) to preserve his exclusive possession of her at all costs. Treachery and jealousy go hand in hand throughout the play, and towards the end are explicitly linked by Mariene when (in the first version) she casts his lowly ancestry in Herod's face:

que eres baxo, y afrentoso
Idumeo, cuya cuna
bárbara es, ¿qué más apoyo
desta opinión, que tus zelos
infames, como alevoso?

(for you are a low-born and base Idumaean, cradled in barbarism; what greater proof can there be of this opinion than your infamous jealousy, like the traitor you are?)[13]

This self-centred ambition gives the Tetrarch a boundless self-confidence. He refuses to be disheartened by presages of disaster:

> Al manánimo barón
> no hay prodijio que le espante.

(The magnanimous man cannot be frightened by any prodigy.)
(469–70) [*BAE*, I, p. 483b]

And even when things are beginning to go wrong, he refuses to believe that it is possible to be unhappy:

> El ser vno desdichado
> todos an dicho que es fácil,
> mas yo digo que es difícil,
> que es tan yndustrioso arte
> que aunque le platiquen todos,
> no le a penetrado nadie.

(Everybody has said that it is easy for one to be unhappy, but I say it is difficult, for it is such a cunning art, that although all practise it, none achieve it.)
(425–30) [*BAE*, I, p. 483a]

Things must inevitably go wrong. An overweening ambition of this kind, an all-embracing possessiveness and self-confidence, must have to come to terms with reality. With Antony's defeat the Tetrarch's political strategy collapses. He is arrested, taken before Octavian, and sentenced to be executed as a traitor. In Octavian's quarters he finds a portrait of Mariene, and the violent jealousy aroused by the thought that she might become another man's possession makes him guilty of a double treachery: he determines to repair his fortune by stabbing Octavian in the back, and he sends an order to Jerusalem to have Mariene killed as soon as news is received of his execution. Both these acts are frustrated. When Mariene discovers the secret order, her indignation at her husband's cruel betrayal makes her flare in a frenzy just as violent as his. '¡Oh plegue al çielo', she cries,

> me le entreguen
> viuo, para que a mis braços . . .
> Pero ¿qué digo? Suspende,
> lengua, otra vez el açento,
> ωi no es que deçir yntentes:
> 'a mis braços, para que
> vengatiba, y ynpaçiente
> en ellos le haga pedaços'.

(Heaven grant that he be handed over to me alive so that in my arms . . . But, what am I saying? Cease speaking, my tongue, unless what I am trying to say is 'so that in my arms, revengeful and impetuous, I may tear him limb from limb')

(2391-8) [*BAE*, i, p.494b]

As her fury calms she decides to break all private relations with him as wife while maintaining public relations as queen. This duplicity (which on a smaller scale parallels that of the Tetrarch towards Octavian) is her undoing: as queen she successfully pleads for Herod's life, while as wife she retires into seclusion and refuses him access to her quarters. His jealousy aroused, he forces his way in, finds evidence that convinces him she is guilty and, although unwittingly, kills her. He then commits suicide in despair.

This is a perfectly adequate account of the tragic action. Two ardent and devoted characters are led by their passionate natures – jealousy in his case, pride in hers – into a conflict that can lead only to death. But though adequate, this is of course an incomplete account of the play. The double prediction adds, unquestionably, an element of strained tension to the action, and this should not be lightly dismissed as alien to the dramatic artistry; but it must be emphasised that it adds nothing to the characters' motivation, which sufficiently accounts for the tragedy already; nor does it add anything to the chain of causality forged by the action: everything would have happened exactly as it did, had there been no prediction. What then is Calderón's purpose in warning his characters, by means of astrology, that Mariene will be killed by the world's greatest monster and that the Tetrarch's dagger will kill what he most loves?

The answer can be seen if the causal links in the dramatic chain are set out consecutively, if namely the dramatic *structure* is analysed. (The purpose of the italics will be explained later; they are not intended as emphasis.) (1) The Tetrarch has plotted treason against Rome. (2) His plans having been discovered, he is arrested and taken to Memphis. (3) *He sees a portrait of Mariene in Octavian's quarters and burns with jealousy.* (4) He attempts to murder Octavian, who decides to have him executed in Jerusalem as a warning to all rebels. (The immediate result of this is (9) below.) (5) Herod's jealousy of Octavian, because of the portrait, causes him to send written instructions to Tolomeo to kill Mariene so that she should not survive his execution. (6) *The letter is seen in Tolomeo's hand by the jealous Libia who struggles to snatch it from him.* (7) *Mariene finds them struggling and demands to see the letter.* (8) in her anger at its contents she decides to separate from her husband and live apart. (9) Arriving in Jerusalem, Octavian sees Mariene, thus learning the identity of the portrait; at her request he pardons the Tetrarch. (10) After saving his life,

Mariene takes revenge on him by severing all relations. (11) *Meeting with Libia who unlocks the door, Herod gains access to Mariene's rooms.* (12) *He meets Tolomeo and attacks him for having shown Mariene the letter.* (13) *Fleeing from his rage, Tolomeo finds himself in Octavian's tent and, as an excuse, tells him Mariene's life is in danger.* (14) *Rushing to her assistance, Octavian meets Herod in her room.* (15) The latter attacks the former, and Mariene, to stop the fight, puts out the light. (16) *In the darkness the Tetrarch accidentally kills her.* (17) He commits suicide.

The main prediction is fulfilled. Mariene does die at the hands of her husband's jealousy, for this motivates his two attacks on Octavian, the second of which fulfills the first. There is an unbroken causal chain between the two attacks, but the important structural feature of the plot is that the causal links do not all work in the same way, which is why earlier it had been said that the action evolves, so to speak, in two different dimensions. This is an example of the intellectual skill with which Calderón can plan his dramatic actions. Each link does not represent a willed decision. The italicised actions are those caused by accident, or chance. If any of these chance events had not occurred, there would have been a break in the chain of causality and the final catastrophe would not have occurred. That this pattern of interplay between willed and unwilled acts is a deliberate aspect of Calderón's plot-construction is borne out by the way the second prediction concerning the dagger is fulfilled. To recall: the prophecy is that Mariene will be killed by the 'greatest monster' and that Herod's dagger will kill what he most loves. The sequence of events is this. (1) To frustrate the prophecy the Tetrarch throws the dagger into the sea. (2) *It pierces Tolomeo and returns with him.* (3) To frustrate the prophecy a second time, the Tetrarch wants Mariene to keep the dagger, but she refuses and makes him guard it. (4) He is therefore carrying it when in sudden anger he tries to kill Octavian. (5) *He strikes at him, but the dagger pierces the portrait.* (6) Octavian keeps the dagger so that it may be the instrument of Herod's future punishment. (7) Mariene, thinking she needs to defend herself against Octavian, snatches the dagger from him, recognises it and drops it in horror. (8) *Herod finds it.* (9) He tries to kill Octavian with it, (10) *but kills Mariene instead.*

In this sequence of events there is a precise pattern of intention and chance. It will be noticed that the deliberate acts are connected with who is to have the dagger and the intention to use it. The chance events concern its actual use: in each case it does what the person wielding it did not want it to do: it wounds Tolomeo; it stabs the portrait; it kills Mariene. So separated are actions and intentions that it might seem justifiable, here if anywhere, to talk of a malignant force twisting events to suit itself.

Equally striking is the fact that the dagger sequence is completely separate from the chain of causality, which it does not influence. It is misguided to see in this the existence of two distinct 'plots' – jealousy and the dagger – which remain unresolved into a unity. What is denoted by this separation is that the dagger is not, cannot be, a *cause* of anything. Herod at the start attributes an independent efficacy to it; he thinks he can annul the horoscope by removing the operative cause: he therefore throws the dagger into the sea. But the dagger is only the cause's instrument; the cause itself is his violent and unruly self-centredness. Herod uses the dagger only twice, in his two attempts to kill Octavian. His jealousy is fully aroused when he sees the portrait in Octavian's possession: his supposed rival is now the object on which his passion fastens. That is why Octavian is made to keep the dagger, which now becomes almost a symbol. In the last scene, Octavian and Mariene are found together in a room into which her husband has been forbidden entry, she and he therefore become the joint object of Herod's jealousy. The dagger is thus made to pass from Octavian to Mariene, and then to lie on the floor between them. Not until the end does the Tetrarch realise, as he constructs in a sonnet a composite monster ('Pues si los çelos difinir hubiera' (for if I could define jealousy), 3064 ff.), that the wild beast which threatens Mariene is the passion within himself that possesses the property of blinding him to its existence:

> ¿Qué pasión ¡çielos!, es ésta,
> de amor hija y madre de odio,
> que es quando más la padezco
> quando menos la conozco?

> (Heavens, what passion is this, the daughter of love, and the mother of hatred, a passion which I recognise least when it inflames me most?)

> (3061–4)

Had Mariene also realised this in time, she would not have returned the dagger when, at the end of Act I, Herod entrusted it to her keeping for her own security, saying:

> para más seguridad
> tuya, cuerdo he prebenido
> que tú, árbitro de tu vida,
> traigas tus ados contigo;
> que mayor felicidad
> nadie en el mundo a tenido,
> que ser, a pesar del tiempo,
> el juez de su bida él mismo.

> (I have prudently determined that, for your greater safety, you, the arbiter of your own life, should always carry your fate with you. There is no greater

happiness in this world than to be arbiter over one's own life, despite the passing of the years.)

(1011–18) [*BAE*, ɪ, p.485c]

This can be taken in a presumptuous sense, in keeping with the Tetrarch's overweening self-confidence; but it can also be given an unexceptionable meaning, whereby every man in the free exercise of his responsibility is the maker of his own destiny. This is the sense favoured by the context, for Mariene proceeds to affirm that a husband is the guardian of his wife's life, not she herself, and that since he cannot wish her harm the dagger is safer in his keeping.

> Así, señor, yo te ruego,
> y así, mi bien, te suplico
> que tú, alcayde de mi vida,
> traigas el puñal contigo.
> Con eso seguramente
> sabré que aquel tiempo bibo
> que tú le tienes.

(And so, my lord, I ask you, and so, my love, I beseech you that you carry the dagger with you, since you are the guardian of my life. In that way I shall be certain that I shall live for as long as you own it.)

(1137–43) [*BAE*, ɪ, p.486b]

But while a normal husband can be called the guardian of his wife, a jealous husband is always potentially an executioner. Mariene fails to take this into account when she argues

> O tú me quieres o no:
> si me quieres, no peligro,
> pues a lo que tú más quieras
> no has de dar muerte tú mismo.

(Either you love me or not: if you love me, I am in no danger, for you yourself cannot kill what you most love.)

(1145–8) [*BAE*, ɪ, p. 486b]

But this is precisely what jealousy does do. Had Mariene not made this miscalculation, had she kept the dagger in her possession, it would not have been at hand at the moment of crisis to serve as the instrument of her husband's violent anger. She thus makes the same miscalculation as he: fatality cannot inhere in a material object, which is not more than the tool of a human will. Only human passions threaten murder. Separation of the dagger 'plot' from the jealousy 'plot' establishes this point.

The fact that the dagger kills Mariene accidentally (which is said to weaken the tragedy) indicates that passion is blind.[14] Under the stress of jealousy Herod never succeeds in doing what he intends to do. It is more fitting that he kill Mariene accidentally than Octavian intentionally, for jealousy is destructive of what it loves as well as of what it hates. Herod's obsession that no other man must ever possess Mariene had already, in Act II, made him kill her in intention so that she should not survive his death. It is an intended irony, which for Calderón was essentially tragic, that actually Herod has to kill himself in order not to survive *her* death. To say that Calderón's drama in general, and this play in particular, is 'anti-tragic' *par excellence*, as Aubrun and others have done, is either to misunderstand him or to uphold a narrow, arbitrary and unhistorical conception of tragedy. His plot here, so carefully and skilfully constructed to safeguard pity and fear on the one hand and expiation on the other, conforms in general to his age's neo-Aristotelian conception of tragedy. His own distinctive type of tragedy, exemplifying what will later be called 'diffused responsibility', is different. His classical and mythological themes conform in general to traditional tragedy; his 'diffused responsibility', learned not from literary theory, but from his actual experience of human relations, is found in his 'real-life' dramas.

The accidental murder of Mariene is the last of a series of fortuitous events that in the causal structure of the plot constantly break into the series of events willed by the characters, diverting them away from the intended ends. These accidents are what Calderón calls *acasos* (chance events). When Libia accidentally encounters Tolomeo with the Tetrarch's letter (an encounter that turns out to be fateful), he says:

> Ya
> que aquesta ocasión ofreçe
> el acaso de encontrarme.

(Since this occasion has given you the chance of meeting me.)

(2152–4) [*BAE*, i, p.493a]

When Octavian tells Mariene how her portrait (which for him represented Venus) had saved his life, he says:

> de manera
> que aunque Venus fuese el dueño
> del acaso, fuysteis vos
> del acaso el ynstrumento.

(so that you were the instrument of chance, despite the fact that Venus might have caused the chance to happen.)

(2666–9) [*BAE*, i, p.496a]

And the Tetrarch, too, speaks of 'los acasos del retrato' (the chance events connected with the portrait) (2705) [*BAE*, i, p.496b]. This perpetual interplay of willed events and unwilled *acasos* means that men cannot control events, for the fortuitous is always outside their command.

How does the introduction of chance affect the concept of Fate? As has just been said, this is no blind force, because the Tetrarch and Mariene are responsible for their fate in the sense that their actions cause it, and these actions are 'free' although done under the stress of violent passion. What chance so clearly indicates is that human actions freely willed do not necessarily produce the willed result and can, in fact, produce the contrary result. Yet men are free to produce miscalculations, and what turns calculation into miscalculation is a force over which men can have no control, namely chance. And this, quite clearly, is *el Hado*, which is something that governs events beyond human control. That these chance events are Fate is shown by the fact that they depend upon the two predictions that govern the actions: that the Tetrarch's dagger will kill what he most loves, and that Mariene will be killed by the greatest monster. The thought and customs of antiquity sanctioned predictions as a means for indicating the turn that Fate would make events take. And these events must always come to pass. In face of Fate man is free only to accept it and co-operate with it, or to resist it. He remains free, however, to be 'the arbiter of his own destiny' by planning, calculating and making decisions. He makes these calculations freely and thus is responsible for their results, but he can never infallibly produce the results he intends. This is not because of any lack of freedom, but solely because he cannot cause events to happen in a universe governed by chance.

In antiquity, the work of chance was attributed to the goddess Fortune, who represented good or bad 'Luck', distributing capriciously wealth or poverty, success or failure. Christian orthodoxy demanded that everything that occurred be the work of Providence, and therefore of Design and not blind chance, but a popular distinction seems to have been constantly made between a blind Fortune and an imperious Fate. One of Calderón's most masterly *autos sacramentales* is entitled *No hay más Fortuna que Dios* (There is no Fortune but God) whose aim is to demonstrate that all happiness and unhappiness comes from God's Providence. Nothing is the work of Chance; everything follows a Divine Plan, and men's efforts should be directed to understanding the purpose of God's Plan for each one of them.[15] When Segismundo leads his rebel army into battle against the king, his father, he says 'Oh fortune, it is to seize power that we march'. It is rare for any character in a play to apostrophise Fate except when he or she lies defeated. If one wished to look for a parallel in seventeenth-century theology for this dramatisation of Fate, with its intermingling of Necessity and Chance, one would be much more likely to detect it in Báñez than in Molina. There is no way of detecting *scientia media* here; the 'physical pre-motion' of Báñez might fit the case – God moves man to act, but moves him according to his nature; in other words, he moves him in such a way that he moves freely. Strictly speaking, such an equation would have relevancy only in a *comedia* developing a theological theme. The suggestion may, however, be made here to weaken further the contention that Calderón is a 'Molinist'.

Men can never be certain of being able to bring anything about or prevent it from happening. Yet, despite the large number of *acasos* in the action of *El mayor monstruo*, the ending of the play is perfectly in keeping with the particular human characters involved and the given situations. Take away the double prediction and nothing fundamental is altered. The catastrophe follows naturally and inevitably from Herod's violent and passionate temperament and from Mariene's resentful pride. Although what happens to them at the end is not, thanks to the *acasos*, what either willed (indeed it is what both sought to avoid), yet each has helped to bring it about by a series of unforced acts, freely determined. As in *La vida es sueño*, what is predictable in life are the consequences of men's free acts. Though Herod and Mariene never willed their deaths, they are nevertheless responsible for them. Because of this consistency between action and character the ending is, dramatically speaking, *predictable*. Given the initial data – the Tetrarch's traitorous ambition and his self-centred, obsessive passion for his wife – it is certain that disaster will befall him. The prediction therefore discloses what actions will follow from a certain human temperament, for a man must act in conformity with what he is. Its dramatic function is thus to clarify, through the interaction of Will and Chance, both the responsibility of the characters for their fate and the tragic irony of human life. The prediction points to the thread through the labyrinth of Fate. This is not a blind and implacably hostile force but a meaningful pattern in the universe, that of guilt and expiation. By knowing himself, a man can know the fate that nature portends for him. The Tetrarch's self-knowledge comes too late: he does not understand the meaning of the prophecy because he does not realise what it is he has to control.

The theatrical interplay of Chance with Fate gives a strong element of irony, which reinforces, in a typically Calderonian manner, the tragic irony that characterised the concept of fate in classical drama. Calderón makes the Tetrarch throw the dagger into the sea from which it was impossible that it could ever be fished out. But it returns to his presence, embedded in the body of one of his servants. When he wields the dagger, striking at Octavian, Mariene's portrait falls in between, and thus the Tetrarch kills her in involuntary anticipation. These *coups de théâtre* have been dismissed as absurdly far-fetched coincidences. However that may be, they are historically in keeping with their age, with its stylistic taste for the 'wittily' unexpected; they are analogous on their different plane to the 'far-fetched' metaphors known as conceits. Calderón is in effect presenting fate as a 'witty' manipulator of human life. This baroque concept is more important than the inverisimilitude of these devices.

At the beginning of the play the Tetrarch throws into the sea the potential instrument of violence, but at the end he realises that the violence is within him, and that he cannot destroy it unless he destroys himself. With the same Calderonian symmetry, linking the end to the beginning, his newly found knowledge makes him throw himself into the sea.

III The tensions of social life

11 The functions of comedy

The preceding chapters have traced the development of a recurring theme in Calderón from his earliest plays to its gradual transformation in plot structure and technique, connected with the movement away from 'real-life' themes and actions towards the symbolism and abstractions of mythology, which are to dominate the last period of his dramatic output. It was suggested that this recurring theme must have been based on a traumatic experience in his boyhood, which he explored by means of dramatic art in a search for understanding and solution of the problems that this aroused for human living. While exploring these real-life problems at the start of his career, he also embarked on other themes, passing from the problems raised by family relationships to the problems raised by living in society. The life of society dominated the stage comedies in all countries that had a well-developed theatrical form of entertainment. The comedies of seventeenth-century Europe exemplified the 'comedy of humours' and the 'comedy of manners'. These had their counterparts in Spain, though the 'comedy of manners' did not develop the elegant sophistication of a Molière. Comedies of manners in their earliest Spanish forms grew into 'comedies of intrigue' which tended to outnumber the 'comedies of manners'.

The comedy of humours was exemplified in Spain by what later was to be called the *comedia de figurón*, the nearest equivalent in Spain to a 'humour' play, namely a satirical piece in which some eccentric or extravagant character is satirised. Such a person was called a *figura*, which with the augmentative ending became the especially ridiculous, pretentious, conceited and opinionated individual who has to be discomfited by the laughter of society. The comedies of intrigue were called *comedias de capa y espada*, or cloak-and-sword plays, a term now always used to denote the characteristic Spanish form of play. The supreme example in Spanish literature of the humour of a *figurón* is of course *Don Quixote*. Calderón wrote a relatively early play with this title which was performed in the palace on Shrove Tuesday, 1637, as part of the festivities celebrating the arrival of the Princesse de Carignan, wife of the king's cousin, the Prince of Savoy, who was the commander of the king's army in Flanders. One of the saddest losses suffered by Spanish literature is the disappearance of this play. Unless it should turn up in some remote archive, we can never know what episode or episodes Calderón selected for dramatisation or how he presented the protagonist. Unless he had concentrated on some of the romantic love stories, like that of Cardenio and Lucinda, it would surely have been a *comedia de figurón*.

'Cloak-and-sword' was a title invented by Francisco Bances Candamo (1662–1704), who was the most reputable of the dramatists in the generation that succeeded Calderón. More valuable than his plays however, is his prose work *Theatro de los theatros de los passados y presentes siglos* (The Theatre of the Theatres of Past and Present Ages), a reasonably full account of the *comedia nueva* from Lope de Vega to Calderón, which describes many kinds of plots with the reactions of the audiences. This interesting work was written in three versions between 1689 and 1694 and was first published by Duncan W. Moir, with an admirable introduction.[1] In the first version, he describes the subject-matter of these plays as follows: 'the wooing of a high-born lady, with the rivalry of another Lover, with various duels between the two, or more rivals, carried out according to the code of gentlemanly conduct, which concludes in one of them marrying her, fully satisfied that he has acted as a man of honour and that the lady did not favour the others, and fully satisfied also that the others are disappointed.' These plays, he says, have already (1689) gone out of fashion, because the limited scope of a single courtship could offer too few incidents that did not constantly repeat themselves. The incidents of these plots are 'duels, jealousy, the gallant having to hide himself and the lady having to cover up her face, in short, all the commonplace episodes of a courtship.'[2] Only Calderón, he adds, knew how to condense such plots in such a way as to give them vivacity and humour, keeping the suspense in the complications of the intrigue, and a pleasing wit in unravelling it.

Sixteenth-century theories of comedy add little if anything to our understanding of these plays. Even after Lope de Vega had accomplished his revolution, theorists of the drama could only look at his plays with the eyes of Aristotle and failed to discern the originality with which he had departed from classical tradition or theory. Literary criticism had to wait a long time before anyone could formulate what *Don Quixote* had done for the theory of prose fiction.

During the sixteenth century, comedy developed in Spain by raising the social standing of the characters on the stage. Laughter remained the effect desired, and laughter was considered to be 'purgative', to liberate the mind of feelings of sadness, melancholy, and depression. The effect of laughter was to remove tension and bring relaxation. But though there is plenty of relaxing gaiety in Spanish comedies, especially those of Tirso de Molina, the dramatic theory of the age placed the cause of laughter in the least admirable type of relaxation. One of the commentators on the *Poetics* of Aristotle wrote as follows in 1623: 'Laughter is a way the mind has of expressing pleasures because of some defect that exists in another person. The origin or first principle of laughter lies in envy and maliciousness, since it is common among men to enjoy the faults and defects of others, and to find entertainment and laughter in them.'[3] Such maliciousness was generally condoned at the time. Don Quixote was a comic figure because of his 'faults and defects'. The commentators writing in Latin used the word *turpitudo,* which is best rendered as 'ugliness' and not 'turpitude', which denotes a viciousness that is not laughable. The defects that cause laughter are either eccentricities of behaviour or inversions in speech (such as Sancho Panza's malapropisms), or else defects of character and conduct like vanity or habitual distortions of the truth. The theorists classed such defects under the term 'disproportion' – the disparity between Don Quixote's aim to be a heroic knight-errant and his age and weak physique, or the social disparity in a young bride marrying an old man, etc. Another word used was *desconveniencia,* or 'inappropriateness', such as offences against social decorum. All this is Renaissance classical theory. An Italian commentator added the new note that laughter also arose from surprise at the unexpected. This came to lie at the heart of baroque treatises on Wit and on the catachresis that is now called the 'conceit'. This surprise was called *admiratio* or wonder in the sense of marvelling at ingenuity.[4] This was the essence of the comic in the astonishing ways in which complex dramatic intrigues were unravelled.

Apart from this innovation, Renaissance theories of wit remained static because they repeated Aristotle and the neo-Aristotelians, without attempting to analyse the new comedies that were appearing on the Spanish stage. For any theory of comedy relevant to European seventeenth-century drama it is best to go to modern treatises. Two of these are now classics: George Meredith's 'An essay on comedy' (1897) and the treatise on Laughter by Henri Bergson (*Le Rire,* 1900).[5] Both these works had a large comic literature to draw on and both have several insights that can usefully be applied to Spanish Golden Age comedies in general and to Calderón in particular.

The main notion to be selected from Meredith is perhaps especially relevant in the present age of Women's Liberation. He finds that the source of comedy lies in the clash of male and female temperaments in a society where men and women are unequal but sufficiently near to equality to make this a practicable aim.

> Comedy is an exhibition of [women's] battle with men, and that of men with them; and as the two, however divergent, both look on one object, namely, life, the gradual similarity of their impressions must bring them to some resemblance. The comic poet dares to show us men and women coming to this mutual likeness; he is for saying that when they draw together in social life their minds grew liker; just as the philosopher discerns the similarity of boy and girl, until the girl is marched away to the nursery.[6]

Meredith saw comedy arising out of the battle of the sexes because since men wielded social power, women could only do battle for equality by means of their wits. The weak outwitting the strong is of course a form of the comedy of the unexpected, and is universal in all literature, especially folk literature. Brer Rabbit escapes the fangs of Brer Fox by deluding him at every turn, and the powerful Fox, discomfited, is a figure of fun. The Brer Rabbit stories are told by a black in a southern state of America, and the stories represent the outwitting and the punishment of the white plantation owners by their oppressed slaves. In countless Spanish comedies of the classical period a vicarious revenge is taken by the oppressed women on their powerful male masters, who find themselves helpless and laughed at. There are plays in which there can be no doubt that this kind of comedy contains a serious feminist protest, especially in the comedies of Tirso de Molina. It would, however, be misguided to take this type of theme seriously as a form of social satire. These are comedies and must be taken lightly for the fun they can provide, and it must have been very funny in a society so thoroughly dominated by male authority and power to see the tables turned. No doubt the women spectators would have laughed with glee at what they would have longed to do themselves, and the men for their part would have laughed at situations which were comic because impossible.[7] We may remember the Feast of Fools in the Middle Ages, when all the social proprieties and respect for authority were forgotten for a short period in the resulting laughter.

There are examples of men outwitting women, but these are invariably against the women who presume to step outside, not the social conventions that enclose them, but against their nature and what this imposes on them. Such women affect to despise men and refuse to accept the burdens that wives and mothers must assume; they seek to retain their freedom. In such cases the men must win these women by attacking *their* weak points, their pride and vanity. Men win this 'battle of the sexes' by pretending to be impervious to all feminine charms. The honour of women demands that such men be humbled; they exert every blandishment to make the men succumb and find to their dismay at the end that their 'wooing' has succeeded in making them fall themselves. Examples of such a theme are *Los milagros del desprecio* (The Miracles Worked by Contempt) attributed to Lope de Vega and *El desdén con el desdén* (Countering Disdain by Disdain) by Moreto. There are examples of this type of theme on a serious (non-comic) level. Whether comic or serious, such plays indicate the limits that seventeenth-century Spain set to 'feminism': women could be allowed goodhumouredly to outwit fathers and brothers, but they could not be permitted to rebel against their natures to the extent of defiantly rejecting marriage.

The stage conventions which set the framework for the 'battle of the sexes' in comedy reflected a society in Spain that was similar to that of the other countries of Western Europe, but the rules of decorum were undoubtedly much stricter. Marriages were arranged between families in order to serve their interests; couples were betrothed before they actually met, and although a young lady was free in principle to withhold her consent to her marriage, it was probably the case that a refusal would have created a serious family difficulty. The system of arranged marriages meant that a girl had to be kept away from unmarried men to prevent her from falling in love with a man before meeting her official suitor. It was difficult for a young man who was not a relative to gain entry into a house if a daughter of the family was unmarried; if he was invited in, the girl might have to be secluded in a room on the upper floor. Seclusion of this kind away from a visitor provided the intrigue of *La dama duende* and was the source of it in many other comedies. A girl could only travel out of doors in the company of a male relative, or a governess and manservant, and she had to have her face covered below the eyes by her shawl, like a Muslim woman. Only in church were young men and women able to see each other's faces; one of the first things that the protagonist of the picaresque novel *Guzmán de Alfarache* did when he arrived in a new city was to go to church on Sunday in order to see the ladies.

It was essential for a girl not to compromise herself in any way with a young man. If she had conducted or consented to a flirtation, her betrothed, when one was chosen, would have withdrawn from the compact. The loss of her virginity would cause a crisis of the utmost gravity. If the man who had betrayed or seduced her refused to marry her, her normal fate was seclusion in a convent for the rest of her life. On the stage her dishonoured father or brother had to challenge the offender to a duel, while the luckless young woman, even if innocent, had to face death at the hands of her male relatives. Death was always the punishment for adultery on the stage, but not always in real life, despite the sanction of a long-standing tradition and popular horror of the act.

The difficulty of any ordinary social intercourse between young men and young women meant that they naturally sought means of circumventing those conventions as far as they could without irrevocably compromising their honour. In plays love invariably happened at first sight, which in any case was a convenient short-cut to dispense with courtship on the stage. Girls would look out from balconies or through windows of the upper floors to see processions and other social celebrations; men in the street would be looking up at the windows in search of pretty faces; when eyes met, and their respective owners were captivated, each party had to do everything possible to discover the identity of the other. If the girl succeeded, a secret letter arranged a nightly meeting at the garden gate; if the girl wanted to pursue the acquaintance, she could arrange meetings in parks or other places where, with her female companion, she had to hold her cloak with her hand to cover her face but for the eyes. If the man succeeded in discovering the woman's identity, he gained entry by stealth or deception into her house; if he succeeded in talking to the girl and was about to be discovered, she had to hide him in a closet or another room.

These conventions required secrecy and therefore deception. Secrecy was in theory jealously guarded and every lady expected that the law of chivalry would protect her from betrayal by the gentleman to whom she trusted her honour. Secrecy, thus intimately bound up with chivalry and honour, led to the intrigues which were the stuff of every cloak-and-sword play and the intrigues grew out of the conventions that have been described. 'All is fair in love and war' applied in Spain, as elsewhere, sanctioning the deceptions that the secrecy of love-making required and thus, going beyond strict comedy, could lead to serious moral conflicts or dilemmas. These conventions are frequently taken for granted as theatrical stock-in-trade, but the better dramatists do not necessarily accept them implicitly. They can insinuate criticism and deal ironically with many of these situations.

The following comedies by Lope de Vega and Tirso de Molina strikingly display the typically seventeenth-century intrigues that exemplify the 'wit of the unexpected'. These examples are so impossible in terms of the conventions they parody that the extravagances of social custom are laughed away. *La discreta enamorada* (The Ingenious Girl in Love) by Lope de Vega presents the situation of a marriageable girl who has no father or brother to look after her, living alone with her mother. The mother must represent social authority, but she falls in love herself with the young man whom the daughter has chosen for herself. Mother and daughter are therefore rivals in love. That a middle-aged woman should so forget the disparity of age is an absurdity that was theoretically possible. The daughter has to dispel it by taking charge. She selects the man who is to be the mother's second husband and tricks her into a compromising situation with him, thus forcing the mother into the unwanted marriage. The daughter usurping authority and imposing obedience on a parent is an outrageously funny inversion of social standards.

Tirso de Molina – that astonishing Mercedarian friar – has several examples of witty inversions that are funny in an imaginatively fanciful way. The theatrical convention whereby a woman who has been betrayed by a faithless lover can only face the world by dressing as a man in order to bring him to book is given delightfully surrealist form in *Don Gil de las calzas verdes* (Don Gil of the Green Breeches). Don Martín, who has won the favours of Doña Juana, throws her over when he sees the chance of marrying a wealthy heiress. He gives himself a new identity, posing as a Don Gil. Juana, following him, becomes the unreal Don Gil that Martín is impersonating and robs him of his identity. The ingenuity of the situation of robbing a man of his identity lies in the woman living a double social life, at times as a man and at times as a woman. The distinctive attribute of the imaginary Don Gil was his dashing green breeches, which when worn by Juana make women fall in love with her, sweeping them off their feet, and breaking up love affairs in the same way as Martín had broken off hers. The green breeches thus constitute a revolutionary element in this society, and in order to appear attractive again in the eyes of their ladies, the discomfited men must don green breeches. At the end, four men, all in green breeches, and all claiming to be Don Gil, are outside the house of one of the ladies. The whole situation has the fanciful absurdity that shimmers like the silk of the green breeches, blinding the audience itself.

In another comedy of this type, *El amor médico* (Love the Physician), Tirso raises the question of the notorious incompetence of contemporary doctors. Why, he makes his play ask, should not a woman succeed where they failed? To answer this question, Tirso presents a young woman who, in order to win her lover, lives as three different persons: herself, a doctor and the doctor's sister. When she is dressed as a doctor and finds herself in a sudden embarrassment, she can claim to be actually his sister dressed as a man. When treating a patient, she assumes this last identity, producing the ludicrous situation of being a man and his sister, both of whom are fictitious, in the same scene.

Another comedy of Tirso's reduces to delightful absurdity the theatrical convention of *la mujer tapada*, the veiled woman, who lifts one corner of the shawl that covers her head, drawing it across her face under her eyes, the obligatory way for a woman to hide her identity when in public. The convention was that this 'disguise' made such a woman unrecognisable, her eyes and voice never giving her away. The play is *La celosa de sí misma* (Jealous of Herself). A young man, Melchor, has arrived in Madrid to meet his betrothed, Magdalena. He leaves his inn on a Sunday morning and goes first to church. At the end of Mass, he enters into conversation with a *tapada* who leaves the church at the same time. He is immediately struck by her dazzling pair of eyes, and by the beautiful white hand that is holding up the shawl. He does not know that she is his betrothed, but she of course recognises him when he is in her house. Haunted by the memory of the eyes and the hand, he is not at all struck by her; she, for her part, cannot understand a coldness so unlike the vivacity of his conversation at the church door. There then unfolds a double relationship: he is uninterested when in her house, but a passionate wooer when they come across each other in the street. Regular outdoor meetings are arranged to alternate with the official meetings at home; she is attracted by him, but has to assume her 'disguise' to make contact. A friend of hers, Angela, is much taken by the suitor and, discovering their eccentric meetings, makes herself a *tapada* with the same kind of shawl and dress. Melchor cannot tell which is which, and has to make love to the counterfeit as well, in order not to lose the original. The result is that Magdalena becomes furiously jealous of herself, and has to 'attack' her rival in order to discover her identity and thus free Melchor from his eyes-and-hand obsession, which is accomplished through the laughter of the audience.

Calderón does not rise to such heights of witty fancy. As he leads into the next generation of dramatists, his intrigues are more 'serious'; always clever but not always humorous, and generally with no touch of frivolity.[8] In Tirso's comedies of the kind described it does not really matter whether 'true love' achieves its right end; the humour lies in the brilliantly impossible situations. With Calderón, on the other hand, the relationships do matter, as does the conventionality of respectable society. In fact, as he develops, he moves away from the inevitability of the opposite, endings that are 'happy' only insofar as they preserve social decorum but are otherwise deeply wounding to the unfortunate young woman who cannot break through to anything better. Even in the happy-ending comedies the intrigue often develops in such a way as to make a possible tragic outcome as fitting to the structure of the intrigue as the happy outcome is seen to be.

On the whole Calderón's women characters, with the notable

exception of *La dama duende*, do not play the same dominant role in the intrigue as do those of Tirso and many of those of Lope. Meredith's theory of comedy does not fit Calderón so well as a later, more subtle and profound theory, that of Henri Bergson. He, too, stresses the social context of comedy and the function of laughter as a corrective. His main emphasis, however, is that comedy expresses a lack of adaptability between individual and society. 'Any individual is comic who automatically goes his own way without troubling himself about getting into touch with the rest of his fellow-beings.'[9] This is what Bergson calls 'absent-mindedness'. Bergson instances Don Quixote as a supreme example of 'systematic absent-mindedness', but this type of humour – the *figurón* in general – is not characteristic of Calderonian comedy. His cloak-and-sword comedies do indeed exemplify the intrigues that surround the 'battle of the sexes' where Calderón's sympathies are with the oppressed young woman who is out to win the man to whom she has given her heart. Like earlier dramatists Calderón is on the side of the woman, but this is no mere stage mechanism to provoke laughter, for all his drama shows that Calderón's sympathies are invariably with suffering women. Bergson's ideas illuminate this sympathy. He instances as one of the main sources of the comic the tendency of human beings to think and act mechanically ('absentmindedly'). 'The rigid mechanism which we occasionally detect, as a foreign body, in the living continuity of human affairs is of peculiar interest to us as being a kind of *absentmindedness* on the part of life.'[10] Man becomes a machine principally because his rigid norms are derived from mechanical standards and conventions imposed by his society. Laughter rebukes him, but laughter also rebukes the society that has formed him. Society itself becomes a machine when its conventions become ossified and when no vital spark can be struck from its standards. Comedy lies in this ossification and in the contrary force that can restore vitality. Bergson's basic idea that what is laughable is the conflict between the mechanical and the vital, with the sudden or subconscious realisation on the part of the audience that the former is taking over, may be said to lie at the heart of so many Spanish comedies where the mechanical is represented by the rigid conventions of honour and social decorum, while the vital is represented by the *ingenuity* of the young women who fight against them. What is laughable is the ultimate powerlessness of the conventional and the rigid, outwitted by those elements in society who are most crushed by the conventions – young lovers.

The application of Bergson's 'absentmindedness' seems apt in the case of the Spanish social conventions that form the stuff of comedies (and of tragedies too). Their inelasticity represents a society going its own way without heeding the principle of natural justice and rational intercourse that should enshrine life-enhancing values within the inevitable restrictions of social living.

12 The vicissitudes of secrecy (1): *La dama duende, El galán fantasma*

Two of Calderón's best-known comedies come early in his career. They are *Casa con dos puertas mala es de guardar* (A House with Two Doors is Hard to Guard) and *La dama duende* (The Ghostly Lady), both of 1629. In chapter 2, it was stated that there are three principal types of dramatic symbols used by Calderón. The first is a place or object central to the development of the action and which therefore has a special significance. It was suggested that the two doors in each of the two houses in *Casa con dos puertas* ... were symbols representing, in the first place, the two poles of convention round which social decorum had to oscillate, secrecy and the dissimulation that has to cover it up: one has to emerge from a door through which one has not entered; and, in the second place, the two-edged character of courtship and love, balanced precariously on a knife-edge – what is sought secretly and kept in secrecy can easily founder in jealousy. Just as the stage action is constructed on this dualism, so is the theme constructed on a constant duality, swaying between secrecy and deception, truth and falsehood, loyalty and betrayal, wooing and duelling, comedy and tragedy. The duality of the doors evokes duplicity in the explanations of the characters' conduct; among the characters themselves, these produce equivocal situations.[1]

The intrigue of *La dama duende* is constructed on the same basic foundation. In each play there is a woman who has been relegated to an upper floor to live in temporary seclusion because a friend has come as a guest into her relatives' home. Unmarried women had (in drama, at least) to be kept away from the inquisitive eyes of men. In *El alcalde de Zalamea* the moment the Captain is billeted in Crespo's house, Isabel has to disappear to the attics. This last play is a tragedy, and it is therefore the Captain who, informed that there is a beautiful daughter, has to find her. In the case of the two comedies, the reverse situation prevails. The inquisitiveness is on the part of the women who, resentful of their enforced seclusion, must spy on the guests. From this basic situation, the two intrigues develop quite differently. Doña Angela is not the normal unmarried girl; she is in fact a young widow who, having had to come to Madrid to settle some legal affairs, is guarded in the house of her two brothers, Don Luis and Don Juan. The fact that she is not an innocent virgin has a bearing on the play's interpretation, though it does not alter the social necessity for her to accept her seclusion. The guest in the second play is called Don Manuel. He is given a room which has a cupboard with shelves which had previously been a door. Angela discovers that the cupboard has not been fastened on both sides, so that it opens like a door. This gives her access to Manuel's room. Escaping one day into the street as a *tapada* accompanied by her maid Isabel, she is followed by her brother Luis. She seeks the help of two strangers (who later turn out to be Manuel and his servant, Cosme) to protect her from the man who is pursuing her. This leads to a duel between the two men.

Later, Isabel sees Manuel in the house and tells her mistress that the man who saved her in the street is living in the house as her brother Juan's guest. Angela refuses to believe this unless she sees him. Isabel then tells her about the cupboard and the two women enter the room while Manuel is out. He returns with Cosme to find that his room has been visited and his belongings ransacked. There is a letter marked 'Private, for Don Manuel alone', which reads 'I'm concerned about your health, since I was the cause of endangering it. Therefore, grateful and worried, I beseech you to inform me about your condition, and make use of my services; there will be opportunity to do both by leaving a letter where you have found this one: be advised that secrecy is paramount, for if any of your friends learn about this, I shall lose my honour and my life.' Don Manuel writes a reply promising to serve her. Cosme is convinced that something supernatural is haunting them.

Angela has a friend, Beatriz, in whom Juan is interested. This gives rise to a secondary intrigue because Beatriz is courted by Luis, the other brother. When Manuel has to leave Madrid for a night on business, Angela re-enters his room. He and Cosme return, because they had left behind an important paper, and catch Angela red-handed. She promises to explain who she is, if they will first make sure all the doors are shut – and promptly escapes as soon as their backs are turned.

A day or two later Angela's letter to Manuel says that she is prepared to let him visit her provided he carries out her instructions strictly. He is to go at dead of night to a certain cemetery, where he will find two men with a sedan chair. He is to enter it without speaking to them and go into the house to which they will take him. They make so many turns that it is impossible for him to guess where they are going, and he does not recognise the door before which they alight. Isabel is there in the dark and guides him through various rooms until they come to Angela's. (Since all dramatic performances were in daylight, darkness had to be represented by the movements: the actors had to walk as if groping in the dark.) Angela is magnificently attired in a lighted room as a great lady, with Beatriz and the servants posing as her maids-in-waiting. Manuel naturally concludes that, since this is a great lady, her honour demands that her identity be withheld. Juan arrives unexpectedly and Manuel is quickly pushed into his own room through the cupboard which he does not distinguish as such as in the dark. At that moment, Cosme arrives from the street, fumbling his way in the dark. Manuel refuses to believe that this can be his room, and says he must go outside to identify the house. While he is away, Isabel comes into the room and takes Cosme's hand, in the dark, and leads him back to Angela's lighted room. Cosme, terrified by all these 'ghosts', falls in a faint. While the ladies are trying to revive him with water, there is a knocking on the door. This, as comedy requires, is Luis arriving at the critical juncture. Isabel grabs hold of Cosme and pulls him back through the cupboard into Manuel's dark room. Luis follows the sound of all this commotion into Manuel's room through the open cupboard and meets Manuel, who has just returned, ignorant of all that has been happening. Angela slips out unseen, begging Beatriz to take her to her father's house for protection. Luis, seeing the previously unknown connection between Manuel's room and Angela's, whips out his sword and the two men fight. Luis has his sword struck out of his hand, and Manuel permits him to go for another. Angela is caught by her other brother Juan when she leaves the house. He brings her back and tells her to wait in her room while he tries to find out what had led her to leave the house at night. Angela is then joined by Manuel, to whom she has to turn for protection against her brothers. She discloses who she is, states that she had fallen in love with him from the start, and explains her present plight. Manuel's predicament is either to be disloyal to his friend and host or to be unchivalrous to a lady in distress. He chooses to defend her. When Luis finds the two together, Manuel asks for permission to escort Angela away, promising to return. Luis says that no man can take his sister out of his house unless he promises to marry her. This Manuel consents to do. Juan reappears, approves of the proposed marriage, and himself proposes marriage to Beatriz. The play ends with Cosme saying he has no time to propose to Isabel because he has to speed up his customary request to the audience to pardon the shortcomings of the performance.

This synopsis does not cover all the complications of the intrigue, which Calderón develops with all the assurance for which Bances Candamo was later to praise him. The play is skilfully constructed in a symmetrical pattern that is characteristically Calderonian; that of a circular movement that ends where it began. In the first scene, Don Manuel is asked by an unknown young lady to protect her from a man who is pursuing her. He gallantly does so without hesitation and a duel results. In the last scene, he is asked by a young woman for protection from a man who will threaten her life. It is the same young woman, and the same threatening brother, and a second duel between the same two men has immediately preceded this second encounter of the three. On each occasion, Manuel has to make a rapid choice, and unhesitatingly he is prompted by chivalry towards a woman. Since the period between the first encounter and the second has been filled with often riotous laughter, this double act of instant chivalry cannot be presented in a solemn light; Calderón does not insist that this is how gentlemen should always respond to a lady's appeal for help. If this were not the accepted standard of behaviour, whether or not more honoured in the breach than in the observance, Calderón would not have made it the double hinge on which the intrigue turns. He presents it with a light, not a solemn, touch. When Manuel reads the first letter from the mysterious lady, he answers it humorously, in fact almost facetiously, using the archaic and florid language of the romances of chivalry, and signs himself 'the knight of the Ghostly Lady'. *Don Quixote* had made out-of-date chivalry laughable, but there is a modern form of chivalry which retains the basic principle of the old: a woman in distress must always come first, no matter what ties there may be towards the other man. Manuel is presented as a 'perfect gentleman': he is entirely rational, refusing to believe in ghosts and marvels of any kind, and being always good-humoured. His good humour makes his acceptance of the marriage entirely right and proper within the conventions of comedy, capped as it is by what can be seen on reflection to be in reality the joking inversion of chivalry, when Cosme puts his loyalty to the audience first before *his* lady.

Because Manuel acts unhesitatingly according to his fixed principle, he in fact acts like an automaton, and in this, as Bergson's theory rightly has it, lies much of the humour. Luis is also an automaton, the conventional male jealously guarding the honour of himself and his family by refusing his sister any degree of freedom, and forcing her at the end into marriage without sounding her wishes. That Calderón intended the audience to take a dislike to Luis is shown by one of the conventional features in the structure of Spanish plots: that of 'poetic justice'. Manuel and Angela, as well as Juan and Beatriz, are 'rewarded' with the marriages they desire (at least, it must be assumed that Manuel does find his marriage desirable), which is a sign that they are meant to earn and hold the audience's approval. The contrary is the case with Luis, who is the only character in the play who wins no lady. Even Cosme and Isabel must be seen, as convention justifies, as future husband and wife. Luis has failed to guard his sister properly and has lost out all round. There is of course no spare lady for him to marry, but this may possibly be significant. Edwin Honig thought that Luis's jealous guarding of his sister . suggested a possible incestuous attraction.[2] A modern theatre audience would almost certainly see 'flickers of incest' in a brother chasing a sister while she makes every effort to elude him. Whether a seventeenth-century audience would have sensed the same perversion is difficult to affirm with any conviction, given the overwhelming acceptance by the Spaniards of the time of the duty of a brother, in the absence of a father, to guard his sister's honour with all the repressive measures permitted by the code. Certainly the features surrounding this aspect of the plot do add weight to Honig's interpretation: not only the disagreeable character of Luis and his failure to find a wife, but also the fact that Angela is a young widow and not the customary unmarried girl.

Angela, on the other hand, is a fine example of a comedy heroine, spirited, able to cope with emergencies, always in control of events until the final crisis. She is able to keep on the right side of social conventions and able to guide the men to the end she desires, while her compromising situation in the last scene and the duel between Manuel and Luis threatens total disaster. Here her control breaks down, and she has to plead with Manuel to protect her, thus putting herself in the power of a man. Perhaps in her heart of hearts she was sure he would respond favourably. In any case, all the way through the play, she has profited from the automatism of chivalry to circumvent the automatism of honour.

The automatism of honour remains the mainspring of Calderón's intrigues. It is an automatism that depends upon the unquestioning need for secrecy, not only to guard one's own reputation but also to defend that of others. Secrecy, however, was not only necessary to safeguard honour and reputation; it was also necessary to safeguard life itself in a society governed by violence and oppression. The tyrannical attitude of fathers and brothers to unmarried girls was, so to speak, itself an extension of the tyrannical concept of authority which governed most national societies at the time, Spanish society perhaps more than most. Rulers of states could oppress their subjects as readily as fathers their daughters. This oppression did not have to be political or religious, it could also be aroused by self-interest.

El galán fantasma (The Phantom Gallant) was published by Don José Calderón, the dramatist's younger brother, in the *Segunda parte de las comedias* (1637). The licence to print is dated 2 March 1637. The title suggests a counterpart to *La dama duende*, with a male ghost, and in fact there is reference to this latter play which suggests a connection.

Porcia Este galán fantasma, ¿qué pretende?
Candil   Que tenga esposo . . .
Porcia   ¿Quién?
Candil   La Dama Duende.

(*Porcia* What's this phantom gallant up to?
Candil He's looking for someone to marry.
Porcia Whom?
Candil The Ghostly Lady.)

(Aguilar, ii, *Comedias*, p. 653b) [*BAE*, i, p. 302a]

It has been assumed that *El galán fantasma* was written shortly after *La dama duende*, perhaps the next year, 1630, while the memory of the ghostly lady was still fresh in Madrid. The second play resembles the first only in the aspect of the intrigue that gives it its title. It is in every other respect very different. The 'haunting' is itself very different, for the 'ghost' is a phantom that is seen at night by a number of people over several days. The second major difference is that its setting is a ducal court; the action thus moves in a higher social sphere, and this is reflected in the verse. It is also reflected in the third major difference, the fact that it is not a funny play, but is a 'comedy' only in the type of intrigue. The 'hauntings' cause fear akin to panic and they could, of course, have been acted in such a way as to arouse amusement, but there is no suggestion of this in the dialogue. Whereas Angela enjoys the effects caused by her apparitions and plays up to them, the Phantom Gallant has no such intention, his only aim being to keep his appearances as secret as possible.

The Duke in this play is not a ruler who stays in the background, but one who takes a prominent part in the action, and whose character and motives make the pretended haunting necessary as an ingenious device to thwart his aims. He is Frederick, Duke of Saxony (it was still a Duchy in Calderón's lifetime). This has no historical significance and, in common with the vast majority of Spanish plays, the play does not aim at any local colour. Like the Poland that is the setting for *La vida es sueño*, this foreign realm is a kind of Ruritania; since this Duke of Saxony is far from an exemplary character, he could not be presented as a Spanish ruler in a near-contemporary setting. An allusion within the play to contemporary theatrical tradition helps to make this clear. Before the Duke actually appears, the heroine, Julia, tells her suitor that the Duke is in love with her and has been pestering her with his attentions, to which she has given no encouragement. She knows that the Duke has discovered that she has given her heart to Astolfo, to whom she is relating this. She has been informed that the Duke is planning to murder him that very night, and she begs him to flee for his life. Astolfo refuses to take the easy way out, and does not necessarily believe what she tells him of the Duke:

> que esto de andar desvalido
> lo augusto, Julia, lo grande,
> es bueno para las farsas
> españolas, donde nadie
> vió querido al poderoso.

(to say that an august and great personage enjoys no favour is all very well for Spanish plays where nobody has seen the powerful man loved)

(p. 637 a–b) [*BAE*, I, p. 292a]

In real life, however, there can be no certainty that such a reputation would be deserved. This is a reference to a whole group of plays, many of them famous, that were popular between 1611 and 1630. Their theme is that of a ruler exploiting his political or social power over a subject or a vassal by seducing his wife. This is the theme of honour at its most powerful, especially when the husband has to defend the sanctity of his marriage against a man to whom he owes allegiance and obedience. Since it was difficult to place such a theme in a contemporary historical setting, dramatists found stories in the late medieval chronicles of the oppression of serfs by their feudal lords and transformed them into a commoner or even a peasant fighting for the right to claim honour and have it respected by the greatest nobles in the land. If the oppressor was presented as a king, the way out of the problem was to make him a medieval king, whose moral character was far from unblemished. The historical theme of the freedom of serfs, or the moral rights of commoners, was transformed into the right of every man, whether rich or poor, to have Honour, thus being entitled to respect and to have his dishonour avenged. The most powerful of these plays involving a medieval Spanish king is *La estrella de Sevilla* (The Star of Seville), attributed to Lope de Vega, whose authorship is very doubtful. The most famous of the plays in which a serf rebels against and kills his overlord is Lope de Vega's *Peribáñez*. Calderón's *El alcalde de Zalamea* is equally famous, but it is a late variant of the theme, in which the king or the grandee is reduced to an army officer, though without any minimising of the powerful conflict of social class. Calderón's Duke of Saxony is clearly, though more remotely, in the line of oppressive *poderosos*, or 'rulers'. Like his dramatic forebears, he violates a subject's rights and tries to over-power a woman on whom his passion is centred. This clear reference to the tradition of the oppressive king or overlord helps to clarify the absence of the comedy one would expect from a pretended ghost. Astolfo will not try to save his life at the cost of exposing Julia, his beloved, to danger. The Duke is a very violent man when his passions are aroused, and his jealousy of Astolfo works him up into a frenzy. The violence of the Duke, it is suggested, parallels the history of violence in the State of Saxony, where his family feuds have often led to riots and murders in the past. This is referred to in the play as paralleling the struggle between the Guelfs and Ghibellines in Italy (p.639a) [*BAE*, I, p.293a]. Two leaders of opposing factions, Crotaldo, Julia's father, and Arnesto, a relative of Carlos, a devoted friend of Astolfo, were conducting so fierce a conflict that the Duke confined Crotaldo to house imprisonment, from which he was never seen to emerge alive. In order to reach Crotaldo, Arnesto constructed a tunnel leading from the house of one of his relatives, Carlos, to Crotaldo's garden which was nearby. It is entered from the stage by a trap-door. The tunnel was nearly finished when Crotaldo thwarted Arnesto by dying (thus frustrated, he died shortly afterwards of melancholia). It was therefore never used and remained known only to Carlos (from whose house it started). The tunnel is called a *mina*, or mine, and is of course the main factor in the intrigue. It has a certain symbolical appropriateness in that it was constructed to further a family feud by murder (feuds and an intended murder are part of the play's action) but is in fact only used years later to effect a union of two families rather than a rupture. But this appropriateness has no dramatic or thematic significance. In a much later play, Calderón was to introduce another *mina* as a cardinal factor in the development of the action, but was then to give it a very significant connection with the theme of the play (*Apolo y Climene*).[3]

These preliminaries to the plot are given in the first scene as 'flash-back' narrations. The action commences when Julia, warning Astolfo that the Duke intends to murder him that night, begs him to escape from the city and go into hiding. He refuses to do this, deciding to remain on guard to protect Julia. There is in this play, as in *El astrólogo fingido*, a garden belonging to Julia's house in which the two lovers meet at night. As in the earlier play there is no suggestion of any impropriety. That same night the Duke finds his way into the garden, challenges Astolfo, wounds him, and departs. It is later announced that Astolfo has died from his wound and he is given a solemn funeral, which is, however, a deception. Enrique, Astolfo's father, nurses him back to health and pleads with him to go into voluntary exile to avoid the Duke's revenge. With the safety of Julia as his primary consideration, Astolfo refuses to leave her, arranging to meet her through the tunnel from Carlos's house, of which his friend had informed him. The garden gate is kept firmly locked, but it proves difficult to keep the night-time visits secret from the servants. Astolfo therefore becomes a ghost and the rumour quickly spreads. In accordance with the tone of the play, his apparitions cause consternation, argument and fear but, although the situation is a comic one, there is no humorous development. The belief gains ground that Astolfo's ghost must be coming back to earth to ask for prayers in order to free him from the sufferings of Purgatory. Believing this to be the probable explanation, the Duke summons Astolfo's father to his presence. Showing for the first time a generous side to his nature, he offers to do what he can to bring rest to Astolfo's soul, asking Enrique if there was anything left undone that would be troubling Astolfo's soul. Had he left any debts unpaid, or failed to make restitution in any way? The Duke then vows solemnly to pay any sum of money that may be necessary, or to redress any wrong committed by Astolfo. He repeats this vow as a man of honour, and Enrique departs. The rumours of the events in the garden continue to circulate in exaggerated forms until the Duke decides on a double course of action, to investigate the truth of the apparitions, and to abduct Julia. The Duke, with a number of servants, invades the garden while Astolfo is talking to Julia. He consents to seek safety in the *mina* only if he can take her with him, which he does. Much then happens. The *gracioso*, of course, falls down the *mina* and finds his way into Carlos's house. There is much rushing to and fro in the garden as people search for the man and the woman who had been seen but had disappeared. The Duke is convinced that the woman must have been Julia, and he orders her to be abducted, but the servants capture the only woman they can find in the garden, who is Astolfo's sister Laura. She has covered her head and face to remain unrecognised. Realising that the Duke must discover the entrance to the *mina*, Astolfo and Carlos, inside the house, decide that there is no way to stop him taking the first *tapada* he should find. Astolfo's dilemma is whether he should allow this to be his beloved or his sister. Finally they decide to let the sister be caught; since the Duke does not love *her*, he is likely to let her go, but would never release Julia. He does in fact discover the sister at once, and is furious with his servants when he finds they have got the wrong woman, but he rushes to investigate when he is told that there is another *tapada* in the house. He then finds himself in the presence of Enrique, Carlos and Astolfo, who are guarding Julia. He has come to realise by now that Astolfo is not a ghost. The crisis must be solved by an 'unexpected' twist to the ending. Enrique steps forward and reminds the Duke of his vow to do anything that would bring peace to Astolfo's soul. The Duke says yes, he did make the vow, and will keep it. Enrique then says that the only way to bring peace and rest to Astolfo is by allowing him to keep Julia. The Duke agrees to what would be a magnanimous act, were his real motive not otherwise. He says

Aunque ofendido pudiera
quejarme de injurias tantas
como de vuestra osadía
me advierten y desengañan
valgo yo más que yo mismo.

(Although I have been greatly offended and could complain because of the
outrages that I am now aware of and because of the deceptions you have had
the temerity to work upon me, I am worth more than myself.)

(p. 669a) [*BAE*, I, p. 310c]

He then hands Julia to Astolfo. This last phrase means that his reputation
as a man of honour means more to him than his own happiness. He
cannot live on, notorious for having broken his word, while seeking
happiness in his love for Julia. Calderón's audience would surely have
taken this as the magnanimity of a man who is at last being true to his
high status. Calderón, however, has introduced this magnanimous act
as a contrast to intended murder and the abduction of another man's
betrothed, which are very far from being the actions of a man of honour.
We are left to draw our own conclusions when we realise that this proud
and fierce man has been tricked into accepting defeat by an appeal that
consists only in not breaking his word.

El galán fantasma is not one of Calderón's most remarkable plays. It is
unusual as a comedy, its greatest virtue lying in what is least comic, the
beauty of much of its verse. It is one of the most poetic of his cloak-and-
sword plays, the meetings between the two lovers having a moving
lyrical quality, despite the stylised imagery and the formal patterns
which express it. The theme concerns the secrecy that must govern a
community ruled by a man who can unscrupulously aim at bending the
rights of his subjects to his own will. It is once again an unnatural
society in which one has to protect one's hope of happiness in a shroud of
secrecy. One of the most unnatural aspects of this secrecy was the
question of 'clandestine marriages', which will be discussed more fully in
a later chapter. In *El galán fantasma* hero and heroine, Don Astolfo and
Doña Julia, had been secretly betrothed for some time, but their marriage
could never be celebrated because of the feuds that disrupted the life of
the city, feuds which eventually cost her father his life. Throughout the
play she has called him 'husband' and their marriage, then postponed for
another reason (the jealous rivalry of the Duke), was looked upon as a
certainty. The danger that then threatened it was what continued to
make the secrecy of their betrothal a paramount necessity.

13 The vicissitudes of secrecy (2): *El astrólogo fingido*

Whether the characters in Spanish plays are strictly bound by the social conventions, or whether they observe them only loosely, marks the difference between tragedies, serious dramas and comedies. *El astrólogo fingido* is much more of a comedy than most of Calderón's cloak-and-sword plays, and in reading it we are at once struck by the disparity between the absurd protestations that the women make about their honour as long as they have their young men firmly on the lead, and the readiness with which they go behind the conventions if the young men threaten to abandon their attentions. The resulting intrigues are a satire on the conventions as well as on feminine protestations about honour, but as befits comedy the satire in this particular case is light-hearted. In the case of serious plays and tragedies there is nothing to laugh at: the conventions are presented in their starkness and the modern reader is repelled; whether the dramatist was also repelled and sought to arouse repulsion in his audience is what critical analysis should seek to determine. There is no such uncertainty or ambiguity in comedies. *El astrólogo fingido* can serve as an example of how far Calderón's humour could go in presenting the social and the stage conventions. It can also serve to demonstrate that Calderón's comedies are works of art, and not just examples of cleverly constructed intrigues.

It is an early play, though the date is not certain. It must have been written before 1632, because it was published in a volume whose licence to print was dated 15 March 1632.[1]

Various suggestions have been made concerning the date of composition. One is purely fanciful (Hartzenbusch thinking that Calderón wrote it at the age of nineteen) and others are not well-founded. There is one passage in the play that can provide evidence. Early on Don Juan de Medrano, thinking that Doña María has rejected his pretensions, comes to bid her farewell as he departs for Flanders to join the army in the company of Don Vicente Pimentel:

Don Vicente Pimentel,
mi señor, hoy apercibe
su jornada: con él voy

(My master, Don Vicente Pimentel, is today preparing for his journey; I go with him)[2]

Don Vicente Pimentel is one of the characters in Calderón's historical play *El sitio de Bredá*, where he commands one of the regiments besieging this Dutch town. This famous siege, immortalised by Velázquez in the painting known as 'The Lances', occurred in 1625. Vicente Pimentel must have been personally known to Calderón; his illustrious name would of course have been well known to the audience, although nothing is apparently known about this particular member of the family beyond his appearance in *El sitio de Bredá*. Don Juan de Medrano's accompanying him to the war in the Netherlands could suggest a date of composition for *El astrólogo fingido*. By 1633 Don Manuel Pimentel, who had the Portuguese title of Conde de Feira, was commander-in-chief of the Spanish armies of the Netherlands, a fact which makes it very topical that Don Juan should travel with a Pimentel to join the army. If the allusion is a topical one, a likely date for composition would be 1631 or 1632.[3] The date of *El sitio de Bredá* has not been documented, but it has been plausibly connected with the celebration in Madrid of the capture of Breda, news of which reached Madrid on 15 June 1625.[4] The alternative dates of composition of *El astrólogo fingido*, 1625 and 1631, are both hypothetical. The first of these dates is convincing only if it is plausible to connect the play directly with *El sitio de Bredá*. The evidence of the manuscript gives weight to the later date.

The play opens with the descriptions of two men who are courting Doña María de Ayala, given by her maid Beatriz who has been watching them from a window. These descriptions are enthusiastic praise of the dashing figures that young men cut at that time in order to impress women. They appeared most splendid and gallant on horseback, aided by their large hats with numerous large feathers, and their riding boots with spurs. The maid's glowing descriptions remind us, not inappropriately, of the exotic birds which parade their brilliant plumage in a display before the female in the form, sometimes, of a ritual dance. In these two speeches, there is an emphasis on the feathers, the spurs, and the horse. Thus, in the second of these speeches, the maid says

le vi en un caballo tal,
que, informado dél el viento
dejó de ser elemento

(I saw him on so fine a horse that as soon as the wind took note of its presence, in order to become so beautiful a creature, it ceased to be an element.)

(p. 128a) [*BAE*, I, p. 573a]

The wind, that is to say, ceases to be one of the four elements, surrendering pride of rank to the horse. Both speeches, especially the second, are full of admiration for the splendour of the male in all his grandeur as, so to speak, a 'centaur'. Each speech describes in some detail the costume that the men wear, especially the feathers, which, pointing as they do to flight, make the 'centaur' vie with the wind. The first of these speeches is intentionally less glowing and eloquent than the latter, because Beatriz thinks her mistress is less interested in Don Juan than in Don Diego, the second gallant. In the second description the splendours of masculine arrogance and horsemanship become more eloquent:

> Saltaron centellas puras
> de las piedras; que el castizo
> bruto, por llamarte, hizo
> aldabas las herraduras.

> (Pure sparks were struck by the horse's shoes; because this aristocrat among horses made of its shoes knockers on your door to summon you.)
> (p. 128a) [*BAE*, ɪ, p. 573b]

This is verse that glows with enthusiasm, intending to arouse the ardour of woman, but this is immediately countered by the cold aloofness of Doña María, who, though obviously interested in hearing these descriptions,[5] and giving her maid the customary gift on receiving good news, cannot allow any feeling of passion to penetrate her wall of reserve. The man she loves, Don Juan, gains entry into the house, but is coldly spurned by María. He departs, protesting that he can no longer wait on her without any promise of success, later returning to bid her farewell before leaving for Flanders. With the certainty of now losing him, Doña María ardently confesses her love, which she says is bursting like a bomb within her, because of having been so long pent up. In explaining her long silence, she expresses very clearly the terrible inhibiting effect of honour upon a woman; if there were a difference here between acting in a play and living in the real world, it would surely have been a difference of degree rather than one of kind. The statement is so clear and full that it is worth quoting at length for the enlightenment of the modern reader:

> De mi silencio la causa
> ha sido, Don Juan, temer . . .
> que tengo honor, que soy noble,
> y que ya la opinión es
> tan difícil de ganar,
> cuanto fácil de perder;
> y no hay desdicha mayor

que rendir una mujer
el santo honor que la ilustra
a la lengua descortés,
no de aquel que ha merecido
su gracia, sino de aquel
amigo poco leal
y criado nada fiel.
¿Hay en materia de honor
desdicha, como temer
en la iglesia, en la visita,
si sabrán que yo te hablé,
si sabrán que te escribí,
y al fin que te quiero bien;
y con este pensamiento,
encogida, no poder
alabarse, que es honrada,
una mujer que lo es?
Porque si acaso blasona
de serlo, teme que esté
desmintiéndola por señas,
el que lo sabe más bien.
En fin, este recelar,
este dudar y temer
hizo llave de mi amor
aquel pasado desdén.

(The cause of my silence, Don Juan, has been fear, for I have honour and am of
noble birth, and because nowadays it is as difficult to acquire a good name as
it is easy to lose it. There is no greater catastrophe for a woman than to
surrender to the tongues of other men the sacred honour that ennobles her. I
do not mean the tongue of the man who has won her favour, but that of a
friend of questionable loyalty and of a servant entirely faithless. Can there be,
in affairs of the heart, a greater misery than to fear, when attending a service
in church or paying a visit, that people might find out that I spoke to you, that
I wrote to you, and, in short, that I love you dearly? Or a greater unhappiness
for a woman than, inhibited by such a thought, to know that she cannot
speak of herself as honourable despite the fact that she is? Because if she
vaunts her honour, she will fear to be belied by somebody who knows better.
In short, this suspicion, this doubt, this fear caused the coldness towards you
which locked up my love.)

(p. 130b) [*BAE*, i, p. 574c]

She concludes: 'now I have broken silence, you must pledge me your
word that you will tell of my love to nobody, neither friend nor servant'.
This unlocking the secret of her heart is the start of the dramatic
intrigue, whose development will depend on whether her confidence is

broken or not. She concludes by assuring Juan that she will tell no-one this new secret other than her maid, because 'I know she can keep silent, and I trust her as I do myself', to which Beatriz replies, 'put aside your fear, my lady, for it insults *my* honour'.

This speech on women's dread of ruining their good name is very serious and unexaggerated. Yet the play is going to develop away from seriousness into the humorous exaggerations of comedy. The juxtaposition of the serious and the comic points not so much to dichotomy as to an inherent artificiality in the conception of honour that women were impelled by society to embody, and the dread that resulted. The contradiction between honour and human happiness forms the stuff of the wife-murder tragedies. Comedy stresses its artificiality. This is brought out in two ways by *El astrólogo fingido*: first by bringing in the artificiality of stage plays, and secondly by exposing the human impossibility of keeping secrets. Beatriz had been firmly convinced that Doña María would favour Don Diego rather than Don Juan, which is why she coloured her 'painting' of Don Diego and his horse with such enthusiasm. Surprised to find that this is not the case, she says to her mistress

> Dama
> de comedia me pareces;
> que toda mi vida vi
> en ellas aborrecido
> al rico, y favorecido
> al pobre, donde advertí
> su notable impropiedad;
> pues si las comedias son
> una viva imitación
> que retrata la verdad
> de lo mismo que sucede
> ¿a un pobre verle estimar,
> cómo se puede imitar,
> si ya suceder no puede?

(You seem to me like the heroine of a play; because for the whole of my life I have seen the rich man abhorred on the stage and the poor man favoured, from which I realised how completely inappropriate stage drama was. If a play is a living imitation that portrays truth in the same way as it happens, how then is it possible to imitate the esteeming of a poor man [in a play] if that in fact never happens?)

(p. 128b–9a) [*BAE*, I, p. 573c]

To which Doña María replies that it is more correct to say that plays find their truthfulness in her, since she is the exception that proves the rule. It is precisely the disparity between the stage and real life that makes both for comedy and for poetry. For an hour or two drama can make the audience live in the realm of an imagination gilding reality. Hence the artificial gallantry with which the ladies are addressed. Stating that he had once entered by stealth into her garden, Juan says

Entre sus flores te vi
con tal belleza, que hiciste
competencia a su hermosura
y ventaja a sus matices.
Corrida naturaleza
de sus pinceles sutiles,
perdió la esperanza, viendo
que imitarte era imposible,
y dijo: 'Pues ya no puedo
excederme, no me estimen;
que ya no tengo que hacer,
después que este asombro hice.'
Un jazmín tu mano hermosa
robaba, y él apacible
rindió sus flores al suelo
porque tus plantas las pisen;
y dijo, viendo que ufanos
blancura y olor compiten:
'Quita a mis hojas las flores,
y tus manos no me quites;
pues es lo mismo tener
tus manos, que mis jazmines.'

(I saw you looking so beautiful among its flowers that you rivalled their loveliness and surpassed their colours. Nature, ashamed of her subtle brushwork, lost all hope, seeing that it was impossible to imitate you, and said: 'Since I cannot now surpass this achievement, do not prize me now; for I have nothing now to create, after fashioning this marvel.' Your hand was stealing jasmine blossoms, and the plant gladly shed its petals on the ground for your feet to walk on, and seeing that whiteness and scent were in proud competition, said 'Take the flowers from my leaves, but do not take away your hands; for having your hands is exactly the same as having the blossoms.')
(p. 129b) [*BAE*, I, p. 574a]

Poetry of this kind is very artificial. It will strike the modern reader as affected and stilted; a modern actor would be able to make fun of this kind of speech, and it is possible, even, that a modern producer would want him to bring out all the affectation in this style in order to arouse laughter. This poetry was, however, to the taste of the audiences of this time; it was a large part of the glamour that the stage could give them but which ordinary life could not. In Spain, as in England, such florid imagery had already gone out of fashion when Calderón was writing this play, being replaced by the more intellectual imagery of the 'conceit'. This change took place in Calderón as he moved out of his first period and approached his maturity. Here it represents the 'unreal' world of the stage, in much the same way as the conception of honour represented natural feelings that had become, on the stage, over-strained and over-tense. In this play, however, this language is found only in the enclosed world of passionate and jealous lovers. Outside of that world, the imagery is normal, but the verse, though less formal, is always elegant. In these Spanish comedies the world of honour and the world of reality are represented respectively by the lovers and by their servants. Beatriz could point to the similarity between Doña María's attitude and that of the heroines of plays. She can also point to the disparity between her protestations of honour and the reality that lay behind such feelings. When Beatriz is left alone on the stage, she soliloquises:

> ¡Ved lo que en el mundo pasa,
> y qué es honor! Por no hablalle
> con escándalo en la calle,
> le entramos dentro de casa.
> Cuando miro estas honradas,
> pienso que sus fantasías
> vuelven las caballerías
> de las historias pasadas.
> Dama, que tus vanidades
> te hicieron impertinente,
> ama al uso de la gente,
> deja singularidades.

(Just look what happens in the world, and what honour is! In order not to cause scandal by speaking to him in the street, we allow him into the house. When I look at these honourable ladies, it seems to me that their fantasies bring back the chivalry of the old romances. Since your vanity, milady, has made you presumptuous, conduct your love affairs in the way of ordinary people, and give up your quirks.)

(p. 134b–5a) [*BAE*, I, p. 577a]

When María had admitted her love to Juan rather than lose him to the wars, she had told him that there would be a handkerchief tied to one of the bars of a window in her house whenever it would be safe for him to visit her at night. If the sign were present, he was to go into the porch, where Beatriz would open a door for him, through which he would enter the garden and converse with María through the bars of a garden window. Beatriz had affirmed solemnly that she would never tell this secret, but she tells it at the very first opportunity to Morón, Don Diego's servant, who then matches her soliloquy with one of his own:

> ¿Aquéste es el santo honor
> que tan caro nos vendía?
> ¡Cuántas con honor de día,
> y de noche con amor
> habrá! Con puerta cerrada,
> pañuelo, Beatriz, zaguán,
> jardín, ventana y Don Juan,
> La Chirinos fuera honrada.
> Mas ¡qué fuerte es un secreto!
> Mucho es no haber reventado
> del tiempo que le he callado.
> Mi vida está en grande aprieto
> si no lo digo. Advertid:
> esto que me han dicho agora,
> mátenme si de aquí a un hora
> no se supiere en Madrid.

(Is this the sacred honour on which she set so high a price? How many ladies there must be who flaunt their honour by day and pursue love by night! With a locked door, a kerchief, Beatriz, a porch, garden, window, and Don Juan, Chirinos herself would be honourable.[6] Oh, the power of a secret! It's a wonder that I didn't burst all the time I kept it. My life will be under an intolerable strain if I don't tell it to someone. [Addressing the audience] Take note: I wager my life that what I have been told now will be all over Madrid in an hour.)

(p. 136a) [*BAE*, i, p. 577c]

Beatriz had immediately broken her pledged word by telling Morón María's secret because he was her special friend whom she will marry after the play ends. Similarly, Beatriz had said she could only tell Morón what had happened if he swore on oath never to disclose this secret, not even to his master; yet he, too, breaks it at the first opportunity, precisely by telling his master, who was Juan's rival in love. Juan had sworn secrecy to María when she made the arrangements for their nightly conversations, and he immediately breaks the secrecy to the extent of telling that he had these meetings, but he does not disclose the lady's identity; that disclosure is made later by someone else. He, in fact, has to break his word, because the arrangement with María depends on his being able to live in hiding in Madrid after announcing that he was off to Flanders. He tells the secret to his friend Don Carlos (after making the customary demand for secrecy) because he wants to be lodged in Carlos's house. It was a commonplace at the time, and still one today, that women were by nature incapable of keeping a secret. In this play, no man is capable of keeping one either, and this must have heightened the comedy, for it was more laughable to see men break their promise of silence than it was to find this in women. The structure of the first Act is the progression in disclosing the secret between María and Juan. It goes from her to Beatriz, then to Morón, then to Don Diego, who tells Don Antonio. The other route, from María to Juan, passes to Don Carlos and finishes with Don Antonio. This last-named character hears the secret twice, asking his friend Don Carlos to confirm what he had heard.

The roundabout journey of the secret ends Act I. Every time that the breaking of a secret is discovered, the culprit has to excuse himself by a lie of some sort. The main part of the play's action is the first cover-up from which all the others will flow – the invention of the 'astrologer'. Act II presents the spread and the progressive embroidery of this mock figure.

Diego, accompanied by his servant Morón, accosts María in the street as she comes out of church and resumes his ardent compliments. She states haughtily that he is offending her honour, whereupon Morón interjects in an aside, 'This honour of hers will be the death of me!' Diego, believing her to be a flighty woman, blurts out the secret about her which he has heard, and rebukes her for claiming a sense of honour by which she does not live. Exasperated by her harping on her honour, Diego loses patience and civility:

> quiero, pues se humana
> el honor que encarecéis
> tan alto, que despreciéis
> más honrada y menos vana.
> No me ofendieron, por Dios,
> los desprecios de honor llenos;
> mas no le echara yo menos,
> a no encarecerle vos.
> No es honra la vanidad;
> que no está en encarecerla
> la virtud, sino en tenerla.
> Y en lo que he dicho, culpad
> vuestra lengua, la mía no,
> si lo dicho se os acuerda;
> pues si vos fuerais más cuerda,
> no fuera tan necio yo.
> De vuestros desprecios fué
> la culpa, no de mis celos.

(Since the honour that you exalt so highly is in fact human and lowly, I should like you to be more honourable in despising me and less vain. Heaven knows that I was not offended by your rejection of me when this was honourable; but I wouldn't have noticed that you are lacking in honour now if you were not emphasising it overmuch. Vanity is not honour; virtue does not consist in making much of it, but in having it. And for what I have said, blame your tongue, not mine, if you remember what I said to you; for if you were more prudent, I would not be so impertinent. Your contempt of me, not my jealousy, was responsible for this.)

(p. 138b–9a) [*BAE*, I, p. 579b]

María turns in anger on Beatriz, who denies that she had given away her secret. Since she had in fact given it away to Morón, he feels obliged to come to her rescue. Diego also is regretting his burst of temper and appeals to Morón to invent some ruse to excuse him. Morón therefore says that his master is a famous astrologer and that by magic means he conjured up in his own house the vision of María talking to a man at night in her garden. Diego has to back him up and invents an elaborate and highly embroidered life-story. 'Astrologer' does not only mean one who casts horoscopes; it also means a man who has practically any supernatural power that any particular context requires: all sorts of magic tricks are later attributed to him. He explains that because such activity is highly dangerous he has had to keep it secret in order to keep on the right side of the law. Having accepted this cover-up he finds himself obliged to add fanciful details as the play progresses. María now finds herself entangled in what she had so much feared – 'Can there be, in affairs of the heart, a greater misery than to fear, when attending a service in church or paying a visit, that people might find out . . .'. She appeals to Diego, ironically enough, as a man of honour: her secret will remain safe with him; his secret, that of being an astrologer, will be safe with her. No sooner does she say this than she feels compelled to break it. Her father, Leonardo, has come upon them in the street and, seeing her in great distress, asks her what is the matter. She has to invent an explanation: this gentleman, she says, has come from the house of a cousin where he had gone as an astrologer to cast the horoscope of the marriage she was about to contract. The cousin had sent him to María to prophesy about her future marriage, and this astrologer had told her that she would marry a poor man, which was the cause of her distress. Leonardo tells her she should not believe in such things, and then turns in excitement to Diego, informing him that in his youth he had dabbled in that science, and would much like to discuss things with him, inviting him round to his house. As he departs, he expresses great concern at the fact that María is going to marry a poor man.

When he next meets Don Antonio, Don Diego excitedly tells him about the huge joke of his astrology. Don Antonio and Morón engage between them to spread this new secret all over Madrid. The reason for Don Antonio's existence now becomes apparent. He is not in fact a *galán*, a young unmarried gentleman in search of a wife. He is much more like an upper-class *gracioso*, in other words an unusual character. In the mature Calderón, there is no character who does not fulfil a dramatic need by exemplifying an aspect of the theme. Don Antonio is a partial exception to this. Morón is a suitable person to spread a lie in the city, were it not for the fact that, being a servant, he can only move among the lower classes. The rumour has to be spread everywhere, and a gentleman is therefore required to mix with the gentry and spread the rumour in that quarter. On the other hand, this activity is not a very gentlemanly one, so Antonio belies his 'Don' by being more like a *gracioso* than a *galán*. Thus Morón suggests this division:

> pregonaré, si pregonas
> tú en salas, yo en los zaguanes,
> yo a lacayos, tú a galanes,
> tu a damas, y yo a fregonas

> (You will announce it in the drawing-rooms and I in the attics; I to lackeys and you to gallants; you to ladies, I to kitchenmaids)
>
> (p. 143a) [*BAE*, I, p. 582a]

When Antonio later reports to Diego the success of his undertaking, he does this with great relish, knowing full well that he has not been living up to his social status. He went first to the two theatres, where he mingled with the audience and spread his news. He then moved to the street corners where idlers gathered to retail gossip. The first thing he found was that they were talking about Don Diego, 'one of them proclaiming that he was absolutely certain you were an astrologer':

> Mas lo mejor de todo no fué esto,
> sino que entré en los trucos, donde estaba
> un hombre que contaba
> cosas que os había visto
> hacer. No sé, por Dios, cómo resisto
> la risa. No pudiendo
> sufrirlo, empecé a hablar contradiciendo,
> de tantos disparates enfadado.
> Levantóse enojado,
> diciéndome: 'Si usted no le conoce,
> yo sí muy bien, y sé lo que aquí digo
> de buen original, porque es mi amigo.'
> Tanto una novedad, Madrid esfuerza,
> que mi mentira la creí por fuerza.

(But that was not the best part. I entered the billiard-hall where there was a man who was relating things that he had seen you perform. (God knows how I can refrain from laughing!) Not being able to stand this, I began to contradict him, annoyed by so much nonsense. He got up angrily and said: 'If you do not know him, I do, and very well, and I know what I am saying because I had it from the horse's mouth, he being a friend of mine.' Madrid gives such heightened colour to any novel gossip that I was compelled to believe my own lie.)

(p. 146a) [*BAE*, i, p. 583c]

Meanwhile, Juan has asked Carlos, his friend and host, to go to a certain Doña Violante to tell her of his absence from Madrid. She is a lady who has become attracted to Juan, and he has encouraged her when María's coldness made him decide to leave her. He must now discourage Violante from any further interest in him. She is distressed at the news of his departure, whereupon Carlos, who is much taken by her good looks, tells her of the astrologer who might be capable of conjuring up the vision of Juan in her own house. She goes with great secrecy and much excitement to Don Diego's house. Diego has never seen her before and is greatly disconcerted by her request that he should conjure up her lover. He is, however, reassured when she mentions her lover's name, because this is his rival for María's hand, and he has already learned that he is hiding in Carlos's house. He says to Violante that he will help her if she will write a letter to Juan, inviting him to her house that evening. Diego gives this letter to Morón, asking him to throw it through a window of Carlos's house. Juan is sitting alone when the letter comes flying in. He has, of course, no idea how Violante knew where he was or why she should wish to see him. Fearing that if he takes no notice of her letter she will tell others where he is hiding, he goes to her house, where his arrival fills her and her maid with terror, and she refuses to let him embrace her, and runs in panic to another room. Juan shouts after the two women, but is left alone in a state of confusion, since he has been summoned to the house by the treachery of a friend (for he thinks Carlos must have betrayed his hiding-place) and the jealousy of a woman anxious to snatch him from María.

Act II has developed the disclosure of the original secret into the invention of the mock-astrologer, to the huge enjoyment of those not directly implicated in his entangled relationships, but to the utter confusion of his rival, Juan, and the panic of one of the two ladies involved. Act III explores the series of cover-ups that are required to prevent any of the characters from having to confess to the numerous breaches of confidence that have characterised Acts I and II. The organisation of the dialogue in this Act becomes very complex, because practically every cover-up produces a misunderstanding. Calderón has to weave his way through the series of misunderstandings while keeping the audience aware of who knows what and of what is true or false. The dialogue of this Act is made up of a large number of asides, as every actor explains his intentions only to become confused by their unexpected outcome. It would be very difficult for modern actors to carry off all these asides convincingly. It was much easier when theatrical convention permitted the actors to communicate asides directly to the audience.

The intrigue of Act III contains three principal attempts to make the astrologer intervene in the course of events. The three are interlinked in the course of the action but it is more convenient to deal with them separately. Juan and María renew their relationship and to confirm her acceptance of him as lover she gives him a precious jewel, a little Cupid studded with diamonds. María is troubled at the thought of the difficulties that will face her marriage to Juan, and her father asks her the reason for her obvious distress. On the spur of the moment, she covers up her real trouble by saying that she had lost her precious Cupid. Leonardo orders the whole house to be searched, and then determines to enlist the supernatural powers of the astrologer. He asks Don Diego to find out where the Cupid is, giving him the necessary particulars, i.e. the place where it was lost and the time. Diego in dismay tries to persuade him that he is not an astrologer and knows nothing whatever about the science. Leonardo, however, is convinced that he is making these disclaimers out of exemplary modesty, because he would never admit that he knows nothing, but would be bound to cover up his ignorance with boastfulness. Diego remains in a quandary until Morón returns from his daily visit to María's house to see how events were developing there. He gives his master the information that he has gleaned from his source (Beatriz) to the effect that Juan had visited María and that she had given him a jewelled Cupid as pledge of her love. Diego sees his way out with Leonardo and tells him that the Cupid is in the possession of the man who had visited his house earlier that morning. Leonardo knows this must be Juan and is greatly upset that so good-looking a young man should have stooped to so mean an action. But with his customary good nature he excuses it by thinking how impoverished the young man must have become. He finds Juan and wishes to obtain the return of the Cupid without offending him. He asks Juan for the jewel, telling him that he knows who gave it to him, thereby hiding the 'theft'. Juan hands over the jewel, greatly relieved because María herself must have told her father that she had given it to him, and since the father is not angry Juan assumes that he must think him an acceptable son-in-law. Full of this sudden confidence, Juan asks him for his daughter's hand. Taken aback by such an unexpected outcome, Leonardo dismisses the request and departs, leaving Juan puzzled at the whole affair.

The other two strands in the intrigue of this Act concern attempts to make the astrologer intervene in the love-affairs. Violante wants him to make María cease to love Juan so that he might return to her. Carlos, by now fully in love with Violante, wants the astrologer to make her switch her affections from Juan to him (Carlos). Diego assures Violante that Juan really does love her and that the sole reason for his remaining behind in Madrid had been the jealous fear that another man might win her. This makes Violante prepared to consider that every sign of coldness on Juan's part towards her is a mark of favour. Thus reassured, she is amazed at their next meeting at the convincing way he feigns his disdain. Thereupon she makes the second part of the 'magic' appear to work by showing marked favour to Carlos in order to arouse Juan's jealousy.

There is a final and more ambitious piece of pretended magic which, very unusually for Calderón, is not linked with these central intrigues and does not constitute a sub-plot on its own. There is an elderly man-servant in Leonardo's and María's household who has appeared from time to time as a messenger or companion to his mistress. His name is Otáñez, and in this last Act he strikes what is bound to be a sympathetic chord in the heart of every old man, when he says that he is wanting to retire from service by returning to his native province of La Montaña,

> que va a buscar buena muerte / quien tuvo mala
> vejez
>
> (because he is going in search of a happy death after having a wretched old age)
>
> (p. 160a) [*BAE*, i, p. 591c]

The journey is a long and difficult one over two mountain ranges; he will carry with him his life's savings and fears to be robbed; furthermore, he has no relish for standing up to truculent inn-keepers. He tells Don Diego that he believes that he is capable of transporting him all that distance in a twinkling of an eye and asks for this favour. Morón intervenes and asks his master to let him deal with this request.

The last scene takes place in María's garden, where she has had the secret visits from Juan. In a scene directly reminiscent of Sancho Panza's flight into space on the wooden horse Clavileño, Morón blindfolds the old man and makes him straddle a garden bench, tying him firmly to it. He readily believes that he will soon be in his old home and promises to make no move or sound no matter what he hears. A lot does in fact happen in the garden but Otáñez believes that the different voices come from the different towns over which he is flying.

Spanish Golden Age plays invariably finish, for the modern reader, very abruptly. Once the intrigue is unravelled and the ending obvious, it was evidently thought that nothing would be gained by spending time on the obvious. *El astrólogo fingido* is more abrupt than most. All the characters come into this garden on this same night, each for different reasons. Juan has to be hidden in the house by María. It is explained that Diego's astrology was a pretence to defend María's maid for having broken her confidence. In the course of these disclosures Juan is brought out of the house by Violante, who expects to see him denounced. Leonardo is dismayed at the sight of this and wonders how he can possibly put right this offence to his honour. With the accommodating good will that he has shown to everybody throughout the play, he realises that if he gives María's hand to Juan, there cannot possibly be any dishonour in the fact that Juan has been found in his house uninvited. He remains an unusual type of gentleman in the Spanish drama.

All therefore ends satisfactorily, except for Don Diego and Otáñez. Violante reconciles herself to having Carlos as a husband and nobody's honour has been blemished. Don Diego explains why he had to accept Morón's invention of his astrology and confesses to the deception that followed. There is no lady for him at the end, but this is of course in line with the Spanish sense of poetic justice. He has been exploiting a lie, to his own amusement and that of his audience, and he cannot be permitted the conventional reward of a happy marriage. Otáñez must put up with the loss of his aerial journey to the north coast as the price of his pathetic gullibility. Though he is an exception to the careful interlinking of all subordinate characters and secondary plots within the thematic unity of the whole play, he does in fact fit into the plot structure of this play. Max Oppenheimer has shown how the structure of the plot gives the play a certain symmetry, very Calderonian in itself, as has earlier been demonstrated. 'A certain symmetry . . . prevails throughout the plot structure, in spite of the apparent confusion. Doña María treats Don Diego in the same manner as Don Juan treats Doña Violante, who in turn treats Don Carlos likewise. The love affair of the valet and the maid reflects that of the mistress and the master. Morón also wants to play his part as astrologer and is given an opportunity to do so in the comic interlude with Otáñez. As Morón puts it:

Que un criado siempre fué
en la tabla del amor
contrapeso del señor

(For in Love's catalogue a servant was always the counterweight to his master).[7]

This study presents the play as illustrating the 'theme of oscillating reality', in which men, as so often in the plays of Calderón or in the baroque period in general, grope through life uncertain whether what is happening is real or fictitious. This uncertainty, for Oppenheimer, is based on the *burla* (deception or practical joke) of turning Don Diego into an astrologer. The characters in the play experience this uncertainty from time to time, but the audience (at least the intelligent members of it) are never in the slightest doubt concerning the truth or illusion of the action. By analysing every possible facet of this *burla*, Oppenheimer made very heavy weather of the play; he never once, for example, suggested that the play is intended to be, or actually succeeds in being funny.[8] The play is a comedy from start to finish and never touches on transcendental problems. Actually the mock astrologer, though of course central to the stage action, is not the *theme* of the play. This, as has been stated, is the confusion and the misunderstandings that arise from the theoretical need to keep secrets, when human nature itself must inevitably seek to break them. The errors and confusions follow from this attempt to impose an impossible rule on human society. Because a comic treatment is required to restore a sense of balance the promises to keep the secrets and the way they are broken are treated in a thoroughly light-hearted manner, and an almost neurotically secretive society is shown its silliness.

14 Secret betrothals and secret marriages: *El postrer duelo de España*

All through the study of selected comedies by Calderón, we have seen that the thematic hinge on which the plays' intrigues turn is the question of secrecy. Seventeenth-century Spain had an obsessive fear of publicity difficult to understand in an age when it is no longer considered necessary to respect secrecy, even when one has given a solemn undertaking. The publication of state secrets that one was in duty bound to withhold has recently been exculpated by a jury in a court of law. In everyday affairs, everything possible is now done to ferret out and reveal in public details of the private lives of individuals in the public eye, especially if any scandal can attach to them. The seventeenth century held up in principle the duty of everybody to preserve the private lives of others from the taint of scandal. This was the social ideal; no doubt Spanish social life more often than not failed to observe this rule, but a moral rule it was.

The potential or actual scandal most often portrayed in Spanish literature are cases where a young girl has accepted a man as her future husband, under a solemn promise on his part, only to find this promise eventually broken. In literature, if the girl has spirit enough not to accept this social humiliation, and the ostracism that would follow if this fact were made public, she proceeds, dressed as a man, to search for her betrayer and force him to keep his word. The most famous Spanish novel of this period has an example of this in *Don Quixote*, Part I, where Dorotea, betrayed by Fernando, is a damsel in distress, whom Don Quixote must succour. The most famous of Calderón's plays, *La vida es sueño*, presents another such situation – Rosaura in search of Astolfo, her betrayer, and championed at the end by Segismundo. Such situations are so numerous in the drama as to be almost hackneyed; clearly the existence of such situations was taken for granted.

Couples could therefore become engaged in secret and could proceed to live as man and wife, but always in secrecy. These were the 'secret marriages', for which both Church and State had to legislate. In many parts of the English-speaking world such unions, with secrecy no longer required, are called 'common-law marriages'. In sixteenth-century Spain, they were called *matrimonios a juras* – 'marriages contracted under oath'. In the drama, such unions frequently succeed in bringing young lovers freedom from the oppression of parental authority; no moral stigma was therefore attached to them.

Secret marriages had been sanctioned in practice by the Roman Catholic Church until they were finally forbidden by the Council of Trent (1545–63).[1] The validation of such marriages rested on sound theology. Marriage in the Roman Catholic Church is a sacrament that depends solely upon a solemn contract by bridegroom and bride; no priest is necessary to administer the sacrament, the contracting parties are themselves the ministers, and the sacrament is confirmed by carnal union. Naturally, such secret marriages could give rise to a number of abuses, since the woman had no witness to the contract and could not in law hold the man to his promise.[2] For this reason, the Council of Trent insisted that no marriage could have canonical validity unless there was a minister and witnesses to sign the register. Previously the State as well as the Church had disapproved of secret marriages and had tried to prevent them, without venturing to deny their validity both *de iure* and *de facto*. The principle reason for this toleration had been the need to apply a brake to the authority of fathers, which had given rise to the contrary abuse of often forcing their daughters into marriages that they had in practice no power to reject. It was also the case that the freedom that allowed a young couple to contract a secret marriage led inevitably to social disorders. *Las siete partidas*, the thirteenth-century codification of Castilian Law, had attacked secret marriages because they led to enmities, murders, fighting, and general dishonour (Part IV, Tit. III, Law v). It is noteworthy that this 'general dishonour' is just as apparent in Spanish literature after the Council of Trent as it was before. It is possible that the Council's prohibition of secret marriages may have reduced their number in real life, but as regards the stage the Council made no difference. It is obvious that secret marriages were a very convenient form of theatrical shorthand for presenting intrigues; in fact it would have been sufficient for a woman to appear on the stage dressed as a man for her situation to be immediately apparent to the audience. At the end of *La vida es sueño* Clotaldo discloses that Rosaura had been not only the victim of a secret marriage, but actually the fruit of one, since for reasons that did not need to be made explicit, but which the audience would assume would not necessarily have been to his discredit, Clotaldo had had to return to Poland before being able to marry Rosaura's mother. This repetition of situation from mother to daughter is a very Calderonian feature, as has been seen in the case of fathers and sons. As has also been suggested, this recurrence of wrongdoing from generation to generation obviously formed part of Calderón's 'philosophy of life'. It could be so easily and simply presented if the meaning of secret marriages were automatically understood despite their prohibition by Church and State. In all the betrayals of women on the stage, the public must still have held to the traditional view that the unions that had preceded such betrayals were implicitly sacrosanct; because all these women (like Dorotea in *Don Quixote*) only surrender themselves to the men after exacting a solemn promise of marriage. In *El burlador de Sevilla* by Tirso de Molina there are four such promises followed by desertion. Modern readers have tended to look upon the Duchess Isabel and Doña Ana as loose women, and this fact increases the sympathy they feel for Don Juan, a sympathy which is quite inappropriate to the theme. This opinion of their easy virtue would not have been that of the contemporary audiences, because these ladies admitted into their bedrooms (under cover of the darkness) the men they thought were their betrothed. The same holds good for Tisbea and Aminta, for they exact from Don Juan the promise of marriage, but in the case of these two women of humble status their own vanity and imprudence had a hand in their downfall.

Behind such secret marriages there lay a long history of condemnation of the secrecy, but also a long tradition of justifying marriages contracted in this way, for theological and also human reasons. In addition to the theological reasons already explained, there is the further point that moral theology had long affirmed that sins of the flesh were less grave than those of the mind (such as pride, envy, avarice, etc.). There can be no doubt that Calderón accepted the general principle that *los yerros por amores, dignos son de perdonar* ('sins committed for the sake of love deserve to be forgiven'). He does not show the same degree of compassion for sins of arrogant pride or measureless ambition. In a later chapter, in his play on Henry VIII's divorce, and the resulting schism (see chapter 19) there is an astonishing difference between his compassionate treatment of King Henry and his total condemnation of Cardinal Wolsey as he interpreted the latter's supposed share in events.

There was an event in Calderón's own life which, on the basis of the meagre evidence available, was most probably a secret marriage contracted by him. The facts are these. Calderón had asked for leave to retire from active service in the army on grounds of ill-health. His brother José had served in the same campaign in Catalonia as an officer in the artillery and had been killed in action. In recognition of the services of both brothers, the king, on 21 September 1645, had granted to Pedro, the dramatist, a monthly pension of thirty escudos. On 4 July 1654, the king acceded to the request made by the Captain General of the Artillery, on behalf of Calderón, to have payment of the pension transferred to 'Don Pedro José Calderón, his nephew, and to the said Don José Calderón, his brother, who can most properly and legitimately receive the reward for the services of the two [i.e. of the two brothers who had served in the war] and because he is of tender years and has no other means of support.'³ In a document of the following year, 2 April 1655, the José Calderón here referred to as 'brother' of Pedro José Calderón, turns out to be the son of the dramatist's elder brother, Diego, who had died in 1647. In this document, this Don José Calderón leaves a legacy to his wife asking her to bequeath it on her death to 'Don Pedro Calderón de la Barca, my first cousin, natural son of Don Pedro Calderón, my uncle, whom at present I am supporting and keeping in my house, and I entreat the said Doña Agustina Ortiz de Velasco, my wife, that she should continue bringing him up and educating him with the same care and gentleness that she has shown hitherto, since we have brought him up in our home as if he were our son, and I trust that she will do this because of the love I have for her and because of the love she has had and has for me, and because of the affection I have for the said Don Pedro Calderón, my cousin, for I shall die comforted in the thought that he [the boy] will remain in her care. I have confidence that her love for him [the boy] will replace my loss.'⁴

A month later (7 May 1655) Calderón signed a legal deed 'as the father and lawful administrator, which I am, of my son Don Pedro José Calderón' empowering his nephew Don José, guardian of the boy, to receive from the Public Exchequer all the money and regular income due to his son from whatever source, and especially the thirty monthly *escudos*.⁵ This is the first recorded recognition by the dramatist that the boy in question was his son. The dramatist was by now a priest, having been ordained in 1651. On 19 May 1657 there is extant an official receipt signed by Calderón for money received from the military pension. The notary issuing the document refers to the recipient as 'heir to Don Pedro José Calderón, my deceased son'.⁶ Sometime between 1655 and 1657 the boy had died, slipping out of his father's life as mysteriously as he had entered it, but not before his father had officially acknowledged him as his son. As Cotarelo states, the acknowledgement was made when it could have been most injurious to the reputation of the father, now in Holy Orders. We cannot but be struck by the repetition in the dramatist's life of what had happened in that of his own father – a repetition that is astonishingly so characteristic of Calderonian drama. There is of course one important difference: Don Diego Calderón had acknowledged Francisco González to be his natural son only after the secrecy had caused such unhappiness in the family and such a disaster to the illegitimate son. Don Pedro, the dramatist, acknowledges his fatherhood while his son is still a minor.

Nothing is known of the boy's mother. It has been naturally assumed that she had already died before Calderón in 1654 makes provision for the boy's upbringing by assigning to him the military pension. It has been conjectured that his entry into the priesthood in 1651 was the result of the sorrow at her death which made him henceforth disillusioned with public life.[7] We can never know whether their union had been a carnal one or intended to have the permanence of a 'secret marriage'. If this had been a marriage, why had it been a 'secret' one and not public? An answer why some marriages had to remain secret well after their condemnation by the Council of Trent, is provided by the play *El postrer duelo de España* (Spain's last Judicial Duel). The play was approved for performance in 1665; the names of the censors are found on a manuscript copy which also contains Calderón's signature on a separate sheet, but there is no record of any performance in the palace. Since the King was in failing health at the time, it is likely that the intended performance was cancelled.[8]

This play throws much light on the social customs and standards of the time, and on the conflicts these aroused. The *duelo* of the title does not refer to the ordinary duels fought in the name of individual honour; it refers to the medieval formal combats before a tribunal and judges that were intended to disclose divine judgement on the justice of the case by the defeat of the wrongful party. The result thus had the force of law.

This play dramatises an event which took place in Aragon in 1522, recorded by Fray Prudencio de Sandoval in his History of the Reign of the Emperor Charles V, which was published in 1604–6.[9] Two Aragonese gentlemen, Don Pedro de Torrellas and Don Jerónimo de Ansa, had been close friends until they quarrelled over a game of *pelota* and fought a duel. Torellas's sword fell from his hand during the duel and he acknowledged himself defeated, imploring Ansa to kill him, or, if he did not do so, to promise never to tell anyone of his ignominious defeat. This was immediately promised, and the two men renewed their friendship, thinking that nobody had witnessed the episode. But there had been a witness and before long the whole city knew what had happened. Torrellas accused Ansa of breaking his word, but the latter swore that he had said nothing. In consequence they determined to renew their combat publicly and went to the Emperor to petition a judicial duel 'in accordance with the laws and customs of Aragon and the ancient laws of Castile'. The petition was granted and the combat took place in the main square of Valladolid before the Emperor and the whole court. The two fought so fiercely that they broke their weapons and continued to fight without them. Thereupon the Emperor ordered the fight to stop since, according to Sandoval, 'it seemed to him that the two men had fulfilled their duty in the restoration of their honour', and that neither had been vanquished by the other. Nonetheless, neither would desist and they insisted so obstinately on fighting that the Emperor ordered their imprisonment. Even after their release, they never consented to become friends again. These judicial duels, like the secret marriages, were condemned by the Council of Trent, which called them 'an invention of the Devil'.

Calderón keeps close to Sandoval's account, presenting first the private duel and then the public one, changing only the ending, making Torrellas and Ansa accept the king's judgement and become reconciled. However, he adds a new detail to the fight and invents of his own accord an explanation for the whole incident; this explanation is in fact the play. Before the duel begins each man has to swear, with his hands on a Missal, by God and the four Gospels that he is not moved to fight by hatred, envy or desire for vengeance, but only by 'the public desire for an honourable reputation'. Nonetheless, despite this less reprehensible motive, Calderón unequivocally condemns this duel for honour's sake. The Count of Benavente, one of the seconds, calls it 'a pagan duel' and expressed the hope that Spain might be free of this custom. Furthermore Calderón, with deliberate anachronism, makes the Emperor declare at the end:

> Escríbase luego al Papa
> Paulo Tercero, que hoy
> goza la Sede, una carta
> en que humilde le suplique
> que esta bárbara, tirana
> ley del duelo, que quedó
> de gentiles heredada,
> en mi reinado prohiba
> en el Concilio que hoy trata
> celebrar en Trento . . .

(Let a letter be written immediately to Pope Paul III who now reigns in the See [of Peter]. This letter shall humbly beseech him that this barbarous, tyrannical law of duelling, inherited from pagan times, should be prohibited during my reign by the Council which he is now summoning in Trent.)[10]

Anachronistically again, Calderón links the duel with the rebellion of the *comuneros*.[11] The rebellion took place in 1520–1 and the duel in 1522. so that the anachronism can scarcely be so called, but it has importance as a detail which Calderón adds to the source. In the play, the Emperor receives the news of the uprising immediately after having to allow the duel to take place: that is, a comparison is drawn between a duel concerning two individuals and a civil war involving a whole nation. When he ends the combat, the Emperor says to the gentlemen:

> porque habiendo visto cuánta
> es vuestra bizarría, quiero
> no me haga a otras lides falta
> más generosas

> (because, now that I have seen how brave you both are, I do not wish you to be absent from other more worthy combats.)
>
> (p. 1593a) [*BAE*, iv, p. 150a]

They, in their turn, admit that if he were to honour them by enlisting their services for the performance of brave deeds, they would ask for nothing more. Honour is gained, in other words, not through fighting over one's personal reputation, but through fighting in the king's service for peace in the land.

Finally, as in several other plays by Calderón, the *gracioso* is the voice of common sense. In the middle of Act III the *gracioso*, left alone on the stage, thus addresses the audience:

> Señores, ¿habrá en el mundo
> dos tan grandes majaderos,
> que les cueste más cuidado,
> más diligencia y anhelo
> saber cómo han de matarse,
> que cuesta a muchos discretos
> saber cómo han de vivirse?

> (Ladies and gentlemen, can there possibly be anywhere else in the world two such egregious idiots, who can spend as much anxiety, diligence and solicitude in finding out how they are to kill themselves as it costs many intelligent and reasonable men to learn how they are to live together?)
>
> (p. 1585a) [*BAE*, iv, p. 145a]

This is common sense and rationality.

The equation of private discord with civil war is an especially Calderonian touch. As will later be seen, in *El médico de su honra*, the discord between husband and wife caused by his overbearing obsession with his honour is associated almost from the start of the play with a quarrel between King Peter I of Castile (1350–69) and his brother Prince Henry (the future Henry II) (1369–79). At the end of the play the prince rides off in disgrace, but the future civil war in which Henry will fight hand-to-hand against the king and kill him is explicitly foreshadowed. The murder of an innocent wife by a jealously self-centred husband is equated with civil war, fratricide and regicide.

The quarrel of the two punctilious Aragonese knights thus symbolises the approaching civil war in the kingdom. This equation does not, however, mean that it was Calderón's intention to condemn judicial duelling, since these duels had ceased for over a century to have the force of law. The duel serves to condemn something else. The irrationality of the duel implies irrationality in the motive of the duellists. In the actual historical episode, the motive was as frivolous and ridiculous as it could possibly have been, a quarrel over a game of *pelota*. This provided no motive for a serious drama, and Calderón therefore had to invent another cause. He did not invent it in order to dramatise the historical event, rather he utilised the duel in order to criticise a social custom that still survived despite its condemnation more than a century previously, secret cohabitation claiming to be marriage.

In *El postrer duelo* don Pedro Torellas is the unofficially accepted suitor of Doña Violante de Urrea. It is made quite clear in the text that they live as husband and wife, because he spends each night in her house, not returning to his own till daybreak.[12] One of the rooms in Violante's house has a secret entrance, known only to a maid in whom Violante has full confidence. Pedro and Violante are not officially betrothed; their relationship is kept a secret because she has made him swear never to mention her, not even disclosing that they are acquainted. She imposes this silence on him because her honour is of course involved. But why should this secrecy be necessary? Why do they not marry? The answer is, for economic reasons. He is expecting an inheritance, but this is subject to litigation. She is the daughter of a gentleman in whose family there was entailed an administrative post with salary, but since the father died without male issue the office of administrator is vacant and she does not receive the income; she petitions the Emperor for the right to receive it. Consequently, if they married they would be relatively poor, unable to uphold the public position with house and domestic service that befits their social status. In other words, they cannot marry because their 'honour' forbids it. People of quality are 'dishonoured' by poverty, and honour produces a situation that might be called characteristically Calderonian because of its irony, or indeed its irrationality: in order to preserve their public honour they must compromise their private honour through the 'immorality' of a secret cohabitation. This does not mean that they are themselves 'immoral'; very much the contrary. They are an upright and honourable couple in every respect other than that of keeping secret their 'betrothal' and their 'marriage'. It is evident that such a reason and others like it in real life prevented or postponed marriages in high society, a fact that must have given rise to clandestine relationships justified in private conscience by the mutual vow of present fidelity and public marriage in the future. All this was demanded by a sense of social honour, since poverty was held to be dishonourable. Let it be recalled that, in *La devoción de la cruz*, Lisardo had said to Eusebio that he could never be allowed to marry Julia because 'es delito la pobreza' (poverty is a crime).

Nonetheless, this ironical private dishonour leads inevitably to the public and tragic dishonour of a judicial duel between friends and kinsmen (Calderón makes them cousins) – inevitably, because if it is not publicly known that a young woman is engaged to a man, someone is bound to fall in love with her. The man who falls in love with Violante is Don Jerónimo de Ansa. Suspecting the existence of a rival, Jerónimo asks his cousin Pedro to find out who this might be. Because of the word he has pledged to Violante, Pedro cannot at the start confess that he is the man; but when it becomes unbearable to Pedro that his friend should persist so strongly in paying attention to Violante, and when it turns out in addition that a house-guest in his own home should quickly become an additional rival by wanting to become acquainted with Violante after seeing her in a public festivity, Pedro decides to break his word, arguing with himself as follows:

> rompa la presa el silencio,
> y ponga mi honor en salvo;
> que si dijo algún proverbio:
> 'Antes que todo es mi dama',
> mintió amantemente necio;
> que antes que todo es mi honor,
> y él ha de ser el primero.

(the nature of the prize must break the silence, and give my honour security in a safe place; the proverb that insists 'my lady before all else' is lying lover-like in its teeth; because my honour comes before all else, and it cannot cede precedence to anything.)

(p. 1561a) [*BAE*, IV, p. 130c]

Silence has turned what was honour for her into dishonour for him, and vice versa. He does, therefore, break his word to her, and this treachery is the first effect of the original secrecy. The second effect is that Jerónimo is unable to understand why Pedro had not declared himself at the outset, and charges him with breaking the laws of friendship, with the duel as the result. Before she learns of the duel, Violante comes to realise how absurd the situation is, and sees how wrong it is to fear poverty and how

wrong it was to impose silence upon her lover. She thereupon proposes to
Pedro that they marry, and in this speech of hers Calderón gives voice to
the condemnation of secret marriages. Like the *gracioso*'s earlier criticism
of duelling, this condemnation is based on reason and common sense:

> Quiebras de hacienda, don Pedro,
> por vuestro lustre y el mío
> el casamiento dilatan;
> pues en dos daños precisos,
> elijamos el menor:
> tratemos de descubrirnos
> a nuestros deudos por medios
> públicos, justos, y dignos,
> y padezcamos desaires
> de cumplimientos altivos,
> poniendo las estrecheces
> a cuenta de los cariños.
> Como yo viva con vos
> en el más pobre retiro,
> y consiga lo dichoso,
> ¿qué falta ha de hacer lo rico?
> Si ha de salir a la calle
> el secreto en desafíos
> de celos, armas y duelos,
> salga por el real camino
> de la fama y del honor;
> y pues casado conmigo,
> no queda al atrevimiento
> el más pequeño resquicio
> que aun pudo quedarle al sol,
> porque es mi esplendor más limpio,
> mejoremos lances, pues
> más enfrena a un desvarío,
> que la espada de un amante,
> el respeto de un marido.

(Financial worries over your reputation and mine, Don Pedro, have deferred
our marriage; faced with two unavoidable evils, let us choose the lesser: let us
now disclose our relationship to our relatives in a public, just and worthy
way, and let us face the insults of lip-serving congratulations and by debiting
our future stringency against the credit of our love. As long as I can live with
you and attain happiness in poverty-stricken withdrawal, what need have we
of wealth? Since our secret will come out into the streets through the
challenges of jealousy, swords and duels, let it emerge on to the king's
highway of Honour and our Good Name. When you are married to me, there
could be no possible chink through which the slur of disgrace could reach me,

not even the smallest chink through which sunlight might penetrate, because my honour is as resplendent as the sun; let us take up a secure position, because the respect felt for a husband will check a mad folly more firmly than could the sword of a lover.)

(p. 1570b) [*BAE*, IV, p. 136b–c]

Having accepted the challenge, Pedro has no alternative but to fight a duel with his friend. This could have ended in senseless tragedy if the Emperor had not become displeased with so 'pagan and barbarous' a way of defending a false conception of honour. An equally false conception of honour is the one that prevents a couple from marrying without a substantial income behind them. To have married on a low income would have been the only way of forestalling quarrels, disorder and reckless behaviour, and of ensuring a peaceful, orderly and rational social life. Secret betrothals and marriages are incapable of solving problems: as Violante says, of two potential disasters, the misrepresentation of reality by hiding the truth is the greater of the two evils involved. She has arrived at the realisation that true honour is a 'public highway'. One should stress this fine image – 'the king's Highway', which is the way of Honour and one's Good Name, because it is the highway of public life: to live in society is and must be life lived in public and not in hiding. Personal honour is a highway and not a tunnel.

We are consequently justified in considering secret marriages to be a blameworthy element in the social life that Calderón's drama puts before us, whether in serious plays or in cloak-and-sword comedies. Secrecy in general is blameworthy in the circumstances presented by this particular play, but this does not apply to secrecy in other respects. Calderón's society considered it essential to maintain secrecy if it meant preserving someone's good name or not betraying a confidence. The titles of several of his plays, so many of them proverbial, are ample evidence of this – e.g. *Nadie fíe su secreto* (Do Not Give Away Your Secret), *Basta callar* (Not a Word More) and *No hay cosa como callar* (Silence is Golden). The first of these plays is an early and rather mediocre one. Its plot deals with a lady's acceptance of her suitor; at the moment of acceptance and before it can be announced in public, the fortunate young man tells it in confidence to a friend, who reveals it to another of the lady's suitors, with foreseeable results. But as soon as the betrothal is publicly announced, all quarrels cease. The title 'Do Not Give Away Your Secret' does not mean that a betrothal must not be made public, but that until it is made public, the secret must be kept. In other such plays, secrecy does not mean hiding something underhand. The theme of 'Not a Word More' is that women are the victims of rules designed to favour men: they are not allowed freedom to disclose the dictates of their hearts and are constantly exposed, in consequence, to the unjust suspicions of their would-be lovers. The heroine, Serafina, who has secretly accepted César, is also courted by two other men who do everything in their power to break down her resistence. César, for his part, is pursued by a woman who has fallen in love with him. When at last the betrothal is publicly announced, the three rivals withdraw; for them 'Not a Word More' becomes the rule to follow, in the sense that each must make no further disclosure of his or her passion because there is no longer any right to further it. In 'Silence is Golden' what has to be kept secret is not a betrothal but something highly tragic – a rape. This powerful play deserves special treatment within this context of secrecy.

The position so far reached in this analysis is that some things should be kept secret while others should be disclosed. In every case, what should determine secrecy or disclosure is the law of Reason in human life. In the social world of Calderonian drama, the enemy of Reason is invariably Honour (in plays with a political context, the enemy of Reason is ambition and the thirst for power). Secret betrothals and marriages, in general, and *El postrer duelo de España* in particular, are evidence of this. Duelling epitomises the social world of honour with its insistence on never allowing anything to cloud one's reputation and doing everything to enhance it whether this is necessary or not. The judicial duel was the supreme example of irrational honour, since it demanded of God that He intervene directly to condemn the guilty party.

15 From comedy to tragedy: *No hay cosa como callar*

El postrer duelo de España is a comedy in its structure, but not in its tone; it deals with duelling and with the intrigues that give rise to duelling. It is akin to a cloak-and-sword play in plot and in the atmosphere of social life, but there is no element of comedy in the way the intrigue develops and in the tone of the dialogue. To celebrate the end of public duelling in Spain was a supremely serious aim, one fully in keeping with the solemnity of a court spectacle. The passage from humour to seriousness within the plot conventions of the comedy of intrigue had been made much earlier by Calderón. Comedy with a light humorous tone and a witty development of intrigue is characteristic particularly of his early period. The comedies so far considered all date from the end of the 1620s into the early 1630s. In this latter decade liveliness of stage movement and entertaining intrigues give way to plays that are comedies in structure and convention, but that have a serious subject-matter that uncovers human weakness and the social customs that give them free rein; but this does not become a satire in a didactic or moralistic sense. These are plays that pull back the curtain on human imperfection to enable the audience to see themselves in this light. In practically every comedy of intrigue a point is reached in the climax (near the beginning of Act III) when the action can easily turn to tragedy. In *Casa con dos puertas mala es de guardar* the intrigues have misfired, jealousy and suspicion are rife. The women are about to betray each other with their honour apparently compromised and the men are about to fight each other with friendship turned into enmity. In *La dama duende* the point is reached where Angela can no longer enjoy herself by playing the 'ghost'. She is faced with owning up to her 'misdeeds' and with taking the consequences. She is saved unexpectedly by the man she has been playing jokes on.

These are the flesh and bones of comedy, and when laughter effects reconciliation the *dénouement* demands a 'happy ending'. The use of this phrase has sometimes been criticised as introducing a Hollywood note into the art of comedy, but it translates the phrase *lieto fine* that the Italian neo-Aristotelian theorists of drama had given as the mark of comedy, because a happy ending is the mark of reconciliation. But of course the happy endings of seventeenth-century comedies are not really such; they merely open the door to what the audience assumes will be a blissful married life with no further complications to prevent the rule of Love. But what if a 'happy ending' leaves little ground for hope of a peaceful life under the rule of Love? Dramatic theorists allowed for the fact that a tragedy did not have to end in calamity and death, and the converse could to some extent apply to comedy. Reconciliation could be effected with the prospect of 'happiness' overshadowed by a large question-mark. Serious intrigue plays with a bitter-sweet ending are characteristic, though not exclusively so, of Calderonian comedy in the middle of the 1630s and the 1640s. *No hay cosa como callar* (Silence is Golden)[1] is perhaps the finest of these works, one that moves the conventions of cloak-and-sword drama very definitely towards tragedy while holding back from the brink.

The play can be dated by internal evidence. In Act II there is mention of the Siege of Fuenterrabía which was raised in 1638. France had entered the Thirty Years War against the imperial forces: Spain's part in the campaigns on behalf of the Habsburg Alliance was to prevent the advance of the French armies in Italy, and along the Spanish frontier. Entering Spain at Guipúzcoa the French aimed to march on Madrid, for which they had first to capture San Sebastián and Pamplona. The fortress of Fuenterrabía frustrated this plan, holding out for two months against the French until reinforcements arrived from Castile and raised the siege on 7 September 1638. Don Juan de Mendoza, the principal male character of the play, leaves Madrid to join the relief army. In Act II, ll. 73–9 [*BAE*, I, p. 557b], we hear that Madrid is celebrating the victory at Fuenterrabía, and at the end of the same Act (ll. 1025–59) [*BAE*, I, p. 563c] Don Juan gives an account, which is mostly invented, of the part he played in and after the battle. The raising of the siege is reported as very recent news, and the play must have been performed in the winter of that year. Calderón's younger brother Don José was in the relieving army and was commended by the commander of the Spanish forces for his bravery in the raising of the siege.[2] This, rather than the possibility (as has been suggested) that Calderón himself fought in this campaign, would probably have been the reason why the battle figures prominently in the play.

The play has the atmosphere of a comedy with no gaiety or caricature about it. The standard figures of earlier comedy (Lope de Vega, Tirso de Molina) are confined to one *gracioso*, who is certainly witty enough. The other servants do not (on the whole) stand out as humorous characters and there are no soldiers to add a touch of lively humour despite the fact that war is taking place outside the play. As befits social comedy, the life portrayed is that of the upper-middle classes; an elegant and restrained world with no exaggeration in its manners. The verse does not have the lyrical quality noted earlier in *El astrólogo fingido*, nor is there any 'elevated' imagery. The whole diction of the play unfolds on the level of quiet good taste. This uniformity of tone is broken by the highly dramatic central episode in the action. This adds no sense of melodramatic exaggeration; on the other hand, it is so serious that it makes the tone merge into sadness and brings a reconciliation that, unlike Calderón's earlier comedies, carries no violence with it. It would be almost a humourless comedy but for the character of Don Juan de Mendoza, the male protagonist, and of his servant Barzoque. The carefree, rather frivolous humour of Don Juan stands out against the seriousness of the play which is in fact directed to overcoming the flippancy of his actions, merging him finally into seriousness. An element of comic humour is required in the presentation of Don Juan, for otherwise the 'happy ending', when it comes, would mar the unity of the play, going counter to the tragic dilemma of Leonor.

The two central characters present a marked contrast. Don Juan de Mendoza is a carefree young man, very susceptible to women's charms, but never to the extent of settling down to a steady relationship. Don Juan is so very common a name that it is impossible to say whether it is intentional or coincidental that he has the name of the most famous of all the libertines of Spanish literature – Don Juan Tenorio in Tirso de Molina's *Burlador de Sevilla*. Doña Leonor is a reasonable, rational young woman, conscious of her dignity. She represents the Calderonian ideal of rational and civilised conduct, that of discretion, keeping silent, not gossiping. Her conduct is rational, primarily because she does not seek vengeance and that is because she always seeks to avoid scandal. It is she who gives a serious tone to the intrigue and makes it border on the tragic, while Don Juan's happy-go-lucky character makes it border on comedy. Calderón does not present Jon Juan with approval, but neither does he present him with total disapproval. He is frivolous, easy-going, but at heart he is a chivalrous young man. He is frivolous because he plays the gallant to women, but has no thought of constancy:

> Yo te confieso que he sido
> tan señor de mis potencias,
> de mi albedrío tan dueño,
> que no hay mujer que me deba
> cuidado de cuatro días;
> porque burlándome dellas,
> la que a mí me dura más,
> es la que menos me cuesta.

(I confess [he says to his servant] that I have been so much in control of my passions and emotions, so much in command of my inclinations, that no woman has ever made me fall in love for as long as four days; because, if I make light of them, the one who holds me longest is the one who costs me least.)

(I, ll. 81–8) [*BAE*, i, p. 549b]

When his servant asks him about Marcela, the lady who is pursuing him with a certain ardour, he replies

> Marcela
> es dama de cada día:
> ni entra ni sale en la cuenta.
> Todo ocioso cortesano,
> dice un adagio, que tenga
> una dama de respeto,
> que, sin estorbar, divierta;
> y ésta se llama la fija,
> porque a todas horas sea
> quien de las otras errantes
> pague las impertinencias.

(Marcela is a lady for everyday: she neither enters nor leaves the reckoning. According to the adage, every idle man-about-town should have an extra lady to spare, who can entertain him without getting in his way. This one is called the fixed [star] because at all times she can pay for everything that the other wandering [planets] make one put up with.)

(I, ll. 168–78) [*BAE*, i, p. 550a]

When talking about Marcela to Barzoque, he says

> Yo pensé que no querría
> a Marcela, cuando vía
> en ella tantas finezas;
> y hoy que su retiro veo,
> la quiero; y basta querella
> sin que anda a caza por ella
> de razones mi deseo.
>
> *Barzoque* Y esa es la mayor, si infiero
> que otra el amor no ha tenido,
> que 'yo olvido porque olvido
> y yo quiero porque quiero.'

(When I felt so much kindness in Marcela towards me, I thought that I did not love her; but now that I find her offhand, I do love her; but it is enough that I do love her without having to go searching for reasons.

Barzoque And that must be your principal reason [for loving her], if I bear in

mind that the only reason there has ever been for loving is that 'I
forget her because I forget her, and I'm in love because I love.')[3]

In this respect, Don Juan has his foil in the person of Don Luis, Leonor's
secretly accepted suitor, who is an old-fashioned lover in his constancy.
While the two men are talking about the same woman without realising
it, Don Juan says

> Aunque tan fino os halláis,
> ¿queréis olvidarla?

Don Luis   No,
> ni que haya, presumo yo,
> tal remedio.

Don Juan   ¡Oh cuánto estáis
> templado a lo antiguo!

Don Luis   Pues
> ¿que medio hay para olvidar
> una hermosura?

Don Juan   Alcanzar
> esa hermosura. Ésta es
> la cura, Don Luis, más cuerda;

(Although you think yourself so courteous, you are prepared to
forget her?
Don Luis. No, nor could such a recourse ever occur to me.
Don Juan. Oh, how well you are tempered in the old style!
Don Luis. Well, how is it possible to forget a beautiful woman?
Don Juan. Take possession of her. This, Don Luis, is the most sensible cure.)

(II, ll. 471–9) [*BAE*, i, pp. 559c–560a]

Calderón neither excuses nor accepts such flippancy. This is only what
can be expected of idle young men who have nothing to do but look for
adventures with women. In Calderón's play it is women more often than
not who present the counterpart to this masculine frivolity; they provide
the constancy, rationality and dignity which give stability to this kind of
society. Through marriage women civilise men; by entering on marriage, men become serious and sensible after having sown their wild
oats. Women today might well make a sarcastic comment on the rôle
assigned to them at that time. It really was taken for granted that,
though they were physically frailer and intellectually weaker, it was
easier for women to behave well than it was for men. It would not be fair
to Calderón to believe that he has his tongue in his cheek when he so
often in his plays makes women the standard of rational behaviour.
Calderón does not of course imply that this is always the case, but his
plays, especially his comedies of manners, do clearly suggest that the

only way a flighty young man-about-town could settle down was by marrying a sensible woman.

This particular Don Juan has only this one defect of inconstancy; in all other respects he is a brave young man, honourable and chivalrous towards friends. This is why he is the 'hero' of the comedy; everything that happens to him has strong comic suggestions; for instance, when the intrigue mounts to its climax he finds himself in a situation that only a cloak-and-sword play could provide. He sums it up to Barzoque as follows:

> En casa estoy de una dama
> a quien ofendida tengo,
> enemigo de su hermano,
> y la causa de todo esto,
> que es Marcela, por testigo.

> (I am in the house of a woman whom I have outraged; the enemy of her brother, and the cause of this enmity, Marcela, is a witness to the situation I am in.)

> (Act III, Il.825–9) [*BAE*, i, p.570b]

He is haunted by a locket containing the miniature portrait of Marcela. This locket is the symbol of his *libertinage* (as will be explained more fully later); he loses it to the woman he has wronged, and the locket is always there to plague him wherever he goes. He invents a tall story to explain the loss of the locket only to have the lie thrown back in his face immediately. He does not know how he can ever escape from the locket. This situation is a comic one, as regards himself, but it is far from comic as regards the woman he had wronged; it is on her account that fate is pursuing him in the form of the locket.

This miniature had been given to Don Juan by Marcela as a gift which she hoped would seal their mutual promise of love. As was customary, he wore it round his neck. One night, by an astonishing sequence of events, he returns home unexpectedly only to find asleep in his chair a woman whose beauty had strongly attracted him when, a few days previously, he had seen her face in church. He could not put her out of his mind as he made the preparations for his journey, which he now did not wish to make, convinced that he would never see her again because he is apprehensive that he is not going to return alive from the war. Whispering to Barzoque that this is the woman whose memory has been haunting him, and without wondering how she has got into his room, he seizes his chance as Barzoque runs away, believing her to be the Devil. The first Act ends at that point – a more impressive 'curtain drop' can hardly be imagined. In a later account, it is explained that he raped her, and that in the struggle she held fast to the chain round his neck, which broke when he escaped, leaving her unconscious with the shock. This woman is Leonor. When she recovers, she cannot tell anybody what has happened because of her terrible disgrace, nor has she any idea who the man was. It had happened the previous evening that her house had caught fire. She was rescued and given temporary hospitality by the gentleman who lived opposite, and who is Don Pedro de Mendoza, father of Don Juan. The latter had left Madrid that afternoon to join his regiment on its way to the relief of Fuenterrabía; as night fell he realised he had forgotten his military papers, and returned. Unconcerned to discover who his victim had been, he had resumed his journey, happy for what had befallen him. The whole of this extraordinary story is so carefully thought out and intertwined with such skill between direct and reported speech that it appears a completely natural incident. This is Calderón at his best in plot construction.

Leonor is not acquainted with the gentleman who helped to rescue her and gave her hospitality for the night, nor does he know who she is. She cannot repay his generosity to her by telling him what had happened, for this could amount to a charge of complicity in the outrage, and he might well have been entirely innocent, as indeed seemed to be the case when, with the greatest concern for her welfare, he returned her next day to her own house where the fire had been put out. Leonor is thus left alone to face her dishonour; a situation that has no precedent, to the best of my knowledge, on the Spanish stage. She is, however, not quite alone, for she has the locket with the miniature of an unknown woman; with this as her only clue, Leonor must hope unaided to identify the woman.

The principal motive that will guide her is to avoid scandal at all costs, not only to avoid publicising her shame, but also to avoid accusing innocent parties. It may not be easy for a modern reader, especially a young one, to appreciate the overriding necessity for such reticence. Our present age is one that feeds greedily on scandal, that ferrets it out and publishes it by every means of mass circulation, heedlessly trampling the feelings of all concerned. The past was not like that, not entirely to its moral credit, because it did not have the means of instantly spreading news throughout the world. Nonetheless, the principle of avoiding calumny and detraction was an ethical rule that did hold sway in theory in social life. Leonor soliloquises thus:

Y pues que ya la desdicha
tan deshecha sucedió,
callemos, honor, tú y yo;
que no ser de nadie dicha

una desdicha, ya es dicha;
y para obligarte a dar
el sepulcro singular
de mi pecho a mi dolor,
honor, en trances de honor,
No hay cosa como callar

(Since this calamity happened so suddenly and so violently, you and I, Honour, must not disclose it; for if nobody mentions a disaster, that in itself is a blessing. To compel you, Honour, to bury my grief in the one single tomb of my breast, let us apply the remedy to all crises of honour, 'Silence is Golden')
(Act III, ll. 51–60), [*BAE*, i, p. 564b]

Leonor's dishonour would be a scandal: for her, it would mean seclusion in a convent; it would also be a scandal for her brother Don Diego and for Don Pedro, the elderly gentleman who gave her refuge in his house. She therefore keeps it to herself in silence and attempts to discover on her own who the rapist was. Her dilemma reaches its climax towards the end of Act II when, having discovered that Marcela was the original owner of the locket, she goes, with her face covered, to Marcela's house. Having told her story, she must either uncover her face, in the presence now of her brother, or else surrender to Marcela the locket which is her only hope of obtaining redress. She takes this sacrificial step.

The events that had led up to this critical situation were as follows. A coach had overturned in the street opposite Diego's and Leonor's house and the lady occupant had been carried in unconscious. With the conventional way of falling in love, Diego is 'thunderstruck' by Marcela's beauty. Leonor, for her part, immediately recognises her as the lady of the locket. Marcela recovers and departs without telling her name, leaving brother and sister anxious to know who she is. A servant is sent to follow her.

Helpless and alone, Leonor is an example of a Calderonian character who puts into practice the positive ethic of *La vida es sueño*, that of 'dreaming with one's eyes open' – the ethical principle exemplified by Clotaldo and, to lesser extent, by Rosaura. Leonor does not attempt to impose herself on events by trying to bring about what she wants to happen. She holds fast to the ethical imperative as she sees it, that of keeping silent. Whatever it may cost her, she will hold back and wait for events to right themselves. As a result, by a series of accidents, and not through any initiative on her part, she comes to discover who her violator was.

The main point of interest for the spectators in the *dénouement* would have been to see how Calderón can solve the problem of honour and vengeance. The locket, representing punishment for the wrongdoer and salvation for his victim, continues to dominate the action of Act III. Marcela plans to make Don Juan jealous, this being the only strategem that might win him back. Realising that Diego has shown a special interest in her, she goes to his house to give him the locket, hoping that Don Juan will see it in Diego's possession (which in fact he never does). Diego declines to accept a miniature painted for another man, but Marcela refuses to keep the locket and rushes away, leaving it on the table. Diego follows her, enabling Leonor to recover the locket. Don Juan does learn of Marcela's visit to Diego's house, and his angry jealousy *is* aroused. The two men meet outside Marcela's house and the altercation that follows leads to a fight in the street, in which Don Juan wounds Don Diego's servant. The *alguaciles* (police) arrive; Don Juan makes good his escape, and, pursued by the police, seeks sanctuary in Leonor's house. He recognises her as the woman whom he had raped, but she of course has no idea who he is. He explains the danger he is in and asks her to hide him, which she does. Because of the hubbub in the street Diego brings Marcela for protection in his house, asking Leonor to look after her. In the conversation the two women have, Leonor comes to realise that the man she has hidden was the owner of the locket. It also emerges from the conversation that the locket with which Leonor had previously challenged her had originally been given by Marcela to the man she (Leonor) is protecting, knowing him now to have been her attacker. She tells the maid to take Marcela to another room, and brings Don Juan out of his hiding-place. Here we have another typical Calderonian inversion of situation. The woman who had received protection in Don Juan's room after the fire is now in the position of giving protection to the man who had so grievously wronged her. Now that Leonor knows who her attacker was, what should she do? Seek vengeance?

> Leonor Ya, honor, todo lo sabemos,
> pues sólo quien hijo fuera
> de Don Pedro, entrara dentro
> de aquel cuarto aquella noche.
> ¿Qué he de hacer? Si aquí le tengo,
> podrá mi hermano venir,
> y no es remediar el riesgo.
> Si le dejo ir, no tendré
> ocasión, como ahora tengo
> para vengarme después.
> Mas ¿qué es vengarme? Que en esto
> mi honor no pide venganza.
> En esto al fin me resuelvo.

(Now, honour, we know everything, for only a son of Don Pedro could have entered that room on that night. What must I do? If I keep him here, my brother will come, and that will be no remedy for my dangerous situation. If I allow him to go, I shall not have the chance later, which I now have, of avenging myself. But why do I think of avenging myself? Because vengeance is not what my honour here demands. My mind is now made up.)[4]

Why does she not seek vengeance? Precisely not to cause scandal, because scandal can only emphasise scandal, not remedy it. She would have to ask for vengeance from her brother or from Don Pedro, both of whom are injured parties, and the only result would be a violent death and the grievous dishonour of the gentleman who gave her hospitality when she was driven from her home by the fire. She therefore renounces vengeance, and tells Don Juan so in these noble words:

La vida vuestra y mi honor
en dos balanzas a un tiempo
puestas están. Pues yo miro
por vuestra vida en tal riesgo,
mirad por el honor mío
vos igualmente; advirtiendo
que soy mujer que pudiera
vengarme, y que no me vengo
porque a escándalo no pase
lo que hasta aquí fué silencio.
Yo no soy mujer que andar
tengo con mi honor en pleito;
yo no tengo de dar parte
a mi hermano ni a mis deudos;
que soy mujer, finalmente,
que moriré de un secreto,
por no vivir de una voz;
que, en fin, hablar no es remedio.
Vida y honor me debéis.
Pues dos deudas son, bien puedo
pedir dos satisfacciones . . .
Una solamente quiero:
y es que si a pagarlo todo
no os disponéis, noble y cuerdo
paguéis la parte en callarlo;
que una clausura, un convento
sabrá sepultarme viva,
quedándome por consuelo
solamente que cayó
mi desdicha en vuestro pecho.
Con esto, idos; no mi hermano
vuelva, donde sólo temo
un lance que a hablar me obligue,
siendo mi honor mi silencio.

(Your life and my honour are balanced on two scales at the same time. Since in this dangerous situation I am considering your life, you should consider my honour to the same degree; noting the fact that I am a woman who could take vengeance, but I do not do so in order that what up till now has been silence should not turn to scandal. I am not the sort of woman who would publicise her dishonour; I will not tell my brother nor my relations anything; I will die from keeping my secret rather than live by telling it; in short, talking will bring no remedy. You owe me your life and my honour; since these are two debts, I could properly ask for a double satisfaction. But I ask for only one: which is, that if you are not prepared to repay the whole debt, I would appeal to your noble blood and your reason to pay part of it by keeping silent; for the enclosure of a convent will be able to bury me alive, leaving me the only consolation of knowing that my unhappiness went no further than your breast. Now go; for if my brother returns, I fear that something will happen that must make me speak; my honour must therefore be my silence.)

(III, ll. 921–54) [*BAE*, I, p. 571a]

Don Juan finds himself brought back to solid earth where flippancy can no longer be of any account. He praises her intelligence and prudence, and the fact that she has found consolation in silence. But he continues, he clearly cannot marry her, because he found her in his room one night, and the reason that made her leave her house might have been . . . He is intending to say that the reason might not have been an honourable one, but she cuts him short, telling him that his lips must not utter the lie that is in his mind, and then begins the explanation of why her honour has a claim on him. At that point her brother returns with Don Luis (her suitor). Don Juan immediately covers his face with a cloak and the brother faces the dilemma of an unknown man in his house. The motivation here becomes extremely complex because of the way the intrigues have been elaborated. Each man faces a clash of loyalties as Don Juan uncovers his face, but only the main thread need be followed here. There is no satisfactory explanation for their situation except that of whipping out their swords. Seeing his master having to defend himself against two men, Barzoque rushes to the house on the opposite side of the street to bring Don Pedro, Don Juan's father. He, seeing two men against one, immediately takes the side of the one (his son). This is the dramatic climax, for Leonor is now in the situation she has all along sought to prevent. She can no longer rely on anybody for any help and can only put a stop to the fight by disclosing the truth of her rape. Leonor intervenes to tell Don Pedro that he must fight against his own son because of the word he had once pledged to her; referring (as the audience would recall) to her reluctance to accept the sanctuary of his house when escaping from the fire in hers. Don Pedro had overcome her reluctance by telling her that she should come to him if any difficulties should arise in the future, because he would be her protector. She reminds him of the occasion by beginning, 'On that unhappy night when my house caught fire, and because you lived opposite . . .' A fortuitous turn of phrase has clarified for the two of them a crisis that a whole series of accidents had provoked. Don Juan cuts her short by approaching her and whispering to her in an aside:

> (*Aparte*) Tente, aguarda, que no quiero
> saber más. Porque si yo
> cobarde estuve, temiendo
> la ocasión que allí te tuvo,
> ya la sé, y así pretendo
> que ninguno sepa más
> que yo. Todo ese suceso,
> ni mi padre, ni tu hermano,
> ni ninguno ha de saberlo,
> porque si en trances de honor
> dice un discreto proverbio:
> *No hay cosa como callar*,
> de lo que hablé me arrepiento,
> y no quiero saber más,
> pues que no puedo hacer menos.
> (*Alto*) Ésta es mi mano, Leonor.

(Stop, wait, I don't want to know any more. For if I was cowardly enough to fear the explanation I asked you for, I know it now, and no-one must know more than I. My father, your brother and nobody must ever know what happened. In affairs of honour, as a wise proverb puts it, 'Silence is Golden', I now regret what I said, and I do not want to know more, because I cannot now do less. (Aloud) Here is my hand, Leonor.)

(III, ll. 1100–15) [*BAE*, i, p. 572b–c]

The five who hear this mysterious interruption to Leonor's speech realise that there is a mystery here that none can honourably probe. Each one in turn states in an aside that for him or her the rest must be silence. It is an extraordinary ending to a play: a young couple in the middle of the stage, holding hands in an unexplained promise of marriage with three previously quarrelling men and with one previously intriguing woman, grouped round the couple in a prolonged stage silence, not 'broken' until the *gracioso* steps forward and addresses the audience:

> Cada uno a su negocio
> está solamente atento,
> olvidados de un criado
> que está herido, porque desto
> se saque cuán malo es

ser criado pendenciero.
Y pues que yo soy criado
de paz, solamente os ruego
que consideréis, señores,
que de yerros ajenos
No hay cosa como callar;
perdonadnos, pues, los nuestros.

(Each of them is concerned only with his own affair, having forgotten a
servant who has been wounded, from which it may be deduced how wrong it
is for a servant to relish a fight. Since I am a servant who relishes peace, I
would only ask you, Ladies and Gentlemen, to consider that when other
people's errors are in question, 'Silence is Golden'; consequently, forgive us
ours.)

(III, ll. 1129–40) [*BAE*, I, p. 572c]

There has been incessant talking on the stage for three Acts. Now the
audience are asked to remember that the serious business of life is better
served by discretion. The point has been admirably made in a very real,
not didactic, way. The way the six characters who have woven the
dramatic intrigue are brought together at the end to face Silence is an
extremely skilful piece of plot-construction. Looked at from outside the
stage, it may well appear contrived, as in fact can the whole intrigue of
the play, from the moment the fire breaks out on the other side of the
street. Yet, dramatically speaking, the motives that have brought the six
together are clear and perfectly reasonable. Once again, we see Calderón
as a past master in the construction of dramatic plots: everything follows
inexorably from a conversation Don Juan has with Barzoque in the first
scene, as he describes going to the assistance of the unknown Don Diego
in a street-fight, and being struck by the beauty of Leonor when he saw
her uncovered face in church. Not till the very end of the last Act does he
come to know that these two are brother and sister. There is no earthly
reason, in real life, why they should be, but it becomes clear at the end
that there is every dramatic and poetic reason why this should be so. For
the family tie points to social relationships. Men, left to follow their own
individual interests, are tossed to and fro between the urge to self-
assertion in quarrelling and fighting, and the irresistible attraction of
women's beauty; only the ethical imperatives imposed by society, if they
are accepted, can free a man from the pendulum swing between self-
assertion in violence and succumbing to erotic passion.

It may not be obvious at first that erotic passion is symbolised by the
fire that drives Leonor from her house into the arms of a man who has no
reason to resist the temptation as she had to resist the danger of the
conflagration. This equation of fire and lust was constantly made in

poetic imagery, as human beings burn in the flames of their desire; but here we have an example of the process described in chapter 2 whereby the development of Calderón's art turns dramatic images into symbols that represent the action. A full development of the dramatic symbol of fire destroying a home comes in *El pintor de su deshonra* (The Painter of his own Dishonour). In the light of this later play, the symbolism of Leonor's house catching fire, making her flee into the house of another, is obvious; but it might not have been so obvious by itself on this first occasion. In the honour tragedies (i.e. wife-murder) war is either the setting of the tragedy, as in *El médico de su honra*, or is brought in at the end of the play, as the husband is sent by the dramatist to take part in a historical battle from which no member of the Portuguese army returned – the battle of Alcázar-Kebir, in which the young king of Portugal led his whole army and himself to destruction (*A secreto agravio, secreta venganza*). It would be tempting to hold that this symbolism is suggested here, but this cannot be the case, because the battle of Fuenterrabía was a heroic victory in national self-defence and not an incredibly rash war of aggression or a civil war in which the king is treacherously murdered. This symbolism would be inappropriate because the play is pulled back at the very last moment from the brink of tragedy, but again in the light of other plays the fact that Don Juan leaves to take part in a war and returns to commit a rape is a clear pointer to a threatening tragedy. This is borne out by two military images spoken by Leonor; one is used in Act II, when Leonor confronts Marcela in her house. She is *tapada*, covering her face with her shawl, but for one eye. Marcela objects that this unknown woman should have the advantage over her by hiding her identity. Leonor replies

> Ventaja en mi no se halla
> que os pueda dar temor tanto,
> que la cortina de un manto
> no es cortina de muralla.

> (I have no advantage that need cause you to fear, for the curtain of a shawl is not the curtain of a fortress wall.)[5]

The other image is more direct and powerful. Recalling, in Act II, the rape that had ended Act I, Leonor describes how she recovered from her faint as she saw the aggressor leaving the room:

> ¡Oh infames lides de amor,
> donde el cobarde es valiente,
> pues el vencido se queda
> mirando huir al que vence!
> (Oh, infamous battles of love, where the brave are cowardly, since the defeated victim watches the conqueror flee!)

> (II, ll. 145–8) [*BAE*, I, p. 557c]

'Traitor, stop!' she cries to Don Juan, as he makes good his escape.

This splendid play illustrates that consistency is the hallmark of Calderón's closely-knit art, where no thread is misplaced or lost. It also illustrates how in his vision of human life comedy and tragedy are so closely interwoven that at the end of the play either can come to the fore. This play has been poised between comedy and tragedy from the end of Act I. At the close *No hay cosa como callar* can scarcely be called a comedy in the technical sense, for can it be said that the play has a happy ending? Every one of the characters connected with the intrigue, with the exception of Don Pedro, is frustrated in his pretensions. Don Juan, who prided himself on never being in love with any one woman for more than four days, finds himself totally unexpectedly tied to a 'fixed star'. Don Luis loses his betrothed. There is nothing to prevent Diego marrying Marcela, but there is no hint that this may happen. In fact any subsidiary wedding would detract from the emphasis on the single wedding that must take place. The modern reader could not possibly look upon this union as Leonor 'living happy ever after'. But this romantic view of the traditional 'happy ending' is quite beside the point. The emotions of the audience would have rebelled if Leonor had not won the hand of the man who had dishonoured her and if he had not been compelled to do his duty. The point of the play is not to construct a complicated intrigue that leads to a happy marriage, but to construct an intrigue that can show the overriding necessity of avoiding scandal. That this is finally avoided would have given the spectators the satisfaction that every play, other than a tragedy, should provide. The story of Juan and Leonor is not a 'slice of real life'; scandal, however, *is* an evil that destroys the harmony that should govern social living. The play therefore has a happy ending in this sense, but of course the human experience that it presents, if divorced from the theme of the play, is an extremely unhappy one, since a woman loses the man she loves, and is compelled to marry one who has so deeply wronged her. An age in which marriages were arranged and not expected to be love-matches would not have looked upon a stage-marriage 'arranged' to avoid scandal as necessarily one that would bring unhappiness. Calderón's audience would certainly have seen this marriage as a 'happier' one than the conventional love-match that it frustrated. Our main conclusion must be that this play has a serious theme, one that is more tragic than romantic in tone. Not all dramatic plots of this kind, however, can be steered away from tragedy, for that would belie the deepest and darkest tensions that lay at the heart of seventeenth-century honour.

16 A Calderónian conception of tragedy: *El pintor de su deshonra*

It used to be considered that Spain had made no original or significant contribution to tragic drama. This was often explicitly stated in general histories of the European theatre, or in studies of tragedy in particular.[1] Hispanists did little to dispel this belief because many of them shared it themselves. As regards the seventeenth century, an explanation for the inability to write tragedy was usually looked for in the religious spirit of the times. No student of Spanish literature need be reminded how horror of the Spanish Inquisition covered every sphere of Spanish history and culture, as an ominously oppressive shadow over everything, even when its activities were not in question. Liberal-minded Spaniards turned against their own history and culture as decisively as did foreigners. Today nobody looks to history to exemplify the dominance of enlightenment in human affairs. For the most part literary historians and critics no longer find in what they study what their general prejudices tell them must surely exist. But some Spaniards went even further than this and ascribed their alleged inability to feel a sense of tragedy to their national temperament, to a supposed contempt for pity, for example. *A priori* assumptions are not the way in which history and culture are now approached. Calderón and his century can now be approached without prejudices, leaving the mind of the critic free to see what his art does in fact offer when properly understood.

Apart from the question of religious background, two fixed ideas prevented the study of Calderonian tragedy, one being that there is such a thing as Tragic Drama, well-rounded and easily definable; if a particular play that deals with obviously tragic material does not conform to this, then its merit and interest are diminished. The other fixed idea is that the Spanish preoccupation with honour was a particularly unworthy motive for writing a tragedy, since it did not emphasise the injustices of life but exalted the self-righteousness of the arrogant obsession of an individual with his own reputation in the eyes of others. Convinced that Calderón was taking his characters at their own estimation, when he made husbands kill their wives out of a sense of duty on suspicion of intended adultery, it was not difficult to feel in practice the moral revulsion aroused by the theory. This came to be considered by Spaniards themselves the extreme manifestation in literature of their traditional sense of honour, which they called 'Calderonian honour'. Only some forty years ago was any attempt made to check this assumption from Calderón's actual plays.

Two developments have altered these *a priori* attitudes. The first is that the full meaning of a play must be looked for in what is special and peculiar to it, its poetic imagery and the details with which its plot is structured. The second is what sociology and social anthropology have taught us, namely that the social traditions, habits and attitudes of a people within a definite culture cannot easily be translated into the terms of another culture. What used to be thought a peculiarly Spanish attitude is now seen to be common to all Mediterranean peoples. Sociologists study these habits of mind and social attitudes within their own context, and do not apply moral criteria evolved from outside them. The literary critic has much to learn from the social anthropologist if he wishes to study dispassionately manifestations of a culture different from his own. This will not necessitate the abandonment of the critic's own ethos, but it should make for fuller understanding.[2]

The belief among literary theorists and critics that true dramatic tragedies exemplify a general theory of tragedy without which no play can properly qualify for the title, is part of the praiseworthy effort to explain the traditions and the structures of literary composition. Critical theory, however, should, where necessary, always follow dramatic practice. Aristotle wrote on Greek tragedy by studying the tragedies that Greece had produced. It was not he but his followers down the ages who worked out rules that every would-be dramatist had to obey.

Definitions, as the history of scholastic philosophy and of literary criticism exemplify, can ossify cultural forms by draining them of their life-blood. Despite what may appear the excessively formal patterns of his poetic and dramatic technique, Calderón's career as a dramatist shows, from first to last, a progressive thread of originality and his conception of tragedy reveals this. By 'conception of tragedy' one does not mean a set of formal rules, but the insight into the problems of suffering and evil that a great dramatist gives to his exploration of human experience. Apart from this personal insight, Calderón's practice is in line with the literary theory of his age, the neo-Aristotelian theory of the Renaissance with such clarifications as were made in the Spanish seventeenth century, but he is not hidebound by them, and what we are concerned with will be his own particular contribution. So far in this book we have noticed tragedies of his that can, broadly speaking, fit into the classical pattern, for instance, *El mayor monstruo los celos*. We have also seen the classical conception of Destiny that lay behind it, and the development of the ideas on Fate and Free Will that also contributed to the seventeenth-century background. What follows now is how a conception of tragedy can be extracted from the dramatic plots that came from his own experience and not from literary theory. This 'conception of tragedy' is exemplified in the plays that reflect the attitudes and the actions of contemporary society and are not, like *El mayor monstruo los celos* or *La hija del aire*, drawn from ancient times. These 'real-life' plots can be set ostensibly in the Middle Ages, while not losing the orientation towards the ideas and customs of contemporary living.

The first version of this present chapter stressed those aspects of modern (post-Romantic) theories of tragedy which seemed to condemn Calderón out of hand. The reader is referred to that essay if he wishes to have a more explicit account of the gulf between Calderón's practice and modern theory.[3] This gulf is a fact of literary history but it is not relevant to the attempt to understand the Calderonian drama. We must look for what he is wanting to give us and look for it only through the poetic and dramatic means of communication which he uses. Modern theory does not like any suggestion that the tragic hero is brought low through his own fault, by imprudence, passion or pride. He is brought low by injustice, not justice, and by an inexplicable injustice at the very heart of the universe. In the light of this fundamental injustice, modern theory maintains that Tragedy should not take sides between belief in a 'patterned' universe where Good and Evil can be clearly differentiated and the former upheld, and a 'chaotic' universe that reveals no principle of order or purpose. For drama to be tragic, it must be poised equally between the two, leaving the dilemmas of life ultimately unresolved. For those reasons it has constantly been asserted that religion can have no place in tragedy and no voice in the judgements that spectator or reader would wish to apply. This rejection of religious values is sometimes quite crude. It is generally said not to matter how much calamity and suffering befalls a dramatic hero in this world if he and the audience believe in an afterlife where all injustice is put right. Drama is concerned with human life as lived in this world, and it is all too evident that suffering and evil can dominate this world despite ingrained beliefs that goodness will triumph beyond it. Calderón, as a Christian dramatist, would not have been poised in uncertainty between two worlds of being, one good and the other evil, nor could he disregard the responsibility of every man for his own actions, or fail to emphasise, where necessary, how far a character fails to uphold the good. Theological 'certainty' has been more often applied to Calderón the dramatist because readers and critics knew that it would have existed in Calderón the man. A close analysis of his tragic drama, free from prejudice about the assumed influence of his religious beliefs, may show that these do not in fact obtrude into the dialogue and the actions of these plays, and that Calderón is far from dispensing praise or blame in a human world that is believed on faith to mirror a patterned universe. These remarks exclude, of course, the specifically religious *comedias*, which need not be defended as Tragedies, however close their plots may approximate to Tragedy.

Two plays that have already been studied in this book will be analysed afresh from the point of view of tragedy. Two other plays will be added to these. The aim will be to disregard modern theories of tragedy and, by starting instead from the meaning we give to the word 'tragic' in everyday life, to see what meaning the term can have applied to these plays.

These introductory remarks have not been intended to disparage every aspect of modern theories of tragedy. It is hoped to show that *uncertainty* between two worlds of being – where does Good lie, and where Evil? can they in fact be differentiated? – is not the only possible equilibrium of tragedy, and that Calderón does in fact show an equilibrium between two worlds of being whereby, though the dramatist (as a Catholic and a neo-scholastic theologian) knew in his own mind that goodness is the positive law of Being, and evil its negation and not a positive counterpart, he none the less leaves us poised between the two.

It is no part of my purpose to decide how many of Calderón's plays deserve to be called tragedies under a more liberal definition than the traditional one. Further discussion of this subject will be needed before any worthwhile classification could be offered. There are many 'near-tragedies' that might well be included, even perhaps *No hay cosa como callar*, despite its use of comedy-like intrigue. There are also some mythological plays that could well deserve the status of tragedies, despite their 'non-human' subject-matter. I am concerned here only to broaden the conception of tragedy in a direction that, as I shall suggest, should be acceptable to any critic or reader not tied to modern definitions. This will be exemplified by plays not hitherto put forward as 'true' tragedies. The treatment of this conception of tragedy will necessitate going back to two plays discussed in chapter 6, but the plays will now be analysed from the new angle.

La devoción de la cruz (see pp. 75–6) has, understandably enough, never been considered a tragedy because of its religiously melodramatic, even superstitious, plot. The young protagonist, Eusebio, meets with a tragic death; but his is miraculously restored to life in order that he may confess his sins and receive absolution from a priest before dying.

This in itself extravagant incident has, of course, a symbolical meaning – it is the concrete representation on the stage of the fact that Eusebio's soul is saved through repentance; and spiritual salvation despite human catastrophe is what Calderón wishes to emphasise at the end in this particular case. The play does not end in the human tragedy to which the incidents of the plot lead, but in a spiritual triumph that is dramatically irrelevant: it is therefore thought to be no tragedy at all. This interpretation, if correct, would offer cogent proof of one aspect of modern dramatic theory: the equilibrium proper to tragedy is lost, because the powers of good come to rescue human beings from the tentacles and suffering of fatality.

I have, however, argued elsewhere that this interpretation is the wrong one because it does not take into account, as one always must in Calderón, the structure of the plot.[4] The whole plot is admirably constructed along an unbroken chain of cause and effect, whereby the final catastrophe that overwhelms Eusebio is seen to be the result of something that happened before he was born – the result of the cruel self-centred and warped sense of honour of his father, Curcio. In this way, Curcio and not Eusebio is seen to be the real centre, because he is the primary agent, of the tragedy, despite the fact that he does not die though Eusebio does. Curcio's tragedy is the ruin in which he engulfs his family, and the social disgrace he brings upon himself by creating a real dishonour in the attempt to avoid an unreal dishonour that was in the first place only the imaginary fruit of his obsessive egotism. There is, however, one important point about this play which was not brought into the discussion of it because it was not relevant to the context of that particular argument on that occasion, but it is relevant here for the different purpose of elucidating a typically Calderonian conception of tragedy. We do not have here the equilibrium between good and evil which has been considered essential for tragedy; and we certainly have an *implicit* insistence on moral responsibility. But where is the moral responsibility for Eusebio's death to be fixed? On Eusebio? Yes and no. Yes, because he commits the crimes; no, because the fact that he was placed in the circumstances that made him commit them was the responsibility of another. Is the responsibility, then, to be fixed on Curcio? Again, yes and no. Yes, because he was responsible for an act that in time produced the circumstances of Eusebio's crimes; no, because he did not himself commit these crimes, nor did he wittingly lead Eusebio to commit them. There is here both a conception of moral responsibility and a tragic equilibrium for which the modern theorists of tragedy have made no provision. It will be suggested that Calderón's tragic equilibrium and his conception of moral responsibility are more subtle than those the modern theorists put forward; for Calderón leaves us suspended, not between two worlds of being, but between sin and guilt: the sin is there – in Eusebio's crimes – but where is the guilt to be placed?

Already at what must have been a point very near the start of his dramatic career Calderón was aware, as most modern theorists of drama are not, that good and evil cannot be differentiated by a simple division into right and wrong and exemplified by a straightforward conception of poetic justice.[5] Eusebio is both guilty and not guilty; while Curcio must share the guilt for crimes that he has not himself committed. If a situation such as this is indeed part of our human predicament (and who can deny it?), is it not something deeply tragic?

This conception of diffused responsibility, of the impossibility of confining the guilt of wrongdoing to any one individual, lies at the heart of the Calderonian sense of tragedy. If, in *La vida es sueño*, Segismundo had been killed in the vain attempt to recover his freedom while Basilio had been forced to see him die before his eyes as the price of retaining his throne, the Curcio–Eusebio situation would have been exactly paralleled. The crime of sedition and recourse to violence would have been clear, but where would the guilt have been placed?

The phrase 'diffused responsibility' has often been misunderstood to imply that everyone who shares in this is *morally* responsible for the calamity that ensues. Even in the case of Curcio this is not strictly true, for Curcio does not share in the guilt of Eusebio's actual crimes: he is guilty of the intended murder of his wife and the abandonment of the child about to be born, but he is not guilty of Eusebio's attempt to abduct Julia and of his subsequent crimes. The point that Calderón is suggesting will be made much clearer as he develops this type of theme. Men are individually responsible for their own sins, but collectively responsible for the evils that human wrongdoing brings to society.

The development and clarification of this sense of tragedy is best exemplified by *Las tres justicias en una*, a splendid play that does not deserve the neglect into which it has fallen despite Fitzgerald's rather free translation. Less passionate and melodramatic than *La devoción de la cruz*, more measured and restrained, it is on that account a work of greater maturity which might tentatively be assigned to the period 1635–40. This play was analysed above (pp.76–7). The analysis brought out how blame for the final catastrophe should be apportioned. The theme of diffused responsibility is more fully developed here than in *La devoción de la cruz*, but the principle at stake is the same. To requote: 'In both these plays this inner family conflict, which must reflect what Calderón had witnessed in his own home, leads to tragedy. The two sons are doomed by their fathers to rebellion and death with the terrible inevitability of tragic drama. In these two plays Calderón certainly did not deprive his audience of the catharsis necessitated by the tragic emotions aroused by his human situation.'

In this latter play the greatest sinner is at the same time the most sinned against, in that others, before he was born, had begun to dig his grave and had unwittingly handed him the spade with which to complete it. Casuistry is not poetic drama. The just legal retribution that follows the deliberate choice of evil is exemplary; it may be lamentable but it is not tragic in any deep sense. On the other hand, without suffering, whether retributive on the theological plane or consequential on the social plane, guilt by itself is also not tragic on the stage. It may be submitted that Calderón's dramatic vision of the nature of moral evil is a tragic and not a casuistical one: all men dig each other's graves as well as their own, for since all human acts engender others in an unbreakable chain of cause and effect, the lesser evil that one man does can combine with that of others to engender a major evil. Calderón's dramatic world in this type of theme is one in which individual responsibility clashes with the fatality of the causal nexus of events.

This being so, the problem of evil takes on, as it were, a new dimension. As an illustration of how Calderón developed this in his mature drama we can turn to *El pintor de su deshonra*, so fine a play in its transformation of ideas into symbols, and of symbols into both action and imagery, that to dissect the structure of the plot is to present only the driest of dry bones. It should probably be assigned to the decade preceding 1650, in which year it was first printed. Being an example of Calderón's maturity it has in large measure all the difficulties inherent in his fully developed technique: the action is stylised, the structure taut and compressed.

The plot deals, once more, with an unhappy marriage. Serafina had secretly pledged her hand to her lover Álvaro, but he is believed to have been drowned at sea; she therefore does not resist the marriage her father has arranged with Don Juan Roca, a man much older than herself. But Álvaro has not been drowned, and he returns to upbraid her with her infidelity and to pursue her relentlessly. Grief-stricken, she resists the man she loves in order to remain faithful to the man she does not love, but Álvaro abducts her and keeps her in hiding; yet still she remains faithful to her husband. The latter sets out in search of his lost wife and eventually tracks her down; without waiting for an explanation and believing her guilty, he kills her and Álvaro.

The catastrophe – the murder of the innocent Serafina – is due to the uncontrolled passion of love in Álvaro and to the impetuous passion of jealousy in Don Juan. These are individual motives arising from the clash of their individual circumstances brought about by the unfortunate marriage which brings suffering to both men as well as to the women; but the two men are not in this respect the victims of fate, since the marriage was itself the direct result of imprudence on the part of each. Don Juan is a painter, and in the first scene of the play it is emphasised that he had wasted his youth and early manhood by allowing himself to become absorbed in study and in his art to the neglect of his social responsibilities. Though urged by all his friends to think of marriage, it was not until well advanced into middle age that he heeded the fact that the preservation of his entailed fortune required an heir. He is therefore guilty of the imprudence not only of neglecting his social responsibilities but of marrying a woman very many years his junior, an imprudence for which her father also shares the responsibility.

One of the structural features of the play is the succession of anecdotes related by Juanete, Don Juan's servant. It was common enough in Spanish plays of this period for the *gracioso* to relate occasional humorous anecdotes. Calderón develops this convention until in the plays of his maturity he often makes the stories ironical comments on the points of the plot that need emphasising. In the first scene Don Juan and his bride are travelling to their home. On the way they call at the house of one of his friends, Don Luis. As Juanete enters the house he gives, jokingly, the salutation given by priests: 'Peace be upon this house'. He then tells two stories; the second is to this effect. One man invited another to a picnic beside the river. He began with a very cold chicken. This was followed by wine that was as hot as the meal was cold. The guest put the chicken inside the jug, and when his host asked him why, he replied 'I am trying to make the chicken cool the wine, or else make the wine warm the chicken.' Since the audience is not yet aware of the situation, it is necessary for the point of this story to be explained immediately:

> Lo mismo me ha sucedido
> en la boda, pues me han dado
> moza novia y desposado
> no mozo: con que habrá sido
> fuerza juntarlos al fiel,
> porque él [cano,] ella doncella,
> o él la refresque a ella,
> o ella le caliente a él.

(The same thing happened to me at the wedding, since they presented me with a young bride and a bridegroom not all young: consequently it will be necessary to balance them on the scales, so that he, white-haired [the Aguilar reading], may cool her, or she, a young maiden, may warm him.)[6]

Don Luis is the father of the Álvaro who has been presumed dead; both will share the blame, in widely differing degrees, for the fatal consequences of this unequal marriage. The latter had kept secret his courtship of Serafina and her acceptance of his hand: had he not done so, she could have resisted the marriage or at least the fact of her attachment would have warned Don Juan that she could not give him her heart. This secrecy was the first link in the chain that the marriage is now going to forge. All the remaining characters in the play, excluding the servants, will have their part in the forging of this chain.[7]

By reconstructing this chain backwards from the catastrophe we find that the sequence of events is as follows. Journeying with his bride to his home after his wedding, Don Juan visits the father of Álvaro, his friend Don Luis, whose vanity it is to be effusive in his hospitality. He importunes Don Juan to lodge in his house despite the latter's clearly expressed wish not to do so. The Prince of Ursino, who is a friend of Don Luis, also arrives, and the latter insists on offering hospitality to him and all his retinue, insisting at the same time that Don Juan should remain, although the latter is, naturally, now more anxious than ever to leave. When Don Luis tells Porcia to get rooms ready for the new guests, she replies that his instructions are unnecessary, because both rooms are always ready, he being more of an innkeeper than a governor. The result of this effusive and ostentatious hospitality is that the prince meets Serafina, with whom he is immediately captivated. He, however, is already secretly courting Porcia, the daughter of Don Luis, who has accepted his suit. He continues this secret courtship, although his heart is now elsewhere, and he is thus guilty of deception towards the women he professes to love. She, to facilitate their secret courtship, arranges for him to meet her at a country house belonging to her father, to which in the meantime Álvaro has secretly taken the captive Serafina. Porcia is anxious that Álvaro should not see the prince, and Álvaro is anxious that Porcia should not see Serafina; the two (Porcia and Álvaro) therefore return together to the city. Their eagerness to hide their respective secrets leaves the prince and Serafina together in the house where they meet for the second time. Though he makes no attempt to take advantage of her tragic situation, the meeting so inflames the infatuation he feels for her that he resolves, now that he knows her hiding place, to commission an artist to paint her portrait which he wishes to possess, since he cannot possess her. The prince does not know that this artist is her husband. The commission to paint the portrait brings Don Juan face to face with Álvaro and Serafina and the murder follows.

The purpose of this strikingly contrived plot is to implicate every single major character, directly or indirectly, in the catastrophe. If at the beginning Don Luis had not been so vain and demonstrative about his hospitality, to the inconvenience of his household and of his guests, the outraged husband would not have been led at the end to the hiding place of his abducted wife. This had been ironically anticipated by Juanete's first story, before the one of the chicken in the wine. A regiment arrived in a village where the soldiers were to be billeted. One of the peasant villagers shouted out 'Two soldiers for me!' Whereupon another said to him 'You are begging for what everyone else is trying to avoid!' To which he agreed, but said that he would welcome being billeted with two because of the extra pleasure this would give him when they left. In the first link of this chain of causality Don Luis does not act evilly, but he acts reprehensibly none the less, since he thinks primarily of himself and is motivated by the vanity of appearing a generous man. The actions of the prince and Porcia that link the beginning of the chain with the end are also reprehensible, since they involve secrecy and deception: each indulges in secrecy because each is concerned only with his or her private world. Their secrecy parallels that of Álvaro and Serafina when they pledged their love to each other. If all four characters had been open instead of self-centred the tragedy would not have happened. Again we have an example, and a still more subtle one, of the equilibrium between sin and guilt. This is no dramatic world of clear-cut black and white ruled by an automatic poetic justice disposing of all problems.

This linking of dramatic causality with some degree of moral guilt in all the major characters of the play constitutes the centre of this particular Calderonian conception of tragedy. The individual human being must base his judgement and actions on 'I and my circumstances'; yet an individual's circumstances are never his own: they are the tangled net of human relationships cast wide in time, a net in which all men are caught up by the inescapable fact that, though individuals, they are cast in a collective mould. The dramatic originality that flows from this sense of human solidarity is to have extended the traditional conception of tragedy as a catastrophe resulting from a flaw in the character of the individual hero or from an error in his judgement. The flaw is not his alone, there is a flaw of varying gravity in each and every character; each single error trickles down and combines with all the others to form the river that floods the tragic stage of life. No single man has the right to protest in indignation against the unjust suffering that is the lot of humanity, since all men in solidarity together make life what it is. In the Calderonian drama individuals are caught in the net of collective circumstances, in which they cannot know all the facts because they cannot see beyond their individually restricted range of vision. The fact that every single human action is a stone cast into the water of social life, producing ripples that eddy out into unforeseeable consequences, makes it the inescapable duty of each man to look outwards towards other men, and not inwards towards himself. Self-centredness, the self-assertive construction of a private world of one's own, is, for Calderón, the root of moral evil. In his drama, the individual cannot see beyond his restricted range of vision; yet with the confidence born of self-centredness he deludes himself into the belief that his vision is complete and aims at what seems a clear goal, only to blunder into something unforeseen.

Don Juan Roca is an example of this. There are three symbols in the action of the play and in the imagery of the verse – fire, sea and painting. Fire, the destructive self-centredness of erotic passion and the sea together represent the passion of love, and its corollary – the self-centred passion of jealousy; painting represents the self-centred activity of the imagination. Fire and the sea are symbols in the action, in that Serafina's house is set on fire before her abduction (cf. the burning of the heroine's house, which leads to her rape, in *No hay cosa como callar*); Álvaro, both the active and the passive victim of love and jealousy, is thought lost at sea, he follows the married Serafina across the sea, he is dressed as a sailor when he abducts her, and he carries her across the sea to their hiding place; Don Juan crosses the sea to discover them.

Only the third of these symbols is important for my present purposes. The general significance of the symbol of painting is obvious from the title: it is not just that Don Juan is commissioned to paint the portrait of his wife when she is in the possession of another man, it is also that his dishonour is imaginary only. When the symbol appears in the first scene, Don Luis praises Don Juan's skill as a painter in these terms:

pues es tanta la destreza
con que las líneas formáis,
que parece que le dais
ser a la naturaleza.

(Such is the skill with which you shape your lines that it seems as if you give life to Nature.)

(p. 123) [*BAE*, IV, p. 65b]

The phrase is very odd: one would expect 'give life to the canvas' or 'give life to what is lifeless'. The departure from the expected image points to a special significance; 'dar ser' is to create: Don Juan 'creates nature', i.e. he imagines reality, he does not see it – which is why in this particular context his painting is blamed for his shutting his eyes to the responsibilities of life. At the beginning of Act II the symbol appears in the action: Don Juan is painting Serafina's portrait and addressing her, but gives up in despair when he cannot capture her likeness. A second odd metaphor makes the symbol explicit: instead of saying that his brush cannot follow his eyes, he says they cannot follow his imagination, although the model is before him:

> Desta arte la obligación
> (mírame ahora, y no te rías)
> es sacar las simetrías,
> que medida, proporción
> y correspondencia son
> de la facción; y aunque ha sido
> mi estudio, he reconocido
> que no puedo desvelado
> haberlas yo imaginado
> como haberlas tú tenido.
> Luego si en su perfección
> la imaginación exceden,
> mal hoy los pinceles pueden
> seguir la imaginación.

(This art requires one (look at me now, and don't laugh) to grasp and represent symmetry, which consists in the measurement, proportion and correspondence of the features; and although this has been my [life-long] study, I have come to recognise that I have not been able, for all my striving, to imagine them in the way that you have possessed them. Therefore, if in their perfection they surpass my imagination, today my brushes can only follow my imagination imperfectly.)

(p. 163) [*BAE*, iv, p. 72c]

On the first occasion his painting is what prevented him from marrying; on the second occasion he is married, but he can no longer paint. The point is beautifully made: his painting was a substitute for reality, now that he has faced up to reality by marrying, his marriage is unreal because it is to a woman who does not love him.[8]

As Juanete had said at the beginning of the play, the warmed wine could not heat the cold chicken. Now, at this juncture, Juanete tells another pointed story:

> Sordo un hombre amaneció,
> y viendo que nada oía
> de cuanto hablaban, decía:
> '¿Qué diablos os obligó
> a hablar hoy de aquesos modos?'
> Volvían a hablarle bien,
> y él decía: '¡Hay tal! ¡Que den
> hoy en hablar quedo todos!',
> sin persuadirse a que fuese

suyo el defecto. Tú así
presumes que no está en ti
la culpa; y aunque te pese,
es tuya, y no la conoces,
pues das sordo en la locura
de no entender la hermosura
que el mundo te dice a voces.

(A man woke up deaf one day, and when he realised that he could not
understand anything that others spoke, he said to them, 'What in Heaven's
name has made you speak in that fashion?' Once again they spoke to him
clearly, and he exclaimed, 'Whoever heard the like! That it should occur to all
of them to speak softly today!' without his being able to see that the fault was
his. In the same way, you presume that you are not to blame; and however
much you don't like to admit it, it *is* your fault, and you won't see it, for you
foolishly turn a deaf ear to the beauty everyone is shouting from the
housetops.)

(pp. 164–5) [*BAE*, IV, p. 73a]

A subsequent story of Juanete's (p. 166) [*BAE*, IV, p. 73b] points, this time
explicitly, to the possibility of cuckoldry. Because his marriage is, so to
speak, a figment of Don Juan's imagination, he is unable to paint his
wife's portrait. He can, however, 'paint his dishonour' by imagining it.
From the evidence presented to his limited and self-centred vision he
imagines her to be guilty and punishes her, without asking for the
explanation that would complete his vision of the circumstances. He
thus creates a non-existent dishonour ('dando ser a la naturaleza')
(giving life to nature).

The evidence of his wife's guilt as presented to Juan Roca could not
have been more convincing. It is cruelly contrived by fatality acting
through Chance or Accident, as we saw fully exemplified in *El mayor
monstruo los celos*. Don Juan has come to the prince's house to carry out
his commission to paint a lady without her knowing. He is led into the
garden by a servant and placed before a ground-floor window with a
grille, and told to wait while the servant fetches her. Serafina is brought
into the room and the servant so arranges it that she reclines in a suitable
position for the painter at the window. In her misery, she falls asleep. Don
Juan is in anguish when he sees who she is. How can she sleep, he asks
himself, while committing so grave an offence against him? Her sleep is
troubled by a nightmare. She awakes with great agitation, calling out in
fear. Álvaro rushes into the room, and she tells him she has just seen her
own death at the hands of her husband. She is about to faint, and so
Álvaro holds her in his arms, upon which she says, 'Never have your
arms been more welcome'. These luckless words fulfil her prophetic

dream, for, taking them in the only sense that fits the circumstances, Don Juan takes out a pistol and shoots the two of them.

Here Calderón uses the device of not letting the tragic hero meet with death as a means to deepen the sense of tragedy by imbuing it with a bitter irony. All the major characters in the play, who all in their various ways have been responsible for bringing the tragedy to pass, have come rushing into the room at the sound of the pistol. Don Juan turns to them, asking for the death he presumes they will think he deserves. But all of them, deprived by the murder of hearing Serafina assert her innocence, believe in her guilt and exonerate Don Juan because in their eyes he has acted as a man of honour. He therefore paints his dishonour not only in his own imagination but in that of everybody else. By refraining from making him meet death on the stage Calderón is neither upholding vengeance as morally legitimate nor departing from the principle of poetic justice: he is accentuating the tragic tone of the play, for the act of vengeance, which in Don Juan's eyes and those of everybody else restores his honour and gives him the right to continue living, is in fact what creates the dishonour he will carry with him to the grave – the dishonour which, together with the ruin of his marriage and the consequent frustration of his purpose in marrying, constitutes his 'punishment'.

In short, the good that Don Juan sought to achieve by murder for honour's sake is an imaginary good only. Many other examples could be given to show that in the Calderonian drama all moral evil lies in the divorce of the imagination from reality, in that tragic capacity of men to go counter to truth by distorting, through their self-centred and limited vision, something that is unworthy of their human nature into a worthy good for themselves. This, of course, is the traditional Christian conception of moral evil; yet Christianity, we have often been told, is incompatible with a tragic sense of life.

The ending of this tragedy, and, indeed, of all other Calderonian tragedies, is not that sense of exaltation – of 'triumph in defeat' – which, according to so many theorists, it should be the aim of tragic drama to excite. The human world, as Calderón presents it, is not one to arouse in us any exaltation; his view of the human predicament is not a heroic but a sad one. It is the predicament of man individualised from all other men yet in intimate solidarity with them, caught in circumstances that are the responsibility of all, whose ramifications the individual cannot see, prisoner as he is of the partial perspectives of a limited time and space, yet both the sufferer of acts that come in from outside the partial perspectives and the agent of acts that have their repercussions beyond them. From the recognition of the human predicament as consisting in the solidarity of all men in this inextricable intermingling of their actions, and therefore in their solidarity in wrongdoing, flows that sense of sadness which is the hallmark of the most typical Calderonian tragedies, and with this sadness a sense of compassion – not only pity for the wrongdoer because, although he is guilty, he is so to a large extent because others, both before him and with him, are guilty too, but also 'co-suffering' – the realisation that the solidarity in wrongdoing of each of us with the whole of humanity makes us sharers in the afflictions of human life.

If this expansion of the Aristotelian catharsis is clearly grounded in the facts of experience, and as such adds to our understanding of life, then the Spanish drama of the Golden Age has a contribution to make to the theory of tragedy and to tragic drama which should not have been for so long ignored.

It should scarcely be necessary to point out in conclusion how misguided is the contention that Spanish honour plays cannot be 'true' tragedies – as misguided as the, until recently, exclusive preoccupation of critics with the formalism of the code of honour. What, one may ask, would any man do if, like Don Juan Roca, he were to find his abducted wife in the arms of another? It would need no acquaintance with or training in Spanish seventeenth-century *pundonor* to feel, under the stress of emotion, the instinctive urge to violence. Why then say that the violence committed in these circumstances is 'in response to external imperatives'? To proceed from this to the conclusion that the experience of such a husband, since it 'results in the death of others than himself', may be 'painful' but is not 'truly tragic',[9] is to fall far short of the comprehension that Calderón possesses of the pain of human experience. Even more misguided is the following contention about these Spanish plays:

> Honour led to plays with violent endings, but these are rarely tragedies proper, because they are concerned more frequently with pointing a moral, the moral that at all costs honour is sacred, than with showing the individual at odds with fate.[10]

Need one, in the light of *El pintor de su deshonra*, insist that this is rather childish? The Calderonian tragic hero, caught in the tangled net of interrelated human actions and imprisoned in his own limited vision, is not at odds with fate in the ordinary sense of the term – he is the victim of something more profound and more tragic, the victim of the sad irony of human life itself, in which each man is compelled to construct, and act upon, his own individuality in a world where the human individual, *qua* individual, cannot exist.

Postscript

Calderón utilised the plots of a few of his *comedias* as allegories for the theological Morality plays he wrote each year for Madrid for performance on the Feast of Corpus Christi. *La vida es sueño* and *El pintor de su deshonra* are the most significant transpositions of this kind. Both these *autos* allegorise the dogmas of the Fall and Redemption of man. Segismundo becomes El Hombre (Mankind), while King Basilio is transposed into God, Who is represented through the Three Persons of the Trinity; Power, Wisdom and Love. When considering these allegorical transpositions of *comedias*, it is essential to bear in mind that what is transposed is not the *character* but the *dramatic function*. Failure to realise this has made some critics question whether Calderón was actually criticising his treatment of Segismundo, since if in Calderón's mind he represented God, this could not have been possible.[11] The transposition was, of course, only this: Basilio begat Segismundo and brought him up in prison to prevent the rebellious behaviour he had foreseen in the stars; God creates Man and places him in the 'prison' of Original Sin, after his rebellious transgression.

The question of transposition from *comedia* to *auto* becomes crucial in the case of *El pintor de su deshonra*. The metaphor is given a surprising twist. The painter does not become Mankind but God: justifiably so because in the allegory of Creation God is presented as painting the world of Nature and placing in it His finest artistic achievement, Man. The concept of Painting is analogous in both cases – the mind and the imagination in the act of creation, but whereas Don Juan cannot paint Serafina's beauty, he can and does imagine his non-existent dishonour. God's dishonour, on the other hand, is Mankind itself. It is God's finest handiwork that dishonours Him. The transposition thus turns Juan Roca from the agent into the victim (he was, of course, the victim of his own dishonour). Here the analogy between the double metaphor must stop: God is the victim but not the agent of his dishonouring. Don Juan Roca in effect disappears conceptually from the allegory. Dramatically this is rendered as follows: the world asks the painter to paint a portrait of humanity who has succumbed to temptation and is held prisoner by *El Lucero de la Noche* (the Evening Star who represents the Devil) and his confederate, *La Culpa* (Guilt or Sin). The Devil thus allegorises Alvaro. As in the *comedia*, the Painter has to paint the portrait without being seen. This he does by withdrawing behind a tree, which symbolises the Cross. When Humanity appears with her two jailers, the Painter, seeing her in the Devil's arms, fires the pistol. Humanity is restored to the Painter's favour (this symbolises the fact that Christ's Atonement for Man's Original Sin removed the Guilt but not the effects). This is one of the less successful of Calderón's theological allegories of the Atonement. There is one explicit connection with the *comedia* when the Painter says

> que es la diferencia que hay
> en los duelos de la honra
> entre Dios y el hombre, pues
> si a los dos vengarse toca,
> se venga uno cuando mata,
> pero otro cuando perdona.

(In the duels of honour the difference between Man and God is that when both have to seek vengeance, one seeks it by killing and the other by forgiving.)[12]

The date of composition and performance of the *auto* is not known, but it was probably a year or two before 1647.[13] The *comedia* would have been written a year or two previously.

17 The tragedy of honour: *El médico de su honra*

At the beginning of the previous chapter, when discussing the allegedly untragic Spanish treatment of honour we noted the opinion that 'the Spanish preoccupation with honour was a particularly unworthy motive for writing a tragedy, since it did not emphasise the injustices of life but exalted the self-righteousness of the arrogant obsession of an individual with his own reputation in the eyes of others'. The analysis of *El pintor de su deshonra* will, it is hoped, have shown how badly misunderstood the play had been if it had given rise to such a total misconception. The play now to be considered was for long the stumbling-block *par excellence* in the understanding of honour in general and of Calderón in particular. This is due in large measure to the fact that here the husband's murder of his innocent wife is due not to a passionate impulse but to a coldblooded and carefully calculated attempt to comply with one aspect of the code of honour concerning the need for vengeance. Since dishonour destroyed one's public reputation, honour could only be restored by an equally public act of vengeance: honour had not only to be restored, but to be seen to be restored. If, on the other hand, a man's dishonour was not publicly apparent, the act of vengeance had to be secret in order not to publicise what vengeance was intended to remove.[1] This requirement led dramatists to devise ingenious and sinister ways of accomplishing the act of wife-murder, as part of the dramatic demand for 'surprise' in the solution. One of the most unpleasant examples is the secret vengeance in Lope de Vega's *El castigo sin venganza* (Punishment without vengeance). The Duke of Ferrara has married a young wife for reasons of state in order to have a legitimate heir, the heir presumptive being a bastard son. The wife and her stepson are of the same age, while the duke is elderly. After his return from a military campaign, he discovers that his new wife and his son have dishonoured him. He devises the secret vengeance as follows: he gags his wife and binds her, while unconscious, to a chair, covering her with a sheet. He tells his son that he has discovered a plot against his life and that he has captured the traitor, whom he wants his son to execute. He forces his astonished and reluctant son to run the bound figure through with his sword. The son pulls off the cover and sees his stepmother. The duke shouts to his courtiers, telling them that his son has killed his stepmother because he was going to lose the dukedom when she produced a son. In fury he orders them to kill his son on the spot as a traitor and murderer. The duke is thus avenged on both the guilty parties, and the son is 'executed' for a murder he did not commit justified by a terrible calumny. This play was written in 1631. Its first performance was not followed by a second, perhaps because the duke's night-time expedition in search of amorous adventures might have been taken as reference to similar proclivities in Philip IV. It was apparently followed by Calderón's two plays in which the murder of a wife involves a cunning secret vengeance, *A secreto agravio, secreta venganza* (1635) and *El médico de su honra* (1635?). His second and more notorious tragedy of this type was performed in the Royal Palace on 10 June of the same year; it was published in the 'Second Part' of Calderón's plays in 1637. The secret vengeance devised in it was apparently drawn from an incident in real life when a husband intent on avenging himself on a secretly adulterous wife engaged a 'surgeon' to bleed her but removed the bandage so that she bled to death.[2] This incident was elaborated into a play with the title *El médico de su honra* and published in an edition dated 1633 and attributed to Lope de Vega. The attribution is now considered mistaken. This is the source of Calderón's play, in which he recast this first play, retaining the title.[3] Calderón's *médico* keeps surprisingly close to the plot of the early play, but the extraordinary thing is that it is quite a different play in its poetry, its technique, and its structured theme.[4]

As was noted earlier, where Calderón has a plot involving social conflicts between husband and wife or any other disruption affecting the honour of a woman, he is apt to place the plot against a historical background of civil war or warfare between nations (*El postrer duelo de España, No hay cosa como callar, El galán fantasma*). *El alcalde de Zalamea*, which deals with the rape of a young woman by an army officer, is placed in the invasion of Portugal by Philip II when enforcing his claim to the Portuguese succession. *A secreto agravio, secreta venganza*, which deals with intended adultery and the husband's secret vengeance, is set in the reign of King Sebastian of Portugal and closes when the husband, having secretly restored his honour, feels free to join the king's campaign against Morocco, a historical campaign from which neither the king nor any of his nobles returned alive. *El médico de su honra* is the most striking example, since the king is fully implicated both in the plot and in the civil strife.

The setting is the reign of King Peter I of Castile, the only legitimate son of Alfonso XI, who left five bastard sons of whom the eldest was Prince

Henry. Peter succeeded his father in 1350. Spanish medieval kings were given cognomens by which they are generally known. Peter was given two: *el justiciero* and *el cruel* – 'the just' and 'the cruel'. 'Just' denoted the strictness and severity with which he dispensed justice; 'cruel' denoted that he did this with the utmost severity, never tempering it with mercy. The period was marked by the struggles for power between the Crown and the feudal nobility. The bastard Henry became a permanent rival to his half-brother, finally becoming the leader in the civil war against the king. When the rival armies were encamped near each other, Henry penetrated the king's camp at night, found his way into the king's tent and, fighting in a hand-to-hand struggle, killed the king with a dagger, succeeding to the throne of Castile as Henry II in 1369. He was remembered by later generations as a fratricide and regicide, and therefore as more villainous than he had actually been. This villainy coloured the whole of this civil war in the popular mind; the numerous ballads recounting these events were known to all. Part of a ballad of this kind is actually sung in the play in mysterious circumstances. The whole of this is important for interpreting the play.

The action of the play and its antecedents are as follows. Don Gutierre and Doña Leonor are unofficially betrothed. Visiting her one day, he finds there is a strange man in the house. He will not listen to any explanation and, thinking that she is guilty of betraying him, he breaks off their relationship and departs abruptly. Leonor, feeling herself dishonoured by this behaviour, goes to the king to demand justice. He promises that he will give her justice, and restore her honourable reputation. When the king asks Gutierre to explain his rejection of Leonor, the latter replies that he believed he had good cause. Leonor defends herself and Arias, who is among the courtiers in the palace, explains to Gutierre that he was in Leonor's house on a perfectly innocent errand. Gutierre refuses to believe this, and the two men are prepared to fight it out when the king intervenes, and has them both arrested. The jailer, a relative of Gutierre's, releases him on trust for the night so that he can go home and reassure his wife.

After jilting Leonor, Gutierre had married Doña Mencía. Previously, she had been assiduously courted by Prince Enrique, King Pedro's brother. Having discovered where she now lives, he resumes his advances, and accuses her of betraying him. She explains that she was not of high enough standing for him to marry her, but she had too honourable a status to be his mistress. Enrique visits her on the evening that Gutierre was due to spend imprisoned in the palace, but when the latter returns unexpectedly, Mencía is compelled to hide Enrique in the house. In case her husband should find him, she warns that she has seen a man in the house, but Enrique escapes, dropping his dagger as he leaves. Gutierre finds the dagger and his suspicions are aroused by the coincidence of his wife's having given the alarm just as he arrived home. Next day in the palace, after the king has released him from prison, Gutierre notices that the dagger he found in his house has an ornamental hilt exactly matching the hilt of Enrique's sword. Persuaded by this and by other circumstantial evidence, he complains to the king of his brother's behaviour, and produces the dagger. He is then ordered to wait in a side-room, while the king interrogates the prince. He is angered by the prince's cynical comments on Mencía and Gutierre, and produces the dagger. As the prince takes it from him, he accidentally cuts the king's hand. The king's anger becomes fury, and in what the audience would see as a prophetic foretaste of his own death, he violently accuses his brother of trying to murder him, and departs. Enrique runs away and decides to escape from the king's anger by leaving Seville. Gutierre has heard this violent quarrel and with his suspicions of Enrique now fully aroused, he picks up the fatal dagger.

These events cover Acts I and II and the first third of Act III. With this synopsis in mind, the reader will be able to follow the structural analysis. The play is remarkable for its compact structure and concise diction; for the causal interrelation of the events. The causal structure is the key to the interpretation of the play. The pathetic Mencía is so much more human and interesting a character than the forbidding Leonor, that the plot concerning the latter used to be disregarded, until she re-emerged in a strange sort of 'triumph' at the end. But the fact that each woman has the same structural significance with each of these two plots' centring in her, and with a remarkable duplication of incidents and their circumstances, shows that each plot must carry equal weight in the theme. This double plot is developed in parallel as follows:

1 Leonor is courted by Gutierre, but he marries Mencía.

2 The Leonor–Gutierre relationship is ruptured by the appearance of another man in her house.

3 Leonor appeals to the king.

4 Leonor is made to hide and listen to Gutierre's explanation.

5 While Leonor is hiding, Arias and Gutierre quarrel and draw

1 Mencía is courted by Enrique but she marries Gutierre.

2 The Mencía–Gutierre marriage is threatened and finally ruptured by the appearance of another man in her house.

3 Gutierre appeals to the king.

4 Gutierre is made to hide and listen to Enrique's explanation.

5 While Gutierre is hiding, the king and Enrique quarrel over

their swords. This angers the king, and both men are imprisoned. the dagger. The king is frightened when this accidentally cuts him, and to avoid the king's fury the prince banishes himself.

There is one further parallel that must not be overlooked. Near the beginning of Act II Mencía, seeing a dagger in Gutierre's hand, is terror-stricken by the ominous foreboding of her death:

> Al verte así, presumía
> que ya en mi sangre bañada,
> hoy moría desangrada . . .
> Toda soy una ilusión

(Seeing you like that, I thought that, already bathed in my own blood I was dying with my blood draining away . . . I am obsessed by imaginary fears.)[5]

Near the beginning of Act III the king, seeing the same dagger in his brother's hand, is agitated by the omen of his own violent death:

> ¡O qué aprehensión insufrible!
> Bañado me vi en mi sangre;
> muerto estuve.

(Oh what an unbearable apprehension! I saw myself bathed in my own blood; I died [with fear].)

(III, 236–8) [*BAE*, I, p. 361b]

In the light of the other parallels, this doubling also indicates that the two events are linked in significance.

The two plots are therefore inseparably connected by the structure of the action; the two initial events lead to the same catastrophe: the fact that Gutierre had courted Leonor, and the fact that Enrique had courted Mencía, both lead to the latter's death. What is more, her death leads to the marriage of Leonor at the end, which the rupture of the courtship had prevented at the beginning. The importance of the causal structure in a Calderonian tragic plot needs no further emphasis. *El médico* is an excellent example of a two-plot structure, in which the two independent strands of causality merge together to produce the single action that fulfils them both. The confluence takes place as early as the beginning of Act II, when Enrique returns to Mencía's house and finds her in the garden. From this point the single action comprises development as well as climax and *dénouement*, when as a result of this visit Gutierre finds the dagger in the house. From then on the inevitability of the plot becomes oppressive. Working backwards from there, the two strands of causality are the following. First the Mencía plot: Enrique visited her because she had encouraged him to do so (A), because he had accused her of disloyalty (B). The Leonor plot provides most of the unfolding of the action in Act I: effects and causes proceed thus: Enrique visited Mencía because Gutierre was under arrest and would not be returning home, because he had fought with Arias, who had defended the honour of Leonor because Gutierre had felt compelled to impugn her honour, because the king had insisted on learning the reasons for Gutierre's refusal to marry Leonor (C), because she had complained to him to the king (D_1), because Gutierre had repudiated her (E), because he had seen another man (Arias) in her house (F, D_2).

There are five main characters, and one secondary character who contributes at the beginning to the course of events. The six capital letters in the above summary mark the initial involvement of each one as a contributory cause in the action. In every case this is an act that can be characterised as imprudent.

The disaster is precipitated by Mencía (A) and Enrique (B); the imprudence of their actions needs no new emphasis.[6] The ground had been prepared by a series of imprudent actions of which the first was entirely innocent in intention. It was perfectly natural that Arias should wish to enter Leonor's house at night to visit her guest, the lady he hoped to marry (F), but this was an *atrevimiento* (rashness) against the social standards of honour:

> Yo, amante fiel
> de su hermosura, seguí
> sus pasos, y en casa entré
> de Leonor, (atrevimiento
> de enamorado) sin ser
> parte a estorbarlo Leonor.

> (I, a faithful lover of her beauty, followed her, and entered Leonor's house (the rashness of a lover) without Leonor seeking to prevent it.)
>
> (I, 958–63) [*BAE*, I, p. 353a]

We must note the complicity of Leonor in this act (D_2) as stated by Arias: her intentions were also innocent, but it was rash for an affianced lady to permit it. Later she admits to Arias that she, not he, must take the blame for this particular act and its consequences:

> Confieso que me quitasteis
> un esposo a quien quería;
> mas quizá la suerte mía
> por ventura mejorasteis;

pues es mejor que sin vida,
sin opinión, sin honor
viva, que no sin amor,
de un marido aborrecida.
Yo tuve la culpa, yo
la pena siento; y así
sólo me quejo de mí,
y de mi estrella.

(I confess that you did take from me a husband whom I loved; but perhaps this was my good fortune; perhaps a lifeless life, without reputation and honour is better than a loveless life, hated by one's husband. I was to blame, I suffer the punishment; and therefore I complain only about myself and my luckless star.)

(II, 713–24) [*BAE*, i, p. 358a]

The fateful irony of the consequences is that she herself placed the question mark against her honour and must spend the rest of the play fighting to have it removed; and that by succeeding she brings upon herself the unhappy fate that here, in a, for her, rare moment of rationality, she knows she has fortunately avoided – that of possessing honour but being unloved by her husband.

Leonor's second and greater imprudence (D$_1$) follows from this rejection of her initial good fortune. She goes to the king among the ranks of the *pretendientes* (claimants at court), ostensibly to request the 'dowry' that will enable her to enter and live in a convent, after the social disgrace of being jilted by her betrothed. This is an unhappy decision, but in the circumstances the only prudent one, and it is right and proper to appeal to the royal bounty. But the request comes, like an afterthought, at the end of a long speech that had been prefaced by a solemn petition for justice (royal and divine) 'de parte de mi honor' ('on behalf of my honour') (I, 594–9) [*BAE*, i, p. 351a]. To her maid, as they entered the audience chamber, she had acknowledged that justice, in effect, would be vengeance if the king heard her plea.[7] Her plea therefore is a disclosure of her grievance – a breach of promise and the subsequent denial of legal redress – and at the very end comes the accusation with the naming of the offender. She acknowledges that redress is now no longer possible: 'since it is impossible for me to recover my honour, since he has married' (I, 667–8) [*BAE*, iv, p. 351b]. Hence the convent; but it is clear that this will be acceptable only as a last resort; for the time being it is merely the pretext for an impossible appeal against a court decision. Gutierre sees her action in this light:

Leonor, mal aconsejada
(que no le aconseja bien

quien destruye su opinión),
pleitos intentó poner
a mi desposorio, donde
el más riguroso juez
no halló causa contra mí,
aunque ella dice que fue
diligencia del favor.
¡Mirad vos a qué mujer
hermosa favor faltara,
si le hubiera menester!
Con este engaño pretende,
puesto que vos lo sabéis,
valerse de vos;

(Leonor, badly advised, for it was not good advice that destroyed her honour,
appealed to the court against my marriage, where even the strictest judge
found no case against me, although she claims that this was favouritism. As
if, your Majesty, a beautiful woman would lack favour if she needed it! Thus
misled she lays claim to your justice since she has informed you of this matter)
(I, 857–71) [*BAE*, i, p. 352b]

Leonor's sense of personal outrage appears trivial to us today, but
according to the standards of the age it was very comprehensible and
very human; the imprudence lies in not accepting the verdict of the
courts and in appealing to the highest judicial authority for an impossible
reparation. Her real motive is revealed in her outburst at the end of the
Act:

¡Plegue a Dios,
ingrato, aleve y cruel,
falso, engañador, fingido,
sin fe, sin Dios y sin ley,
que como inocente pierdo
mi honor, venganza me dé
el cielo!

(Thankless, treacherous and cruel, perjurer, deceiver, hypocrite, a man
without faith, without God, knowing no law, God grant that, since I am
deprived of honour, though innocent, Heaven give me vengeance.)
(I, 1007–13) [*BAE*, i, p. 353b]

This passionate desire for a vengeance beyond the law goes, of course,
beyond imprudence.

The king, in his first involvement in the action, pays no heed to the
request for a dowry and never refers to the convent. Instead, piqued at
her charge that in the courts of a kingdom ruled by *el rey justiciero* (the
just king), the poor cannot expect justice, he speaks of satisfaction for
her and of taking up her cause himself:

Señora, vuestros enojos
siento con razón, por ser
un Atlante en quien descansa
todo el peso de la ley.
Si Gutierre está casado,
no podrá satisfacer,
como decís, por entero
vuestro honor; pero yo haré
justicia como convenga
en esta parte; si bien
no os debe restituir
honor, que vos os tenéis.
Oigamos a la otra parte
disculpas suyas; que es bien
guardar el segundo oído
para quien llega después;
y fiad, Leonor, de mí,
que vuestra causa veré,
de suerte que no os obligue
a que digáis otra vez
que sois pobre, él poderoso,
siendo yo en Castilla Rey.

(Madam, I rightly sympathise with your anger, since I am Atlas on whose shoulders there rests all the weight of Law. Since Gutierre is married, he cannot, as you yourself admit, satisfy your honour completely; but I shall give you the justice that is proper in this case; although he does not owe you the restitution of an honour which you still possess. Let us hear what explanations the other party can give, for it is right to keep my second ear for the person who comes after you. Have confidence in me, Leonor, for I shall so consider your cause that you will never again be able to say that you are poor, and he powerful, while I am king in Castile.)

(I, 673–94) [*BAE*, i, p. 351b]

If it were simply an appeal against a decision of a lower court, his telling her to rely on him would be no more than a promise to re-examine her case without favouritism to the successful defendant. But since, as he states, Gutierre's marriage subsequent to his acquittal makes reversal of the decision impossible; since, in any case, her honour does not need to be restored because she has not lost it, what is the cause he is going to take up? What is the partial satisfaction he implies might be possible? A public apology? This is never mentioned, now or later. The king's imprudence lies in ignoring the practical solution (the convent) and, out of the injured pride of a *rey justiciero*, in offering the false hope of a redress that is in fact impossible.

Gutierre's initial imprudence (E) was to jump to the conclusion that

Leonor had dishonoured him and, subsequently, to nurse his affront despite exculpations that he knew to be plausible:

> Y aunque escuché
> satisfacciones, y nunca
> di a mi agravio entera fe,
> fue bastante esta aprehensión
> a no casarme; porque
> si amor y honor son pasiones
> del ánimo, a mi entender,
> quien hizo al amor ofensa,
> se le hace al honor en él;
> porque el agravio de gusto
> al alma toca tambien.

(And although satisfactory explanations were offered, and although I never fully believed in the affront, the fear of it was enough to prevent my marrying; because if, as I understood it, love and honour are passions of the spirit, if love is offended, honour is offended at the same time; because if one's senses are hurt then the mind is also affected.)

(I, 922–32) [*BAE*, I, p. 352c]

As with Leonor, there is more than imprudence here. There is a rigid pride that does not shrink from or relent at injuring the woman he loves. The initial, more or less innocent, rashness of Arias and Leonor is thus turned into an unpardonable offence. This act of injustice sets the play in motion; on it is based the marriage with Mencía. Gutierre had thought he could shrug off this act of injustice, but it rebounds to strike at his marriage, to affront his pride a second time and to make him repeat an injury to the woman he loves – this time by murdering her. His unjust repudiation of Leonor turns her into a Nemesis to which he must bow at the end, fulfilling the promise of marriage he should never have broken, but fulfilling it at the cost of a terrible injustice of a far graver kind.

The plot of *El médico* therefore has the structure of tragedy. Not only does it illustrate with a grim irony the inescapable Nemesis of an error that seeks and finds a retribution out of all proportion to the harm it originally caused, but all the characters have a collective responsibility for the disaster that overwhelms Mencía, a responsibility they share through miscalculation, imprudence or pride. They bear a collective guilt for the injustice and suffering that enter their world. This conforms to the previously detected pattern in those Calderonian tragic plots that are related to real life, as distinct from ancient history or mythology. What *El médico* adds to the other plays studied in that context is a particular technique for communicating the sense of an overriding Fate: the contrast, namely, between what the characters seek to build for themselves and what life actually builds for them. Fate is suggested here by a series of repeated situations, unsought by those involved in them; each repetition brings unforeseen consequences and makes the problems more painful and intractable than before, until the main repetition, which encircles all the others, turns 'the man in the house' from a well-meaning Arias into a dishonourable Enrique, and turns the rejection of a betrothed into the murder of a wife.

Fatality, as we have already seen, in Calderón is represented by the way accidents constantly intervene in the affairs of men, creating problems and directing events away from the ends planned as solutions to these problems. The problem of the play is created by two accidents: Gutierre happening to see Arias emerge at night from Leonor's house, and Enrique happening to fall off his horse near Gutierre's house. Four further accidents are decisive causes in the subsequent nexus of events: Gutierre is unexpectedly allowed home for the night and so returns when Enrique thought he could meet Mencía with safety; Gutierre finds the dagger; the dagger accidentally cuts the king's hand as Enrique takes it from him (this precipitates the latter's flight and breaks off the explanation of his relations with Mencía at a point where her complicity is suggested). The last fateful accident occurs when Mencía is informed that Enrique has decided to leave Seville. Her fears immediately make her think that this will confirm Gutierre's suspicions of her infidelity, so she begins a letter asking the prince not to leave the city, but at that point Gutierre appears. Her terror makes her faint. Gutierre reads what she has written, and her guilt is confirmed in his mind not by the prince's departure but by her attempt to make him desist from departing. Gutierre then hires a 'barber-surgeon' to bleed his 'sick' wife. Threatened with death by Gutierre, the surgeon is obliged to leave Mencía's wound unbound, so that she bleeds to death. He remains unaware that the blindfolded surgeon pressed the palm of his bloodstained hand against the door of the house, leaving on it the imprint of the deed.

All the acts which follow from the accidents outlined above are voluntary acts; this intermingling of volition and accident means that fate does not predetermine events but it does constantly frustrate the ends willed by men and demand unexpected decisions.

A 'tragic structure', however well planned and wrought, cannot by itself provide a tragedy. Tragic emotions are aroused by the significance of the action and by the tone in which it is presented. Irony has already been noted in the play; the supreme irony lies in the fact that the murdered wife was innocent in deed and in intention of the crime imputed to her, and that by killing her the avenging husband can never know the wrong he has done. Nor can anyone else ever know it because of the effective concealment of the truth by the 'secret vengeance'; this dissembled version of the event becomes the official one when the King accepts it. Both Leonor and the King are accomplices in the concealment. The former must obviously guess what has really happened, for her conversation with Arias in Act II had made her perfectly aware of the remedy that Gutierre is certain to apply if the situation worsens:

> [*D. Arias*]   Gutierre pudiera bien
>   decirlo, Leonor; pues quien
>   levantó tantos desvelos
>   de un hombre en la ajena casa,
>   extremos pudiera hacer
>   mayores, pues llega a ver
>   lo que en la propia le pasa.
> *Doña Leonor*   Señor don Arias, no quiero
>   escuchar lo que decís;
>   que os engañáis, o mentís.
>   Don Gutierre es caballero
>   que en todas las ocasiones,
>   con obrar, y con decir,
>   sabrá, vive Dios, cumplir
>   muy bien sus obligaciones;
>   y es hombre cuya cuchilla,
>   o cuyo consejo sabio,
>   sabrá no sufrir su agravio
>   ni a un Infante de Castilla.

> ([*D. Arias*] Gutierre could very well illustrate this [that heaven makes a jealous lover suffer when he becomes a husband]; for he who raised so many alarms about a man in somebody else's house could create even greater disturbance when he saw what was happening in his own.
> *Doña Leonor* Don Arias, I will not hear another word; either you are mistaken, or you are lying. Don Gutierre is a gentleman who on any occasion will know (in God's name!) how to fulfil his obligations either by word or by deed; and he is a man whose blade or whose wise counsel will not tolerate any affront even from a Prince of Castile.)

(II, 794–812) [BAE, I, p. 358b]

But her connivance in the cover-up is not due solely to the concern for Gutierre's good name with which she silences Arias; it is, above all, her own interests that are served by this pretence.

It depends upon the king whether he believes Gutierre's story that Mencía's death was accidental. The king knows far more about it than anybody else, for he has heard both Ludovico's account of what has actually happened, with the dying Mencía's assertion of her innocence,[8] and Coquín's account of the events leading up to her death with its virtual corroboration of this innocence. The king cannot be acting through ignorance in condoning what he himself calls a 'cruel' act.

> Gutierre sin duda es
> el cruel que anoche hizo
> una acción tan inclemente.
> No sé qué hacer; cuerdamente
> sus agravios satisfizo.

> (Gutierre, without any doubt was the cruel man who committed such a merciless act. I don't know what to do; he has satisfied his honour with prudence.)
>
> (III, 741–5) [*BAE*, i, p. 364c]

The momentary doubt is due to his concern for justice; his decision to condone the act is due to Gutierre's prudence in so skilfully covering his tracks that the king is enabled to let the question of justice drop in this particular case and fulfil, instead, his rash promise to bring justice to Leonor.

Ironically, it is a crime and not his judicial impartiality that enables the king to redeem his promise to Leonor. This he realises at once. Immediately after hearing the evidence of Ludovico and Coquín, he had said to Leonor:

> pues sois acreedor, por Dios,
> de mis honras, que yo os di
> palabra, y con gran razón,
> de que he de satisfacer
> vuestro honor; y lo he de hacer
> en la primera ocasión.

> (You are the creditor for what I owe you; I gave you my word, and very rightly, that I would satisfy your honour; and I will do so at the first opportunity.)
>
> (III, 760–5) [*BAE*, i, p. 365a]

The first opportunity has now presented itself, and *el rey justiciero* becomes an accomplice in the cover-up of justice for exactly the same reason as Gutierre and Leonor – to vindicate his honour. The irony runs deep: what made him embark on the course of action leading to this was his sense of outrage that justice was administered in his kingdom not with impartiality but with favour.

In other words, King Pedro by making his rash promise to Leonor, and she by accepting his advocacy and hoping for his justice, unwittingly established an interest in the only means by which this could be accomplished – by Mencía's death. Already by the end of Act I the catastrophe had been made inevitable. This is not to say that the king and Leonor are evil people. Like Gutierre they are upright, guided rigorously by what they understand to be moral principles; as such they are in their own way admirable people (which does not mean that in real life we should enjoy their constant company). The integrity of all three would be absolute were it not, like the moral principles of every individual human being, dependent upon self-control, which is itself dependent upon temperament. Although upright, all three are passionate, and thus, under certain conditions, liable to rashness and impetuosity. These conditions apply when their honour is involved – in other words, their integrity in the eyes of their society.

This is what makes Gutierre's conscience clear, and what makes the king and Leonor whitewash not only his conscience but their own. They can accept as justice what in reality is a travesty of it, because their society upholds the legitimacy of private vengeance for honour's sake, and the possible doubts of conscience are silenced when the individual honour of each is involved. To affirm justice by injustice, to sustain honour by creating a non-existent dishonour, to assert human values by denying them – if this is the society men have created (created precisely, as philosophers and theologians had long taught, to enable human nature to attain to its perfection), if this is the society upright men believe in, then all are trapped in a tragic situation, not the tragic heroine alone. Though Fate exacts a single victim, it is not really possible to speak of a tragic protagonist; all the characters are 'agonists'; there is a direct community-involvement in a tragic situation: it is humanity itself that is inescapably trapped.

The king is the symbol of this society: he is both Pedro *el justiciero* and Pedro *el cruel*. It is clearly incorrect to apply the epithet 'cruel' to Calderón's Rey don Pedro in a literal sense; he neither inflicts pain nor enjoys seeing others suffer. At the same time it is equally incorrect to think that Calderón completely disregards the traditional *cruel* to emphasise only the *justiciero*. His king is 'cruel' because he is rigorous and over-severe in his attitude to his subjects, as countless incidents and references make clear.[9] His personal honour as king is involved in this appearance of unbending sternness; hence his confidence, to be noted later, that nothing will make him laugh. The society he governs is one which demands a stern, unswerving loyalty to moral duty inflexibly conceived.

The three people who at the end of the play represent this society with its restored honour are, in their own way, good people for whom we should not abandon all sympathy. Each has been placed in a real dilemma in which each has wanted to do the right thing; but none is as perfect as he thinks he is, and none has been able clearly to separate the cause of justice from the cause of self-interest. All therefore have adhered rigidly to a system of social values that has enabled them to keep their consciences clear in obeying the law of duty while in practice violation of the law of love is clinched in the marriage that fittingly but grimly brings the play to an end. This is brought about as follows.

On the night of Mencía's murder the king, as *justiciero*, leaves his palace to do the rounds of the streets to see for himself that all the citizens are law-abiding. As he emerges from the palace, he hears the following sung:

> Para Consuegra camina,
> donde piensa que han de ser
> teatros de mil tragedias
> las montañas de Montiel.

> (He journeys towards Consuegra, where he thinks that the mountains of Montiel are to be the theatres for a thousand tragedies.)
>
> (III, 586–9) [*BAE*, I, p. 363c]

These four lines, as everyone in the audience would know, recall the old ballads recording the life of Peter the Cruel, Montiel being the place where he was to die at the hands of his half-brother. Furious at the singing of this song, he gives chase, but does not catch the singer. Instead, he meets with Ludovico, the barber-surgeon, from whose story he guesses that Mencía has been killed. He then meets Coquín, Gutierre's servant, from whom he hears more evidence to this effect. Proceeding to investigate for himself, the king reaches Don Gutierre's house at the moment when Leonor and her maid are passing. In typical Calderonian fashion, the three main characters of the drama are brought together for the action and theme to be clinched. First he encounters Leonor and reminds her of his promise to restore her honour. Cries are heard from within Gutierre's house, and the latter rushes out to disclose the 'terrible accident' that has happened to Mencía. On hearing Gutierre's story the king in an aside calls it an extraordinary event, one in which he now has to show his own prudence (i.e. by accepting Gutierre's cover-up and so to avoid greater scandal by effecting the reconciliation between Gutierre and Leonor). He says to Gutierre 'Give Leonor your hand' (in marriage), and retorts to the objections of the astounded Gutierre: 'this must be so, no more.' Again Gutierre objects, and receives the reply 'Your king commands it.' But Gutierre persists in declining another marriage, recalling to the king how Prince Enrique had been in his house, and the various stages by which his suspicions had mounted until he had found a letter from his wife asking the prince not to depart from Seville. What should he do if that situation were to recur?

Rey	Para todo habrá remedio.
Don Gutierre	¿Posible es que a esto le haya?
Rey	Sí, Gutierre.
Don Gutierre	¿Cuál, señor?
Rey	Uno vuestro.
Don Gutierre	¿Qué es?
Rey	Sangrarla.
Don Gutierre	¿Qué decís?
Rey	Que hagáis borrar
	las puertas de vuestra casa;
	que hay mano sangrienta en ellas.
Don Gutierre	Los que de un oficio tratan,
	ponen, señor, a las puertas
	un escudo de sus armas;
	trato en honor, y así pongo
	mi mano en sangre bañada
	a la puerta; que el honor
	con sangre, señor, se lava.
Rey	Dádsela, pues, a Leonor;
	que yo sé que su alabanza
	la merece.
Don Gutierre	Sí la doy.
	Mas mira que va bañada
	en sangre, Leonor.
Doña Leonor	No importa;
	que no me admira ni espanta.
Don Gutierre	Mira que médico he sido
	de mi honra: no está olvidada
	la ciencia.
Doña Leonor	Cura con ella
	mi vida, en estando mala.
Don Gutierre	Pues con esa condición
	te la doy.

(King	There is a cure for everything.
Gutierre	Is it possible there can be one for this?
King	Yes, Gutierre.
Gutierre	Which, Sire?
King	Your own cure.
Gutierre	What is it?
King	Bleed her.
Gutierre	What are you saying?
King	That you clean the doors of your house; for there is a bloody hand on it.

Gutierre Those who exercise a profession put, Sire, a coat of arms on their doors; I deal in honour, therefore I put on the door the mark of my hand bathed in blood; honour, Sire, is cleansed by blood.

King Give your hand, then, to Leonor; for I know she is praiseworthy and deserves it.

Gutierre Yes, I will give it. But see, Leonor, that it goes to you stained with blood.

Leonor That does not matter; for it neither astonishes nor frightens me.

Gutierre Note that I have been the surgeon of my honour: and I have not forgotten this science.

Leonor Cure my life with that science, should I fall ill.

Gutierre I give you my hand on that condition.)(III, 878–903) [*BAe*, I, p. 365c]

This is a remarkably impressive exchange between the three agents of and connivers at the cover-up to a murder. For long this was read as a grossly shocking defence of murder for honour's sake, even the murder of an innocent wife. It is hard to believe nowadays that it was possible to take at their face-value the words used by each of the three persons, and to have assumed that the king's command to Gutierre to marry Leonor should have been unquestionably taken as a sign of Calderón's own approval of the murder, with no realisation of the distinction that must be made between a dramatist 'speaking in person' and 'speaking in character' – it is the king who approves of the murder because it enables him to fulfil his rash promise while upholding the appearance of justice. The other two characters also approve of the murder. But what sort of human beings are they, and what are their real motives?

The new bridegroom has killed a wife he loved; the new bride had earlier voiced the passionate desire to kill the man she professed to love, and had cursed him.[10] This curse at the end of Act I is fulfilled at the end of the play, literally in Gutierre's having witnessed his own dishonour, metaphorically in his seeing himself stained with his own blood, which is that of his wife, the two being one flesh. This bloody hand he offers in marriage and his new bride accepts. Justice has been achieved through the stain of blood on the door of her new home. The murder of Mencía had been presented between two prophetic announcements of the King's own death at the hands of his brother, being thus placed on the same level as civil war and regicide, the gravest form of treason.[11] The husband's murder of his wife is an act of treason to the values of life, love and fidelity. The evils of individual human relations are one with the major evils that afflict the political commonwealth.

Though the play is very compact, each of the main characters is delineated with unmistakable clarity. In this hard world ruled by the pride of individual honour, Mencía and Coquín are the only human characters. Mencía is an upright and reasonable woman; faced with the agonising problem of the return of the man she had once loved when she is now married to another, she faces up to her problem rationally and humanly. Instead of stridently dismissing the prince from her house as Leonor would have done, she argues with him sensibly, pointing out that she had no other choice, and that if the prince will return to discuss the matter further she will be able to prove to him that she was right to get married. Unwittingly her reasonableness is what persuades the prince to return; she is thus sealing her own fate. If there is a character who may be considered Calderón's mouthpiece it is Coquín – not the only time, as we have seen, that a *gracioso* has this function.

The common charge that Calderón nowhere condemns Gutierre's action implies that we must accept the king's approval since there is no-one else in the play to act as Calderón's mouthpiece and tell us otherwise. The point, of course, is that the whole play condemns the murder by every detail of its structure, and Calderón wrote the play. Nonetheless, there is one character who stands outside the society of the play and serves as an explicit and implicit critic of its standards. The essentials have already been said about Coquín, but some additional points may be added.

In his first encounter with the king. Coquín's fear that he may be hurled out of the window is due not only to the latter's reputation for severity but also to his realisation that the king can never need his services:

> *Coquín* teniendo un oficio yo
> que vos no habéis menester.
> *Rey* ¿Qué oficio tenéis? . . .
> *Coquín* Soy cofrade del contento;
> el pesar no sé quién es,
> ni aun para servirle; en fin,
> soy, aquí donde me veis,
> mayordomo de la risa,
> gentilhombre del placer,
> y camarero del gusto,
> pues que me visto con él.
> Y por ser esto, he temido
> el darme aquí a conocer;
> porque un rey que no se ríe,
> temo que me libre cien
> esportillas batanadas,
> con pespuntes al envés,
> por vagamundo.

> (*King* What is your trade?
> *Coquín* I belong to the confraternity of happiness, I don't know who Gloom is,

and would not even be his servant; in short, as I stand here, I am the majordomo of Laughter, gentleman in waiting of Happiness, and the valet of Pleasure, since he dresses me. And because I am all this, I have been afraid to let myself be known here; because I fear that a king who doesn't laugh will let fall on me a hundred blows on my back to drive me out of town as a vagabond.)

(I, 739–69) [*BAE*, I, p. 351c][12]

These are two contrasting worlds, that of merriment and laughter and that of severity and inflexible honour. The opposite of cheerfulness and laughter is pain and tears. This, apart from the sidelight offered on the temperament and character of the king, is the main point of the wager.

Rey ¿Hacer reír profesáis?
Coquín Es verdad.
Rey   Pues cada vez
que me hiciéredes reír,
cien escudos os daré;
y si no me hubiéreis hecho
reír en término de un mes,
os han de sacar los dientes.
Coquín Testigo falso me hacéis,
y es ilícito contrato
de inorme lesión.
Rey   ¿Por qué?
Coquín Porque quedaré lisiado
si le aceto; ¿no se ve?
Dicen, cuando uno se ríe,
que enseña los dientes; pues
enseñarlos yo llorando
será reírme al revés.
Dicen que sois tan severo,
que a todos dientes hacéis;
¿qué os hice yo, que a mí sólo
deshacérmelos queréis?

(*King* Do you profess to make people laugh?
Coquín That's true.
King   Well then; every time you make me laugh, I'll give you a hundred escudos; and if you haven't made me laugh at the end of a month, I shall have your teeth pulled out.
Coquín You're making me a false witness, because this is an illegal and enormously injurious contract.
King   Why?
Coquín Because I shall be wounded if I accept. Can't you see that? When someone laughs, they say 'he shows his teeth'; therefore, if I show my teeth weeping I shall be laughing 'inside out'. Men say that you are so

severe that you bare your teeth to everybody; what have I done to
you, that you want to smash my teeth and mine only?)

(I, 777–96) [*BAE*, I, p. 352a]

Teeth are shown in three ways: in laughter, in tears, and in aggressive
anger, *mostrando dientes* being defined in the *Tesoro de la lengua castellana*
(1611) of Covarrubias as 'baring one's teeth, as a dog does when about to
attack another'. The king's baring of his teeth can invert Coquín's
laughter into tears. The point of this is driven home when Coquín,
rushing to the king with the news that Mencía is in mortal danger, says:
'for I want to make you cry, since I cannot make you laugh'. (III, 688–9)
[*BAE*, I, p.364b]. When the king realises that there may still be time to
save Mencía, he asks Coquín how he can repay him for this act of mercy.
Coquín replies 'by freeing me from the wager about my teeth'. 'This is no
time for laughter,' retorts the king. ' ¿Cuándo lo fué?' asks Coquín. 'When
was there ever a time for laughter?' is the jester's bitter rejoinder.

The incompatibility of Coquín's world with the stern, rigid rule of
honour is driven home when he suggests to Gutierre that, rather than
return to imprisonment and face possible execution at the King's
command, they should break parole. Gutierre is naturally horrified at
such a dishonourable suggestion, but Coquín's reply puts honour into
the perspective of common sense:

Coquín	Señor, yo llego a dudar
	(que soy más desconfiado)
	de la condición del Rey;
	y así, el honor de esa ley
	no se entiende en el criado;
	y hoy estoy determinado
	a dejarte y no volver.
Don Gutierre	¿Dejarme tú?
Coquín	¿Qué he de hacer?
Don Gutierre	¿Y de ti, qué han de decir?
Coquín	¿Y heme de dejar morir
	por sólo bien parecer?
	Si el morir, señor, tuviera
	descarte o enmienda alguna,
	cosa que de dos la una
	un hombre hacerla pudiera,
	yo probara la primera
	por servirte; ¿mas no ves
	que rifa la vida es?
	Entro en ella, vengo, y tomo
	cartas, y piérdola: ¿cómo
	me desquitaré después?

Perdida se quedará,
si la pierdo por tu engaño,
hasta, hasta ciento y un año.

(*Coquín*   Sir, because I am more mistrustful I have come to doubt the king's
temper; therefore the 'honour' of that law is not to be understood of
the servant; now I have decided to leave you and never to return.

Gutierre   You? Leave me?

Coquín   What else am I to do?

Gutierre   And what will people then say of you?

Coquín   And am I to let myself be killed only for appearance's sake? If death
won't permit a discard or any other way of avoiding it, so that with
two choices a player could make one, I would try the first in order to
do my duty by you; but do you not see that life is a gamble? I enter on
life, I arrive here, I take a card, and I lose: how can I put matters right
afterwards? If I lose my life because you have misled me, it will
remain lost for a hundred and one years.)

(II, 250–73) [*BAE*, I, p. 355a]

Why sacrifice life for reputation? If one gambles on one's life and loses,
there is no second chance. Mencía's life is the one that is lost in the play;
Gutierre does in fact gamble it away with a single stake 'por sólo bien
parecer' (only for appearance's sake). This discussion is abruptly cut
short by the return of the agitated Mencía, and Gutierre makes no reply.
We are left with the sight of her distress and with Coquín's question
ringing in our ears. It is for us to answer. Is honour to one's pledged word
absolute, so that one must proudly choose death rather than dishonour?
Or does the preservation of one's life annul this obligation? Can one really
break a solemn promise?[13] As Calderón presents it, on the one hand there
is extremist, joyless obedience to moral duty at whatever cost to self or
others; on the other hand there is a cheerful, happy life of laughter and
good sense. In whatever direction the reader may feel himself inclined by
the play, there is no doubt that Coquín is allied with Mencía against
Gutierre and the king.[14] Calderón allows him his say, and it is an explicit
counterpart to the official supremacy of honour.[15]

The code of honour is the specific example for the period in which the
play was written – a heightened dramatic example – of the tragedy
inherent in the universal human situation: that men striving after good
do evil, that they construct systems of values in which they are deceived
by the face of righteousness, since this can be the mask worn by evil. The
Spanish 'formalisation' of honour is part of the natural human instinct to
view all one's actions in the best possible light. When this is borne in
upon us we should be filled with pity, horror and fear – pity for the

victims, but also for the proud possessors of clear consciences; horror at the lengths to which human self-righteousness can go; fear for the part each one of us can play in unwittingly fomenting the wrongs that mankind commits and suffers. This, I maintain, is a 'tragic sense of life' whose truthfulness to experience we all can see. In order to devise a dramatic form with which to express it, Calderón had to go beyond his age's neo-Aristotelian conception of tragedy; we should recognise with what originality, subtlety and technical skill he did this. *El médico de su honra*, I would hold, has a more subtle tragic plot than *Othello*. Shakespeare's Moor does the same thing as Don Gutierre Alfonso Solís: he kills an innocent wife in the belief that she is guilty and that he is performing an act of justice. But Othello is the victim of villainy (a villainy not easy to account for), and the villain can be caught and made to confess. The greater subtlety of Calderón's plot is that there is no villainy in it, no conscious, deliberate malice. Nonetheless, evil is committed and condoned in fulfilment of their moral duty by men and women blind to the tragic situation in which they are communally enmeshed.

Othello is a great poetic tragedy because it is said that jealousy is a human passion. *El médico de su honra* was denied the status of poetic tragedy, because the husband kills his wife not out of the passion of jealousy but out of cold calculation. Wilson, in a close analysis of the motives and reactions of all the characters in *Othello*, has shown, with great clarity, that they are identical in kind, if not in degree, with the motives that are explicitly based on honour in *El médico de su honra*.[16] Othello's sense of honour is played upon by Iago and his honour is Othello's justification for killing Desdemona. The conception of honour and the passion it arouses is the same in both plays, though expressed in different forms. Wilson shows that it is erroneous to say that Othello is motivated by the passion of jealousy while Gutierre is moved by the inhuman logic of honour, for this overlooks the fundamental distinction between jealousy for love and jealousy of one's reputation. The former is inability to bear the intolerable burden of allowing the woman one loves to share herself with another man; the latter is due to the equally intolerable burden of having to bear the social disgrace and ostracism of cuckoldry. The latter is just as human, just as real, and just as tragic in its effects as the former.

A further objection to accepting *El médico* as a tragedy is that the tension remains unbroken at the end: there is no 'recognition', calming of emotion, or reconciliation. This departure from the tragic norm is inevitable in this particular case. If the aim of the play is to arouse horror and fear at the authoritarian principle of honour, the audience, conditioned to accept the principle, have to be left unhappy and uneasy. If the tragedy is in effect a criticism of their society, the play must close with a big question mark. Any tranquillisation of emotion would restore the complacency that it is the aim of the play to shatter, or at least to crack. The tragic effect much greater if the audience recognises the truth while the stage characters continue in their blindness.[17]

That tragedies were almost non-existent in Golden Age Spain and the corollary that the genre was virtually impossible in that particular ethos were judgements that followed from certain prejudices, which literally 'prejudged' the conclusions. One was a purely arbitrary definition of Tragedy not arrived at from the plays themselves; the other appeared to be an argument that Spanish plays had to have particular meanings that followed from what was assumed to be the ethos of the age.

A convenient formulation of the prior definition is to be found in Clifford Leech's *Tragedy.*[18] Its kernel is this: 'tragedy, which implies surely, for us in the last two centuries, an exposition of man's powerlessness in his cosmic setting.' Referring to Sidney's definition of Tragedy, he states that it contains elements that seem 'to run counter to our modern conception of tragedy'. The same elements are expounded by Racine in his preface to *Phèdre*, and Leech commented: 'Nevertheless, Racine wrote tragedy in spite of his theory.' Naturally, the literary theory behind a great writer's work will rarely be as significant as the work itself; nonetheless, for Racine, there was no disconformity between his theory and his practice, and the latter exemplified the former. Leech liked the one and dismissed the other: all through western literature every play that does not conform 'to our modern conception of tragedy' was removed from the genre, and very little was left.

This conception of tragedy has followed from a changed philosophical approach, from the emergence of a 'tragic sense of life' (in Hegel, Kierkegaard, Nietzsche, etc.). This implied, briefly, 'that our situation is necessarily tragic, that all men exist in an evil situation and, if they are aware, are anguished because they are aware.' 'So new is all this,' continued Leech, 'that we can say that the concept of tragedy, as it is now generally understood, is a creation of the last two centuries . . .' He was aware of the danger of setting up a narrow, exclusivist definition of a genre ('the preoccupation with Kind – an enforced preoccupation in this present book – can exercise an inhibiting and debilitating influence on our concern with the nature of the individual work'), but this caution did not prevent the conclusion that before 'the beginning of a philosophical concern with tragedy in the nineteenth century' there were 'many people who wrote what they called tragedies,'' but that only since then can 'a sense of what a writer is doing when he undertakes what we agree to call a "tragedy" . . . sharpen the impact of the individual work.'[19]

What *they* call tragedies; what *we* agree to call tragedies . . . 'We' are the privileged heirs of an agnostic world-view, disbelievers in any providential pattern. In fact, however, there is no 'agreement' even among 'us', for there are those who are opposed in principle to this exclusivism. Two examples may suffice of a contrary, less dogmatic, more rational and historical approach.

The first is Walter Kerr:

> the critic will acknowledge that a form called tragedy does, or did, exist, he will have the particular plays which accord with his definition of it, and he will accept the consequences of his definition by being candid about what he must reject. In making his rejections, he is generally careful to point out that he is not calling the abandoned plays bad ones. They remain good and interesting plays, to be placed in categories which may be called failed tragedies, or paratragedies, or perhaps metaplays. They are excluded only from the tragic heartland.
>
> But the exclusions are too many to leave the heartland vitally populated . . . I would rather lose a definition than a tragedy. Put to it, I would rather attempt to construct a theory of tragedy by beginning with the outposts of tragedy – throwing a girdle wide enough to encompass the most difficult, the most bizarre, the most intractable of plays – than by striving mightily to drive a stake through its heart. I would rather circle the city walls, staring up at those watchtowers which face toward the desert – *The Bacchae*, *Prometheus*, *The Suppliants*, *King Lear* – than lay claim to knowing the city from an inspection of the shrine at its hub. I do not think we can say that we have described a form if we have admittedly failed to embrace it in all its existential fullness.[20]

As well as the evidence of literature we have the evidence of experience. Geoffrey Brereton, before examining dramatic theory, philosophy or theology, starts by analysing the meaning of 'tragic' as applied in everyday life.

> We have tried to confine ourselves to normal and spontaneous usage and to carry the analysis of what lies beneath it no further than any unspecialised mind can do after a little reflection. By this means we have discerned what appears to be commonly accepted as the principal conditions of a 'tragic' happening. They can be summarised in a few lines:
>
> A tragedy is a final and impressive disaster due to an unforeseen or unrealised failure involving people who command respect and sympathy. It often entails an ironical change of fortune and usually conveys a strong impression of waste. It is always accompanied by misery and emotional distress.
>
> The last sentence is self-evident, and could be dispensed with for that

reason. The middle sentence contains its own reservations, 'often' and 'usually'. The first sentence is basic, and is put forward as the essential definition.[21]

Tested against dramatic theory and practice, this comprehensive definition is found to achieve Brereton's purpose of including, when discussion is confined to essentials, the 'factors common at least to Sophocles, Shakespeare, Racine, and probably Ibsen and others irrespective of the difference in their historical and ethical backgrounds.' It is comprehensive enough to admit any play to be studied for the specific tragic emotion peculiar to it without *a priori* rejection from the genus. It should be wide enough to encompass, as Kerr puts it, the most difficult and intractable of plays; to make it possible, in other words, to look at Calderón's most problematic play free of the prejudgement concerning the essentially anti-tragic nature of Spanish honour plays; free, that is, to look upon Serafina's and Mencía's murders as 'a final and impressive disaster due to an unforeseen or unrealised failure involving people who command respect and sympathy.'

If, despite the evidence of *El pintor* and *El médico*, this broad definition is not accepted and the narrower 'modern' one is dogmatically re-affirmed, then those of us who admire these plays' spare, taut but complex structure, who are deeply moved by their relentless march to catastrophe and who are left disconsolate by their vision of the human world, will agree with Walter Kerr and would rather lose the definition than these particular tragedies.

IV The tensions of public life

18 The king as centre of political life

It is a special feature of Spanish Golden Age plays from Lope de Vega's time that kings are frequently present, being either referred to or presented on the stage, especially after dramatic writing and performances became centralised in Madrid. The capital city was always referred to as *la corte*. This usage stemmed from the Middle Ages when the 'capital' moved around with the king and his government, being always where his court happened to be at any particular time. The characters in plays are always 'arriving at the Court' or 'leaving the Court', or discussing the latest customs and fashions of 'the Court'.

This traditional use of the term represented a reality of which the inhabitants were very conscious, for the life of Madrid revolved round the actual palace in which the king resided. The presence of a king in a play, whether seen or just felt, was a strong sense of authority (of law and order, as we say nowadays) with all the connotations of justice and the moral law. Philip II had prided himself on being accessible to any of his subjects. With the expansion of bureaucratic government this had ceased to be the case in Calderón's time, but in the drama kings are at hand to hear complaints, to pass judgement, and to right wrongs.

This 'presence' of the monarch meant that there was always a standard to be appealed to. Apart from actual infringements of the law, kings in Golden Age plays are the source of rewards and favours, or of the various ways patronage could be exercised or property and income entailed. In *El médico de su honra*, as has been seen, King Peter the Cruel is not only involved in adjudicating between the private complaints of the characters, he even goes the rounds of the streets at night in order to satisfy himself that his subjects are law-abiding. In the plays of Lope de Vega and Tirso de Molina, kings were not always beyond reproach, either in their political or private lives, but when Calderón began to write it was becoming difficult to suggest that a monarch could be guilty of unjust or immoral actions. Plays requiring such a monarch, one who would openly wrong one of the subjects, had either to be set in antiquity or in medieval times, for the Middle Ages were not short of kings with sullied reputations; or else placed in distant lands like Poland or Muscovy, or, of course, in purely fanciful kingdoms.

The concept of a 'good king' was based on the way he administered justice, or on the morality of his private life. The numerous treatises on ideal kingship dealt not with practical political theory but rather with the ways in which the king's private life should follow the example of Christ. In the drama, a king of immoral life represented a danger to the community in that any of his subjects might find himself suddenly disgraced. Favourites had risen or fallen throughout history and they rose or fell on the stage. The decline of objective justice into subjective tyranny is perhaps the way in which plays come nearest to dealing with political life.

Naturally enough, politics must, in order to be dramatic, deal with royal power as it affects individuals rather than classes or economic issues. One of Calderón's earliest plays is 'political' in this sense and in a very Calderonian way. This is *Saber del mal y del bien* (To know Evil and Good), which was performed at Court on 28 March 1628 (coming very shortly after *La cisma de Ingalaterra*, another 'political' play which will be analysed in this section); but that it was also performed in a public theatre can be inferred from the customary reference to the play made by the *gracioso* at the end.[1] *Saber del mal y del bien* is a good play, and one which presents the tensions of public life as Calderón saw them. The play is set in the reign of Alfonso VII, known as 'the Emperor'. He was crowned King of León and Castile in 1126, and established his overlordship of most of the Northern Iberian states and kingdoms, hence his cognomen. The play deals with the friendship of two noblemen, one Portuguese (Don Álvaro de Viseo) and the other Castilian (Count Pedro de Lara, the name of one of the great families of León). Don Álvaro had fallen into disgrace with his sovereign through the calumny of his enemies, and journeying in utter penury to Castile is attacked and wounded by the king's huntsmen because he had taken a piece of bread given to one of their hounds. King Alfonso takes pity on him and orders Count Pedro, his favourite, or chief minister, to care for him. The two strike up a firm friendship. The count has a sister, Hipólita, whom the king is courting, although she does not respond. She is paired dramatically with another lady, her friend Doña Laura.

At this early stage of his career Calderón is already developing a parallelistic structure. In addition to the two male friends and the two female friends, there are two courtiers who are responsible for the coming downfall of Don Pedro. Further, there are two servants, Julio and García (the latter illustrating the theme on a comic level). These pairs are the main participants in the action, but the balancing of the actors on the stage is completed by two other male characters who are servants, and two female characters, one a lady, and the other servant to Doña Hipólita. Above this whole group stands the king. He and his power are represented in the verse by images of the sun and its light, which can be obscured by clouds, whereupon darkness reigns. The main characters respond to and develop the intrigue, but it is the king who manipulates it for his own purposes.

Count Pedro is aware of the ill-will towards him of a faction at the court and therefore of his potential downfall. This is what attracts him to Don Álvaro when the king takes pity on him and has him brought into the court, because his history up to now is a warning of the fate which may befall him. The one man is a foil to the other: when one falls, the other rises. This 'political' intrigue is paralleled by the amatory intrigue, for Hipólita falls in love with Don Álvaro, who thus finds himself in rivalry with the king, and so faced with disgrace like his friend the count. At the same time Álvaro has also attracted Laura, which means that these two women friends become rivals. Álvaro, for his part, feels gratitude towards Laura because she had helped him to win favour in his new court; he therefore shows special attention to her although Hipólita has already won his heart. The jealousy of Hipólita is aroused and she falsely tells Laura that Álvaro has been ordered by the king to court her, Laura, in order to find out whether she, Hipólita, will respond to the king's advances. This makes Laura angrily disregard Álvaro's courteous attentions, and he now finds that while he is in favour with the king he is in disgrace with the ladies. Bewildered by the fact that they favoured him while he was poor and wretched and now reject him when he is wealthy and a courtier, he can only conclude that life is nothing but confusion, if happiness and unhappiness are the two faces of the same coin. Described in this way, this intrigue seems conventionally silly, but it is so constructed that it illustrates the main theme of the play, that the reversals of fortune follow directly from the king and the effect his service has upon his courtiers. He is, directly or indirectly, at the heart of every problem, and Fate in the form of Accident adds further turns of the screw.

Álvaro and Pedro have exchanged servants so that third parties become confused by their identities and (for perfectly understandable reasons), one is given a jewel intended as a reward for the other, while the other is slashed in the face with a dagger as a punishment intended for someone else. The servants now find life as confusing as Don Álvaro does. The one who is undeservedly punished concludes that when one changes one's lot it is to no purpose, for the man who has been miserable can never be sure that his good fortune will last. Fortune is fickle, and life has no discernible purpose.

The plot develops in the rest of Act II. Iñigo and Ordoño forge the count's handwriting and show the king a letter purporting to reveal that the count is planning treason. The count in vain pleads his innocence and is disgraced. Álvaro advises him to leave court, saying that he will stay behind to clear his friend's name. Don Álvaro has fallen and risen; the count has risen and fallen: and Act II closes as both men recognise that they have known good and evil in equal measure. All this has happened because the frowns and anger of kings are capricious and can bear no relation to justice. The two friends realise that

> los enojos de un Rey
> son cometas cuyos giros
> anuncios son de sucesos
> adversos; por eso huidlos,
> pues no se examinan culpas,
> si se ejecutan castigos.

(The displeasure of a king is a comet, whose revolutions are harbingers of adversity; flee it, therefore, because punishment is meted out without guilt being established.)[2]

The king confides to Álvaro that he does not believe the count to be guilty, but is using his disgrace to blackmail Hipólita: her brother's restoration to favour or his death depends upon her yielding or refusing to yield to the king's wishes. Álvaro is ordered to give Hipólita this message while the king hides himself to hear the answer. Álvaro protests, but finally yields because loyalty to king must come before loyalty to a friend. A despotic king can therefore force a man to 'know evil' not just by suffering it but by committing it. In the event, this does not actually happen because instead of the expected arrival of Hipólita, it is the count who comes in all eagerness to see his friend. Álvaro is so taken aback that he cannot speak to the count; he mumbles disjointed phrases and departs without an explanation, whereupon the count, thinking his friend is abandoning him, laments in a soliloquy the pass to which calumny has brought him. The king overhears this, instead of the message he wanted delivered to Hipólita. The contrary effect is produced because the king is now convinced of the count's innocence, and leaves his hiding-place without waiting for Hipólita's arrival. The situation of king and count is now reversed: the count is not anxious to see his sister, and hides from her in the place where the king had been, overhearing Álvaro deliver the king's message to his sister. He hears Hipólita say that her brother's life cannot be purchased at the cost of her dishonour, but at the same time he is angry with Álvaro for betraying him. He then proceeds to denounce him to the king. What had been making for tragedy now turns into a happy ending, for the king, having been impressed by the answer Hipólita gave to his message, has decided to renounce his pretensions. He restores the deserving to favour and punishes the undeserving; Álvaro's actions are explained, and the king gives him Hipólita in marriage. To complete the symmetry of reconciliation the count offers his hand to Laura, so that the two women friends are reconciled as well as the two men friends.

Thus the theme of the play is the confusion that besets life in the world because of the constant reversal of fortune. Nothing is as it seems. A favourite appears to be a traitor, a lover appears to be pleading another man's cause to his lady, all ties between human beings appear to be unstable; nothing happens as expected and planning ahead becomes impossible. Perplexity and confusion are the law of life, and the plot is skilfully contrived to present this constant uncertainty. The *gracioso* proves this confusion of life on the comic level: whenever he thinks his situation is being bettered, it turns out to be worsened. The innocent are struck down and the guilty are rewarded for one reason only: the arbitrary will of an all-powerful king who need consult no law other than that of his own desires and inclinations. He compels a man to act dishonourably because he can count on his obedience; he expects to barter a man's life in order to subdue his sister to his will. The pursuit of a monarch's private interests instead of the public defence of honour and justice makes for uncertainty and disorder. The play would have been a better one if this disorder had been allowed to work itself out in a way that brought tragedy to the subjects and moral disgrace to the king, but such a play could scarcely have been performed at court. A happy ending could serve as a mild warning, a tragic ending might have been construed as an invitation to subversion. Calderón does give a political message, but he is more concerned to meditate on the social effects of 'the knowledge of good and evil' and above all to give this meditation on the reversals of fortune a symmetrical dramatic plan with a striking interplay of coincidences and accidents in constantly confusing the results of good and evil in human intentions and actions.

Only with this kind of fiction could the inner life of *la corte* be presented to the people who lived directly under its lights and shadows. It is typical of Calderón that he requires more than an appropriate fiction to establish the point about the absolute will of a reigning monarch; he needs a 'philosophical' concept of life through which to universalise the particular life of *la corte*. The application of dramatic plots to the realities of public life had become clearly established by the end of Calderón's life. In his survey of the drama in the age of Calderón, Francisco Bances Candamo had written that a dramatist should aim at showing on the stage *historias* ('histories' or 'stories') that represent the king's problems in action in such a way that the king can work out the problems and the solutions for himself. Such plays, continues Bances, are didactic, but in a special way, developing the subtle art of *decir sin decir* ('to speak without telling'): 'Plays for sovereigns are living stories, which without speaking directly to them must instruct them so respectfully that it should be their own reason that takes heed of what they see, and not the dramatist who explains it. Who can doubt that great art is needed for this speaking without telling?'[3]

It is possible, indeed probable, that though *Saber del mal y del bien* develops a 'philosophy' of life in *la corte* within a 'political' fiction, it nonetheless could have had in general terms an application to contemporary events. While the uncertainty of life is the theme of the play, its fictional plot is one that was often treated in the literature of this period, the rise and fall of royal favourites. The great exemplar in Spanish history was Don Álvaro de Luna, all-powerful favourite of John II of Castile (1406–54), who was publicly executed in 1453. His career was dramatised by Mira de Amescua (born between 1574 and 1577, died 1644) in *La próspera y la adversa fortuna de Don Álvaro de Luna* (The Rise and Fall of Don Álvaro de Luna). Calderón's treatment in 1628 of the same reversal of fortune followed a sensational example. The death of Philip II in 1598 ushered in a century of government by royal favourites or chief ministers. The favourite of Philip III was the Duke of Lerma, who amassed a vast fortune during his rule; he also appointed favourites of his own who likewise enriched themselves. On Philip III's death in 1621 Count (later Count-Duke) Olivares became the chief minister of the sixteen-year-old Philip IV. So great had been the decline of Spain under Lerma and so scandalous the corruption, that Olivares began a campaign of reform. Lerma was dismissed from office in 1618 as a result of a palace revolution led by his own son, the Duke of Uceda, who succeeded him in office and fell himself on the rise of Olivares. Both the fallen favourites, father and son, had parts of their ill-gotten gains confiscated. The origins of all the fortunes made under Lerma were investigated but proved so difficult to determine that the investigation was finally dropped. The most sensational fall of a powerful public figure was that of Rodrigo Calderón (unrelated to the dramatist), who was arrested in 1619 and brought to trial for corruption. He was sentenced and publicly executed.

These three reversals of fortune are the historical context for Calderón's choice of theme in *Saber del mal y del bien*. The fact that the *dénouement* illustrates the reversal from evil to good may well be due to the public optimism engendered by Olivares' campaign for reform. It would have been too early in 1627/28 to suggest the continued decline that was actually to take place. The sudden change that marks the policy of the king in the play and his attitude to his subjects may well represent the hopes raised by the new reign. Even though the connection of this plot with sensational contemporary events would have been obvious to all theatre-goers, the fact remains that no lesson concerning the past was necessary for Philip IV. His father had been guilty of bringing Lerma to power and keeping him there, but he himself was bringing in the necessary reforms. The rise and fall of Lerma and his minions was utilised by Calderón as the background of reality to exemplify the confusion of life and the need always to tread warily when the sun's light is obscured by clouds.

The direct connection of the stage with public events existed in countries other than Spain. It has been recognised for Shakespeare's time by Lily Campbell, in *Shakespeare's "Histories": Mirrors of Elizabethan Policy* (Los Angeles, 1947). Anthony Watson has plausibly argued that the same process was earlier at work in Spain in the plays of Juan de la Cueva. This Sevillian playwright (1543–1610) wrote fourteen plays which were performed in his native city from 1579 to 1581. Eight of these plays are on 'historical' themes from classical and Spanish history or legend, or on near-contemporary European history. All deal with different aspects of a single large theme, that of usurpation of power, conquest, fratricidal struggles between kindred nations, in short, tyranny threatened or achieved by war. During the years when these plays were performed the crucial political issue was the succession to the Portuguese crown. When the young King Sebastian was defeated and killed in 1578 in his Moroccan campaign, he was succeeded by the aged and celibate Cardinal Henry. Among the claimants to the throne when he should die was Philip II of Spain. He probably had the strongest claim in law, but he did not have majority support among the Portuguese people and their parliament. The period during which the plays were performed covers the unfolding of these events: King Sebastian died in 1578, and in 1580 Philip assured his conquest of Portugal at the battle of Alcántara. Watson interprets the plots of these plays of Cueva in the light of contemporary opposition in Spain to Philip's policy towards Portugal, especially his resort to war. His thesis is skilfully argued and the background of political opinion is well documented.[4]

It is clear that in the years following the performance of Cueva's plays, years which see the rise of the new star in the theatrical firmament, Lope de Vega, the stage could be used as a forum for public opinion, which had no other means of expressing itself. An example is the theme of a feudal lord's attempt to seduce the beautiful wife of a peasant vassal, safe in the assurance that he is not acting dishonourably, since peasants have no honour, a theme culminating in the peasant's assertion of his honour by killing the offender, as any nobleman would. This theme is exemplified among others by one of Lope de Vega's best known plays, *Peribáñez y el comendador de Ocaña* (Peribáñez and the Commander of Ocaña). Such plays used to be seen as a remarkable assertion of the moral and civil rights of the common man in a highly class-conscious society. It is now interpreted as originating in opposition to the selling of titles of nobility to people whom popular prejudice considered to be of Jewish stock ('new Christians') and in the indirect plea for creating a new aristocracy among yeomen farmers, whose agricultural background placed their 'purity of blood' beyond suspicion. At least one of these vicious feudal lords is openly identified by Lope de Vega as a living personage. In *Peribáñez* (published 1614) he is a member of the military Order of Calatrava and the Knight-Commander of the fief of Ocaña. In 1614, when the play was printed, and in 1612, when the play may have been written, the actual Knight-Commander of Ocaña was the aforementioned Don Rodrigo Calderón, a plebeian of known Jewish ancestry who was knighted by and became the favourite of the Duke of Lerma, Philip III's Chief Minister. In October 1618 Lerma fell from power; Don Rodrigo was arrested for corruption in February 1619, and executed in 1621.[5] The plot of *Peribáñez* is set in the fifteenth century, but by making the villain of the play *comendador de Ocaña* Lope was ensuring that no intelligent theatregoer could fail to understand this particular example of 'speaking without telling'.

While, therefore, the corruption of government by favourites and their fall from power was the immediate historical context when Calderón began to write plays, the tradition of 'speaking without telling' with implied advice or reproaches to king and ministers was the established background to playwriting. Calderón does not do anything as openly pointed as Lope de Vega's use of the commandership of Ocaña, nor does he directly associate any of his characters with a living public person, but the 'historical context' is often present in his mind when his plots touch on public life. Examples of how he 'speaks without telling' will be given later. For the moment we may pass to a play that, when it was written, had a direct bearing on an important political event, a play, moreover, that uses a historical example to illustrate one of the main themes of *Saber del mal y del bien* – that disaster overcomes a kingdom when a king follows his private interests rather than the common good of his kingdom. For this subject Calderón goes to English history with the divorce by Henry VIII of Queen Catherine. This play also raises, obliquely, an issue of paramount importance in national and international affairs, as well as providing a comment on a contemporary event.

19 Religion and the state: *La cisma de Ingalaterra*[1]

The reign of Henry VIII is one of the most momentous in English history because of its far-reaching consequences. On the level of Henry's private life, the reign is also one of the most sensational because of his six marriages and the fates of the rejected wives. His first marriage was the cause of the schism from Rome, which led to the English Reformation and the ecclesiastical settlement under his daughter Queen Elizabeth. Henry, who was born in 1491, came to the throne in 1509. He married Catherine of Aragon, the daughter of Ferdinand and Isabella of Spain, in the same year. She was the widow of his elder brother Arthur, who had died in 1502. Doubts had been expressed, even by the Pope, about the validity of Catherine's second marriage to her brother-in-law, since marriage to one's brother's widow could be possibly construed as incestuous. This did not trouble Henry's conscience at the time, but when it became certain twenty years later that he could have no further issue from the marriage than his daughter Mary, Henry alleged the canonical impediment as a reason for divorcing Catherine in order to obtain a male heir. There had been no queen regnant in English history and since Henry's father had won the throne after a long civil war, Henry felt it expedient that Mary's right of accession should not be challenged. He therefore decided to obtain a divorce from Queen Catherine which was only canonically possible if his marriage could be considered invalid. Henry therefore petitioned for a divorce on the grounds of consanguinity. The question was debated by Pope and theologians, the support of parliament was obtained, and Thomas Wolsey, Archbishop of York, persuaded Henry that the Pope would invalidate his marriage. The Pope never did, but Henry went ahead with the support of the English church, and married Anne Boleyn. This ruptured the allegiance of king and church to the Roman Pontiff. This is the theme of Calderón's play.

Henry's second marriage was of short duration. Three years later Henry had Anne beheaded on the charge of adultery; the marriage had lasted long enough to provide another daughter, the future Queen Elizabeth. Jane Seymour, the third wife, bore Henry his desired male heir, the future Edward VI, but she died in childbirth. The fourth wife, Anne of

Cleves, was rejected; the fifth, Catherine Howard, was beheaded, and the sixth, Catherine Parr, was able to outlive him. Henry died in 1547.

Little attention had been paid to *La cisma de Ingalaterra* because it is a travesty of history. This covers two aspects, the events and the implied judgement on King Henry. As regards the first, the fact that Henry is made to abdicate and to appoint his daughter Mary as his successor is surprising enough, but the second aspect is perhaps more so. Calderón's treatment of the schismatic king is extraordinarily compassionate, and totally at variance with the source from which he learned his history. The omission of Edward VI's reign can be excused as a not unreasonable telescoping of the effects of the schism, but to have gone against what all continental Catholics had been told about Henry is not so easily explained. When Calderón's 'shaping of dramatic plots' was discussed in Part I, chapter 4, it was emphasised, in accordance with Aristotle's distinction, that 'Historical Truth' had to give way to 'Poetic Truth'. The history of Henry VIII's divorce and the resultant schism did not present to Calderón, in the historical account of it that he had studied, a potential dramatic action with a coherent beginning and a logical development and end, nor did it offer him a humanly understandable motive and a satisfying explanation from the point of view of poetic justice. We must of course accept the fact that Calderón's co-religionists could not see the English Reformation as other than a disaster for England and Europe; the fact that this is not how English historians have seen these events and their consequences is beside the point. The dramatic significance of a historical play cannot be judged with the benefit of hindsight. What has to be judged in the light of the sources available to the dramatist is the way the events are selected, shaped and unified to present human and political problems with a universal significance.

For an English dramatist, writing for an audience who had lived under Elizabeth, the theme of Henry VIII's divorce had an inherent duality, which Shakespeare, for his part, did not attempt to resolve. There is a difficulty inherent in the historical subject. The divorce and the new marriage could only be treated with unity of tone if a really worthy motive justified them both. If Henry were presented as sincerely convinced of the invalidity of his marriage, and convinced also that the good of the state required a male heir – if he had genuinely grieved at the suffering his conscience compelled him to inflict upon Catherine, and if he were to marry Anne to fulfil a king's duty to the nation – there would be no confusion of tone, no conflict in our sympathies. But Shakespeare fails to present the king's plea of conscience in a serious light.[2] It is not likely that any unfavourable comment would have been acceptable even ten years after Elizabeth's death, when the play was probably first performed. Insofar as rights and wrongs are considered, they are shown to be unfavourable to Henry. Yet what Henry wishes must, because of his position, be right; and that he achieves his wishes is therefore a matter for congratulation to all concerned. Our sympathies are pulled towards and away from Queen Catherine, towards and away from King Henry, and the final vision of Elizabethan England fails to resolve this duality and does not give the play significance as historical drama, for, however fine it may be as a poetic statement, it has no inner relation to the dramatic action: it is not a conclusion that inevitably follows from the interpretation and treatment of the theme.

For Englishmen who had lived through Elizabeth's reign, her father's divorce could not be considered a political disaster; for the compatriots of Queen Catherine, for whom the divorce could not have any canonical and moral justification, it was a different matter. For a Spanish dramatist, therefore, the moral issue of the divorce and the second marriage would be quite unambiguous, and the religious issue would coincide with it; he would also have the added advantage of being able to make the theme historically more complete by introducing the downfall of Anne Boleyn. Nonetheless, the theme viewed from the Catholic standpoint presents a dramatist with a difficulty of another kind – evil triumphs, and the protagonist does not suffer for his wrongdoing. Either dramatic fitness or historical truth must therefore be sacrificed. Calderón was able to place the claims of dramatic poetry first, because he was not writing for an English audience. The 'suspension of disbelief' demanded by a historically fanciful *dénouement* would have been much less of a strain on his audience, if it was a strain at all, than one that was dramatically inappropriate. But a historically fanciful conclusion is only part of a surprising deviation from his source. Obviously what is dramatic and stage-worthy in the history of the schism is not the problem of canon law involved or the theological issues of Papal versus Royal supremacy. Theme and action must be reduced to the human dimensions, and these are a powerful king's rejection of an innocent wife out of love for another woman.

Either the first Book of Pedro de Ribadeneyra's *Historia ecclesiastica del scisma del reyno de Inglaterra* (1588) or (though this is much less likely), Ribadeneyra's own authority, Nicholas Sander's *De origine ac Progressu Schismatis Anglicani* (completed by Edward Rishton and published in Cologne in 1585) provided Calderón with his source.[3] This is proved by two details: Wolsey's antagonism to Catherine owing to a soothsayer's prophecy (a Calderonian predilection, as we have several times seen) that a woman would be his undoing, and Pasquín's reference to Wolsey's tomb. Ribadeneyra reported the prophecy as follows: 'some say that he was also impelled to repudiate the Queen by the fact that an astrologer had prophesied that a woman would be the cause of his ruin and perdition.'[4] Wolsey's tomb is introduced as follows:

Volseo Pues ¿qué has visto?
Pasquín   Vuestro entierro.
¡Oh qué gran capilla hacéis!
Para un pájaro pequeño
Muy grande jaula es aquélla.
Mas ¿no sabéis lo que pienso?
Que no os habéis de enterrar
vos en ella.

(*Volseo* Well, what have you seen?
Pasquín Your funeral. What a large chapel you are building! For a little bird
that's a very large cage. But can you not guess what I'm thinking?
That you are not going to be buried in it.)[5]

This derives from Ribadeneyra: 'Some say that Wolsey during his life was building a sumptuous monument for his tomb, and that when he went one day to see it a Fool among his retinue, who was accompanying him said to him: "Why are you spending so much money to no purpose? Do you intend to be buried here? Well, I tell you that when you die you will not have the money to pay for your burial."' (p. 203b). Ribadeneyra, as one would expect, differs widely from the sixteenth-century English chronicler Holinshed in numerous details, but the main historical outline is roughly the same. Where the discrepancy in the two sources is important for a dramatic plot is, of course, in the interpretation of the characters of the main personages. Ribadaneyra's treatment of Wolsey, Anne Boleyn and Henry is, briefly, as follows.

Wolsey is held initially responsible for the schism, being the first to suggest to Henry that his marriage could be annulled. His principal motive for this is revenge on the Emperor for not furthering his candidature for the Papacy, a secondary motive being hostility to the Queen. He is presented as vain, ambitious, insatiable in his longing for wealth and unscrupulous in his flattery of Henry; but Ribadeneyra's attitude is one of pity rather than of anger, and Wolsey's disgrace is considered sufficient expiation of his guilt.

Though Wolsey bears initial responsibility for the schism, it is from Anne that the full evil flows. The beliefs current among Catholics that she was Henry's illegitimate daughter, and that she had incestuous relations with her brother, are recorded as certain facts. She is also presented as a woman of extreme depravity, unashamedly dissolute both before and after her marriage.

Ribadeneyra faithfully transcribes Sander's judgement of Henry, omitting none of his good points, such as his generosity and love of learning, but he stresses of his own accord, and in the blackest colours, the king's lust, avarice and cruelty, and does not shrink from recording his conviction that the magnitude of his wickedness made him incapable of repentance and that, dying in despair, he was damned in hell.

Calderón's source, therefore, from the point of view of a dramatic plot, presents him with three villains of the deepest dye. Their personal wickedness overflows into the politico-religious sphere and infects a whole nation with the virus of schism. The saintly Queen Catherine is the victim of their personal wickedness and England is the victim of their religious wickedness. Wolsey and Anne are punished in this world, but Henry is punished only in the next.

Had Calderón faithfully followed Ribadeneyra, he would have produced a lurid melodrama. The first necessity, therefore, in order to extract dramatic significance from this material, is to tone down the high colours. The irrelevant scandals of Anne's origin and past life are, of course, omitted. But so also is her depravity as Queen, for Calderón reduces her dishonourableness to a jilting of a formerly accepted French suitor and to a hint of a willingness to restore him to favour by being unfaithful to Henry. It is true that in one respect he goes beyond Ribadeneyra, because he implies that Anne murdered Catherine by enclosing poison in a letter. This is not required to justify Anne's execution, and may have been introduced partly in order not to go counter to an accepted belief among Spaniards (though Ribadeneyra merely states that Catherine died 'not without suspicion of poison' (p. 217b)), and partly because his *dénouement* required Catherine to be dead, and her murder was in keeping with his presentation of Anne's character – a woman who was not dissolute, but who was led by an overweening and calculating pride to seek to dominate everybody.

But it is in the presentation of Henry that Calderón tones down Ribadeneyra beyond all recognition, for his treatment of him is extraordinarily compassionate. From the historical point of view this is the most astonishing thing in the play. Henry is endowed with a conscience: he does wrong only after agonising hesitation, his reason blinded by a passion that he finally cannot resist. He sins not out of lust but out of love. And where he sins he also finds salvation, for in the assertion of his honour as a husband, in view of Anne's concealment of her former acceptance of a suitor and of her prospective infidelity, he reasserts his honour as a king, and struggles through to repentance and such restitution as the terrible consequences of his sin make possible.

With Wolsey, however, Calderón is sterner than Ribadeneyra. He, not

Henry, is incapable of repentance. In order to bring Wolsey to the sin of despair Calderón takes two minor liberties with history. First, his dismissal is brought about by Anne, because of his threat to depose her if she does not further his interests. Secondly, he is then confronted with his victim, Catherine. Her charity to him so strongly reinforces his conviction, arrived at through the ingratitude of Anne, that he is suffering evil because he did good –

> ¡O cuánto yerra
> el que bien hace!   (229a)

> (Oh, how wrong is he who does good!) (229a)

– that seeing no order but only utter confusion everywhere,[6] he takes his own life in despair. For this latter licence Calderón's source offered him this measure of justification: 'It was spread around that the Cardinal himself, in order not to suffer public dishonour, had killed himself with poison: I believe this to be a false imputation.'[7]

These alterations in Ribadeneyra's presentation of the moral iniquity of his three villains, and the reversal of his moral judgements in the case of Henry and Wolsey, point to the significance Calderón gives the human as distinct from the political aspect of the theme in transforming it into dramatic art. Anne's licentiousness is rejected because she is the incarnation solely of pride. Wolsey is the incarnation of unscrupulous ambition and self-seeking. Both these are intellectual sins of a calculating, cold-blooded kind, and as such far graver than sins of the flesh. Henry sins through a physical passion that cannot be suppressed. The evil of Wolsey and Anne is a deliberate and crafty evil: they distort and degrade human nature, whereas Henry, in his weakness, bears the tragic burden of all humanity.

La cisma de Ingalaterra is marvellously constructed, its three Acts presenting an exposition, a development and a *dénouement* that are tightly knit together. There is no ambiguity of tone, no shifting centre of interest and no uncertainty of aim. The issues at stake are presented with forceful clarity, and the action is raised from the very outset to a plane of ominous foreboding from which it never descends until the tragic fatality is made manifest. There is no lingering on the way to make capital out of the pathetic: the action is compressed and its course relentlessly swift.

The opening scene, so effective dramatically, and in its subtlety so characteristic of Calderón's technical originality, presents the *confusión* in Henry that is to be the seed of the tragedy. He is a learned man who sincerely strives to make his intelligence the champion of truth. Writing in defence of the Catholic faith he is 'awake':

> . . . la defiendo, asistiendo
> con el ingenio y las fuerzas:
> pues ahora que Marte duerme
> sobre las armas sangrientas,
> velo yo sobre los libros.

(I defend it, bringing my mind to bear on it as well as my strength: for now that Mars is sleeping beside his bloodstained weapons, I am keeping awake over my books.)

(215b)

But when he writes of matrimony, his mind becomes clouded and he falls asleep:

> . . . cargada la cabeza,
> entorpecido el ingenio
> de un pesado sueño.

(my head grows heavy, my mind is dulled as sleep overtakes me.)

(215c)

Waking or dreaming – reason or passion. He is therefore a man whose passion can be aroused so strongly that he is then not master of himself:

> ya no acertaba a escribir;
> pues cuanto con la derecha
> mano escribía y notaba,
> iba borrando la izquierda.

(I was now unable to write distinctly; for what I was writing with my right hand my left hand kept rubbing out.)

(215c)

The unrealistic action of falling asleep when he reaches the subject of matrimony indicates that sensuality clouds the intellect. Matrimony immediately suggests the passion that is to prove King Henry's downfall. From this conception of the relation of sensuality to reason there followed the scholastic doctrine that sins of passion are less serious than sins of the mind (an idea that becomes very important in the presentation not only of Henry, but also of Wolsey and Anne Boleyn), the reason being that the clouding of the mind affects the degree of one's responsibility for the actions concerned: one cannot be clear-headed morally if one is not clear-sighted where a moral choice has to be made. The lack of grip on himself on this occasion frightens and bewilders Henry.

Even in this early period Calderón's technique is clear. Instead of presenting strong emotions and letting them speak for themselves, he is intellectualising the whole situation, and thus clarifying the conflict. Henry does not know whether he is awake or dreaming:

Con esta imaginación
que hizo caso y tuvo fuerza
de verdad, estoy despierto
considerando las señas,
tanto que ahora la miro
con aquella forma, aquella
imagen que antes la ví,
y aun pienso que el alma sueña;
pues en tantas confusiones,
tantos asombros y penas,
si puede dormir el alma,
no debe de estar despierta.

(With these imaginings which took account of what I felt and gave a strong illusion of reality, I am now awake and pondering on these signs, so much so that now I am seeing her in that form, in the self-same image in which I previously saw her, and it even seems to me that my soul is dreaming; since in so much confusion, so much amazement, so much distress, if my soul can sleep, it cannot now be awake.)

(215c)

This physical passion is no brutal lust. There is another lover in the play who parallels this aspect of Henry. Before the latter actually meets Anne, Carlos, in the most vividly colourful and sonorous poetry in the play, gives the sensuous reaction by placing love in the setting of natural beauty:

Allí el silencio de la noche fría,
el jazmín que en las redes se enlazaba,
el cristal de la fuente que corría,
el arroyo que a solas murmuraba,
el viento que en las hojas se movía,
el aura que en las flores respiraba,
todo era amor: ¿qué mucho, si en tal calma
aves, fuentes y flores tienen alma?

(There the silence of the cold night, the jasmine entwined in the lattices, the crystal of the splashing fountain, the stream which murmured in its solitude, the wind that rustled the leaves, the gentle wind that breathed upon the flowers, all spoke of love: is it surprising, then, that in such quiet birds, streams and flowers all have souls?)

(217b)

But in men love is not calm. Its impetuousness, its fierce power to blind and enslave, and the helplessness of the lover to offer any resistance, are stressed:

Yo que entonces de libre blasonaba,
quedé al mirarla envuelto en fuego y hielo;
que como amor es rayo sin violencia,
crece y crece en su misma resistencia.

(I, who then boasted of being free, became, as I looked at her, wrapped in fire
and ice. Since love is lightning without violence, it grows and grows in the
very resistance it builds up.)

(217a)

Thus deprived of his freedom, Carlos sacrifices his duty for love when he
offers Anne his hand in marriage. Henry, also caught up in this vital
force, will do the same:

Puesto que mi albedrío
a quererte me fuerza
sin que mi amor se tuerza,
ya no es libre, ni es mío.
Dame esa blanca mano.

(Since my will is making me love you without forcing this love, it no longer is
free, no longer mine. Give me your white hand.)

(223b)

Carlos, in his love for the beautiful Anne, has our full sympathy. By
introducing him, and by presenting love in this way, Calderón ensures
that we shall not lose sympathy with Henry.

This sensibility to passionate love, which is to be Henry's conflict as a
man, is immediately widened into the religious conflict to which, on the
plane of his kingly duty, he will be led by his inability to resist his passion.
Significantly, it is Wolsey who is responsible for connecting the two.
When he brings the letters from the Pope and Luther, Henry's agitation
and uncertainty vanish. On the rational level there can be no shadow of
doubt which represents the truth. Here, then, there is something he can
hold fast to; here there can be no sleeping, no crossing out, no confusion:

estas cartas son
lo que acabo de soñar.

    La mano con que escribía
era la derecha, y era
la doctrina verdadera,
que celoso defendía:
    aquesto la carta muestra
del Pontífice. Y querer
deslucir y deshacer
y con la mano siniestra
    su luz, bien dice que lleno

de confusiones vería
juntos la noche y el día,
la triaca y el veneno.

(these letters represent what I have just dreamt. The hand with which I was writing was my right one, and this was the true doctrine which I was zealously defending: this is what the Pontiff's letter has made clear. My wanting to make its light fade and vanish with my left hand clearly means that in the midst of my confusion I was going to see side by side, day and night, the antidote and the poison.)

(216a)

But since passion can blind reason, the universal–religious and the personal–moral planes are not discontinuous. Henry's emotional agitation embraces both alike: he places Luther's letter on his head and the Pope's at his feet, which greatly increases his distress and sense of foreboding. These actions of throwing to one's feet or raising to one's head are strikingly original devices, by which Calderón makes Henry's inner dilemma *dramatic*: by which, that is to say, he makes them visible on the stage while expressing them as poetic metaphors, this being a technique that makes the actions symbolical. This method of creating dramatic metaphors was analysed in chapter 2, above, where it was demonstrated how Calderón turns metaphors into stage actions, which subsequently turn the metaphors into symbols, the symbols first being spoken in the dialogue and later made visible on the stage. The reader is referred back for this analysis. Here, it is necessary to analyse the significance of the two actions of throwing one letter down to one's feet and raising the other on to one's head. Ludwig Pfandl was the first to see a special significance in these actions and the first thereby to broaden one's understanding of Calderón's technique.[8] It must first be noted that Wolsey, not Henry, is responsible for the error; Wolsey, in delivering each letter separately, identified them wrongly. His attempt to allay Henry's agitation by passing this off as an accident thus becomes an ironical pointer:

¿qué agüero es
al dar dos cartas, señor,
trocarlas yo por error,
o entenderlas tú al revés?

(What omen is there, sire, in my mixing up two letters when I hand them to you, or in your misunderstanding what I said?)

(216a)

He it is who is going to confuse the whole issue by devilishly fanning Henry's passion in order to involve Church and State in his own personal revenge. Henry will sin grievously, but the gravity will be Wolsey's responsibility. Henry's proneness to an emotional–rational disorder lies at the very root of human nature; the cold-blooded, the satanic rather than human, sin – the craftily deliberate introduction of an intellectual disorder – will be Wolsey's alone.

That this scene is consummate dramatic art is made further apparent by another important purpose that this incident fulfils. It introduces (as was previously noted) a type of imagery that runs through the verse of the play as one of its constant strands. The head and feet positions represent an 'up-and-down' imagery – on the one hand, ascent; on the other, being on the ground or having something at one's feet. Up and down – right and wrong, either absolutely or relative to a particular character's interpretation of the desirable good.

The relativity of human moral judgements – the liability to confusion and error, to self-delusion – is shown in the speech in which Henry finds reassurance by seeing an appropriateness in the two letters being placed as they are. For the Pope is the foundation stone of all order, Luther a menace to that order, a burdensome responsibility that Henry, as a Catholic king, must face. Henry is the pillar grounded in the one, supporting the burden of the other; and Luther is a destructive flame ending in smoke. Both letters thus find their proper place in the order of natural values: the stone drops, the smoke rises.

The original interpretation of the head and feet positions is absolute: one cannot reverence with one's feet and spurn with one's head. But Henry's later metaphors are in themselves perfectly acceptable. While values are absolute, the interpretation of them is relative to the human being; and since passion can be blind and blinding, mistakes are all too easy. Henry, because of his passionate nature, is not guaranteed against mistakes by his intelligence and learning. Thus, though separately valid, the two interpretations of the up and down together constitute confusion. The foundation stone, because it is down, can be spurned; the smoke, because it is up, can be reverenced. Therefore, Henry's perfectly legitimate statement here:

> Baje la piedra oprimida,
> suba la llama abrasada,
> ésta en rayos dilatada,
> y aquélla del peso herida;
>   que yo de las dos presumo
> que buscan en esta acción
> su mismo centro, pues son
> una piedra, y otra humo.

(Let the weighted stone descend, let the burning flame ascend, the latter spread out in rays, the former struck by its own light; for I presume that in these actions each seeks its proper centre, since one is a stone, and the other is smoke.)

(216a–b)

is later echoed when he does reverence the smoke by succumbing to his passion:

No en balde el alma mía
que ausente de ti estaba,
errando me guiaba
dónde tu luz ardía;
que en tan feliz encuentro,
llama ha sido mi amor, subió a su centro.

(Not for nothing did my soul, which was absent from you, in its wanderings guide me to where your light was shining; for in this happy encounter, my love has been a flame, which has risen to its centre.)

(223b)

Even here the judgement of value is legitimate in itself. Viewed in isolation from all the other circumstances that make up the complexity of human life, the end Henry is here seeking is good: the movement of passionate love, being in itself noble, *is* an upward movement. But all good ends are relative to others, and Henry introduces confusion by making a relative good absolute: his love for Anne can only rise if both Queen Catherine and the Pope fall.

This *confusión* (which in various forms is a keystone of many of Calderón's *comedias*) accounts for one of the special features of this remarkable play: the extensive use of dramatic irony. For statements have both an absolute meaning and one relative to the intention of the speaker. Thus when Anne, in telling Henry that she loves him but cannot be his mistress, says: 'Más vale que tú reines, y yo muera' (It is better that you reign and that I die) (223b) she is stating something that events prove true in an absolute sense which is the exact opposite of what she intended, though her intention is in fact also realised.

There is a quite different relativity in Cardinal Wolsey's moral judgements. Unlike Henry he has not to decide between the use and non-use of what is a natural good in itself. His mistake in the up-and-down movement is an inversion of absolute values clearly recognisable as such. It is not that his reason is confused, but that his will is corrupt. When Henry departs to answer the letters, Wolsey immediately places the image of ascent in this different perspective:

Aunque yo desde la cuna
hombre humilde y bajo soy,
subiendo a la cumbre voy
del monte de mi fortuna.

> A su extremo soberano
> sólo falta un escalón:
> dame la mano, ambición,
> lisonja, dame la mano;
>   que si por vosotras medro
> a tan excelso lugar,
> me pienso altivo sentar
> en la silla de San Pedro.

(Although I have been from birth a man of low and humble station, I am approaching the summit of my fortune. To its sovereign peak there remains but one step: hold out your hand, ambition; flattery, hold out your hand; if through you I reach this lofty place, I aim in my pride to sit on St Peter's chair.)

(216b)

This is one aspect of the ascent–descent imagery, the inversion of humility into pride. Wolsey is perfectly clear-sighted, he is never uncertain of his aim and never at a loss for the means to employ. He is absolutely confident of his ability to control events, having the same proud self-reliance as Basilio: 'because the wise man can control the stars' (222c). Yet, like him, he cannot master fate. He misinterprets the soothsayer's prophecy. And because he inverts the natural order, what he actually achieves is the opposite of what he aims at: 'nothing turns out right for me' (222b), he cries in his anger. And when he thinks to damn Henry –

> pues pienso hacer de modo,
> que el que engañado ahora y ciego queda,
> cuando se quiera arrepentir, no pueda

(for I intend so to act, that he who now is deceived and blind will be unable to repent when he wants to)

(224b)

– it is only his own clear-sightedness that is proved to be permanent blindness; it is only himself he damns.

The up-and-down imagery dominates the presentation of Wolsey and Anne in the first Act and recurs throughout the play. Catherine says to Wolsey:

> aquesta púrpura santa,
> que por falso y lisonjero,
> de hijo de un carnicero
> a los cielos os levanta

(this sacred scarlet that raises you, a butcher's son, through flattery and deception to the sky)

(218c)

and to Henry:

> . . . tengo a Volseo
> por lisonjero, y que entabla
> más su aumento que el provecho
> del reino: que sólo trata
> de subir al sol, midiendo
> la soberbia y la arrogancia.

> (I judge Wolsey to be a flatterer, who has in mind more his own advancement
> than the good of the kingdom: for he is aiming at nothing less than the sun by
> means of pride and arrogance.)

(221b)

Anne applies the imagery to herself with dramatic irony, for her remarks
are only a conventional courtly compliment to her hearers, but denote
for herself the intention of reversing the absolute significance of her
humble position at the Queen's feet. Her first speech (it is to Catherine) is:

> Si favor tan soberano
> hoy merece mi humildad,
> deme vuestra Majestad
> a besar su blanca mano.
> Llegará mi aliento ufano
> a la esfera de la luna,
> y no habrá pena ninguna
> que tema mi suerte, pues
> tendré la envidia a mis pies,
> y en mi mano la fortuna.

> (If my humility today deserves so sovereign a favour, give me, Your Majesty,
> your hand to kiss. I shall be encouraged proudly to reach the sphere of the
> moon, and there will be no suffering that I need fear, since I shall have envy at
> my feet, and my fortune in my hand.)

(217c)

And a little later she says, interpreting in a favourable sense the irony of
Pasquín's prophecy:

> Yo tomo por buen agüero
> aquesta vez su locura;
> pues siendo yo vuestra hechura,
> tanto levantarme espero,
> que en el sol me considero.

> (On this occasion I take his folly as a good omen; for since you have made me
> what I am, I hope to ascend so high that it would seem as if I were in the sun.)

(218b)

Anne, therefore, has the same clarity of aim as Wolsey. She also will ascend, at no matter what cost to others or the State: for to be on the ground – to accept her rightful subordinate status – is intolerable to her:

> Llegar a verme
> a los pies de una mujer,
> ¿qué gloria, qué triunfo es éste?

(for if I come to see myself at the feet of a woman, what glory, what triumph will this be?)

(219a)

And the reason is tersely expressed:

> nunca envidiada de alguna,
> de alguna envidiosa siempre

(never envied by another woman, always envious of another)

(219a)

For the summit of her happiness is to have 'la envidia a mis pies' (envy at my feet). She hates to have to kneel even before the king:

> ¡Otra vez tengo de verme
> con la rodilla en la tierra!
> ¿Ésta es gloria? Agravio es éste.

(Once again I must put my knees to the ground! Is this glory? This is an outrage.)

(219c)

Yet despite their having the same clarity of aim, and therefore the same manner of ascent, Anne's downfall is different from Wolsey's. She does not primarily fall because she inverts humility into pride, but because she also overturns another order of values: she inverts love into self-interest:

> Carlos, perdona
> si tu firme amor ofendo,
> cuando hoy aspirar pretendo
> al lustre de una corona.
>
> Mujer he sido en dejar
> que me venza el interés:
> séalo en mudar después
> y séalo en olvidar.
>
> Que cuando lleguen a ver
> que el interés me ha vencido,
> que he olvidado y he fingido,
> todo cabe en ser mujer.

(Forgive me, Carlos, if I offend your steadfast love, when today I aspire to the splendour of a crown. I have been a woman in permitting self-interest to overcome me: let me be a woman in my subsequent inconstancy, and let me be a woman also in forgetting. For when people come to see that I have been overcome by self-interest, that I have forgotten, that I have feigned, they will explain it all through my being a woman.)

(223a)

This womanly fickleness to which she falls victim is several times stressed throughout the play.

Two of the passages quoted to illustrate the imagery of ascent in connection with Wolsey and Anne contained the phrases 'subir al sol' (to rise up to the sun) and 'en el sol me considero' (it is as if I am in the sun). This is important. Anne's ambition is to live in a kingdom:

donde ceñidas las sienes
de rayos del sol, me vea
adorada de las gentes

(where with my brow encircled by the sun's rays, I shall see myself adored by humankind)

(219a)

and Wolsey, when about to tempt Henry to repudiate Catherine, says to himself 'al sol te atreve' (aim daringly at the sun) (224a). This sun image in association with the idea of ascent of course represents proud ambition: Wolsey and Anne aim at the sun, but the wax of their wings melts. It is also, however, part of a wider image-complex running through the play: light (or day) with its counterpart darkness (or night). Light represents the ability to see – certainty of aim and self-reliance; darkness represents blindness – confusion, groping uncertainly, and especially error, failure and death. There is no character in the play who is actually able to see his way through the maze-like obscurity of life with an absolute clarity of vision – except Pasquín, who (and here the irony of the play is almost unbearable) had once been learned, but is now mad and does not act at all. All the other major characters are either totally or partially blind. Wolsey, Anne and Catherine all think they see clearly, but all three are plunged in the end into blindness and darkness. When the disgraced Wolsey becomes a beggar, he says

una luz ciega
a quien el sol le vió así.

(any light now blinds [me] whom the sun once beheld [in my glory])

(228c)

And Anne, who has also risen to the sun, will be sent to a dungeon:

a esa Bolena prended,
y en el castillo invencible
de Londres, que del palacio

está enfrente, en noche triste
viva presa.

(seize that Boleyn, and let her live in sad darkness, a prisoner in the impregnable Tower of London, which faces the Palace.)

(230a)

The sun brings death to her, not life. From the commonplace of the almond-tree foolishly blossoming too early Calderón extracts, through this wider context, a subtle depth:

¿Qué importa
que a sus giros ilumine
el sol tus flores, si luego
airados vientos embisten,
y hechos cadáver del campo
tus destroncados matices,
aves sin alma en el viento
fueron despojos sutiles?

(What does it matter if the sun in its revolutions should have lit up your flowers, if later angry winds struck, and your colours, fallen from their stems, have become the corpse of the meadows, the soulless birds of the air being its flimsy spoils?)

(230b)

And Catherine says of herself at the end:

Púsose el sol: ¡ay de mí!
tinieblas y sombras toco.

(The sun has set, alas! I face shadows and darkness.)

(225c)

Henry, when he confuses the two letters, uses the same imagery of conflicting light and darkness. As already quoted, he explains his confusion by saying 'my wanting to make its light fade and vanish with my left hand clearly means that in the midst of my confusion I was going to see, side by side, day and night, the antidote and the poison' (216a). At the end of Act I, Henry meets Anne Boleyn for the first time and is greatly shaken at the sight of her as she kneels before him:

¿Cómo te nombras
mujer que deidad pareces,
y con beldad me enterneces
si con agüeros me asombras?
Entre luces, entre sombras
causas gusto y das horror;

entre piedad y rigor
me enamoras y me espantas;
y al fin entre dichas tantas
te tengo miedo y amor.

(How can you call yourself a woman if you seem a goddess, and if you move
me with your beauty while omens cast their shadows over me? Between light
and darkness you fill me with both pleasure and horror; swaying between
gentleness and sternness, you inspire me with both love and dread; in short,
in the middle of such joy, you fill me with fear and love.)

(220a)

Appropriately it is the jester Pasquín who introduces this new
imagery. He, we are told, had once been what all acknowledge Henry to
be, a learned man. On his first appearance he compares himself to a blind
man who walks at night in the pouring rain, carrying a lighted taper, not
that *he* may avoid groping, but that others may avoid stumbling against
him:

yo con mis locuras
soy ciego, y alumbro a oscuras.
Huid de mí, pues que veis.

(with my madness I am blind; I carry a light but I remain in darkness. Shun
me, since you can see.)

(218b)[9]

A blind man in the dark, carrying a lighted taper in the pouring rain,
unable to help himself and able only to warn others – this is the
atmosphere that pervades the whole play: it is an impression not of
misguided folly but of a tragic helplessness. The humour of Pasquín is of a
bitter, helpless kind: with his 'cargo figurífero'[10] he moves through the
play, pulling to pieces the artificiality of the courtiers' lives, and he alone
tells everyone the truth – but they pay no attention to him, or if they do, it
is not to understand what he says. At the moment of crisis, when Henry
has to make the agonising decision between Anne and Catherine,
Pasquín appears with his joke – but with a pointedly ironical joke, for
Henry, who will be false to the truth both as man and king, is the 'figura
de a dos', the *figura* twice over; forced to 'pagar dos veces', to pay twice
over for his weakness both as man and king. Henry makes up his mind
and departs without hearing Pasquín:

No quiso responderme. ¡Peligroso
alcance sigue el hombre que es gracioso!
Pues llega en ocasión donde se enfría,
cuando dice una gracia, y no hay quien ría.

(He did not want to answer. The man who is a jester follows a difficult prey, for he may arrive when the scent has grown cold: he makes a joke, and nobody laughs.)

(224c)

La cisma de Ingalaterra is indeed a play where no-one laughs. The madman's humour is too grim for laughter.

On all these occasions Calderón employs his imagery of ascent/descent, light/shadow with skill, in a diction that is extraordinarily neat and concise.[11]

At the end of the first Act Henry meets Anne for the first time. She is indignant at having once more to kneel on the ground, but she is made to remain at his feet while Henry, overwhelmed by seeing her, struggles to retain his composure. The act closes on the note on which it began, and both the up-and-down and the sun imagery recur. Able to speak at last, and perturbed by his dream-vision having come to life, Henry says:

> Y si el cielo me condena
> a haber sus luces tenido
> a mis pies, disculpa ha sido
> el haber, Ana, quedado
> entre tanto fuego helado,
> y en tanta nieve encendido.
>
> Pero esta disculpa en mí,
> más que me absuelve, condena,
> pues no es ésta, Ana Bolena,
> la primera vez que os vi.
> Levantad, no estéis así.

(If heaven condemns me for having kept its light at my feet, my excuse, Anne, has been that I was held frozen in the midst of so great a fire and burning amid so much snow. But this excuse, instead of absolving me, condemns me, for this is not the first time, Anne Boleyn, that I have seen you. Arise, do not stay kneeling.)

(220a)

The Petrarchan conceits of 'frozen in fire' and 'burning in snow' reflect the moral uncertainty, the *confusión*. And the courtly deference of Anne's reply reinforces both the imagery and the dramatic irony of the whole Act, by expressing first the value, relative to her, of Henry's inverting the moral order, and secondly the absolute value of its non-inversion:

> Si en tus brazos me levantas,
> tocaré las luces santas
> del sol: mas no será bien

que vuele más alto quien
está, señor, a tus plantas.

(If you help me to rise with your arms, I shall touch the holy light of the sun;
but it would not be right, sire, that she who is at your feet should fly any
higher.)

(220a)

It should be noted that this closing scene of the first Act is a most
effective symmetrical counterpart to the opening one. Henry has not
appeared in between and Anne has dominated the whole Act, carrying
the sinister portent from possibility to probability, from the sphere of
dreams to that of action. This symmetry extends to the whole play,
because the dream vision of the first scene becomes the dead body of the
last. The imagery completes the circle: the shuffling of the letters points to
the tragic disorder; when Henry and Anne first meet she is in her rightful
place at his feet; but Anne refers to her ambition to be Queen as:

        después
que tenga el cetro a mis pies
y la corona en mi frente

(after I shall have the sceptre at my feet and the crown upon my brow)

(223a)

and Henry raises her to be his head when Anne, in dancing, trips and
falls at his feet:

Rey A mis plantas has caído.
Ana Mejor diré que a tus plantas
    (pues son esfera divina)
    me he levantado . . . (*Aparte.* Tan alta,
    que entre los rayos del sol
    mis pensamientos se abrasan
    más remontados.)
Rey   No temas,
    si mis brazos te levantan.
    (*Aparte.* Quiera amor que sea, Bolena,
    al pecho en que idolatrada
    vives)

(*King* You have fallen at my feet.
Anne I would rather say that I have risen to your feet, since they are the sphere
    of [kingly] divinity . . .
(*Aside* So high, that my thoughts are burning in the rays of the sun to which
    they have soared.)

King   There is nothing to fear, since you are being raised by my arms.
(*Aside* May love grant, Boleyn, that it be to my heart, in which you live idolised by me.)[12]

and at the close of the play, as the beheaded Anne lies at *her* feet, the Princess Mary says:

¡Qué bien vuestra Majestad
satisfizo mis ofensas,
pues que me ha puesto a los pies
quien pensó ser mi cabeza!

(How fully has your Majesty given satisfaction to my injuries, for you have put at my feet the woman who sought to be my head.)

(231b)

Clearly, this play, from start to finish, reveals a poet who, even in his twenties, was a master of subtle dramatic construction, interweaving thought, imagery and movement into the symmetrical pattern of a whole play.

The full tragic significance of the human situation presented in the first Act is expanded in the second. The opening scene is again an admirable pointer, this time to the approaching national catastrophe. Henry is in the throes of his struggle of conscience. His prophetic dream had been a portent comparable with those that presage the death of kings: it is the life of his kingship that is at stake. To Pasquín he discloses that he is distressed and sad because

las pasiones del alma
ni las gobierna el poder,
ni la majestad las manda.

(the passions of the soul are governed neither by power nor commanded by kingship.)

(220b)

Pasquín then lays the issue bare with an anecdote that stresses by implication the dangers of kingship, contrasting the absoluteness of political power that is his as a king with the moral weakness that is his as a man. Henry, in being unable to be happy, is, he concludes, a sorry sort of king. The rest of the play develops the issue here stated: the tragic situation will follow from Henry's human weakness whereby his passion blinds his reason and, by making him thus a prey to the villainy of Wolsey and Anne, overwhelms his conscience; but the tragic significance of this and the extent of the disaster will be immeasurably increased by the greatness of his social responsibility.[13] In the bewildered and, as he realises, hopeless pursuit of his own happiness, he will use the sacred trust of his royal power to violate right and justice with fateful consequences to the whole kingdom.

The divorce is Wolsey's idea. He cunningly points out that it is Henry's royal power that makes a divorce not only easy but safe. He is king, and a learned one, nobody will therefore think that he is acting otherwise than as his conscience and the good of the State require. What has he to fear? Henry knows that the argument in favour of the invalidity of his marriage is specious, but he knows also that under the stress of his passion for Anne he is a blind man groping in the dark. There can be no bearable life for him now; whichever alternative he chooses – whether he sacrifices Anne or Catherine – he is fated to be unhappy. The argument that no political harm can come to him since he can make it appear that he is not conscious of any wrongdoing is something he can clutch at:

> Confieso que estoy loco y estoy ciego,
> pues la verdad que adoro es la que niego.
> Pero si un hombre el daño no alcanzara,
> aunque errara parece que no errara;
> que en tan confusa guerra,
> sólo errará el que sabe cuándo yerra.

> (I confess that I am mad and blind, for the truth I adore is the truth I deny. But if harm never befell a man, it would appear that, although he had done wrong it would seem as if he had done right; for in such a confusing struggle, he alone will do wrong who knows that he is doing it.)

(224b)

This means that the balance between the two kinds of unhappiness is not affected by any consideration of his position as king; it becomes, therefore, a straight choice between two kinds of death – and, being now only a suffering man, a private person, he chooses the less painful. But painful and agonising it is, nonetheless, for there is still nothing but darkness and death before him:

> Pues ya estoy desta manera
> muera de gusto, y no de pena muera;
> pues de cualquiera suerte
> voy pisando las sombras de la muerte.

> (Since this is the condition I am in, let me die from pleasure and not from suffering; for either way, I step into the shadow of death.)

(224c)

But, with the tragic irony permeating the whole play, this decision destroys its own safeguard, for it is in reality his death as a king that he chooses, however much he may think his kingship will be unaffected.

This inversion of values, this placing his kingship at his feet – or at Anne's feet: compare her statement

> después
> que tenga el cetro a mis pies

> (after I shall have the sceptre at my feet)

(223a)

– is made apparent in his speech to parliament when announcing his decision, for he claims to be acting not as a private individual but as a Christian king ('Esto es ser césar cristiano') (in this way I am being a Christian ruler) by sacrificing his personal happiness to the rule of the moral law:

> ¡Sabe el cielo si sintiera
> apartarme de mí propio
> tanto! pero donde es ley,
> es obedecer forzoso.

> (Heaven knows whether I would feel as much if I were divorced from myself! But where law rules, obedience is obligatory.)

(225a–b)

And his final degradation as king comes when, at the end of his speech, he states that his decision will be enforced with the whole might of his political power:

> Y el vasallo que sintiere
> mal, advierta temeroso
> que le quitaré al instante
> la cabeza de los hombros.

> (And the vassal who disapproves should note, in fear, that I will instantly cut off his head.)[14]

Queen Catherine, in refusing to accept the decision, places the fate of the nation above her personal tragedy, foreseeing the momentous consequences which Henry has openly disregarded:

> Menos sé que tú, señor;
> mas cuando las cosas toco
> de la fe y su religión,
> creo, cerrados los ojos,
> que el peregrino en el mar
> fin tuviera lastimoso,
> si el gobierno de la nave
> tiranizara al piloto.

Las cismas y los errores
con máscaras de piadosos
se introducen; pero luego
se van quitando el embozo.
,Mira no vayas, señor,
deslizando poco a poco;
porque el volver sobre ti
será más dificultoso.

(I am less learned than you, sire, but in matters of faith and religion I believe,
with my eyes shut, that the pilgrim sailing the seas would come to a sad end if
the pilot were to usurp the command of the ship. Schisms and errors are
introduced behind the mask of piety; but soon they throw off their disguise.
Take heed, sire, that you do not slip little by little, because it will be more
difficult for you to reverse direction.)

(225b–c)

On this point Catherine is the only one who sees clearly. But it must be
noted that she is not, as in Shakespeare's play, an innocent victim; for
she has brought her own disaster upon herself. This departure from his
source is further evidence of Calderón's dramatic skill, of his impressive
transformation of this theme into moving art. For in the world of tragic
human error that the play presents, a world in which only the mad are
not blind, there is no such thing as innocent suffering. Catherine had
permitted Wolsey's rigid obedience to Henry's orders to enrage her, and
had rashly attacked him to his face, comparing him to Haman and
herself to Esther (218c). In view of this undisguised threat, Wolsey
determined to safeguard his position by having her removed. Catherine
does, indeed, see the truth: she and not Henry had read Wolsey's
character rightly, and in the matter of the divorce she is the only one to
place first things first. But previously her vision had not been clear-
sighted: her belief in what is right is, as she herself states, a belief held
'with her eyes shut'. In other words, she gropes in the dark, and through
her lack of political prudence (there were other ways of getting rid of
Wolsey), as well as through her lack of charity (her intolerance and
violent scorn), she frustrates the righteousness of her anger by aggravat-
ing its cause. Her last lines as she faces her abandonment (lines which so
impressively close the Act) have in this context a dramatic irony which is
truly tragic:

¡Ay, entierro para vivos!
¡Ay, corte, ay, imperio todo!
¡Dios mire por ti! ¡Ay, Enrique!
¡El cielo te abra los ojos!

(Oh, burial for the living! Oh, court, woe on the whole kingdom! May God look
after you! Alas, Henry! May Heaven open your eyes!)

(226b)

In the light of all the preceding imagery this last sentence should be
carefully noted. The darkness into which her closed eyes have plunged
her is a suffering from which there seems no escape. Margaret Pole
invites her to a new hope (note the gentler, more subdued form of the
light image, which is not Wolsey's and Anne's noonday sun):

sal a ver la blanca aurora,
que la torre no es prisión,
pues nunca della saliste.

(Go out to gaze on the white dawn, for the tower is not a prison, and you have
not yet been outside.)

(228a)

But Catherine retorts that there is no hope:

Mal dijiste;
que a un triste sólo consuela,
Margarita, el estar triste.

(You have not spoken wisely, for the only consolation for sadness, Margaret,
is to remain sad.)

(228b)

Nonetheless, her eyes do open to the light of the dawn, for she finds
consolation and hope in the expiation of her fault, in feeling now the
charity she had not felt for her enemy, and in doing now the good she
had not done him. To Wolsey she is now able to say:

Tú has hallado
en mí remedio felice.
Y yo hallé consuelo en ti

(You have found in me easing for your suffering. And I have found
consolation in you)

(228c)

and thus finds her redemption:

La vida y alma te diera
por consolarte, Volseo.

(I would give my life and soul to you, Wolsey, if I could only console you.)

(229a)

Contrasted with her ability to forgive Wolsey is his inability to forgive
Anne. The liberty taken with history in this moving scene fulfils a

dramatic necessity: the final touches are given to the significance of these two characters, the one finding redemption in suffering, the other despair.

Catherine's repudiation marks the climax of the play. In the third Act Calderón is faced with his *dénouement*. The downfall of Wolsey and Anne has been made inevitable (though that of Anne is brought about by means that perhaps show a temporary falling away from the high level of dramatic skill so characteristic of the play). What, however, is to become of Henry? Ribadeneyra, in viewing his history as a stage on which providence unfolded a design he was confident he could interpret, had faced a similar problem. Villainy demands expiation; and so, with a gratuitousness unbecoming in both a theologian and a historian, Ribadeneyra consigned Henry to hell.[15] Since Calderón has departed from his source by not making Henry a villain, he cannot now follow it by making him die in despair. But history, even when viewed with more charitable eyes than Ribadeneyra's, offers no ready-made solution to the dramatic problem of finding an ending consonant with condemnation of the divorce. Calderón must therefore devise one for himself. Actually his solution is not as remote as might be thought from history as he read it in his source. Henry's remorse; his desire to make restitution by summoning parliament to swear allegiance to Mary; his temptation to despair; his submission to his subjects' will – all this is to be found in Ribadeneyra, but Calderón reverses the outcome. Ribadeneyra's account of Henry's death will reveal both the points of contact and the divergence between him and Calderón.

> The king fell ill with a serious and dangerous malady, and seeing that he could not be cured, tortured by the cruel executioner of his conscience, he began to enquire of some bishops how he could become reconciled to the Apostolic See and return to communion with the Church. But he who had so barbarously and cruelly executed many for having told him the truth and for having spoken freely to him as he had ordered did not deserve to find anybody to tell him the truth now. Therefore there was nobody now who dared to tell him what it was in his interests to hear. Rather, one of the bishops, sensing danger, and thinking that he was deceitfully asking for his opinion, replied that the king was above all other men wise in the extreme, and that he had rejected the primacy of the Roman Pontiff through Divine Inspiration and with the public authority of the whole kingdom, because of which he had nothing to fear. It is said that Stephen Gardiner, bishop of Winchester, advised the king secretly to summon all the Estates of the Realm, and inform them of a matter of such importance. If there was not time for this, he could announce his intention in writing; for our Lord is satisfied with our good intention when it cannot be carried out. After the Bishop had given this advice, the king was surrounded by a gang of evil flatterers who dissuaded him from his intention, overcoming

the scruples he had had; because they were afraid of losing the spoils that had come to them from the dissolution of the monasteries, if the king should return to the allegiance of the Pope. The king easily enough abandoned his good intention, as is usually the case with those who are not grounded in the love and fear of God . . . When his end was approaching, with all hope already abandoned by his doctors, and when he was informed of his danger, he asked for a goblet of white wine, and turning to one of his confidants, he said: *Omnia perdidimus*; we have lost everything; and with mortal anguish he uttered some bitter words, and naming several times some clergy and monks, he is said to have expired.

(231b–232a)

And:

[Opposition to the accession of Elizabeth] was voiced by the king of France, because he had seen that King Henry himself, when not swayed by passion, had ordered the parliament of the realm to declare that the Princess Mary would be his heir, and that the kingdom was not bound by the oath it had sworn to Anne Boleyn and to Elizabeth, her daughter.

(255b)

In Calderón's ending Henry does resist the temptation to despair and does therefore make restitution by restoring the Princess Mary to her position as his heir and leaving responsibility for righting the religious wrong done to her. This ending, as will be seen, is from the dramatic point of view an effective and satisfying solution to the theme in its two aspects – Henry's actions as a man, and his actions as a king. As regards the latter – the politico-religious aspect of the theme – Calderón concludes by pointing to the future. As a Catholic he points to Mary rather than to Elizabeth. He cannot, however, point to Mary as a hope that will be permanently realised. Not only would that be completely false to history, it would also (and this is much more important) be false to his theme as he has so far developed it. Calderón's ending has a close inner connection with what has preceded. A world in which men blindly grope for life in the darkness of error, suffering and death; a world in which men move with their eyes shut, or have them open only to turn values upside down; a world in which the blind carry lighted tapers in the pouring rain – such a world cannot suddenly be flooded with light and hope. And the Princess Mary does not so flood it.

By the shattering realisation that in passionately loving an unworthy woman he has degraded his honour as a man, Henry's eyes are opened to the magnitude of the disaster he has brought upon himself. Torn with remorse, the man who had previously sought advice only from Wolsey now humbly turns for guidance to God. Enlightened by prayer he determines to make restitution to Queen Catherine, but the news that she is dead removes restitution from the personal to the political plane. Here he realises that, as she had forecast, it is not easy to retrace his steps. Not only must he bear the weight of his personal grief, he must also bear bitter humiliation as King – helplessness in face of his subjects. So crushing is the burden, that he is tempted to despair:

> ¡Qué mal hice! ¡Que mal hice!
> Mas si no tengo remedio
> ¿de qué sirve arrepentirme?
> ¿De qué sirven desengaños
> y deseos? ¿De qué sirven,
> si está cerrada la puerta?

> (What harm I have done! What harm I have done! But if I cannot remedy it, what is the use of repenting? What is the use of disillusion and good intentions? What use are they, if the door is shut?)

> (230c)

His royal power was sufficient to enforce what he knew to be wrong; it is insufficient now to enforce what he knows to be right. For political difficulties make restitution impossible. He realises that the nobles will not suffer the restoration of the monastic property he permitted them to seize, nor will the people agree to return to the yoke of religious obedience from which he freed them. He failed in his duty as king to enforce the rule of right and justice, and is compelled to bow to, rather than command, his subjects' will, and to acquiesce in the perpetuation of injustice and wrong. But instead of despairing he places on his shoulders the burden of his political helplessness, and makes the only restitution that he can. Parliament must be summoned to take the oath of allegiance to Mary. Accepting also the burden of his personal grief, he orders (in the whispered aside to Thomas Boleyn) Anne's dead body to be placed at the foot of the throne on which Mary will sit, thus exposing to public ignominy the woman he had loved, and thus also exposing his own shame and dishonour. He hesitates as he enters the parliament chamber, fearful of being unable to face his double ordeal, but with a prayer he musters such courage and composure as he can:

> ¡Ayuda aquí, poderoso
> Señor, que el bajel va a pique!
> ¡En qué piélagos navega
> de confusiones Enrique!

> (Almighty God, grant me your help here, for the ship is sinking. On what a sea of dilemmas Henry is sailing.)

> (231b)

Despite the solemn proclamation of his royal authority, the people in parliament show the unruliness Henry has foreseen. They will accept Mary as heir only if she is prepared to preserve the existing state of affairs: if she swears not to compel them to change their new religious opinions, not to take ecclesiastical property from laymen, and not to look upon the despoiling of the Church as robbery. Indignantly refusing to accept these conditions, Mary affirms that her first duty as queen will be to truth and justice, and that the Law of God cannot be violated in the interests of political expediency. With this deadlock Henry tastes the full bitterness of his humiliation.

> ¡Pobre Enrique!
> ¡Qué de daños que te esperan!

> (Unhappy Henry! What disasters await you!)

(231c)

Mary is right, as he acknowledges to her; but even in what is right the choice of an end is relative to the possible means. He pleads with her to view her duty in the light of the means that are alone available to her:

> María, moza y mujer
> sois, y la poca experiencia
> os hace hablar dese modo.
> Tocaréis las conveniencias,
> y veréis lo que os importa.

> (Mary, you are young and a woman, and lack of experience makes you speak like that. You must do what can be done, and you will see what matters most)

(231c)

But she remains adamant.

Henry is thus again placed between two irreconcilable extremes. This time, humbled by grief and disaster, he makes the right choice; but it is a tragic choice that is the measure of his own helplessness and degradation. Excusing Mary's impetuousness as youthful inexperience, he advises the people to swear allegiance to her now, and later to depose her if as queen she is not to their liking; while to Mary he recommends silence and feigned consent, telling her that the time will come when she will be able to act on her zeal.

Judged by an absolute standard this compromise is an abject one. On one of the levels of significance in the play this conclusion thus represents the working out of dramatic justice. The once learned and conscientious king, who used his political power to place his private happiness above the spiritual good of the State, suffers the degradation of political impotence, with the consequent enforced transference of his responsibility to his daughter, whose steadfast resolve to rule according to right lays bare his own failure to fulfil his high duty.

But the play has another and a deeper level of significance. All through it there has run the contrast between the fixity of the absolute order of values and the confusion introduced by men through their inability or refusal to maintain it. On this level Henry's compromise is the only right course of action in the circumstances. For in the world of men there is no absolute clarity of vision, and there are no shoulders strong enough to bear the weight of absolute justice. Henry's human shoulders supported a learned head, but they were too weak for the burden of his kingly responsibilities. Now his eyes are open to his weakness, but Mary's are closed to hers, for with her intolerance and violent threats she exactly parallels those of her mother, Catherine. It is clear that she too will aggravate by her rashness what justly angers her. For righteousness and absolute justice belong to God alone. In the darkness that is the world of human affairs, especially of politics, men must grope warily and walk humbly, falling and rising, recognising themselves to be men not gods, viewing their ends in the light of their own frailty and always measuring them by the means at their disposal.

> de cualquiera suerte
> voy pisando las sombras de la muerte
>
> (either way, I step into the shadow of death)

– death and failure everywhere; nowhere, where men of themselves can find it, is there life. For the darkness can only partially lift. Only those can face the difficulties of life who ask in penitent prayer for God's mercy. Only those can emerge to view the suffused light of 'la blanca aurora' (the white dawn) who have been humbled by suffering into charity and compassion. Any attempt to stare boldly at the sun will cause its light to turn to fire. Mary threatens her future subjects with the fire of persecution if they do not bow to her intransigent and uncompassionate will:

> al que me jure, y faltare
> a lo que mi ley profesa,
> si no le quemare vivo,
> será porque se arrepienta.
>
> (Whoever swears allegiance to me, but fails in observing the religion I profess, if he is not burned alive by me, it will only be because he repents.)
>
> (231c)

In *La cisma de Ingalaterra* the theme of Henry VIII's divorce is therefore transformed into a significant and impressive dramatic action. Since it has a powerful dramatic idea unifying the action with intricate subtlety into an admirable coherence, and leading it to an inevitable conclusion, we are surely compelled to admit that as a piece of dramatic construction and execution *La cisma de Ingalaterra* should be considered a masterpiece.

Despite all this *La cisma de Ingalaterra* is a travesty of history. Must a historical play that is a successful example of dramatic art be nonetheless condemned if it alters historical fact? Or to put it in another way, must Calderón be condemned for choosing a historical theme that he could not dramatise without travestying? We must distinguish between contemporary theatre and the drama of past ages. No modern dramatist would be likely to take such liberties with history, but in Calderón's lifetime the freedom of the dramatic artist to mould historical material by adding, rejecting or altering in order, in Sir Philip Sidney's words, 'to frame the history to the most tragical conveniency', was a commonplace of literary theory, which was exemplified in dramatic practice as frequently in England as in Spain.[16] Whatever restrictions would now be imposed by public and critics on the writer of a historical play, the fact remains that a work of art cannot be merely history decked out in a more pleasing garb than that provided by the historian.

Not only is each minor departure from Calderón's source necessitated and therefore justified poetically by his dramatic plan, but the major departure itself – the sympathetic treatment of Henry – is, on the level of poetry, a 'truer' presentation of history. The historical fact to which *La cisma de Ingalaterra* must be related is not the history of Henry VIII's reign as we know it but as Calderón knew it. Ribadeneyra did not depart from what he was convinced was true fact, but the truth is distorted by the violent feeling with which he presents it. No human history is a sharp contrast of black and white, and by rejecting the crude invective of his co-religionists Calderón in effect showed Ribadeneyra how history should be written – with a tolerant mind and a compassionate heart open to the tragedy of human life. It may be objected that, nonetheless, Calderón is even here straining our credulity too far, that the historical Henry, as a man, does not in fact deserve so much sympathy. But Calderón, on the high level of poetic drama, is concerned more with the tragedy of humanity than with the tragedy of one particular human being.

Further, it is not as if the significance Calderón reads into the historical events is itself fanciful. To view Henry VIII, in the first place, as a tragic example of a catastrophic abuse of political power in order to attain an unworthy personal end, is not a false interpretation of history from the Catholic standpoint that the schism was a national disaster. But Calderón's aim is also wider than that: wider than the genuine concern for a right order that lies behind the ill-informed invective of Ribadeneyra's History. Calderón perhaps derived his head and feet imagery from Ribadeneyra, for in dealing with Elizabeth the latter had written:

> But human malice perverts and destroys everything, and turns her who cannot be the head of a man into the supreme head of the Church [i.e. Queen Elizabeth's assumption of this title after the rejection of Papal supremacy]
>
> (258b)

The English

> confuse and pervert the order of everything divine and human, giving primacy to the body over the soul, to civil government over spiritual, and to the kingdom of this earth over that of heaven, to the lower over the higher, to the sheep over the shepherd, and turning the head into the feet, and the feet into the head.
>
> (320a)

Calderón's aim is a vaster one than that of relating a particular historical issue to the universal standard that should govern it. Is it being false to history to view Henry VIII and all the other actors in his drama as symbols of tragic humanity, falling under the weight of unbearable responsibilities, confused by the conflict of passion and reason, blinded by pride, ambition or a self-righteous over-confidence, all erring in the darkness that is human life?

Calderón alters fact in order to achieve these two connected and historically valid ends. By suggesting that his Henry is to be considered as Mankind I do not mean that it is the writer of *autos sacramentales* who is here interpreting history. The sense of hopelessness, the pessimism, of *La cisma de Ingalaterra* is not the spirit of the *autos*. Calderón is interpreting history strictly within the context of history, and this context is a wider one than that of Henry VIII's reign; and this seems to me another reason why Calderón departed from his source, and why he omitted any reference to the reign of Elizabeth.

Henry VIII's divorce was but part of a long period of tragic human error and strife, of hopeless and fruitless wars of religion, which it had itself helped to usher in. And Calderón transposes *this* history into dramatic art, without travestying its meaning in any way.

We may conclude, therefore, by not only maintaining that *La cisma de Ingalaterra* is an impressive example of dramatic art, but by also suggesting that it is, despite its deliberate departure from fact, an impressive *historical* play, in the way in which poetic drama can most significantly be historical, in that it shows insight into history as the stage on which humanity struggles for its salvation.

There is, however, more to be added to the question of the play's 'historicity'. It can be argued that Calderón turned to this English theme because it had a direct bearing on contemporary history. This point will now be discussed.

20 The issue of religious freedom

All new history alters the significance of all previous history, and for Calderón the present could not but alter the past. Ribadeneyra's interpretation of history (his first Part was published in the year of the Armada) was dictated by the spirit in which he approached it: 'Who will not abhor so diabolical a sect? Who will not wonder at the patience of the Lord, who endures them? Who will not fight against these monsters? Who will not believe that victory is certain?'[1] No intelligent Spaniard could approach the history of England in that spirit some thirty-four years later. When the original paper, which the last chapter largely reproduces, was published, it was generally accepted that Calderón's play must have been written after 1639 and before 1652, probably therefore after the outbreak of the English Civil War, and perhaps even after the execution of Charles I (an event which aroused consternation and horror in Spain). My essay gave this as the probable reason for Calderón's compassionate treatment of the earlier English king.

After the publication of that original paper it was discovered that a private performance of *La cisma de Ingalaterra* had been given to Philip IV in the palace, for which payment was made on 31 March 1627. We do not know whether this was the first performance, nor whether the play then performed was the play as we now have it. Assuming that this is the case, the likelihood is that the play was begun, if not completed, in 1626. This is a remarkably early date for so well-constructed a play. The question why Calderón should have treated Henry VIII so much more compassionately than did Ribadeneyra, as well as the question why he should have turned to this theme of English history, cannot be answered by Spanish sympathy for a king at war with his subjects or executed by them. A reason for a dominant Spanish interest in England and the English monarchy prior to 1627 must be sought in the protracted negotiations for an Anglo-Spanish alliance through the marriage of the Infanta María, sister of Philip IV, to the Prince of Wales, the future Charles I. This does in fact provide a more satisfactory explanation in current affairs for the ending of Calderón's play.

In 1626 the sensational event of the secret visit of the Prince of Wales to Madrid and the protracted negotiations, which took place in 1623, for his marriage to the Infanta María were still fresh in the memory of the inhabitants of Madrid, despite the fact that war with England had just broken out. During the last years of Philip III's reign Count Gondomar, the Spanish Ambassador in London, had been actively promoting this marriage. James I and his favourite, the Duke of Buckingham, were strongly in favour of this alliance. The young Philip IV and Olivares kept the negotiations going as a possible means of converting Charles, and possibly King James, to Roman Catholicism, thus preparing the way for England's return to the Old Faith. Gondomar advised that the prince should travel incognito to Madrid where his presence would force the Spanish Government's hand. Charles and Buckingham presented themselves early in March 1623 at the residence of the astounded English Ambassador in Madrid. Gondomar, who was in Madrid, informed Olivares of the prince's arrival. The gravity of this situation was immediately apparent. How could the marriage be refused and the prince sent back to England without the danger of war? These apprehensions were disguised by the polite cordiality with which the English party were welcomed and 16 March was fixed as the date for Charles's formal entry into Madrid. In all the conversations concerning the marriage it was assumed by the Spaniards that Charles's conversion to Catholicism would follow. Although King James's correspondence seemed to foresee no difficulties, the English party in Madrid were alarmed at the way the conversion was being taken for granted. The festivities lasted for three days, and the official negotiations then began, while the arrival of the dispensation from Rome was awaited. The conversion of Prince Charles was felt to be certain, and the Spaniards did not demand it, but as a condition for the marriage they requested the removal of all the penal restrictions on English Catholics, despite the fact that Buckingham was never sanguine that such a condition would ever be accepted by parliament. In April it was reported that the dispensation for the marriage was on its way from Rome, but that this included further demands for religious freedom for English Catholics. However, opposition in England to these conditions remained firm, and on the Spanish side all possible compromises were rejected. Thereupon in June, King James ordered the English party to return, the date fixed being 17 July. In a valedictory address to King Philip, Spanish reports state that Prince Charles astonished everybody by pledging himself to obtain from his father freedom of worship for English Catholics. This made the Spaniards think that the marriage was now certain, and Olivares would not permit Charles to depart until he and his father were committed to this measure; as for Charles's conversion, Olivares said that this would rest with

Charles himself. Charles and Buckingham tried to persuade King James to agree to the repeal of the penal laws, writing that if he would promise this they could return to England immediately, taking the Infanta with them. On Sunday 20 July King James, still extremely anxious to achieve the Imperial and Spanish alliance, privately took an oath before a Spanish emissary, a Catholic priest and two Secretaries of State that he would remove all the disabilities on English Catholics. Olivares, however, did not trust James and refused to permit the Infanta to leave Spain before the removal of the penal disabilities became effective. Charles and Buckingham realised that they had been fooled by Olivares, and bade farewell to king and government. Diplomatic efforts were made in both Madrid and London to keep the negotiations alive, but they ultimately foundered on the intractable issue of religious freedom in England.[2]

Other stipulations made by Spain had been that all children of the marriage should be brought up as Catholics by their mother and should remain so without forfeiting the right to succession to the throne. That such demands were extravagant shows how little Spaniards at that time knew of the nature of the English Reformation. Calderón was of course correct in referring to it as a 'schism' during Henry VIII's reign, but Spaniards in 1623 seemed not to have realised that the breach with Rome was wider than this.

> Gondomar seems to have believed that most Englishmen were either Catholics who disguised their real religion through fear of persecution, or Protestants whose religion had been assumed to please the head of the state and who would revert to Catholicism if the penal laws were repealed.[3]

Because of this ignorance it is surely not fanciful to see the close of *La cisma de Ingalaterra* as mirroring the events of 1623 rather than the supposed end of Henry VIII's reign. Calderón was bringing the English schism 'up-to-date', which would be why he omitted the reigns of Edward VI and Elizabeth as irrelevant for his purpose, since they had no bearing on the events of 1623 that he and all the inhabitants of Madrid had lived through in the exciting prospect that Spain through her Infanta (with whom the Prince of Wales had appeared to be genuinely in love) could reverse the unhappy outcome of Henry VIII's passion for Anne Boleyn.

The dispute between King Henry and the future Queen Mary with which the play ends, centering as it does on the question of religious freedom in England, with Henry (like the English party) counselling moderation and compromise, while Mary (like the Spanish Government and Church) insists on firmness, must have taken the minds of king and court back to the still very recent months of the Prince of Wales's love for the Infanta María who, they all hoped, would be instrumental in bringing England back to Rome, just as the Princess Mary is determined to do when the curtain falls. Such a hope was still not fanciful in 1626, for Charles had indeed married a Catholic, Henrietta Maria of France, in 1625. The contract for this marriage allowed members of the queen's household to be Catholics and had also permitted the suspension of the penal laws. This nonetheless was never granted by the English parliament. In 1626, the year the play was most probably written, France made peace with Spain and therefore English parliamentary hopes of an alliance with France against Spain and the Empire were abandoned. James's cherished plan, the opposite, an Anglo-Spanish alliance, had failed and his reign ended as it had begun with war against Spain (1625–1630).[4] This war is probably reflected in the threat of disaster at the end of the play. The Prince of Wales had been generally popular during his protracted stay in Madrid, and Calderón's sympathy for his English king probably reflects this popularity. In any case, the high hopes in Spain that England might return, through a Spanish marriage, to the union with Rome, which had been ruptured by the divorce of a Spanish-born queen, significantly accounts for Calderón's unhistorical treatment of the outcome of the English schism.

The fact that reconciliation had been effected by Queen Mary, who had married a Spanish Catholic Prince (the future Philip II); the fact that this reconciliation had been marked by persecution of Protestants and did not survive Mary's death, leading finally to open war with Spain under Elizabeth, to be followed still later by the disappointment at the reconciliation between England and Rome apparently promised during the Prince of Wales's stay in Madrid (and whose only outcome was in fact renewed war with England), may have contributed to the pessimism of Calderón's ending.

The threat of persecution and religious struggles, expressing the pessimism with which the play ends, had already been a reality in Spain's government of the Low Countries. The Dutch, who had embraced Calvinism, began in 1566 a revolt against the rule of their Spanish sovereign. The revolt had been fired by the religious wars in France in 1562 and the growth of 'international Protestantism' had thus grown roots in the Spanish dominions. Philip II had promulgated the decrees of the Council of Trent in all his realms, and this was a major cause of disaffection with the Dutch. In deciding what course of action he should take in face of the Revolt, Philip followed the long-standing practice of the Spanish Crown in seeking advice from theologians in all affairs of State that impinged directly on moral issues. A *Junta*, or council, of theologians was the keeper of the king's conscience in such matters. In

1566 the king asked this council to tell him whether he would be justified in suspending the Tridentine decrees in the rebellious province. His theologians advised him that he could withhold the promulgation of the decrees, but Philip sent back the comment that he had not asked whether he *could* but whether he *should* suspend them. Faced with this stricter demand, the theologians answered that he should not. The king's conscience was more rigorist than that of his theologians, and he imposed strict principle upon them as well as on himself rather than political prudence. As a result the struggle in the Netherlands became in Philip's eyes a religious crusade against heresy and not just a political issue. Consequently the Dutch were denied freedom of conscience and freedom of worship and became liable to persecution for heresy if Spain could reassert her authority over them. In the long-drawn-out struggle Philip slowly conceded the Dutch everything they were fighting for except this single issue of freedom of religion. Thanks to a conscience that could not compromise on strict principle, Spanish power had to suffer a drain of economic resources and the increasing weakness of her military power, which led more than any other single issue to the disaster that was to overcome Spain's position in Europe. This disaster was averted by the Twelve Years Truce with Holland that lasted from 1609 to 1621. This truce was finally broken by the Thirty Years War, which ended in the Treaty of Münster (1648). Spain had eventually to recognise the independence of Holland, and the crusade against Dutch Calvinism proved a failure.

Calderón wrote *La cisma de Ingalaterra* while the fruitlessness of the struggle was still unrecognised. The play closes with a dispute between King Henry, counselling prudent expediency in the forthcoming religious struggle in England, and his daughter Mary Tudor, threatening bloodshed and persecution while adamantly refusing to move an inch on the principle of religious uniformity. It is surely not fanciful to see in this unhistorical dispute a true lesson in history applicable retrospectively to the difference of opinion between Philip II and his Council of Theologians; applicable also to the contemporary issue of religious freedom, which Spain with diehard conservatism was still refusing some of her subjects. This could well be in the sweep of sixty years of history, a subtle instance of 'speaking without telling'. Everything in the action and the tone of *La cisma de Ingalaterra* points to the message that crusades cannot succeed, and that it would be better for public policy not to be governed by intransigence. It is possible that the same judgement on crusades could have been conveyed, to those who had ears to hear it, in the play that followed *La cisma de Ingalaterra* two years later, *El príncipe constante*.

21 Religion and war: *El príncipe constante*

Part 3 of this book dealt with representative themes covering the problems of social living. These are problems affecting individuals; although most of them are universal in the sense that they can arise for all men at other periods in cultures that have, broadly speaking, similar *mores* and ethical standards. They are essentially problems of private lives. Other problems of moral and social living arise in the context of public life. All men have to live in this sphere, and all men can face the problems that can arise within it. The problems are mainly political, dealing with the relation of the individual to authority, either the authority of government, or the authority of the law. In the case of seventeenth-century Spain, there was another overriding authority, that of the Church. In Habsburg Spain it was not just the question of state religion; it was rather that Spain was, properly speaking, a 'Religion State', one in which the doctrines of the Church and her jurisdiction covered in theory the life of every individual, and if there was any conflict it governed the life of the individual in practice also. Religious belief and observance could be literally matters of life and death. Monarchy and government were as authoritarian as the Church, and no-one could be exempt from the sanctions of either.

One can speak of political plays in the output of Calderón only by broadening the range of the term in the way suggested by the outline given in chapter 18 to *Saber del mal y del bien*. With religion it is a different matter. Apart from the special case of the *autos sacramentales*, in which problems of belief and the acceptance of dogmas were rendered allegorically and symbolically, religious *comedias* fell into two broad groups – historical, dealing with biblical stories or episodes from the early history of the Church, or they dealt with a special type of history – that of hagiography. These latter plays were, and still are, called *comedias de santos*. Deriving directly from the Jesuit school plays, they dealt with the biographies or legends of saints in order to bring out how men and women could become saints. Most of these plays dealt with Christian martyrs, understandably the most dramatic and the most moving examples of sanctity. Following the principles laid down by the Jesuit drama, a strong tradition of martyr-plays was established in Catholic Europe which survived for over a century. The Jesuit plays were written by the fathers of the society in Latin, and performed in their schools on special occasions such as prize-giving. Plays of martyrdom proved so popular that secular dramatists in France, Spain and Germany wrote them in the vernacular for performance in the public theatres. There is even an English example of one of these martyr plays – Massinger's *Virgin Martyr* on the life of Saint Dorothy. The general theme is the persecution of a Christian for his faith, and how he suffers death rather than recant.[1] The two best-known of Calderón's martyr plays are *El príncipe constante* (The Steadfast Prince) and *El mágico prodigioso* (The Wonder-Working Magician); the date of the former is 1629, the date of the first version of the latter is 1637. The latter play establishes a special tradition of Calderón's own within the general theme. It deals with the legend of Saint Cyprian and Saint Justina, martyred in Antioch under Diocletian. What Calderón adds to the theme is the conversion of the martyr as part of his philosophical enquiry into the nature of God. Having realised that only the Christian God fulfils all the attributes of the Divine Nature which Reason must postulate, Cipriano is distracted from actually receiving Christian instruction when the Devil tempts him to abandon philosophy for erotic experience in the person of Justina, who has been a Christian since birth. Faust-like, Cipriano signs a pact with the Devil, offering him his soul in return for the possession of Justina. When put to the final test, the Devil can bring him only a skeleton in Justina's garments; a symbol of the end to which the search for happiness in sensuality must lead. Realising this, Cipriano comes back to his philosophical search, is converted, and dies a martyr's death together with Justina.[2]

Though an early play, *El príncipe constante* deserves to rank as one of Calderón's most beautiful and moving plays. It deals with the capture and death in captivity of Prince Ferdinand of Portugal (1402–43), who was revered as a saint and martyr. There is no question here of any conversion to Christianity; the play is not set in the early history of the Church but in the late period of the Iberian crusades against the Moors. From the conquest of the whole of Spain in 711 by the Berbers from Morocco under Arab leadership, the history of the Iberian kingdoms had been that of a slow reconquest for Christianity, completed in 1492 by the Castilian conquest of the kingdom of Granada. The long Reconquest had left an indelible mark on the history and literature, especially the ballad poetry, of Castile, and it coloured the imagination of all Spaniards for long after 1492. That year saw also the discovery of America, and the beginning of the transference of the crusading spirit overseas in the conquest and subjugation of the American Indians to Spain and the Church. The crusading spirit was further fostered by the Protestant Reformation and the Wars of Religion which were its legacy, in which Spain was deeply committed. Calderón wrote *El príncipe constante* in the middle of the Thirty Years War. It is the product of centuries of religious strife and conquest, and representing as it does an episode in the seven-century-long conflict between Christian and Moor, it can be looked at, as has been said, as an epilogue to a long struggle in which political and religious ends had always been inseparable. Its theme is one of the last expeditions of the Portuguese against Morocco. It was very much part of the epoch of the Iberian crusaders, and the contemporary struggle of Catholic against Protestant was a continuing part of this religious war. The European struggle with the attendant religious persecution is what helped to give the martyr drama a certain actuality. Because of all this, the theme of *El príncipe constante* is essentially one of public and not private life. Spaniards could still be fighting unbelievers (Moors and Turks) or fighting heretics, and persecuting or being persecuted by them. How did such a world affect and control the lives of individuals?

Furthermore, prisoners of war and their ransom or slavery were very topical issues which must have affected large numbers of families. The most famous of these prisoners of war was Miguel de Cervantes, who was captured by the Turks in 1575 as his ship was sailing from Italy to Spain. He was a soldier, returning to Spain with letters from his commanding officer recommending him for a commission. If prisoners of war were people of standing or judged to have families with money, they were held for ransom; in other cases the prisoners were sold as slaves. The order of Mercedarian friars had been founded to raise money for the ransom of captives and negotiate their freedom. When no ransom was forthcoming for Cervantes after five years, his owner decided to sell him in the slave market in Constantinople, but before this could happen, he was ransomed by money that the friars had brought for another prisoner but which proved insufficient. Captivity under the Muslims and slavery were therefore events of everyday life; even if there was no war, piracy ensured that prisoners were never lacking in the Mediterranean.

El príncipe constante thus dramatised a historical theme still connected in 1629 with the national life of Spain, but the play itself cannot be called historical. The capture and enslavement of a royal prince and his martyrdom for the faith was too sensational an event for it not to be been transformed over the course of a century. Prince Ferdinand was the youngest son of King Edward (Duarte) of Portugal. The eldest of this distinguished family of Princes was the famous Henry the Navigator. He appears in Calderón's play but with his rôle and that of Ferdinand inverted.

The Portuguese campaigns against Morocco began in 1415 with the capture of Ceuta. Prince Henry took part in this campaign. In 1437 he commanded another expedition which sailed to Ceuta and the army marched by land to capture Tangier. The King of Morocco sent reinforcements and the Portuguese sued for peace. In the battle, Prince Ferdinand, who is presented in the play as the commander of the Portuguese forces, was made prisoner, and was kept as a hostage in Fez pending a successful outcome to the peace negotiations. The conditions were that Henry should be given freedom to embark his troops on condition that Ceuta was returned to Morocco. From Ceuta Henry began negotiations with the King of Portugal for the release of Ferdinand but insisted that Ceuta should never be handed over. The Moroccan king was adamant that Ceuta was the only price for Ferdinand. While the Portuguese parliament (Cortes) was discussing the terms, Ferdinand wrote a letter pleading for his release and asserting that the retention of Ceuta was not of supreme importance, either on strategic or religious grounds. The Cortes, however, decided that Ferdinand should be freed by other means. The King of Portugal tried to obtain help from other countries for another expedition to free the prince but was unsuccessful, and Ferdinand remained in captivity in Fez. Henry was confident that his brother could be rescued with a larger army than had been available for the attack on Tangier, and refused to consider the transfer of Ceuta. King Edward died in 1438. In his will he demanded the release of Ferdinand, even with the surrender of Ceuta. The Queen Regent decided to surrender Ceuta and emissaries were sent to receive Ferdinand in 1441, but the Moroccan king demanded total evacuation of Ceuta before Ferdinand would be exchanged. The Portuguese refused this and the Moroccan government demanded, and persuaded Ferdinand to ask for, an exorbitant sum of money. Ferdinand was left to die in captivity under ever more rigorous conditions of solitary confinement, dying in 1443. His embalmed body was exposed at the gates of Fez to the mockery of the inhabitants. The other Portuguese prisoners, however, had preserved his heart and entrails, and when they were released in 1451 they took these relics back to Portugal. Alphonso V (Ferdinand's nephew) renewed the war against Morocco, capturing Arzila and Tangier in 1471. In a treaty with the Governor of Arzila he obtained Ferdinand's body in exchange for the wives and son of the Governor of Arzila, whom Alphonso had captured. These remains were transferred ceremoniously to Lisbon and interred in the Mausoleum at Batalha. Ferdinand had never voluntarily chosen captivity and indeed had constantly requested freedom through ransom; but at the same time he endured his five and a half years of suffering with steadfastness, never wavering in his Christian faith. He soon came to be revered by the Portuguese as a saint and martyr.

Up to this point, the outline of Calderón's plot is reasonably faithful to history. He gives the Moroccan king's insistence on ransom, but he makes Ferdinand refuse it. The prince, however, had always demanded and expected to be ransomed, and in all his letters had pleaded for freedom. There was never any question in his mind that he had to suffer enslavement and death in order to preserve the religious freedom of the Portuguese inhabitants of Ceuta. He was not, therefore, properly speaking, a martyr, since he did not willingly accept enslavement and death, but hoped always to avoid them.

Calderón introduces the expedition of King Alphonso but makes its aim the freeing of Ferdinand. When Alfonso arrives at Fez and hears that Fernando has died, he asks for the return of the prince's body, the ransom of which for Christian burial in a Church becomes now the aim of the expedition. Historically, the body was exchanged for the wives and son of the Governor of Arzila, whom Alphonso had captured on his march. The exchange of living captives for a dead body is retained in Calderón's play and given a special significance, but the living body exchanged is that of Fénix, the daughter of the king of Fez, who is the most important of the characters contrasted with Fernando.

The telescoping of chronology and the exchange of prisoners in the play cannot be considered deviations marring the spirit of the history. What does make the play fundamentally unhistorical is the fact that Ferdinand renounces freedom and chooses slavery against the wishes of King Duarte and Prince Henry. This fundamental deviation, however, was not Calderón's invention. He is in essence true to his sources. The change from an unwilling captive to a willing martyr on religious grounds, to safeguard the religion of Ceuta and its inhabitants, began fairly soon after the prince's relics were brought to Portugal. The glorification of Portugal's heroic martyr is fully developed in the national epic, *Os Lusíadas* by Camões (1572). It provided the plot for a play, *La fortuna adversa del Infante don Fernando de Portugal*, first wrongfully attributed on pulication to Lope de Vega. It was published undated but composed after 1595, and was probably written by Canon Francisco Tárrega. This play was Calderón's source.[3]

Arguments have been brought for and against considering *El príncipe constante* a tragedy. Whether it is, is really immaterial. But in the course of debating it various arguments are used that seem to be inaccurate statements of what actually happens in the play. As previously noted on several occasions, it is essential for understanding a Calderonian play to analyse the details and coherence of the plot's structure and not to assume that what the characters in his plays say of themselves and their actions necessarily represent the author's opinions. These misunderstandings are due to preconceived notions of what a play about a crusader and a martyr *must* be.[4] The principal reasons for denying *El príncipe constante* this status do not in fact apply.

Although the alleged incompatibility of Christianity and tragedy has been stated perhaps *ad nauseam*, it is advisable to repeat it here in the words of a contemporary writer:

> There has been no specifically Christian mode of tragic drama even in the noon-time of the faith. Christianity is an anti-tragic vision of the world . . . Christianity offers to man an assurance of final certitude and respose in God. It leads the soul towards justice and resurrection. The Passion of Christ is an event of unutterable grief, but it is also a cipher through which is revealed the love of God for man. In the dark night of Christ's suffering, original sin is shown to have been a joyous error *(felix culpa)*. Through it humanity shall be restored to a condition far more exalted than was Adam's innocence. In the drama of Christian life, the arrow beats against the wind but points upward. Being a threshold to the eternal, the death of a Christian hero can be an occasion for sorrow but not for tragedy . . .
>
> The Christian view knows only partial or episodic tragedy. Within its essential optimism there are moments of despair; cruel setbacks can occur during the ascent toward grace. But, as a Portuguese proverb has it, *Deus escreve direito por linhas tortas* (God writes straight on crooked lines).[5]

'Optimism' (invariably repeated in this kind of context) is a relative term in association with this impressive proverb. If one could imagine God, like the wise old monk Pimen in *Boris Godunov*, writing the chronicle of humanity through the night, one would feel his infinitely weary sadness at the perversity of men's unendingly crooked lines. Calderón never loses sight of the crooked lines and makes them the centre of his religious plays. It is to forfeit a sense of proportion to say this of one of his martyrs, Cipriano in *El mágico prodigioso*:

> The Christian hero has the card of immortality and beatitude with which he can trump the last tricks of his opponents, Paganism and Death. Heads may be severed from bodies, but there is no suffering: what seems to be agony is unreal because it is willed, not undergone – the victim remains in control.[6]

In control of what? Precisely because Cipriano is no longer free *not* to see and love the truth that reason and experience have put before his mind and heart, he is *not* in control of his death; those who are free not to die are the *graciosos*, enslaved to the *ignorancia a vista de la ciencias* (ignorance within sight of knowledge) which (in that play) is the crooked line of human life. The search for truth and not the actual act of martyrdom is the dramatic centre of *El mágico prodigioso*. This drama is not a tragedy; but neither has its *dénouement* the crudity of a trump card.

In the light of this general consideration let us examine the reasons why *El príncipe constante* has not been accepted as tragedy:

> Yet, in the end, both the Portuguese arms and Christian faith triumph on both levels, the secular and the religious. Fernando's spirit leads the Porguese army to victory. His dead body is exchanged for the living *hermosura* of captive Fénix, thereby symbolically expressing the superiority of spiritual values over the worldly ones. Fernando receives a Christian burial, Ceuta is kept in Christian hands. The Portuguese national honor, which suffered defeat in Act I, is restored through victory in Act III. Even in the light secondary plot, Muley and Fénix will be happily united in marriage.

> The world order, upset and threatened in the course of the dramatic action by frightening changes of fortune, both personal and national, has been restored. There are no unanswered questions left at the end of the play.

> *El príncipe constante* lacks the one essential quality for tragedy, catastrophe at the end. Fernando is a flawless character who lives unflinchingly by a code of hierarchically arranged values, both secular and religious. His death, chosen by himself in the exercise of his free will, is the logical conclusion of his Christian constancy. His re-appearance as a spirit after death brings on the triumph of right. Fernando is a martyr and a saint, but not a tragic hero.[7]

Does Portugal in fact 'triumph' in the end? Does Alfonso's 'victory' achieve the purpose of his campaign? Was this in fact to give Fernando a Christian burial? Was it to keep Ceuta in Christian hands? (Had Ceuta ever actually been threatened by the Moors? Had it not been the Portuguese themselves who decided to hand it over to the infidel?) Is the ending really a 'restoration' of world order? Are not the conditions for Portugal at the end actually worse than when the first expedition set off? Is it then a 'triumph of right' to gain nothing, and to 'restore' something worse than the *status quo*?

Exactly the same questions are posed by Elida Maria Szarota's presentation of the issues. Of Fernando the slave she states: 'But this slave will live aware that he has rescued Ceuta for the Catholic faith, and that is his greatest triumph.' His 'triumph' to have 'rescued' Ceuta for Catholicism? Wasn't it his military failure in the first place that exposed it to danger? Is not 'triumph' too strong a word to denote doing what one can to prevent the consequences of one's failure? If it is a 'triumph' it must imply a corresponding disaster for the enemy. 'Fernando's heroic resistance is the moral defeat of the King of Fez, not only his political loss. Fernando's uncompromising attitude is a fiasco for him all along the line.'[8] 'Political loss'? How can the king lose what he has not got? He is frustrated in his hopes of getting more than he has, but this is not a 'fiasco'. The fiasco is surely Portugal's in being defeated and so being placed in the position of handing over Ceuta without even a siege. As regards territory, the King of Fez, 'defeated all along the line', retains at the end everything that he had at the beginning.

This tendency to present the political and military facts as other than they are is, of course, perfectly understandable. The reader is dazzled by the moral splendour of Fernando's death. Calderón intends him to be. He wants his audience to be stirred by the appearance of Fernando's ghost holding a lighted torch aloft, and he presents the 'ransoming' of Fernando's dead body through the exchange of Fénix and the freeing of Tarudante, king of Morocco, as an apotheosis of his martyrdom. The exaltation of the dead saint is such that it is only too easy to project the sense of triumph on to the political sphere and the second military expedition. But what kind of apotheosis is this? Not a political triumph over an infidel enemy, but the personal triumph of an individual in rising to sanctity not only over the natural human fear of pain and death, but also through and above the warring ambitions of politicians and the human suffering they cause. It will be argued here that the apotheosis of Fernando's sanctity is the opposite of any patriotic exaltation of the politics of territorial aggrandisement and of crusading warfare; that, in fact, it is necessary to distinguish clearly between the religious and the political levels in the play in order to see the full extent of its originality.[9] The nature of Fernando's sanctity – how he rises superior, as a human being, to the other characters – has been excellently studied already.[10] It is not my intention to repeat this by showing how Christian values are incarnated in an individual, but to examine instead the relation of Christian values to the form in which the conflicts of the human drama are conceived, for they pervade the structure of the plot as well as the poetry and the symbolism.

If we shut our eyes for the time being to the moral triumph of Fernando's death and look at the main action as a conflict between two nations, we must conclude that, on the political level (with political aims sought through military means), the play is a story of failure. At the start each side is aiming at territorial conquest. The King of Fez is planning an expedition to capture Ceuta. On his mission to reconnoitre the defences Muley discovers that King Duarte of Portugal has forestalled the Moors by sending an invading army to capture Tangier. The defence of this city takes precedence over the capture of Ceuta. The Portuguese are defeated and Tangier is not captured. Instead their commander, Prince Fernando, is taken prisoner. The Portuguese are presented with the choice of losing either their prince or Ceuta; they decide to surrender Ceuta, but this decision cannot be implemented and Don Enrique has to return to Lisbon with the news that the non-ransom of the prince means his degradation into a common slave. This military defeat represents political disaster, for either alternative means national ignominy for Portugal. Fernando says that the surrender of Ceuta, with the consequent conversion of Christian churches into mosques, would be

un epitafio, un padrón
de nuestra inmortal afrenta

(an epitaph for and a monument to our eternal disgrace)[11]

This ignominy *he* cannot face; on the other hand, the ignominy of having a prince of the blood enslaved causes King Duarte's death of grief and is something that his successor, Alfonso, cannot face. A second expedition to Africa is therefore despatched, not to capture Tangier but to free a prisoner. This is a marked decline in the political aim; it is in fact not achieved (despite a military victory) because the prisoner is already dead. Don Enrique (the voice, throughout the play, of political prudence) says:

¡Válgame el cielo! ¿Qué escucho?
¡Qué tarde, cielos, qué tarde
le llegó la libertad!

(Heavens! What do I hear? How late has his freedom come!)

(92) [261b]

The first expedition fails through over-confidence, the second fails through being too late. What political advantage has been gained through the expense and labour of two expeditions and two battles? None at all; only a coffin. And the loss? The degradation of a Prince's cruel death, through starvation and ill-treatment, in a captivity which the might of the nation was powerless to prevent and to relieve. The failure of Portugal's aggressive policy is total; on the political level her last state is worse than the first and there is therefore not even the consolation of 'restoring' the status quo. It would have been better – politically, militarily and economically – if the first expedition had never set sail: in other words, if Portugal had never aspired to conquest.

Does Fez's aspiration to conquest produce the desired result? The successful defence of Tangier offers the opportunity to gain possession of Ceuta through reliance on the legal rights of a victor, and so by quicker and easier means than war. But the policy, first of ransom, then of attrition through enslavement, fails. Ceuta is never won. The balance of power does not alter, but this does not mean that the status quo is maintained. The last state of Fez is also worse than the first, not only because in the quest for Ceuta the king so abuses his power as to be accused by his own subjects (Muley and Fénix) of harsh cruelty, but also because at the end he has to suffer the indignity of defeat, the ignominy of seeing his daughter, the princess, and his royal ally made captives, and of having her exchanged – as being of no higher worth – for Fernando's dead body. The King of Fez could not but resist the attack on Tangier; but it would have been better for him and his kingdom if he had limited his political aims to defence, and if he, too, had never aspired to additional territory.

This structure of events – a succession of failures in the two conflicting policies of conquest, with continuous deterioration in the political situation of either side – might well imply some criticism of the policies themselves. There is further evidence to support such a conclusion.

What are the motives that impel each side to aggression? Ceuta, for the King of Fez, is a standing reproach to his political honour (in the same way as the loss of it would be a disgrace for Portugal). The city is thus described to the king by Muley:

aquella, pues, que los cielos
quitaron a tu corona,
quizá por justos enojos
del gran profeta Mahoma;
y en oprobio de las armas
nuestras, ya vemos ahora
que pendones portugueses
en sus torres se enarbolan,
teniendo siempre a los ojos
un padrastro que baldona
nuestros aplausos, un freno
que nuestro orgullo reporta,
un Cáucaso que detiene
al Nilo de tus victorias
la corriente, y puesto en medio,
el paso a España le estorba.

(that [city] therefore, that Heaven took from you, perhaps through the just anger of the great prophet Mohammed and on whose battlements we now see the standards of Portugal unfurled to the shame of our armies, since we have an obstacle that is an insult to our fame, a brake which holds back our pride, a Mount Caucasus which dams up the Nile of your victories, and which, placed in the middle, blocks our way to Spain.)

(7) [246b][12]

particularly, it most stands in the way of his invasion of Spain, this being an ultimate objective whose desirability is taken for granted. For the king his army is 'arrogante', and the Portuguese have 'bríos arrogantes' (arrogant spirit' (13–15)) [247a] The same adjective is applied by Don Enrique to the king himself:

porque Tarudante
al Rey de Fez socorre, y arrogante
el Rey con gente viene

(because Tarudante [King of Morocco] is going to the aid of the King of Fez,
and Tarudante is arrogantly approaching with his army)

(29) [249c]

In this sort of context this ambivalent adjective bears its secondary
meaning of valiant and full of martial ardour, qualities that these
warriors unquestioningly impute to themselves and to their enemy; but
in other contexts it may bear the condemnatory sense which is its
primary meaning and which is always potentially present. The desired
end of all this ardour is glory, national and personal, and this is what the
capture of Fernando brings to Fez. As the King of Fez says:

Suspéndanse las armas, que no quiero
hoy más felice gloria;
que este preso me basta por victoria.

(Let the fighting cease, for there can be no greater glory for me today; this
prisoner suffices for my victory.)

(31) [250b]

What moves a nation to self-assertion is thus, on the vaster level of
international war, what also moves the individual – honour: fame,
prestige and the need to remove *oprobios* (shame). Writ large or small, the
human goal is glory.

When Muley reports the arrival of the Portuguese fleet, he calls its
commanders:

Enrique y Fernando, gloria
de este siglo que los mira
coronados de victorias.

(Enrique and Fernando, glory of our age which looks on them crowned with
victories.)

(12) [247a]

He calls the king who sends it:

Duarte de Portugal,
cuya fama vencedora
ha de volar con las plumas
de las águilas de Roma

(Duarte of Portugal, whose victorious fame flies with the eagles of Rome)

(12) [247a]

Fernando, when he lands on the African beach, glories in the power he brings which he (unaware of the irony) says will enslave that continent:

> Yo he de ser el primero, África bella,
> que he de pisar tu margen arenosa,
> porque oprimida al peso de mi huella
> sientas en tu cerviz la poderosa
> fuerza que ha de rendirte.

> (I will be the first, beautiful Africa, to tread on your sandy shore, so that you oppressed by the weight of my foot may feel on your neck the power that shall overcome you.)
>
> (16) [247c]

The first order he gives is full of confident reliance on his military might:

> haced a la ciudad la primer salva.
> Decid que defenderse no pretenda,
> porque la he de ganar a sangre y fuego,
> que el campo inunde, el edificio encienda.

> (Fire the first warning guns at the city. Tell it not to try to defend itself, because I will win it through blood and fire, which will flood the battlefield and set alight the buildings.)
>
> (17) [248a]

And of his first victory, the capture of Muley, he says:

> Yo ufano con tal victoria,
> que me ilustra y desvanece

> (I, proud with this victory that brings me renown and earns me undying applause)
>
> (21) [248c]

This pride in a prowess that brings fame is part of the *arrogancia* of the warrior. The play does present the goal of honour – bravery in the pursuit of fame, and pride in victory – as the glory that men bring to life, as a noble end whose pursuit can foster the chivalrous virtues that Christian and Moor alike show both on and off the battlefield. Bravery and chivalry are exalted by Calderón as real virtues. But while they can be exercised in the activity of war, whatever its result, the honour that they aim at depends on victory; defeat is a disgrace. It is a disaster to be avoided. Enrique, cautious and suspicious, fears defeat and advises withdrawal; Fernando confidently overrides him and is defeated. He makes a mistake and is therefore to blame for the defeat. The drama thus requires him and not Enrique to become the prisoner (or rather, working from the sources, since Calderón wished to present the two commanders divided between prudence and overconfidence, he had to give the latter quality to the historical prisoner, who dramatically, has to redeem his error).[13] A new note is now struck, that of condemnation of the expedition by the Portuguese themsleves. Enrique thus describes it:

> Rota y deshecha la armada,
> que fué con vana soberbia
> pesadumbre de las ondas,
> dejando en África presa
> la persona del Infante,
> a Lisboa dí la vuelta.

(Damaged and scattered are the ships of the fleet which had burdened the sea with vanity and pride. Leaving captive in Africa the prince's person, I returned to Lisbon.)

(42–3) [252b]

'Vanity and pride': the other face of 'arrogance'. Fernando's overconfidence had stemmed from the vain pride of the politics of conquest but he himself had not been touched by this pride. He had been able to disclaim any desire for national or personal glory, and to believe that he and his men were motivated only by God's interests:

> no se emplean
> nuestras armas aquí por vanagloria
> de que en los libros inmortales lean
> ojos humanos esta gran victoria.
> La fe de Dios a engrandecer venimos:
> suyo será el honor, suya la gloria,
> si vivimos dichosos.

(We do not here wield our weapons out of the vainglory of having human eyes read of this great victory in the chronicles of immortal deeds. We have come to spread God's faith: His will be the honour, His the glory, if we succeed and survive.)

(19) [248b]

He will indeed glorify his religious faith, but not in the way he thinks – not by victory, but by defeat; not by political and military honour, but by the humiliation, suffering and death of a slave.

That God is not to be glorified by wars of conquest – or, at least, that there can be no such thing as a purely disinterested war of conquest – is made clear by the preliminaries to the second expedition early in Act III. Tarudante and Alfonso, arriving in Fez incognito to deliver their messages to the king, give a bombastic exhibition of personal arrogance. They quarrel over the question of precedence:

Tarudante ¿Cómo mientras hablo yo,
          tú, cristiano, a hablar te atreves?
Alfonso   Porque nadie habla primero
          que yo, donde yo estuviere.

(*Tarudante* How do you, Christian, dare to speak while I am speaking?
Alfonso   Because no-one speaks before I do, wherever I am.)

(70) [257a]

And they spit out their challenges in language reminiscent of the diabolical figures in the *autos sacramentales*:

Alfonso   Pues en campaña te espero.
Tarudante Yo haré que poco me esperes,
          porque soy rayo.
Alfonso   Yo viento.
Tarudante Volcán soy que llamas vierte.
Alfonso   Hidra soy que fuego arroja.
Tarudante Yo soy furia.
Alfonso   Yo soy muerte.
Tarudante ¿Que no te espantes de oírme?
Alfonso   ¿Que no te mueras de verme?

(*Alfonso*   Well then, I shall await you on the battlefield.
Tarudante I shall not keep you waiting long, because I am lightning.
Alfonso   I am the wind.
Tarudante I am a volcano spitting out flames.
Alfonso   I am a Hydra breathing fire.
Tarudante I am fury.
Alfonso   I am death.
Tarudante Are you not terrified at hearing me?
Alfonso   Do you not fall dead at seeing me?)

(72) [257c]

Doubtless many, even most, of the spectators would have been stirred to patriotic excitement by this exchange, but would there not have been some thoughtful ones among them, wondering if any good could come of such arrogance? However that may be, as he prepares for battle Alfonso gives, according to all the early texts, so outrageous a sign of arrogance that later editors have not felt able to accept what these make him say. In contrast to Fernando's 'suyo será el honor, suya la gloria' (His will be the honour, His the glory), he says:

Fernando, si el martirio que padeces,
pues es suya la causa, a Dios le ofreces,
cierta está la victoria:
mío será el honor, mía la gloria.[14]

(Fernando, if you offer to God the martyrdom you suffer, victory is certain,
since the cause is His: mine will be the honour, mine the glory.)

(88) [260b]

Since it is God's cause, God will make victory certain, but the honour and
the glory will be the young king's. Enrique comments: 'Tu altivo orgullo
yerra' (Your haughty pride errs.) (88) [260b]. The 'error' – the fact that
this self-confidence is misplaced – is seen in the appearance at that point
of Fernando's ghost to take over command of the army. The battle is then
won, but it is not Alfonso who wins it. There is no honour and glory for
him because he fails in his objective: he arrives too late. This realisation
deflates Alfonso's self-conceit (of which there is no further sign), and we
may presume that the actor would have indicated this deflation well
before Alfonso himself says to the dead body he has failed to free:

Dadme, tío, vuestra mano;
que, aunque necio e ignorante,
a sacaros del peligro
vine, gran señor, tan tarde,
en la muerte, que es mayor,
se muestran las amistades.

(Uncle, give me your hand; for although foolish and inexperienced, I came
Sire, so late, to rescue you from danger, in the greater danger of death
friendship is shown.)

(94) [261c]

Alfonso does not carry back in triumph a liberated prince; nor at the end
of all this military endeavour is there a Tangier to be added to his
territory; only a new church to be added to his capital city. Alfonso's
frustration (a failure politically), together with the fact that not he but
the dead Fernando leads the army to a military victory, are surely
intended to indicate that political ambition and arrogant self-conceit do
not deserve success. What is needed in human life is not bellicosity and
the pursuit of fame, but a selfless faith, a faithfulness unto death, which is
what alone can triumph over failure and the ravages of time.[15] The only
triumph at the end of the play is the dead slave's, because he had
achieved sanctity. This is represented symbolically by his relics being
carried off the stage on their way to a shrine in a new church. That the
humility of prayer is better than the arrogance of territorial expansion is
what this ending can signify, and this is the lesson that Alfonso might
learn from the fact that he had not led his army to victory, but was led by
Fernando's example to a victory which was no victory on the political
field.

If this is the correct interpretation of the dramatic facts, then it necessitates a criticism of Alfonso's youthful and arrogant ardour and the retention of the original reading of 'mío será el honor, mía la gloria'. The common opinion, which I once held, that Alfonso is presented in Act III as the counterpart to the Fernando of Act I, paralleling his faith and intrepid ardour, and avenging his defeat, does not really seem tenable. The view, here argued, that there is no real military victory and no patriotic triumph to celebrate at the end, in no way minimises the spiritual triumph that is certainly presented. One must not confuse the political (human) and the religious (spiritual) levels, but see how Calderón keeps them distinct in the facts presented by his action. The essential point that emerges from this distinction is that Fernando's spiritual victory rests on, is indeed only made possible by, political failure. Only by seeing the human failure can the nature of the spiritual victory be properly understood. The 'optimism' that is said to be intrinsic to Christianity and to deprive it of any tragic sense of life is not really a very appropriate term to apply to Christian values as Calderón presents them here.

These religious values are not confined to the final scenes, beginning with Fernando's prayer that in recompense for his martyrdom God may grant him burial in a Christian church, and concluding with the ransom of his bones so that a shrine may be built over them.[16] This is a triumphal ending on the religious level, but the tone of the play as a whole is far from being 'triumphalist'. Nor are religious values asserted in the rather truculent defiance Fernando hurls at the king before dying, and in his confident belief that by his sufferings he has placed God under an obligation. This is a necessary level for communicating the theme, but the most superficial: there has to be the appeal of excitement for the less understanding and less sensitive members of the audience, whose spirits need to be raised at these points. But the real religious values lie deeper: they are the corollary to the way in which human values are presented throughout the play, from the song which the captives sing to alleviate Fénix's melancholy, to Alfonso's aspiration for honour and glory: 'mío será el honor, mía la gloria'. Despite this sabre-rattling quest for glory (because, in fact, of its failure) the dominant poetic tone of the play is one of sadness. There is no play of Calderón's more moving in this particular way. Sadness can dominate some of his maturer work, but in a reflective and detached way. Here in this youthful work there is a tenderness that justifies one agreeing with Wolfgang Kayser and Leo Spitzer that the scene between Fernando and Fénix, culminating in the two famous sonnets, is one of the most beautiful in all drama.[17]

Fénix (whose name means, of course, Phoenix) is a character that Calderón adds to the historical source. She is the daughter of the King of

Fez. She scarcely adds anything to the action of the play, but the theme would be disastrously truncated if she were lost. She is needed to add the feminine dimension to the human values presented by the play. The masculine values are the valour and chivalry of the soldier, whose aspiration is glory and renown. The feminine values are Love, which is aroused in men by the sight of beauty. Women by their beauty attract men away from self-seeking conquest to love and an altruistic chivalry. The degradation of masculine values are ambition and cruelty, the degradation of female values is self-centred vanity. The opposite of masculine values is represented by the king's rigorous treatment of the captive Fernando and his refusal to let it be tempered by compassion. Both sets of values enter into the play when Fernando is made a captive hostage and when Fénix is agitated when she hears her fortune told.

Fénix is the principal character in the opening scene. The Christian captives are at work in the palace gardens of the King of Fez. They are singing as they work and when they cease the request comes for them to resume singing, for the princess takes pleasure in hearing their songs. Is it possible, one asks, that anyone could take pleasure in songs whose accompaniment is the clank of the fetters of unhappy captives? They sing to bring some relief to their own unhappiness, not to please others. But the command is repeated and the captives then sing a short song that epitomises the two aspects of the play's theme:

Al peso de los años
lo eminente se rinde;
que a lo fácil del tiempo
no hay conquista difícil.

(All eminence succumbs to the weight of the years; for there is no conquest too difficult for the easy victory of time.)

(1) [245a][18]

When Fénix appears and asks for a mirror in which to gaze at herself, it becomes clear that her beauty is her sole preoccupation and that she is obsessed with a sadness that she cannot explain. She says it is not properly 'sadness', for then she would know the cause; since she does not, her suffering is 'melancholy'. Her insensitiveness to the suffering of others is explained by this self-centredness and the song hints movingly at the double aspect of the play's theme. First Fernando's fall from the status of a royal prince and army commander to the abject misery of a slave, and secondly the inevitable destruction of the princess's beauty by the ravages of death. That her incurable melancholy is due to an unconfessed fear of death is revealed at the beginning of Act II. Fénix has been confronted with an old hag, 'like a living skeleton', who took her hand and said, 'Alas, unhappy woman! Alas, inescapable misfortune! For indeed, this beauty is to be the price for a dead man!' (pp. 35–6) [251a]. From that moment Fénix lives in terror of this prophecy's fulfilment, haunted by the thought of this dead man.

After Fernando is kept as hostage by the King of Fez he keeps company with the Christian slaves in the gardens. Fénix asks for flowers to be picked for her. Her mind keeps turning on her fears and while waiting for the flowers she asks. 'Who will this dead man be?' At that moment Fernando, who has decided to take the flowers to Fénix himself, says, 'I . . .' Before he can continue with the sentence, Fénix trembles with fear at the answer to her question and cries out, 'What do I see?' in astonishment at having the prince wait on her; and after this interruption Fernando continues the speech he had begun.[19] 'I, Fenix, who wish to serve you humbly, was bringing you flowers, hieroglyphics of my lot, for born with the dawn they die with the day.' *Fénix* 'The marvel was given its name when the flower was discovered.' *Fernando* 'What flower is not a marvel if I am the servant who brings it to you?' (pp. 54–5) [254b–c].[20] Fénix cannot believe what she is told, that a prince has become a servant. Such, he says, is the lot of all mankind, symbolised by flowers. Then he speaks the famous sonnet:

> Flowers which were glory and joy when they awoke with the day, by evening will be pitiful nothing, sleeping in the arms of cold death.
>
> These colours which vie with the sky – a rainbow striped with gold, white and purple – will be the warning of human disillusion, so much can happen in the space of one day.
>
> Flowers awake early in order to bloom, and they bloom in order to grow old: they find grave and tomb within a bud.
>
> In them men have seen their own destiny. In one day they are born and die, for when centuries have passed, they have been but hours.

Fénix expresses horror at these words and wants to run away. 'What,' (asks Fernando), 'do I do with the flowers?' 'If you have found hieroglyphics in them, I can be cruel enough to shred them to pieces.' 'What', (asks Fernando), 'is wrong with flowers?' 'That they resemble the stars,' replies Fénix, adding that Woman is subject to the rigorous fate of Death and she has seen her own spelt out in that star. When Fernando expresses surprise at the equation of flowers with stars, Fénix recites a sonnet that complements his.

> Those flashes of light, those sparks which are the warnings of Fate as their shining lights draw nourishment from the sun live only for as long as one grieves over them.
>
> They are the flowers of night; although they are so beautiful, they burn ephemerally: for if one day is a century for flowers, a night is an era for the stars.

Thus from that fleeting springtime, we can infer, sometimes our harm, sometimes our good; whether the sun is dying or being born it is the book in which our births and deaths are registered.

What duration can Man expect, or what mutation will he not receive from an orb that every night is born and dies?

(p. 58) [254c–5a]

The brevity of life and the mutability of fortune are the two themes reflected in the fears of Fénix at the withering of her beauty and in the fall of Fernando from prince to slave. These two characters are inextricably linked together because Beauty (which is what impels men to Love) and Honour are linked as the supreme aspirations of humanity, that represent the happiness which all human beings must desire and for which they must strive. Beauty and Honour are linked together not only in this way, but also (since nothing in Calderón is accidental or pointless) by the etymology he gives for Ceuta, the city which symbolises the glory to which political power aspires:

que Ceido (Ceuta, en hebreo
vuelto el árabe idioma)
quiere decir hermosura,
y ella es ciudad siempre hermosa

(for Ceido, which is the Hebrew form of the Arabic Ceuta, means beauty, and she is an ever-beautiful city)

(7) [246b]

The supreme human values are therefore centred in the Beauty of Woman and the Power of Empire: these are what give honour and glory to humanity – 'lo eminente'. But these values, precisely because they are human, are inevitably conquered by time.[21] Decay, destruction, and therefore ultimate failure, are the natural end of all human glory.

Fernando and Fénix, prince and princess, must both face failure – he, the warrior, in dishonour and degradation; she, the beautiful woman, in old age and death. Fénix, having no other value to live by, cannot face her destiny, and thus fails from the start to find happiness in the honour nature intended for her, wasting her life in emotional inadequacy as a prey to morbid fear of death. Fernando also fails to find happiness in the honour that is his due; but he wastes his life willingly in a suffering that negates honour, because, having other values than human glory to live for, he can face and accept his destiny. But with regard to the honour that gives social glory to human living, Fernando is a total failure; his fate denies every human value – royal status, military success, power, prestige, wealth, health and life itself.

Within the general failure represented by the warrior-kings – the waste of effort that is politics – we have the particular human failure

represented by Fernando and Fénix. Completing this presentation of the
failure of the human world, as representatives of the ordinary people
(apart from the *gracioso*) there are the Portuguese captives in Fez,
enslaved to their captors. They are the victims of the political failure of
their rulers, forced to waste their lives in a meaningless misery, which is
stressed through the play until in Act III Fernando, for dramatic
purposes, is made to bear alone the weight of human suffering. When
Fernando chooses slavery rather than surrender Ceuta, one more drop is
added to the ocean of human suffering, one more corpse to dig its own
grave:

> moros, un esclavo os queda;
> cautivos, un compañero
> hoy se añade a vuestras penas;
> cielos, un hombre restaura
> vuestras divinas iglesias;
> mar, un mísero con llanto
> vuestras ondas acrecienta;
> montes, un triste os habita,
> igual ya de vuestras fieras;
> viento, un pobre con sus voces
> os duplica las esferas;
> tierras, un cadáver os labra
> en las entrañas su huesa

> (Moors, a slave is left for you; captives, a companion to your sufferings added
> today; heaven, a man restores your churches; sea, a wretched man adds to
> your waves with his weeping; forests, a miserable man inhabits you, the equal
> now to your wild beasts; wind, a poor man with his cries adds to the music of
> your spheres; earth, a corpse is digging his grave in your bowels)
> (47–8) [253a]

In the darkness of human misery only two lights shine to guide men in
their relations with each other: compassion and loyalty. They cannot
remove suffering, but they can alleviate it. The companionship of their
prince in their misfortunes is a consolation for the captives:

> the only one, they say,
> that heaven offers them
> (37) [251b]

And for the prince, too, it is a companionship that helps him to face his
misfortune:

> *Muley*   Aquí estoy viendo el amor
> con que la desdicha fiera
> de esos cautivos tratáis.
> *Fernando* Duélome de su fortuna,

> y en la desdicha importuna,
> que a esos esclavos miráis,
> aprendo a ser infelice

(*Muley*   I am seeing from here the love with which you counter the
wretched misery of those captives.

Fernando   I grieve at their ill-fortune and in the importunate unhappiness
which you see in those slaves I am learning how to be unhappy.)
(38) [251b].

When he sinks lower than they in wretchedness, Muley and Fénix are
deeply moved to pity and plead for mercy to the king. The latter retorts
that compassion does not rest with him: Fernando is responsible for his
own condition and it is he who must show compassion to himself by
fulfilling the Portuguese side of the political bargain – let him abandon
resistance and conform. In pursuit of the overriding interest of the State
its ruler must gainsay the overriding interest of men, their claim to
sympathy, compassion and freedom. The argument would have been
used by an Inquisitor concerning the torture of a heretic; it will have
been used in our own century by representatives of totalitarian states
endeavouring to force individual consciences into submission in the
name of the common good. The King of Fez, as a politician, is right to
desire the reincorporation of Ceuta into his dominions. The territorial
integrity of a nation is a legitimate political goal, but the individual
human beings whose lives will be affected should not be left out of
account. The Portuguese government, pursuing honour, is prepared to
expose the Christians of Ceuta to persecution. Only Fernando sees them
as subjects with rights, looking to Portugal for the protection of their
consciences. There is an inevitable clash of values in the relations of the
government to its subjects in Ceuta and of the King of Fez to Fernando.
The clash of values, with irreconcilable conflicts between diverse
legitimate rights, is for Calderón the inescapable condition of the human
world. Caught in this strife, it is the lot of men to suffer in their passage
towards the death that casts its shadow over all things, even over the
beauty of the world. The pursuit of national honour through warfare is,
in practice, this:

Alfonso   Ya mi ira
> ningún consejo alcanza.
> No se dilate un punto esta venganza:
> entre en mi brazo fuerte
> por África el azote de la muerte.

(*Alfonso*   My anger can no longer tolerate advice. My vengeance must not be

postponed a moment longer: let my might bring to Africa the scourge
of death.)

(87) [260a]

Men cannot therefore look to their rulers for any mitigation of their
misery; they can look only to themselves for the mutual loyalty that in
love and friendship make the human values, which are denied by
political ends, realisable on the personal level.

Two characters are examples of this. One is Don Juan Coutiño who
(with Brito) shares his prince's misery by never abandoning his side.
When Alfonso receives Fernando's dead body he turns to Don Juan and
says, 'My friend, you have given me a good account of the prince.' Don
Juan replies, 'I kept him company until he died, until I saw him freed; I
was with him while he was alive and while he was dead. See where he
lies.' (93) [261c]. The other is Muley, the general of the Moorish army. In
the preliminary skirmish, Fernando takes him prisoner, and is surprised
to see him take this fate so hard. When he is told that Muley is grieving
not only at his captivity but at the fact that he will never see Fénix, whom
he loves dearly, again, Fernando gives him his freedom, and as he rides
off Muley promises to repay him. When it is Fernando's turn to be
captured, the king places Fernando in his charge. Later, when Fernando
is enslaved, Muley shows the human compassion that the king must
deny himself.

The friendship between Muley and Fernando surmounts the political
and religious divisions between Moor and Christian; nonetheless, these
divisions prevent this friendship from reaching its natural fulfilment and
Muley must stand by and witness Fernando's slow martyrdom. He is
willing to risk his life to facilitate his friend's escape and repay the debt he
owes him; but when this means disloyalty to his king, Fernando refuses
to accept his freedom, and Muley must acquiesce in this because both
know that loyalty to king must take precedence over loyalty to friend.
Muley, in acting as a political subject, must fail to act as a human being
when the greatest demands are made on his compassion and love. His
dilemma is insoluble: either way he must fail to do what is right. That,
precisely, is the human world. Priorities must be found among values,
and no priority can be perfect. The King of Fez in trying to break
Fernando's will is applying a priority that on his level can be justifiable.
Calderón condemns his cruelty but does not condemn his priority. As for
Muley, he is not condemned at all. Calderón uses dramatic convention –
his marriage, at the end, to Fénix, unnecessary for either theme or action
– to indicate approval of his conduct. Nonetheless, the fact remains that
he has failed in the task he set himself, the repayment of his debt of
honour to his friend.

Purely human solutions to the dilemmas of life, even when they are the best possible, must always be unsatisfactory. Only Fernando, in the dilemmas of conscience presented by the play, chooses a priority that is absolute in the sense that his loyalty to conscience neither conflicts with any other loyalty nor creates disloyalty on another level. This it can only do because, accepting the failure of his political ideal, he can reject every single value on which men pin their hopes of happiness – power, prestige, honour, wealth, health and life – and choose to die of starvation as a slave on a dunghill, as the total negation of all human glory. From the purely human point of view he is a total failure: setting out, full of confidence and with all the majesty of human power, he has gained nothing and lost everything in ignominy, suffering and death.

There is no triumph whatsoever in the human action of the play. *Everybody* fails, to a greater or lesser extent, in the aims they set themselves. Fénix is, of course, no exception, for she cannot find release from her tormenting melancholy. In a sense she is a deeper failure than anyone else, for while the others fail to achieve the positive ends they set themselves, she fails to find any positive aim in life at all to prevent her from fearing death. But while there is no *human* triumph, there is of course a *spiritual* triumph. This is no mere quibble with words but a fundamental dichotomy. Spiritual values, as here presented, necessitate the inversion of all human values and the denial that they can be efficacious in constructing a satisfying and reasonable framework for living. Fernando's loyalty to his conscience, surviving the degradation, torture and death of his body, is the only victory there is in the whole play. Charity and compassion for all men and self-sacrificing loyalty to one's conscience, constitute sanctity as Calderón presents it here. As such it is the triumph of the human spirit over the turmoil and failures of life in the world, but it is the triumph of individual men, not the triumph of mankind over its destiny. Nor should it be said that the play represents the triumph at least of the crusading ideal, since through this ideal Fernando's sanctity is achieved. He, being a Christian warrior, achieves sanctity through his participation in a crusade, which gives him the opportunity to exemplify compassion, charity and loyalty. But sanctity can emerge out of any human disaster: there is no need to have a crusade in order to make a saint (or, symbolically, to build a church). But if there is to be a crusade, it is necessary (the play would seem to imply) for it to fail before it can produce a saint. Otherwise it will achieve the end of human glory and so pander to arrogance and pride. Perhaps the profoundest dramatic element in the play, if it is looked at closely in order to see what exactly it is saying, is the one that has generally been taken as its greatest weakness – the symbolical emergence of the lighted torch out of the night-time of human life (that is, out of political and military failure, the conflicting clashes of values, the darkness of suffering and death), the torch being in the hands of a ghost, of a *dead* man's spirit. All through the play the plot is constructed on the fact that Christian values invert worldly and human ones. Nothing would show greater mis-understanding of Calderón's conception of Christian values than the assumption, against the evidence of the plot he devises, that because Christianity is an 'optimistic' religion, a martyr's death must mean for a Christian dramatist a triumphant answer to all problems: in this case, the triumph of the Cross over the Crescent, military victory, the recovery of national honour and the restoration of world order. On the contrary, *El príncipe constante* is Christian drama because, on the plane of natural human values, it is a story of defeat and failure.

Nor should one assume that since those who are defeated and fail are Portuguese, Calderón is here, in 1629, criticising the sister nation for beginning to lose her overseas empire, and thus by implication exalting Spain as the morally superior power.[22] There is no criticism of the public activity of anybody in the play; all are presented as acting according to their legal rights; there is only sadness at the fact that political aims are self-frustrating and that the values of this world are unrealisable in practice.[23]

22 The drama as commentary on public affairs

Las armas de la hermosura and the Catalan Rebellion (1640–52)

At the commencement of his dramatic career, as has been seen, Calderón raised politico-religious issues that had been prominent in recent events. These provided a 'historical context' for dramatic plots, and no well-informed member of the audience (which would have included king and councillors) should have failed to see the analogies. But apart from the general implication in the plays that have already been considered, namely, that conciliation and peace are likely to prove more successful than intransigence and war, none of these plays can be taken as 'speaking without telling' in Bances Candamo's sense. There are, however, two plays that may clearly come into this category.

The first is *Las armas de la hermosura*, and its source play, *El privilegio de las mujeres*. The former was analysed in chapter 5 as an example of the dramatic requirement to transform 'historical truth' into 'poetic truth'. The analysis and the interpretations of the play previously given still stand, but the theme of pardon instead of vengeance and the restoration of privileges has a special application to the aftermath of the Revolt of Catalonia, which lasted from 1640 to 1652.

The causes of the Revolt lay in the 'regionalist' structure of the Spanish State, so different from the centralisation that had been achieved in France. Regionalism versus centralisation was to remain a perennial Spanish problem, as the new democratic state that succeeded the dictatorship of General Franco eventually conceded. Weakness of central government invariably produced a tendency to disruption of 'The Spains', as the state was officially known. This disruption was the situation in the 1630s. In the long struggle with France and with the Dutch Protestants the difficulties of recruiting and supplying Spain's armies abroad were aggravated by the constitutional structure of the monarchy. The Spains comprised kingdoms, principalities and lordships, which had independently developed their own systems of government, with separate parliaments or assemblies, different laws and customs (*fueros*) and different methods of raising government subsidies. As each unit was incorporated into the Castilian–Leonese monarchy before he could count on its allegiance, the king had to promise to govern in each region in accordance with its *fueros*. This meant that a Viceroy or other official had to apply, according to the *fueros* of each region, the policies and laws emanating from Madrid. The system was cumbersome and slow and proved a great handicap to Spain. In the difficult period of the Thirty Years War with its struggle against a centralised France, Olivares saw that for Spain to compete successfully he would have to impose a centralised system of government. The attempt to impose the Castilian system of taxation led to a number of revolts, the chief of which were in the Principality of Catalonia and in the kingdom of Portugal. Catalonia was eventually subdued, but Portugal was finally lost to the Spanish Crown. To ensure the defence of Spain against France, an army had to be quartered in Catalonia. Since this army consisted of soldiers drawn from regions other than Catalonia, the Catalans condemned it as a violation of their *fueros* which prohibited the billeting of 'foreign' troops on Catalan soil. This was the signal for revolt and Barcelona was occupied by the insurgents. Olivares had to choose between conceding independence, conciliation or military repression. He favoured conciliation, but was forced into war by the march of events. The Catalans withdrew their allegiance from the Castilian Crown and transferred it to the King of France, who however did little to defend the Catalans in the war. Calderón, as a Knight of the Military Order of Santiago, fought for a time in this war until invalided out of the army.

As a result of his failure to prevent the secessionist movement, Olivares fell from power in 1643. Peace with the Dutch came with the Treaty of Münster in 1648, to be followed by the Peace of Westphalia, which ended the Thirty Years War but not Spain's war with France, the wars in Catalonia and Portugal. In 1651 Barcelona was finally besieged, and it surrendered in October 1652. The Spanish Government had to decide what to do with the vanquished Principality: either it could be made to suffer the full consequences of defeat by having its system of government and its *fueros* abolished, thus being incorporated into the Castilian system as Olivares had originally hoped, or else the Crown could show magnanimity in victory, pardon the insurgents and restore the traditional liberties of the Principality. For three months debates and discussions continued until finally Philip IV decided on the general pardon.

During these three months the situation of defeated Barcelona was in all essentials analogous to the situation facing the defeated Romans in *El privilegio de las mujeres*, with the added analogy that the point at issue between Rome and Coriolano had been the 'rights and privileges' of the women of the city, and the point at issue between Barcelona and Madrid was the constitutional rights and privileges of the Principality. Thus the feminist thesis of *El privilegio de las mujeres* came to suggest, in *Las armas de la hermosura*, a national issue of extreme importance.

El privilegio de las mujeres refers specifically to a government decree forbidding lavish expenditure on women's dresses. Sumptuary laws like this were a feature of Olivares' campaign to reduce public expenditure and to reform the moral tone of the country. The decree made farthingales illegal, banning them as immoral because they made it possible to hide pregnancies, thus enabling women of loose life to wander about more easily than previously. The reference to this decree occurs in the first Act, which was the one written by Calderón; the other two Acts were written by Montalbán and Coello. Cotarelo, in calling attention to this, points out that the decree against farthingales and other extravagant fashions was issued in October 1636, the year in which *El privilegio de las mujeres* was published. The play must have been written before the sumptuary decree and must have been intended as advance criticism of the government's known intentions. If farthingales were popular among the court ladies, as they no doubt were, the court dramatist might have been urged to attack this insult to women.[1]

The tragic and stirring events of 1640–52 thus altered the criticism of the government for abolishing a ridiculous feminine fashion into a vital issue for the future of Spain. From having been, in *El privilegio de las mujeres*, a comment on feminine fashions, the reference to the decree prohibiting farthingales becomes, in *Las armas de la hermosura*, an indirect plea for the pardon of Catalonia and the retention of its traditional privileges and freedoms. If the play was written after the general pardon (issued on 3 January 1653) its ending would have lost its force by praising a *fait accompli*; in that case the play would have been written in 1653. It would seem logical, however, to suppose that the play was written in 1652 and performed at Court during the three months in which the conditions of the surrender of Barcelona were being debated; the play would then have been a plea on behalf of magnanimity and pardon, and therefore a good example of 'speaking without telling', the topical reference occurring in its closing lines:

> ¡Viva quien vence!
> Que es vencer perdonando
> vencer dos veces.

> (Long live he who conquers! Because to conquer by pardoning is to conquer twice over);[2]

but impossible to miss in the noble lines of Veturia's plea:

El desagravio del noble
más escrupuloso y grave
no estriba en que se vengó,
sino en que pudo vengarse.
Tú puedes, y también puedes
dar tan precioso realce
al acrisolado oro
del perdón; que en el semblante
del rendido luce más,
con el primor de su esmalte,
lo rojo de la vergüenza,
que lo rojo de la sangre

(The satisfaction required by the injured honour of the most punctilious and correct nobleman does not lie in the fact that he did avenge himself, but in the fact that he could have avenged himself. You can do so; and you can also give added lustre to the pure gold of forgiveness; the red blush of shame shines forth with a finer colour on the countenance of the vanquished man than would the red of his spilled blood)

(p. 1311a) [*BAE*, iii, p. 208b]

Amar después de la muerte and the Morisco problem

A more indirect but not dissimilar case of 'speaking without telling' is provided by *Amar después de la muerte* (Love after Death). This is a play of Calderón's in which historical colour, and historical events, are most impressively fused with the main plot. It deals with the rebellion of the *Moriscos* of Granada in 1568.

The terms of the surrender of the kingdom of Granada in 1492 had been generous. The Moors were guaranteed freedom in the use of their law and the practice of their religion, their customs, and their dress. The policy of religious tolerance advocated by Archbishop Talavera might have kept the conquered kingdom peaceful but few converts to Christianity resulted, and it was felt that a stronger policy was needed. In 1499 Cardinal Jiménez de Cisneros put into effect a policy of forcible conversion and mass baptisms, which had the effect of creating Christians in name only, and this led to antagonism between the Moorish minority (now called *Moriscos*, the name for baptised Moors) and the Christian State. A first revolt in 1499 was quelled in the following year. Those among the defeated who would not submit to the practice of Christianity were expelled to North Africa, and in 1502 this policy was extended to all adult Muslims. Since the vast majority had no alternative but to submit, the religion of Islam officially ceased to exist in Spain; its former adherents were now the *Moriscos*, a substantial minority in Southern Spain.

Since the resources of Government and Church were insufficient to build schools and re-educate this recalcitrant minority in the new citizenship, disaffection grew. The *Moriscos* remained 'an unassimilated racial minority' in touch with the Moors of Morocco and the Turks. The anti-Islamic rules had not been enforced in practice. The Edict of 1567 attempted the enforcement: it prohibited the use of Arabic and the wearing of Arab dress and also various traditional Moorish customs. This was an attempt to enforce a radical assimilation, which several contemporary historians thought too rigorous. All warnings from officials on the spot were ignored by Madrid, and fighting broke out in 1568 throughout the whole of the kingdom of Granada. Don John of Austria, a bastard son of the Emperor Charles V and soon to be the victor at the battle of Lepanto, was put in command and the revolt was crushed in 1570. Philip attempted to forestall the *Morisco* danger by removing large numbers of the Granada *Moriscos* to other parts of Spain and by bringing in new settlers from as far away as Galicia. The immediate danger of further revolts was removed but only at the cost of storing up trouble for the future.

The *Moriscos* now in the former kingdom of Valencia had come to form a close-knit community which bore the name of 'The Nation of the Moorish New Christians of the kingdom of Valencia'. Threats of a Turkish invasion of the south-eastern coast were felt to be real, and this 'Nation' had established connections with Spain's enemies abroad. As a result, the Spanish government decided on a policy of total expulsion of *Moriscos* from the whole of Spain. They were deported to the Moroccan coast where they were for the most part not welcomed. The numbers expelled are estimated at 275,000 out of a total *Morisco* population of over 300,000. The expulsion was carried out largely in response to popular feeling, for most people were glad to see the end of 'unbelievers' on Spanish soil. But the aristocratic landowners had been against the expulsion because their estates depended on *Morisco* labourers. The economic consequences of the expulsion varied from region to region; in Aragon and Valencia they were disastrous. The real consequences of the policy were not brought home to the government until Olivares' policy of reform and retrenchment.

Amar después de la muerte (which has the alternative title of *El Tuzaní de la Alpujarra*) covers the outbreak of the rebellion and the defeat of the *Moriscos* under Don John of Austria.[3] This impressive play contains the personal tragedy of one of the *Morisco* leaders, framed most effectively within the wider tragedy of a nation (that of the *Morisco* 'Nation') who after the Edict of 1567 rose in defence of their civil rights against its harsh rulings. The play opens with this rising in the city of Granada, and the sympathies of the audience are thus aroused for the rebels. The leaders of the rebellion are gentlemen of standing, even members of the City Council. One of them, Don Fernando Válor, is proclaimed king and takes the name of Abenhumeya. Another is Don Álvaro Tuzaní, who is the protagonist in the main plot. Both of them are historical figures, as indeed are most of the characters of the play.

Tuzaní is married near the beginning of the play, but as a military leader he is never able to live with his wife. When they come together, their meetings are always interrupted by the summons to battle. She is murdered and robbed by a Spanish soldier, and dies in her husband's arms. He vows vengeance, discovers who her murderer was, slays him while avenger and murderer are both in prison. The act of vengeance is the 'fulfilment' in death of the love destroyed by the war. This epitomises the destruction of the Moorish 'Nation' in their struggle for their civil rights.

Calderón's departures from his historical sources all accentuate the heroism of the rebels in a hopeless struggle. One of these changes is the transformation of Abenhumeya from the weak and indecisive historical leader into a determined and valiant man of action. The most significant alteration of history comes with the final defeat of the *Moriscos*. Historically, the punishment of the rebels was cruel; after the town of Galera was destroyed by an underground mine, all the survivors were killed. Rebels from the other towns were deported to other parts of Spain. In the play, Calderón follows history by making the victorious Don John of Austria determined to exact implacable retribution on the defeated *Moriscos*, but Calderón prevents this in the play by making his generals plead for the vanquished and Don John does issue a general pardon to all the rebels. Once again in these plays there is a plea for reconciliation between enemies. Don John of Austria tells Mendoza, his general, to go to Berja and find the rebel leader, Abenhumeya:

le diréis que si rendido
se quiere dar a partido,
daré perdón general
a todos los rebelados,
con que vuelvan a vivir
con nosotros y asistir
en sus oficios y estados;
que de los daños pasados
hoy mi justicia severa
más satisfacción no espera:

(tell him that if he will surrender, I will grant a general pardon to all the rebels, so that they may once again live among us, practise their trades and professions; for today my stern justice does not ask for more satisfaction for the harm that has been done).[4]

Calderón thus makes the terms of surrender produce the complete reintegration of the rebellious dissidents into Spanish life. The whole message of the play is that war and vengeance bring no solution to conflicts.

The whole campaign is not presented as a triumphant victory for Spanish arms. One of the Spanish commanders refers to the campaign as a victory which has brought no honour with it. Don John of Austria himself is perplexed in the course of the play by being unable to determine whether he is fighting a campaign on land or at sea. In 1570, immediately after the victory in the Alpujarras, he was to take over command of the Allied fleet in the Mediterranean and win the decisive battle of Lepanto. This curious confusion was Calderón's way of expressing doubt at the value of any kind of victory in war. The three Granadan towns and villages in which the action takes place are Galera, Gavia and Berja, all of which are nautical terms.[5] Margaret Wilson has acutely analysed the way in which the mountains of the Alpujarras are themselves described in nautical terms, and shows how the rocks of the fortresses, like the victory, like the ideals and hopes of the *Moriscos*, are all dissolved into ruin. '[The morisco community] trusted in its mountain strongholds, and the rocks turned to water beneath it.' (p. 423); and she concludes that the play was written by someone who 'knew how to draw attention through powerful drama to the rights and sufferings of minority peoples' (p. 425).

Once again we note how Calderón refused to follow patriotic ardour. He was not the only one in court circles who was sensitive to 'the rights and sufferings of minority peoples'. There was an influential voice at Court expressing itself to this effect when consulted by the Council. J. H. Elliott states that: 'In 1633 the royal confessor [Fray Antonio de Sotomayor] wrote: "It is a very short time ago since the *Moriscos* were expelled – an action which did such harm to these kingdoms that it would be a good idea to have them back again, if they could be persuaded to accept our Holy Faith"'[6] It is not far-fetched to associate the play with the opinion expressed by Fray Antonio de Sotomayor. It is significant that Calderón wrote an enlightened play on the *Morisco* revolt at a time when an enlightened view on the expulsion of the *Moriscos* existed in an influential quarter at Court.[7] For the purpose of this chapter, which is to discover the climate of political opinion that Calderón's plays reflected, the whole document from which Elliott quoted is significant and most interesting.

The context of this document is a series of discussions initiated by the royal confessor and reported by him to the king. These discussions centre on the persecution of Portuguese New Christians (converted Jews) and their request for a 'general pardon' made directly to the king by them in order to remove the reasons for the persecution. These New Christians were the descendants of Jews who had earlier chosen to accept Christianity rather than be expelled from the Peninsula. From 1630 to the secession of Portugal there had been many attempts to negotiate such pardons.[8] The royal confessor was the keeper of the king's conscience, providing him with the spiritual and moral background for the social and political decisions he had to make. It was the duty of the confessor to advise the king privately on the moral rights and wrongs of policy. The documents which here concern us show that he was also asked for his opinion by the Royal Council before they decided on the advice to tender the king. In this particular case he was reporting in full to the king on 1 January 1633 on a petition forwarded to the king by the Bishop of Coimbra that all New Christians should be expelled from Portugal.

The royal confessor's report states that it is not in accordance with justice to condemn a whole group of people for what might be the errors of a few. Whatever insincerity might have existed originally among the Jews who accepted Christianity, it is not legitimate to assume that subsequent generations were not now, on that account, sincere in their practice of Christianity. The Jews after their conversion had brought great intellectual, cultural and social distinction to the Iberian kingdoms, and had for long contributed notably to the spiritual life of the Church through their membership of religious orders. The attempt to justify expulsion of New Christians by citing the recent expulsion of the *Moriscos*, he continued, is invalid. The *Moriscos* of Granada had not been assimilated into the Christian social structure by intermarriage, as the Jews had long been. When the *Morisco* rebellion was crushed, only those who had actively taken part in it were included in sanctions; those who had not been guilty of rebellion were not punished. The *Morisco* rebellion was put down by reason of the defence of the realm. No such reason exists in connection with the descendants of the convert Jews; there are no licit grounds whatever for punishing them, either on religious-moral grounds or for reasons of practical politics. Then there comes in the confessor's report the passage quoted by Elliott. If, the report continues, the great harm done to the Spanish realms by the still fairly recent expulsion of the *Moriscos* has not been remedied, how much more irremediably harmful would be the consequences of the expulsion of the far larger numbers of Christianised Jews? In firmly advising against such a drastic measure the king's confessor took the opportunity of condemning the expulsion of the *Moriscos*, and suggesting that this would not still be irremediable if the *Moriscos* could be persuaded to return.[9]

Such a suggestion was obviously Utopian. The New Christians were not expelled from Portugal, but it is not known whether the Royal Council actually discussed the secondary idea of repatriating any *Moriscos* who wished to return. It would seem clear nonetheless that Calderón who, it must be remembered, was a court dramatist, knew of this suggestion and must have discussed it sympathetically with others at Court. This supposition gives us an approximate date for the writing of *Amar despues de la muerte*, c. 1632–3.[10]

Historical allusions in El alcalde de Zalamea

Two ways have so far been considered in which history can be used by Calderón for dramatic plots without losing its function as history, namely its connection, direct or indirect, with real events. The first of these supplies a context by which a plot that is dramatic in its own right sheds light on current affairs without destroying the dramatic autonomy of the stage action and theme. The second way is an implied analogy with a contemporary event, whereby the dramatic plot is given a political intention beyond the immediate significance of action and theme.

Plays can also show an awareness of history that, if properly grasped, can add greatly to the impact that the play would have made on its audience. A good example of this is *El alcalde de Zalamea*, a play so full of the atmosphere of real life within a historical context that it seemed to Max Krenkel impossible that it could not be dramatising an actual event. A regiment of the army sent by Philip II to support by conquest his claim to the Portuguese crown is passing through the country town of Zalamea where the tired troops are to be billeted. The troops are commanded by Don Lope de Figueroa, one of King Philip's notable generals. The Captain has the best house in the town chosen for his billet. This is the residence of Pedro Crespo, a yeoman farmer, who has property and wealth beyond that of the other inhabitants. He also has a beautiful daughter who is the real reason why the Sergeant in charge of the lodging arrangements has picked on the house for the Captain. Crespo is apprehensive, and orders his daughter Isabel to confine herself to the attic. Not finding her anywhere else, the Captain penetrates into her room. An altercation follows between Crespo, his son, and the Captain, which is cut short by the arrival of the General, Don Lope, who orders the Captain to find another billet, and who remains himself in Crespo's house to prevent further disorder, but this fails to prevent the serenading of Isabel during the night. Outraged at this conduct, Don Lope decides that the regiment must move on, and the march starts on the evening of the second day. The Captain and some soldiers return under cover of darkness, Isabel is abducted and raped.

During that day, Crespo had been elected mayor and magistrate by his fellow citizens, and he decides to use his new judicial authority by arresting and trying the Captain himself, instead of handing him over to military authority. He pleads with the Captain to right his daughter's and his own honour by marrying her, offering to endow her with his substantial property. The Captain scornfully rejects the offer, laughs at Crespo's reference to his honour, and at the father's belief that a Captain and a nobleman would ever marry a village girl. Thereupon Crespo draws up the indictment, takes the evidence, and finds the crime proved. Without any delay he carries out the legal sentence of death by inflicting the added indignity on the nobleman of garrotting instead of beheading him.

By then the General, having become aware that his Captain is missing, returns, and in his anger at Crespo's abuse of his authority by imprisoning and sentencing an army officer instead of handing him over for court martial orders an attack on the village while Crespo's fellow-citizens are prepared to resist. Once again, this conflict between army and town is interrupted by the arrival of Authority, no less a person than the king himself, following his army on the march to Lisbon. The infuriated General demands the arrest and sentence of the Mayor for exceeding his authority, but the latter defends himself by showing that the indictment was validly drawn up and that the sentence was just. To the charge that he ought to have handed the Captain over to the army for trial Crespo replies that if the trial and sentence were in conformity with justice, what does it matter whether the left hand of the king's law should carry out the execution rather than the right hand? The king recognises the justice of Crespo's case, says that this is not affected in essentials by the technical usurpation of authority over an officer and a nobleman, and decides to let well alone.

All the details are precise, the town, the occasion of the army's march, the General is a real commander, and the king whose campaign this is, is the right one, and the military and political purpose of the campaign is correctly given. Krenkel, in his detailed study of the play for his edition of it,[11] saw that it had the stamp of historical accuracy, yet when he examined the action he found that none of it squared with history. Philip II's army on its way to Lisbon never passed through Zalamea, nor did Philip II when he travelled later; Don Lope de Figueroa never commanded one of its regiments. While Pedro Crespo is frequently mentioned in the literature of this period as a magistrate famed for championing the rights of the poor,[12] there is no evidence that he actually existed; in all probability he was merely a legendary folk-hero. Calderón follows his source-play by the same title, by Lope de Vega, in making the magistrate 'Pedro Crespo'. Though obviously disappointed at finding no historical corroboration, Krenkel affirmed that there was nothing in the play that was contrary to history, citing the facts, first, that Spanish troops were notorious for their riotous behaviour on their marches through Spain, that townspeople and villagers feared having them billeted in their homes, and that all offences committed by them were very leniently treated by the courts martial: secondly, that Philip II was famed for the way he would listen to any of his subjects, even the least important among them, who claimed redress in law for offences against them. In accordance with the critical principles of his age Krenkel obviously thought that the literary value of the play would have been immeasurably enhanced if it could have been proved historically true in every important particular. He was not, however, looking for the right kind of historical corroboration, and did not attach full importance to it when he in fact found it.

Hartzenbusch, in volume IV of his edition of Calderón's plays (*Biblioteca de Autores Españoles*, 14, Madrid, 1926, p. 692a), quotes extracts from news items (*Avisos*) that circulated in Madrid. One reported on 20 September 1639 that the *Alcalde mayor* (a magistrate of lesser status than a judge) arrested a nobleman, Don Alonso de Torres y Sandoval, for having been called a *cabrón* (a man who connives at or promotes the adultery of his wife) by him. That he arrested him, tried him, sentenced him, and had him executed all in the space of six hours, without (it was rumoured) allowing him to make his confession. As extreme indignity, the man was beheaded in prison by a slave. This *Aviso* stated that the whole capital was deeply moved at the news of this execution. The judgement and the ignominious execution were obviously a punishment far in excess of the crime. This magistrate must have been tried and sentenced to death himself, because a later *Aviso* of 24 January 1640 reported that the king had suspended the sentence for reasons that were not given. The sentence, however, was eventually carried out, because an *Aviso* of 14 February 1640 reporting the appointment of a new commander for the coastal defences of Málaga, added 'where a short while ago the city's *Alcalde mayor* was publicly executed.'[13]

The parallel between these events and the plot of Calderón's play are too striking to be coincidental. They probably induced Calderón to rewrite 'Lope's' *Alcalde*. Calderón's version is generally thought to have been written shortly after 1642, when the events in Málaga would still have been fresh in popular memory.[14] Obviously the *Alcalde mayor* of

Málaga was not a magistrate of the same stature as Pedro Crespo. Calderón would perhaps have been saying no more than that a summary trial and execution is not in itself a miscarriage of justice if the magistrate is an upright man and if the spirit of the law had not been contravened, despite the infringement of the letter.

But there is more behind Calderón's re-writing of this part of 'Lope's' play than the Málaga affair can indicate. He gives his villanous captain a definite name and surname, Álvaro de Ataide, which are the name and surname of a historical personage who attained great notoriety. This was overlooked until Ángel García Gómez brought it to light in his paper '*El alcalde de Zalamea*: Álvaro de Ataide y el Capitán de Malaca'.[15]

Álvaro de Ataide was the name of a son of Vasco da Gama, the great Portuguese navigator and ruler of the Portuguese settlements in India. Ataide was the commander of the Malacca sea at the time when the great Jesuit missionary, St Francis Xavier, following his successful evangelisation in Japan, was about to fulfil his life's ambition by entering China. The proposed journey to China had the sanction of the Portuguese king, of the Viceroy of India, and of the Bishop of Goa. Diego Pereira was appointed Portuguese envoy to China and was to sail with Francis Xavier in order to give the latter diplomatic protection. Ataide as Governor of Malacca refused Pereira permission to sail to China. Francis Xavier could not sail without him. He tried every form of pleading, leaving to the last his official authorisation from king and Viceroy. Even this was to no avail, and eventually the missionary had to sail without Pereira, arriving at the island of Sanchón within sight of the Chinese mainland in December 1552, where he died. He had been refused entry into China, which he would have received if he had accompanied the official Portuguese envoy. During these months of frustration, Francis Xavier sent letters to Europe describing his tribulations. These circulated round Jesuit houses and furnished material for the biographies which became widely known after the saint's canonisation in 1621. These present Álvaro de Ataide as an arch-villain who prevented the great plan for the Christianisation of China. Ataide himself was deprived of his command, arrested in Goa by the Viceroy, sent to Portugal to face the king's justice, and sentenced to life imprisonment after being exposed to public ignominy. He died in prison of leprosy. The histories of the Jesuit missions in the Far East were read throughout Catholic Europe, and the name of Don Álvaro de Ataide became notorious.

The main parallels (which are not in 'Lope's' *Alcalde*) between the historical personage and the dramatic character are indeed striking, despite the dissimilarity of the backgrounds. First, Crespo pleads with Don Álvaro to marry his daughter, offering to surrender to her his whole fortune; only when Don Álvaro scornfully rejects this offer does he invoke his authority and arrest him; Francis Xavier tried every means of conciliation with Ataide and only when these proved fruitless did he invoke the powers conferred on him by king, Viceroy and Church, which were scornfully disregarded as is Crespo's appeal to his authority. Secondly, Don Álvaro is executed by Crespo by what for a nobleman was the most ignominious method, garrotting rather than beheading; Ataide was exposed to public ignomiy in Lisbon by the king's orders before being confined to prison for life.[16]

What could have been the reason for Calderón, circa 1642, giving his fictitious character such a well-known name? That he did so merely to brand him as a villain would have been using a sledge-hammer to crack a nut. García Gómez speculates on the reason by invoking the historical context of the 1640s. The Catalan revolt of 1640 fired a simultaneous insurrectionary movement in Portugal. The king's advisors were divided into two parties, those who counselled moderation and conciliation and those who favoured strong military action. The war waged to suppress the revolt did not go well for Spanish arms, but it was not until 1644 that the Spanish public was informed that Portugal was lost. It is to be noted that *El alcalde de Zalamea* is placed in the historical context of a successful conquest of Portugal, while contemporary events were pointing in the opposite direction. It would be unlike Calderón not to bring out, by implication, a parallel or a contrast between the two Portuguese wars. It may be the case that Calderón wanted to associate the rebellious contempt of his Captain for the authority of the law with the rebellion of Portugal against the Spanish crown which, as García Gómez has noted, would introduce current affairs into the play with a caustic implication.

It is generally agreed that Calderón must have written this play after his return from military service against the rebellious Catalans. The use of the name Ataide was his way of referring to the rebellious Portuguese, as García Gómez suggests. Calderón may have been implying that repressive measures should only be used after all efforts at conciliation have failed. When the Catalan Rebellion was quelled by civil war the Spanish Crown had to choose between the policy of punishing Catalonia by suppressing the measure of autonomy she enjoyed or by pardoning her and restoring this autonomy. As was noted above in *Las armas de la hermosura*, Calderón was clearly on the side of reconciliation, like his Philip II in *El alcalde*. García Gómez centres this advocacy of conciliation in the scene in the play where Crespo pleads on his knees with Don Álvaro to marry his daughter, offering to impoverish himself in order to enrich his offender. This, for García Gómez, is the main reason for introducing the Portuguese rebellion through the person of the historical

Ataide. He equates Crespo's Christian and forgiving attitude with those of the king's ministers who advocated conciliation rather than repression in 1637, when the Portuguese rebellion was threatening. This would be more plausible if it were likely that the play were written at that time.[17] If, however, we take the date of composition as more probably 1642, we are in a different historical context. Portugal has been lost, but this disaster has not been admitted. What was the government to do? Should it plan to pursue the war in order to vindicate its authority or should it accept defeat with as good a grace as possible? To make the attempts at conciliation in 1637, the main point of the Portuguese analogy would not be feasible with the earlier date of composition. In any case, Crespo's humble plea to Don Álvaro is not the climax of the play. The climax is whether (like the real-life Málaga magistrate) Crespo should be punished for the grievous illegality of his action, as the irate army commander demands. Calderón was provided with a ready-made solution by his source- play, and he did not alter it. It fitted perfectly in what, as is here being suggested, was his purpose in reviving and re-writing 'Lope's' play. The fact that Philip II takes the line that what is done cannot be undone, and that the *de facto*, and not the *de jure*, solution should be accepted, despite the protestations of the military, may well point to the political discussions before the Spanish defeat was made public. By making his criminal Captain a notorious Portuguese villain, Calderón not only associates his re-working of the first *El alcalde de Zalamea* play with Portugal and the contemporary Portuguese war, but safeguards himself from condoning the rebellion *qua* rebellion, but nonetheless advocating a peaceful and conciliatory acceptance of the result.

Calderón has long been thought a dramatist concerned with abstract problems, and therefore remote from the real world of human passions and conflicts. The realisation that history is a formative element in the elaboration of his themes through his special technique of allusions, analogies, and contrasts, may help to right the balance. History is indeed present in his drama with the past brought to bear on the problems of the present, suggesting possible solutions in the light of historical experience.

V From symbol to myth

23 The court drama

That Calderón is a predominantly religious dramatist cannot be substantiated statistically, if we limit ourselves to his *comedias*, or plays for the public theatres and the palace. There are 109 of these plays, only twelve of which have religious subjects; in the remainder religion does not enter at all except in so far as its practice was a natural part of the social world portrayed on the stage; but there are some forty plays that do not portray this social world, and among these there are a group of seventeen in which it is impossible to detect that they were written by a Christian. These are his mythological plays. Calderón could not have written these had he not been an heir to Renaissance Humanism. The classical myths coloured every poet's way of thinking and determined his metaphors. It also invaded the stage, especially in that least realistic of dramatic forms: opera. This had begun in Italy with mythological themes. The first opera, produced in Italy in 1597, had as libretto the myth of Daphne. Orpheus and Cephalus were the subjects of the next two operas, also of course in Italy. Calderón plays an important part in the early stages of the development of opera in Spain:[1] many of his mythological plays are music dramas in whole or in part. Mythology and music, each in its own way, elevated dramatic art well above the sphere of prosaic reality. This was not theatre for the ordinary people, but for an aristocratic élite. All Calderón's mythological plays are court plays, although not all his court plays are mythological.

Spanish court plays, or *comedias palaciegas*, constitute a sub-genre of the *comedia*, or secular drama as a whole. They differ from the rest because of their staging, their special audience, and, in the case of the plays with which we are here concerned, their subject-matter. Four chapters in the standard history of the Spanish stage are devoted to the rise of the court theatre and its development in the seventeenth century.[2] Plays in the Palace were first performed in a suitable hall or room until, in 1623, just after the accession of Philip IV, a special room was permanently reconstructed as a theatre, known as the *Salón Dorado*. In that year, Calderón was at the commencement of his dramatic career. This private theatre was in the Alcázar, the royal residence within the city of Madrid. In 1640, the new Palacio del Retiro was completed and inaugurated outside the city in what is now the Park of the Retiro. This contained a special building for a theatre known as the Coliseo.[3] The theatre was of the then modern type, with a large stage, separated from the auditorium by a proscenium arch and by a curtain. Stage machinery of a kind not possible in the public theatres, and the provision of stage sets for scenery made possible elaborate productions not previously seen in Spain. The first performance of a court play to the sovereigns and the Court was followed by private performances to officials and finally to the ordinary inhabitants of Madrid, who were enabled to see the spectacles that their own theatres could never have produced.

The development of the court theatre in both the Alcázar and the Retiro was directed to producing theatrical spectacles that were conceived as elaborate homages to the king. A point was selected in the auditorium where the eyes of the audience and the actors could be naturally drawn to the two Royal chairs which were placed on it. The stage scenery was so set up that it could be seen to best advantage from this focal point. This meant that 'for the courtier . . . the king is the true spectacle, the play being merely of secondary importance'.

> The palace spectacle is a heightening of the metaphor which the Court as a whole plays out, for if the Court theatre is a mirror in which can be seen reflected the king's taste, his ambitions, his virtues, his nobility and, above all, his regal power, than we must always remember that the Court itself is theatre, a play in which the king is the sole protagonist.[4]

The very special nature of these dramatic performances raises a difficulty for the student of Calderón and for literary critics in general which should be put into proper perspective. John Varey is a specialist in the history of the Spanish stage and on every aspect, including the administrative and financial, of theatrical productions in the Spanish Golden Age. From his special scholarly point of view he defines the problem in this way: 'literary scholars are professionally book-oriented, and tend to consider primarily the text' (p. 399). 'The moral for us is clear: critical interpretations based on the literary text of a court play studied in isolation must be suspect' (p. 405). John Varey's specialist erudition can supply his imagination with all the ingredients of these spectacles, and he is of course right to be more interested in such reconstructed spectacles than in the texts to which they gave body on the stage. But the rest of us cannot do without the printed texts, which alone recorded plays before the age of film and television. We are of necessity 'book-oriented' when facing the drama of the past. Opera is the closest example today of a multi-faceted theatrical spectacle, the nearest equivalent to a Spanish court play when re-performed without the king and Court. The fusion of music and dramatic text is, *mutatis mutandis*, a parallel to the fusion of stage performance and court spectacle which the Palace of the Retiro could provide. An opera as a theatrical entertainment can only exist when well-produced on the stage. The music (the orchestra and the singers) with the sung words of the text and the visual spectacle are all essential elements. A silent film of a performance on the stage would be pointless; the libretto must be read, but in isolation this would be a mere skeleton. But a recorded playing of the music of an opera can be a highly satisfying experience. This cannot give a full aesthetic appreciation of the opera as a work of art, but the music is the *raison d'être* of the artistic creation, and must be the only part that can be isolated. Though not offering a total experience, the recorded music of an opera could not in any sense be called 'suspect' as a musical experience. In what sense can the *reading* of any Calderón play lead to 'suspect' interpretation? It will do so, of course, if the interpreter lacks poetic sensitivity and dramatic insight, and if he does not understand Calderón's technique, but that is not, of course, what Varey means. He means that any interpretation of the theatrical *entertainment* must be suspect if based on the reading of the printed text alone. There can be no disputing that statement. But this implies that we must await the discovery of the drawings or paintings of the stage sets and of the music and, further, await a good integrated production, before we can understand the poetic and dramatic meaning of a particular text. Though Varey would not, indeed cannot, admit it, the Calderonian text, with its poetry and its drama, is the only part of these seventeenth-century spectacles that, in the present state of our knowledge with very few exceptions, can have universal validity. We should not want to recreate the impact of these spectacles on their first audiences; we should aim at understanding them within the framework of Calderón's dramatic art as a whole. This means, as it does with all his plays, looking for the *meaning* of the text, for Calderón could never have envisaged a text without meaning.

In defence of his point of view, Varey quotes a comment made on the visit of the Princesse de Carignan to Madrid in 1637, that in a court performance she could see its whole idea embodied in the king, and see the performance of the play as accessory to it, ('como en idea en los Reyes la representación, y por accesorio lo representado de la comedia') (pp. 401–2). Since the king was the person to whom everything was directed, this is of course acceptable. But Varey also quotes (p. 404) words of Calderón himself from the *Loa* (Prologue) to another of Calderón's mythological plays, *Andrómeda y Perseo*, the definition given by Poetry of her function:

> *Poesía* Pues yo soy la Poesía,
> en mis números daré
> a tus coros y a sus líneas
> el alma que han de tener

> (I am Poetry; in my numbers I shall give to your choruses and to your outlines the soul that they must have.)

In other words, Poetry is to the other aspects of the production (Music and Painting) what the Soul is to the Body – it gives them life and significance.

The only scholar to put on paper in book form an integrated view of the spectacles in which Calderón's mythological plays were produced is Sebastian Neumeister. He interprets the function of mythology in these spectacles as that of portraying for king and courtiers their place in society. Mythology represented a hierarchical society, because it represented a cosmos with a supreme deity (Jupiter) at its head, and in descending scale a host of lesser gods, demi-gods and human beings. The cosmic splendour of the gods is mirrored in the brilliance of the décor. This mirror of the cosmos gave king and court the illusion of a stable world order in which they could hold fast despite awareness of the dangers that threatened from without and within. This is no doubt true in a general sense. But the ways in which Neumeister sees particular analogies between myths and court life may be illustrated from the fable of Cupid and Psyche. He visits her only at night, and she is forbidden to see him by the light of a lamp. When she succumbs to temptation and looks on him as he lies by her side, the whole palace he has built for her disappears. Neumeister interprets this as the secret plots which threaten the political stability of the monarchy. There is no objective correlation in the text of contemporary political plots with the disappearance of the palace in Calderón's handling of the fable in *Ni Amor se libra de amor* (Not even Love is Immune from Love) (1662), but the inadequacy of such an interpretation lies in the fact that it presents Cupid as a man and not a 'god', and that Psyche becomes only a woman. Cupid of course represented erotic desire, as his name indicated: he is the 'God of Love', and Psyche, as her name also indicates, was the Human Soul. On the appropriate level of meaning, therefore, court conspiracies can have nothing to do with this. The only ways to discover the meaning Calderón gives to any myth are first, from the concepts that the classical gods represented, and secondly, from the indications, direct or indirect, given in the dialogue, or by isolating the changes that Calderón introduces into the myth's structure. In this play, there are four such changes, and a long discussion between Cupid and Psyche, all of which point to an elaboration by the dramatist of the tradition that goes back to Fabius Fulgentius (467–532), whereby the fable signified that the innocence of true love is destroyed by lust, which can only be purged by expiation involving suffering.[5] The final reconciliation of Jupiter and Cupid and the restoration of Psyche's union with the latter is interpreted by Neumeister as an illustration of the need for a prudent monarch to govern his court with magnanimity. This, he maintains, is how the audience would have interpreted the *dénouement* of the play. This may be so, but it is clearly not how Calderón presented the meaning of the fable. Neumeister, who in general follows structuralist principles, does not admit that arguments and discussions between the characters in the dialogue can throw any light on the meaning of the plays. Perhaps we may state that an attempt to analyse the meaning of any Calderonian play, including the mythological ones, that is not based on a close analysis of the text and of the dramatic action is suspect.[6]

To illustrate the kind of meaning that can be arrived at from a study of the myth and its transformation by Calderón into a dramatic action, we may take the most complex of these plays, *La estatua de Prometeo* (The Statue of Prometheus). The play was published in 1677 in the spurious *Quinta Parte* of Calderón's plays. It was probably written in 1670 to celebrate the birthday of the Queen Mother, Mariana of Austria (22 December).[7]

It is a complex play, and certainly one of Calderón's finest achievements, but not easy to interpret. The source myth, like all myths, has several variations. Prometheus as the friend of man against the tyranny of Zeus and punished accordingly, is a late form. Originally he was a trickster arousing the anger of Jupiter by his deceptions of the gods. In the best-known form Jupiter fashions a statue of a woman which he sends to Prometheus hoping he will fall in love with her when she is brought to life, but Prometheus is suspicious, and it is his brother Epimetheus who becomes enamoured of her and marries her. She is then Pandora, and Jupiter sends as her wedding gift a box containing all the evils of life which she lets loose on the world. In another form of the myth Prometheus fashions two statues from clay which are the first man and woman on earth: he gives them life from the fire that he steals from Heaven. Calderón runs these two versions of the myth together to create an original conception. He also introduces other significant changes of detail.[8]

Calderón's play deals with the passage of humanity from barbarism to civilisation. Prometeo has clearly the status of a demi-god, although the term is never applied to him. He lives and moves in a kind of wilderness, which the opening scene identifies as Mount Caucasus, a mountain that for the ancients was inhabited by numerous savage tribes. There are no cities or even villages, only a series of caves in the mountainside, one of which is the dwelling of Prometeo. The setting, according to the stage directions, can be changed from a forest to a wilderness of boulders: 'upstage there must be a cave of bare rocks, and with a door of the same material large enough for a person to pass through, until at the proper time the whole of this upstage area opens, and Prometeo emerges, shouting'.[9] When this type of setting occurs in Calderón, it means one of two things. In a *comedia* it denotes the domain of a 'wild man' or 'wild woman', and portends a violent action of some kind.[10] In an *auto sacramental* it denotes the place where Man is lying asleep awaiting Creation. This is one of the features allying *La estatua de Prometeo* with the theological symbolical drama. This will be discussed in chapter 25 below when the analysis of this *comedia* is completed. Other examples will be quoted of this type of setting and its significance explained. Here, in *La estatua de Prometeo*, this setting establishes the human 'wilderness' before the birth of culture. This wilderness contains inhabitants who are beneath Prometeo in intelligence. It is also a place where gods and goddesses can be summoned by Prometeo. The only building that exists is a temple to Saturn: their only 'religion' being this barbarous cult of a god who devoured his children, and whose worship required human sacrifice.

Prometeo has a brother Epimeteo. The former represents the reasoning faculty of man; his brother Epimeteo represents the passionate and violent side of human nature. Prometeo, given to speculation, has worked out the principles of jurisprudence and politics. Deploring the barbarity of his rustic companions, he tries to give them laws and government, but they turn against him accusing him of tyrannical ambition. Withdrawing into the solitude of his cave, he becomes a devotee of Minerva; he sees her so vividly in his imagination that he fashions a statue of her in clay. He summons the people and shows them the statue: since they did not accept laws and government, let them accept religion, worship this goddess and build a temple to her. Prometeo, that is to say, has seen the ideal of civilisation, beyond the limitations of politics, and this ideal he puts before the simple rustics.

The rustics receive his suggestions favourably and agree to suppress the cult of Saturn and to build a temple to Minerva larger than the one they already have to Saturn. Epimeteo, staring in wonder at the statue, is strongly attracted by its physical form. He tells Prometeo to keep it hidden while the temple is being built, having the secret intention of visiting it from time to time. All begin to celebrate the new cult with singing and dancing, when the alarm is given that a wild beast is roaming the countryside,[11] and the men depart to kill or capture it. Prometeo is successful, and leads the beast on to the stage, whereupon it throws off its skins and reveals itself as the goddess Minerva, who proceeds to thank Prometeo for his service and for introducing her cult. No unusual device is meaningless in Calderón, and this unexpected transformation from dangerous wild animal to goddess can be no exception. It symbolises the suppression of the cult of Saturn in favour of the worship of Minerva; that is to say, human intelligence, which has been suppressed under barbarism, is now dawning as the supremacy of Minerva is recognised. She can reveal herself to Prometeo, her first devotee, because he is effecting the transition among men. Minerva, grateful to Prometeo for his service, tells him to ask for a boon. He asks first for a glimpse of heaven: he wants to see how the gods live so that he may know what to ask for. In heaven he is dazzled by the light of the sun (which symbolises the light of knowledge); he asks for one of its rays so that he can take light and fire to the earth. As Apolo's chariot passes by, Prometeo seizes one of its torches. This is theft because the Earth has no natural right to the fire of heaven. Minerva, however, connives at the theft, and protects him while he carries it out. Apolo does not notice the theft. Returning to earth, Prometeo puts the torch into the hand of his statue, and the statue comes to life.

Whereas Minerva was grateful to Prometeo for the service he renders her, her twin sister Palas is violently angry with Epimeteo for his admiration of the statue, and orders him to return to her cult. This interplay is developed into an intrigue of attraction and repulsion, love and jealousy, of the type so common in the social comedies. While the grateful Minerva wishes to reward Prometeo with an embrace, he is repelled and leaves her; on the other hand, Epimeteo pays more and more attention to her, and she is repelled by him. Palas, who desires Epimeteo's attentions, becomes jealous of her twin sister. The similarity of situation between the love and jealousy situations of the social comedies goes further. At one point, Minerva wants to see how Prometeo reacts to the statue but, not wishing to be seen by him, hides behind it in the same way as a *dama* hides in a closet or behind a curtain. For the modern reader, it is doubtless disconcerting to have similar dramatic conventions used for two such totally dissimilar settings. Perhaps it had become so much second nature with Calderón to give this kind of movement to the situation of attraction and repulsion that he might have thought that the dissimilarity between the two levels of stage action did not matter. On the other hand, he might have known that his audience did not have the intellectual equipment necessary to grasp his philosophical distinctions and therefore gave them the stage presentation they would have understood. Furthermore, it may be the case that his power of conceptual abstractions and distinctions was keener than his imaginative power to vary their dramatic form. In any case, this book will have made it abundantly clear that what his symbolic actions represent in his mind is always something that repays unravelling.

What he is saying behind the social comedy type of intrigue is one of the most difficult problems of ancient metaphysics, one that Platonism and Aristotelianism bequeathed to scholasticism, and which Neoplatonism kept in the foreground. The myth presented Prometheus's bringing the fire of heaven to mankind as a theft, which immediately indicates the Platonic dualism of Spirit and Matter. Matter and Spirit are essentially incompatible; man's material brain has no natural right to be the vehicle for abstract reasoning and the spiritual Powers of the Mind, much less for those of the Soul. This was the source of the tension that Renaissance Neoplatonism saw as the tension of love. The human soul has a natural desire for the spiritual, while the human body has a natural desire for physical love. What satisfies the soul starves the body, and vice versa, but the intellectual and the spiritual are the goods proper to man's rational nature. Reason ennobles, passion degrades. This tension has already been noted in Calderón's mythological plays.[12] Mythology gave him a variety of fables and symbols with which to clothe and express it; in the particular case of *La estatua de Prometeo*, he uses the conventions of the secular stage. Man's soul and rational nature are due to his being made 'in the image of God', but the human soul is never fully at home in the 'Prison' of the Body. Prometeo, who represents the reasoning and speculative powers of the human being, is more at home in the world of the gods than he is on earth. What he loves in Minerva/Pandora is the fire that gives life and knowledge: he cannot love the clay that harbours the fire and is thus insensitive to physical beauty as such. Epimeteo is, of course, the reverse: he can love only the clay, not the fire.

Pandora, the epitome of all feminine graces, is hurt at the way Prometeo shuns her. She cannot marry him in Act II, because Palas, and her confederate Discordia (Discord) release the black cloud of conflict by removing the stopper from the vase. In Act III, Prometeo is asked by Minerva to account for his constant rejection of her. He answers with this very neat description of the dualism of human nature:

> ¿Cómo puedo sin saberlo
> decirlo tampoco yo?
> Pues si deidad te contemplo,
> te adoro; si hermosa, te amo,

si discreta, te venero,
si prodigiosa, te admiro,
y si todo, te aborrezco;
Que hay otro yo que sin mí
manda en mí más que yo mismo.

(How can I, if I cannot explain it even to myself? For if I look on you as a Divinity, I adore you; if I see you as beautiful, I love you; if I consider your intelligence, I venerate you; if I see the wonders you work, I admire you; but if I think of you as a whole, I hate you; for there is another self within me, who, without my consent, rules me more than I rule myself.)

(III, 848–56) [*BAE*, III, p. 716a]

As the black cloud from Pandora's vase envelops the earth, there is thunder, lightning and earthquakes, and the frightened people call on heaven for mercy, and as Act II merges into III, the scene changes to a heavenly setting and Apolo, Palas and Minerva appear. Palas appeals to Apolo arguing that he must punish the theft of heaven's fire. Minerva argues that he must *pardon* the theft because more beneficent results have been produced thereby than if it had remained in heaven. Translated into the mythic terms of the theme, this means that human civilisation, despite its terrible abuses, is better than the original state of barbarism. Apolo, being unable to state whether Prometeo's theft had been wrong, determines to stand aloof from the ensuing battle. The fighting starts, and Discord appears to pronounce judgement on Prometeo and Minerva/Pandora. They are both seized by the rustics, led by Epimeteo. Minerva fights with Palas, and chaos ensues until Apolo reappears to order the fighting to cease. He disperses the smoke, and restores harmony. Palas and Discord flee; the two brothers are reunited and Epimeteo announces the wedding between Prometeo and Pandora.

On the face of it, this seems a rather contrived 'happy ending' not in keeping with the strength of the action, but what of course justifies it is its meaning on the thematic level. Apolo or the Sun is the god of the fine arts, especially of music and poetry – in short, the god of civilisation. Only he can reconcile the duality in human nature, the clash between the twin brothers, Prometeo and Epimeteo. Only in the creation of an artistic civilisation can the clay of humanity justify its usurpation of the fire of heaven. At first sight this is still the optimistic humanism of the Renaissance, but the passage of time has made a difference. The optimism is implicitly qualified by 'only if' – only if Apollo rules rather than Pallas, only if warfare is supressed by artistic creativity, can a peaceful civilisation be created; but this means that the violence of passion must be subjected to reason in the pursuit of art and learning. Bembo and Castiglione and the Italian Neoplatonists in general had believed, or had professed to believe, that since reason could deduce that a spiritual, non-sensual love was superior to a carnal one, the human will would automatically accept the judgement of reason and carnal appetites would automatically be stilled. For Calderón this is not so. Discord lurks behind all human activity and will inevitably keep coming to the fore because good and evil are inseparable. Minerva the goddess of civilisation and Pallas the goddess of war are the same, and they rule in human nature, the one in reason, the other in passion, but in human history it is possible from time to time to strike a balance, as the Humanism of the Renaissance in fact did. In Calderón's mythological plays, the conflict between Eros (sexual passion) and Agape (spiritual love) is part of the inseparability of Good and Evil. The obverse and reverse of the same coin: Eros is to be subordinated and stilled but not destroyed. An important aspect of Calderón's originality in re-working the myth is that he makes Minerva and Pallas twin sisters, while tradition has it that they are one and the same. They are a single 'double-sided' character, in exactly the same way as Prometeo and Epimeteo are twin characters, also inseparably joined together, a similarly original addition of Calderón's.

What, more than anything else, might make Calderón's ending seem artificially contrived is the fact that in no version of the myth does Prometheus marry Pandora. Is this the conventional 'happy ending' of the Spanish *comedia* with the hero giving his hand to the heroine? As this book has several times emphasised, any change made by Calderón in the history or known stories that he uses in any plot is not an arbitrary change but one that specifically points towards the meaning he wishes his play to convey. Because this is the ending of the play it will be the meaning Calderón has been leading up to. This change in the myth will point to the essential theme of the play. What Greer calls 'The Myth of Royal Power' and 'The Political Myth' (as will be explained in chapter 25) are subordinate themes: they cannot be the essential theme. This has two closely related aspects: the unity of Soul and Body is a *real* unity which must overcome the metaphysical duality; and secondly, that human intelligence and reason can be positive forces for good if harnessed, not to war, but to culture and art. On this level the intervention of Apolo is not a hoped-for intervention of any royal or political figure within the period during which the play must have been written and performed. It is an intervention that must be consonant with the symbolical meaning of the mythological god.

Such is the theme of *La estatua de Prometeo*, but the significance of the play has not yet been fully expounded. There is one further section, when the statue comes to life, which represents, within the originality of

Calderón's treatment of the myth, a further remarkable deviation from his sources. It is here, in connection with the symbolic creation of mankind, that Calderón introduces the second of his own mythic archetypes, which is in effect a permutation of the archetype of the fatherless son. This, like the symbol of imprisonment, is obsessively repeated by Calderón in the *autos sacramentales* as part of his general mythic presentation of human destiny. The discussion of this, and therefore the completion of the analysis of *La estatua de Prometeo*, may most conveniently be left to the last chapter.

Calderón's Prometheus play has here been dealt with through its stage-action but always in the light of the traditional approach to mythology in late classical times and in the Renaissance and Post-Renaissance. The author of the present book has of necessity been 'book-oriented'; it is unlikely that any of its readers, now or in the future, will ever be able to see and hear a fully satisfactory production of this play along the lines intended by the poet, the composer, the producer and the designers of the scenery and the costumes. Such a hypothetical production might or might not alter the meaning of the text as set out here, but until such a production materialises the student and critic of drama must analyse the text as it exists on printed pages. In this elucidation the nature of classical mythology with its religious orientation through allegories and symbols must always be taken into account, and Calderón's re-working of the myths must be deduced from the poetic and imaginative structure given in his conception of them. It is in this light that Calderón's mythological *comedias* must be approached – from the point of view of their dramatic themes. *La estatua de Prometeo* has demonstrated what kind of intellectual life he could extract from myths and embody in dramatic characters and actions. A further example of such treatment can be provided by *Andrómeda y Perseo*. It must of course be understood that when one speaks of 'intellectual life' in relation to the mythological *comedias* one refers to ideas expressed in a form proper not only to drama but also to myth. This means that they are suggested as universal truths and can therefore be more easily expressed 'philosophically'. As will now be shown, Calderón gave clear expression to the importance of classical mythology in the sphere of *quasi*-religious thinking. Here, we shall have to depart from the rigid separation of the *comedias*, or secular plays, from the *autos sacramentales*, or theological plays, a separation that was valid as we began the exploration of Calderón's mind and art, but that is no longer valid as we approach its climax.

24 Mythology and Humanism

All men have a guide within their own traditions to the problem of human destiny. One such was mythology in the ancient pagan world. Calderón considered classical mythology to be a variant or deviant form of the original revelation given to Mankind. Ten of his *autos sacramentales* use classical myths as allegories of Christian dogmas, including the Incarnation and the sacrificial death of Christ. In the earliest Christian centuries Orpheus had appeared as a symbol of Christ, because he broke down the gates of Hades in order to restore his beloved, Eurydice, to the world. Very soon, however, the early Church fathers scornfully attacked the Greek and Roman gods, ridiculing especially their licentiousness and marital infidelities. The stern judgement of Lactantius was that 'if one were to call out to Jupiter, Neptune, Vulcan, Mercury, Apollo, and Saturn, the father of them all, they would all reply from the depths of Hell.'[1] Calderón, however, justifies his use of mythology in the *autos* by pointing to the numerous parallels between the fables and the Bible, because Renaissance mythographers had more than an inkling of comparative anthropology.

Our modern culture finds nothing extravagant in such a parallel. In fact, the modern anthropologist would accept the parallel but would invert its interpretation. The Christian doctrines of the Virgin Birth, God made Man, His sacrificial death as the means of freeing Mankind from enslavement to sin and guilt, might themselves be considered myths, alternative forms of the Graeco-Roman fables. In 1881, the great scholar and critic Marcelino Menéndez Pelayo could say: 'the use of mythology in the sacramental drama of Calderón will strike some as irreverent; it seems to me nothing more than doubtful taste'.[2] This was a prejudice that prevented him from recognising some of Calderón's most beautiful poetry, and the full range of his ideas on human life. True to the heritage of Renaissance Humanism, Calderón saw in mythology an imperfect but not distorted echo of Divine Revelation. In Spain this view was argued at some length by the Franciscan Fray Baltasar de Vitoria, in the opening section of his *Teatro de los Dioses de la Gentilidad* (Theatre of the Pagan Gods), first published in 1620, republished several times and widely read.

In the *Loa* to *El Laberinto del Mundo*, an *auto* allegorising the myth of Theseus and the Minotaur, Calderón justifies his use of classical mythology for a sacred theme by reference to Paul's Epistle to the Romans (i, 20–3), which he paraphrases in this way:

> Dígalo el texto
> de Pablo: Entre los Gentiles
> asienta, que convirtieron
> en fábulas las Verdades:
> porque como ellos tuvieron
> sólo lejanas noticias
> de la Luz del Evangelio,
> viciaron sin ella nuestra
> escritura, atribuyendo
> a falsos dioses sus raras
> maravillas

(Let this text from Paul explain: he asserts that the Gentiles converted truths into fables; since they saw the Light of the Gospel only as a faint glimmer they were unable without it to preserve uncorrupted our scriptures. They attributed to false gods the wonders of the Gospel)[3]

The most extensive expression of this relationship between mythology and scripture in Calderón's *autos sacramentales* comes in the early section of *El Sacro Parnaso* (1659). The Mount Parnassus of the ancients, home of Apollo and the Muses, is allegorised as a foreshadowing of the Holy Mountain, Mount Zion, that leads the faithful to Heaven. The play opens with a song summoning men to a poetic contest. Judaism and Paganism come on the stage. Entranced by the beauty of the voice and the instruments, they move towards it, questioning what it might be. Judaism thinks it must be the earthly paradise, Paganism the Elysian Fields. It is not the time now, says Paganism, to argue which of the two is right; let them await the answer that will settle the argument. Faith tells them that neither is right, but also that neither is entirely wrong. The prize in the contest, as Faith later explains, is to go to the one who writes a poem (a *canción real*) on the life of Christ and to the Holy Eucharist and its superiority to all earthly nourishment. Before the contest begins, Faith urges Judaism and Paganism to clarify their respective religious doctrines, the one from Genesis, the other from Ovid's *Metamorphoses*. As they begin with the creation of the world, she points out where they agree. She then tells them to open their respective books at random, and to read out loud. There follows a lengthy passage in stichomythia, a passage in which Judaism reads out one of her truths and Paganism parallels it with one of his. The passage may be summarised in this way: the battle between the dragon and the archangel – Phaethon, who is hurled down from the heavens to the earth; the apple whose poison infects the human race – the Goddess Discord, throwing an apple labelled 'for the fairest' at the banquet of the Gods, the apple that led to the ruin of Troy; Noah, contrasted with Deucalion and Pyrrha; the Tower of Babel built, according to Jewish legend, by the mighty Nimrod in order to dominate the earth – Typhoeus leading the revolt of the Titans against Jupiter; Gideon's fleece giving promise of victory over the Midianites[4] – the golden fleece restored to Thessaly when Jason eludes the fiery bulls and the dragon that guard it in Colchis;[5] Isaiah prophesies to Ahaz that 'a young woman (Vulgate: 'virgin') shall conceive and bear a son, and shall call his name Immanuel' (Isaiah, ch. 7) – this prophecy is fulfilled in the Virgin Mary)[6] – Danae conceives Perseus by Jupiter in a shower of gold, he will rescue humanity from the monster Medusa.

In this enumeration of parallels between scripture and mythology Calderón goes further than Fray Baltasar de Vitoria. In the first chapter of his *Theatre of the Pagan Gods* the latter had given parallels only between the supposed etymologies of names and between persons and events. Calderón goes further by introducing symbols like that of the Golden Fleece. Whether Calderón's parallels are mostly coincidences, or whether it is possible to postulate a mythical affiliation between others is immaterial. What matters is that Calderón believed that mythology belonged, although remotely, to the revelation of Scripture, which meant that he was sufficiently respectful of the ancient deities to utilise them as allegories for his Eucharistic plays. In the *Loa* of *El laberinto del mundo* (1654) Faith announces that the theme of the play is to be the 'fable' of Theseus and the Minotaur. Surprise is expressed that such a 'fable' could be relevant to the Feast of Corpus Christi, but Faith then reiterates the idea that mythology is a vitiated form of revelation, and continues:

> que no
> hay fábula sin misterio,
> si alegórica a la Luz
> desto se mira

(there is no fable without a mystery, if it be interpreted allegorically in this light)

(III, p.1558a)

One further illustration of this thesis must suffice. In the second or final version of *El divino Orfeo* (1663) Calderón makes the Prince of Darkness justify to Envy, his confederate, the use of the myth of Orpheus in these terms:

La Gentilidad, Envidia,
idolatramente ciega,
teniendo de las verdades
lejanas noticias, piensa
que falsos dioses y ninfas
atribuya las Inmensas
Obras de un Dios solo; y como
sin Luz de Fe andan a ciegas,
hará con las ignorancias
sospechosas las creencias.
¡Cuántas veces se verán
los Poetas y Profetas
acordes, donde se rocen
verdades en Sombra envueltas!
¿Qué más Faetonte que yo,
que por gobernar la Excelsa
Carroza del Sol caí?
Y de esta misma manera
habrá infinitos Lugares
que por repetidos deja
mi voz, en que se confronten
Divinas y Humanas Letras
en la consonancia amigas
y en la Religión opuestas.

(Paganism, blinded by idolatry, possessed only remote knowledge of Truth. It thinks that it can attribute to false Gods and nymphs the marvellous handiwork of one single God; and as the Pagans stumble blindly without the light of faith, they make the beliefs of faith suspect by their ignorance. How often poets and prophets will be found in agreement, where truths, enveloped in shadow, brush against each other. Who could be a better Phaethon than I, who fell through driving the lofty chariot of the Sun? In common with this one, there will be an infinite number of examples in which Divine and Human letters confront each other, in friendship because of agreement, in enmity because of religion. (I omit them on this occasion, because they have been so often repeated on others.))[7]

This aspect of Calderón's thought has been brought in to reveal his respectful attitude to classical mythology, which in the *autos* he always refers to as 'Poetry' as against the 'Scripture' of Revelation. It must not be thought from this exposition that Scripture can automatically be turned into Poetry whenever an analogical parallel can be extracted. It is a serious error to think that when Calderón has worked out an allegory that turns a myth into Christian dogma, that particular theological meaning must always be implicit whenever that particular myth recurs in his plays. The allegorisation of myth into theological dogma is dependent solely upon the purpose of the festival in which the play is being produced. The *autos* were written for public performances in the open air on the feast of Corpus Christi, and were so written and produced to make that purpose abundantly clear. The purpose was to expound the truths of the Christian faith, in their Tridentine Catholic form through what the feast established as the theological and devotional centre of theology, the mystery of the Holy Eucharist. Calderón devises a very careful technique to make it plain that he is allegorising his theme and not merely representing it naturalistically through dialogue and action. The allegories are always explained either directly or through symbolism. The conditions of performance for the Corpus Christi drama were totally different from those of the court drama, though both were 'spectacles' of different kinds. It is a serious error of interpretation to read a mythological *comedia* as if it were a mythological *auto*.[8] Nothing that has so far been said about Calderón's use of mythology must be taken as justifying this: it does not take long when studying Calderón's plays to be able to differentiate an *auto* from a *comedia*. It must, however, go without saying that a myth that can suggest the principal dogmas of the Christian faith must always be taken seriously as a vehicle in Calderón's hands for conveying ideas and not just as a means for spectacular stage settings. Because the classical myths are so far removed from 'reality', Calderón's mythological palace plays have in the past been removed from the realm of dramatic and intellectual significance. In the age of the metaphysical conceit Calderón took pains to elaborate in the *autos* the complex analogies between the mythical and the theological, and just as clearly he found as much intellectual satisfaction and pleasure in doing this as poets found satisfaction and pleasure in developing their elaborate conceits. Every conceit in the hands of a major seventeenth-century poet ultimately satisfies the mind, and the same will be true in Calderón's dramatic handling of mythology, whether it be the working out of the analogies between the mythical and the spiritual in the *autos*, or the implicit presentation of the analogies between myths and philosophical ideas, in the broad sense, in the mythological *comedias palaciegas*. Calderón, like Homer, sometimes nods, but being Calderón, he cannot fail to infuse his dramatic themes with intellectual life. It is in this light that Calderón's mythological *comedias* must be approached from the point of view of their dramatic themes. *La estatua de Prometeo* has demonstrated what kind of intellectual life he could extract from myths and embody in dramatic characters and actions.

One of the parallels between Scripture and mythology quoted from *El sacro Parnaso* was the Old Testament prophecy that a virgin would conceive and bear a son called Immanuel, a prophecy that Christianity saw fulfilled in the announcement by the Angel to Mary that she would conceive a son by divine power. Calderón saw this twofold Scriptural passage paralleled in the fable of Danaë, who was confined by her father Acrisius in a tower because an oracle had foretold that if she bore a son he would kill Acrisius, his grandfather. She conceived as a virgin when Jupiter entered her bed as a shower of gold. When she gave birth to Perseus, the two were placed in a boat and set adrift on the sea, and were blown to the island of Seriphus where Perseus grew to manhood. The adult Perseus was sent to fight the Gorgons, a trio of monstrous women who turned to stone all those on whom they gazed. Only one of these, Medusa, was mortal, and with the direct assistance of the gods Perseus was able to cut off her head. On his way back to Seriphus Perseus rescued Andromeda, whom he found chained to a rock by the king, her father. The parallel between mythology and scripture as outlined above by Calderón made it easy enough to turn the myth into a theological allegory, which Calderón in fact did in *Andrómeda y Perseo*, which he wrote for the Corpus Christi festivities of 1680, the year before his death. Perseus is of course Christ, and Andromeda is Human Nature, chained to the rock of guilt through Original Sin. The power of evil is represented by Phineus, Andromeda's uncle, who violently opposes her marriage to Perseus. The marriage of Christ to Human Nature is a frequent allegory in the *autos* for the Incarnation, the union of the two Natures, Human and Divine, in the one Person of Christ. In the theological *autos* of his maturity, Calderón always pairs Satan with an abstract character, generally called Guilt (or Sin), as here, otherwise Fury, Discord, etc:[9] Christ atones for Humanity's fault by making it possible for men to receive the Grace that removes the Guilt of Original Sin.

The full title of the corresponding *comedia* is *Las fortunas de Andrómeda y Perseo* (1653). This is a perfect example of the Myth of the Hero, which is the most universal and, in essence, the most unchangeable of Jung's archetypes. The noble and valiant hero battles victoriously against forces of evil to rescue their victims. Perseo slays Medusa, the sight of whose face turned men to stone, and with her severed head he can slay the sea monster ravaging the coast, and rescue Andrómeda, bound to a rock as a sacrifice to placate the monster. Calderón's play was written exactly midway in his long dramatic career. It is perhaps not one of his most successful mythological plays, though it has some fine moments. Its action is too crowded, and this is because there are three other myths that form part of the Perseus legend and Calderón brings in all three: the myths of Danae, of Medusa and of Andromeda. All three are women, and it is significant for Calderón's dramatic thought that each one is a suffering victim, suffering undeservedly: Danaë was violated by Jupiter through no fault of her own, but only because he saw and loved her. She was punished by her father, being set adrift in an open boat with her baby, Perseus; Medusa was violated by Neptune inside the temple of Minerva and for this sacrilege her beauty was changed into the hideous serpent-covered head that turned men to stone; Andromeda was the daughter of Cassiopeia who insulted the god Neptune by claiming that she and her daughter were more beautiful than his Nereids. In revenge he sent the sea monster to which Andromeda was ordered to be exposed as sacrifice. That it is the lot of women to suffer is one of the leitmotifs of the Calderonian drama (as has been noted in previous chapters): to suffer the violence of male passion, or suffer male infidelity and the cruelty of male domination under a rigid code of honour, to which men are prepared to sacrifice their womenfolk.

Of these three women Danaë is one of the numerous examples of the Calderonian archetype (first met with Segismundo of *La vida es sueño*) of the imprisoned youth or maiden deprived of freedom in order to prevent her from doing wrong. Calderón alters the first of these three myths: his Dánae is imprisoned by her father because she is loved by a young man and her father cannot trust her to behave honourably. But love cannot be warded off; Dánae's tower cannot exclude a god who enters as a shower of gold. Júpiter violates her *disguised as Cupid*. This idea is repeated at the end when Júpiter appears on stage to acknowledge Perseo as his son: he does so dressed as Cupid. This may sound laughable to us, but the idea that Calderón is repeating here has already been referred to in the preceding chapter. In the early Christian centuries Jupiter's unedifying amours aroused scorn; what kind of religion was this, Christians asked, which presented the so-called King of Heaven as a lecher and an adventurer? Calderón is not only rejecting this scorn, he is in effect saying that to deprive a young woman of the freedom to love is the evil, not the sexual experience that is prevented, for there is nothing evil in sexual experience as such; on the contrary, it has the sanction of the gods. At the end of the play Júpiter says that his assumption of the role of Cupid was the first cause of Perseo's heroism, which all are celebrating. Against the beneficent force of love there stands Jealousy, which breeds revenge and hatred. Jealousy is represented by Juno, who seeks revenge on all the recipients of Jupiter's favours, and who summons Discord and the Furies to her aid. Perseo and Dánae are protected by Mercurio and Palas, the children of Júpiter. The rivalry of these gods dominates the action: we see again how mythology enabled Calderón to portray good and evil as supra-terrestrial forces which direct and influence the fortunes of men.

Perseo, conscious of a spirit within him that makes him superior to the shepherds among whom he has been brought up, acquires arrogant airs. Irritated by this, they taunt him with his origins, telling him he landed as a baby on their shores with his mother in an open boat – an obvious sign that he was the offspring of adultery or of some other act of treason: his origin is therefore a disgrace. His mother confirms the truth of this story but beyond this her lips are sealed. She cannot tell him who she is or who he is, the problem facing Faetón in *El hijo del sol, Faetón*. Fired with the conviction that he has it in him to be more than a simple shepherd, Perseo seizes with courage every opportunity for heroic endeavour that his destiny puts before him until at the end he is acclaimed as the son of no less a being than Júpiter – as the final chorus puts it, he has proved himself Júpiter's son by deserving to be so.

In the corresponding *auto* no doubt is left in the spectator's or reader's mind that Perseo stands for Christ, since there are clear indications throughout, but if each play is kept in its proper context it is equally clear that in the *comedia* Perseo is a human hero and not the Second Person of the Trinity. Nonetheless, mankind has an element of the divine within itself, which is here called Heroism. Man can prove worthy of this by creating civilisation, like Prometheus, and by defending it heroically, like Perseus, against the monsters that would destroy it. This is Calderón's version or transposition of Renaissance Humanism.

25 The destiny of man

Ángel Valbuena Prat, who emphasised the 'baroque' quality of Calderón's art in order to bring him into favour with Spanish readers in the wake of the restoration to favour of baroque poetry in the complex art of Góngora, saw *La vida es sueño* as a watershed in Calderón's dramatic production. Conflicts and themes of political and social life recognisably 'real' had led up to it, but *La vida es sueño* itself introduced a new type of philosophical and symbolical drama, which was gradually to expand until his death. Valbuena called these 'las dos maneras', Calderón's two manners or styles, with no clear-cut chronological division but with a clear progression towards what he defined as baroque, the court plays with their lavish spectacle being the culmination of baroque drama. There is more to this 'watershed' metaphor than just the progress towards a more complex type of stage play. What the 'watershed' metaphor indicates is a new conception and handling of dramatic plots, initiated in *La vida es sueño*. Its plot could not be called 'realistic', although this never bothered its readers, nor did it need to, because there was a poetic pattern that conveyed a life above and beyond that of contemporary society. The unrealism of its basic plot – the imprisonment of a new-born baby in a tower, who acquires no knowledge of other men or of the world, until he grows to manhood and is released – was explained in chapter 7 as a symbolic mode, meaning more than it said, and the Prison–Tower was there called a Calderonian archetype. It was pointed out that this had grown from the recurring theme of a father–son conflict with the leading motif of a young man who did not know who his father was, because he had been abandoned or disowned as a baby. This motif of the fatherless son had first appeared in one of Calderón's earliest plays, *La devoción de la cruz*. Symbols and archetypes are associated with myths, and this was the direction in which Calderón's dramatic thought and feeling were from then on orientated. The themes of classical mythology were a natural development of the symbolical and archetypal motifs which, if the argument of this book is acceptable, had grown out of the traumas and obsessions of Calderón's early life. Classical mythology had furnished Calderón with the symbol and archetype of the

Tower–Prison and the archetype of confinement from infancy, but with and after *La vida es sueño* Calderón makes these, by constant repetition, peculiarly his own. From this archetype, he develops two myths which keep on recurring in his plays right down to the end of his life in places where one would not expect them. Before the motif of the fatherless and rebellious son is developed in *La vida es sueño*, Segismundo, in chains, steps out of the door of his tower and recites his poignant soliloquy. Why is every creature that he can see, even the lifeless stream as it falls down the rocks, free to move, while he is not? What crime has he been guilty of, that he should be confined like this? he asks. The only answer he can give is the fact of being a human being, because 'Man's greatest crime is the fact that he was born'. The problem of Life and Guilt was not pursued in *La vida es sueño* on this existential plane, but Calderón never forgot it, and the question of guilt and destiny keeps returning, especially in the mythological plays and in the *autos sacramentales*, which, by reason of their symbolism and allegory, share the mythic mode of the former. There is one motif in *La estatua de Prometeo* which was not mentioned during the analysis of this play. Guilt and punishment are of course crucial to the Prometheus myth. In Calderón's play, Prometeo is denounced by Palas to Apolo for having stolen the fire of heaven; but previous to this, Prometeo had denounced himself, acknowledging that his theft of the fire had been the cause of the discord that was now raging in the world. Would it not have been better if he had left men to fester in the state of barbarism? As we shall see in the theological transposition of the theme of *Life is a Dream*, this same question is asked by God the Father, reproaching himself for having created man. With this universal problem of Birth and Destiny, as has already been stated, the mythological court plays and the theological drama of Corpus Christi come together, not by each one overstepping its proper bounds of dramatic technique, but because both, on the plane of myth, must face the problem of Existence.

The two motifs of the rebellious son and the prisoner appear together in *La vida es sueño*. Both had derived from that early seminal play, *La devoción de la cruz*, with Eusebio as the 'rebellious son', or a violent young man of unknown parentage, and with Julia as the 'prisoner', confined not in a jail but against her will in an enclosed convent. After they come together in *La vida es sueño* the two motifs are more frequently separated. Thus in *Las fortunas de Andrómeda y Perseo* the girl, Dánae, is the prisoner, deprived of freedom because of a prophecy that had foretold that if she bears a son he will kill his grandfather. The disowned Perseo, born in a prison, is therefore a derivative of the rebellious son, although he kills his grandfather by accident, not because of rebellion.

In *La estatua de Prometeo*, there is a mythological character representing a derivative of Segismundo at his prison door with his anguished cry for freedom and his haunting sense of guilt. This is Pandora, the statue fashioned by Prometeo and to which he gave life. In chapter 23 above the original features of Calderón's presentation of her were described: first, she is identical in features with Minerva, the goddess of wisdom and civilisation; when Minerva, in gratitude for Prometeo's establishment of her cult among mortals, tells him to request a boon, he asks for a glimpse of heaven in order to see how the gods live. Then, while Minerva stands guard over him to ensure his safety, he seizes the divine fire of the Spirit in the form of one of the torches of the Sun as it moves by; taking it to Earth, he puts it into the hand of his statue. This is not the primitive Prometheus who stole fire from the Gods; Calderón's Prometeo, because of his cult of knowledge and wisdom, is permitted by Minerva to take fire from the Sun in order that the human clay may, through knowledge and wisdom, acquire a soul. That is why his Pandora and Minerva have the same face and why both rôles had to be performed by the same actress; in fact, the name Pandora does not occur among the *dramatis personae*. It is always 'Minerva' who speaks. Pandora for the ancient Greeks represented the first mortal woman, a more beautiful conception than the Eve of the Jews. The Gods in turn endow her with every grace. Not until the end of the play is Prometeo able to love and marry Pandora; till then he has recoiled from the clay of which she was formed. Only Epimeteo can love her because sensuality and passion are his domain; he recoils from the Spirit within her. In this new symbolical form Calderón represents once again the dualism of matter and spirit in the human being. The dualism reaches its climax in Palas's present to Pandora, the box containing every gift: the box of Discord whereby the black smoke of passion clouds the fire of the spirit.

The most striking novelty in Calderón's dramatisation of Pandora's coming to life is to place her in a similar situation to that of Segismundo when he steps out of his Tower. He does not know who he is, why he is chained in a prison or what the world is that he sees before him with all other creatures enjoying freedom. Minerva/Pandora does not know who she is, whence she has come and whither she is going. She cannot understand what the mortals tell her or how they can say they have seen her before (i.e as a statue). The dramatic and thematic reason for this is that the Divine Spirit as it combines with the Human Clay is overcast and loses its way. This uncertainty of whence and whither will torment every mortal man as he steps into the world.

When Epimeteo comes on stage to steal the statue, she talks for the

first time and Epimeteo asks in astonishment: Who is inflaming her with
a new spirit? The answer is given by the chorus off-stage:

> Quien triunfa para enseñanza
> de que quien da ciencias, da
> voz al barro y luz al alma

(The one who triumphs by showing that he who gives knowledge, gives
speech to the clay and light to the soul)[1]

The 'triumph' has been Prometeo's in stealing the torch from heaven; it
is he who has thereby given speech to the clay and illuminated the soul.
On the symbolical level, this is Humanity being born into the new world
of intelligence. Minerva/Pandora cannot use it properly, having as yet
no experience of life: that is why she is bewildered and puzzled by the
place in which she finds herself:

> ¡Qué estancia
> tan pavorosa, tan triste,
> tan trémula, oscura, y vaga!
> Si no fuera por el astro
> que me influye . . . mas, ¿quién anda
> allí? ¿quién va? ¿quién es?

(What a fearful place, so sad, so indistinct, so dark, so formless! If it were not
for the star that is influencing me . . . but who is moving? who goes there?
who is it?)

(II, 248–53) [*BAE*, III, p. 708a]

Uncertainty about the place gives way to uncertainty about the two
men, Epimeteo and Merlín, who had come to steal her. Merlín draws
back in terror, but Epimeteo tells her that he has loved her from the first
moment he saw her and has surrendered to her his soul and his life.
Unable to understand this, she replies that she does not hold his soul or
his life, unless they are inside the lighted torch that is animating her. She
moves it towards him, asking him to take them back. But he is terrified by
the light, which he says does not illuminate *him*, rather does it dazzle. He
departs in search of someone who can explain this mystery to him. (This
of course means the light of the mind is not the fire of passion, which is all
that Epimeteo can react to.) By deft touches like these does Calderón
expand his symbolism until he leads it on to a different level.

As he moves away, Epimeteo calls out to the shepherds, telling them
to wake from sleep and leave their huts in order to see the new prodigy
that has appeared in their land. As he speaks each line departing,
Prometeo repeats it like an echo, approaching until Epimeteo is off the

stage, with Prometeo reaching the centre stage at the moment when voices of the shepherds ask him offstage, '¿Quién a esta hora nos despierta?' (Who awakens us at this early hour?) (II, 294) [*BAE*, III, p. 708b]. The answer is the repetition of the preceding chorus off-stage, 'He who triumphs' etc., which refers to Prometeo, as he approaches centre stage. From the other end of the stage Minerva/Pandora asks,

> Músicas el aire, espantos
> la tierra, y el fuego ansias;
> ¿quién soy yo, Dioses, q[ue] he puesto
> el orbe en confusión tanta?

> (The air plays music, the earth gives out frightening sounds, and the fire in my hand produces in me dread and longing; who am I, oh gods, who have caused so much confusion on the earth?)
>
> (II, 298–301) [*BAE*, III, p. 708b]

Prometeo, who does not see the statue, says that he will await here the coming of the people who are bound to have been awakened now by 'el nuevo imán del reflejo' (the new magnet of the reflection) (i.e. the light of the torch which reflects the sun and the divine light of wisdom). At this point he sees the statue, which he takes to be the goddess Minerva, and whom he addresses as such. The statue is utterly confused by the references to Minerva and by his asking why she now frowns upon him, without accepting his cult. The statue cannot understand why he speaks as if he had known her already, or why he does not run away as the others did, dazzled by the torch's light. Prometeo for his part is equally confused, especially by the fact that previously the goddess has always sung, but now the beautiful harmony of her voice is lost (this continues the main symbolism: that the divine light of the spirit and its message of harmony are dulled when expressed through human clay. Not only can the statue not sing, it has not been able to talk coherently.) The last lines of Minerva/Pandora's answering speech bring this high level of symbolism down to the first human and social level, harking back to Calderón's first mythic expression of human destiny with Segismundo in his prison giving utterance to his unruly passion, which was awakening at the stage of adolescence. Thus the statue finishes:

> ¿Cuándo yo (dime) te hablaba?
> si son éstas las primeras
> razones q[ue] articuladas
> fueron de mí, transcendiendo
> las rudezas de la infancia
> a los discursos de joven.

(Tell me when it was that I spoke to you. For these are the first words that have been put together by me, passing beyond the inarticulate sounds of infancy to the reasoned speech of youth.)

(II, 349–54) [*BAE*, III, p. 708c]

Prometeo is distressed that the goddess should be angry with him and he not know why. He refers to when he modelled the statue of her and to the fire he stole from the sun, but Minerva/Pandora interrupts with the ejaculation 'What statue?' He is astonished at her refusal to admit what he had told her. Why, she asks, should he be surprised at her ignorance, if she has just come to life and acquired knowledge now? Who are you then? he asks. 'I do not know,' is the reply. 'All I know is that, illuminated by this torch, the winds said of me . . .' (and here she joins in the last two lines of the refrain which is sung again, 'for he who gives knowledge gives speech to the clay and light to the soul'). So that the audience should not miss the point Calderón makes Prometeo say

O moralidad envuelta
en fabulosa enseñanza,
qué de cosas que me dices;
pero ninguna más clara
que al ver que el monte discurras,
ver que de la gruta faltas

(Oh morality play, whose teaching is cloaked in a fable, what a number of things you are telling me! But nothing is more clear than that you are out of your cave and moving around the mountain)

(II, 388–93) [*BAE*, III, p. 709a]

It is not surprising, he continues, that the winds should be saying loudly, and the echoes repeating more softly . . . Here Epimeteo, off-stage, joins in the dialogue, repeating his earlier call to the shepherds to awaken from sleep and come out of their huts. The two levels of the theme must not be lost sight of: the 'morality play' is Mankind's awakening to knowledge and purposive action as Pandora, guided by Minerva, gropes her way towards self-realisation. The shepherds emerge to follow Epimeteo, asking 'Who is illuminating the shadows of the night? Who is brightening its darkness?'

Minerva/Pandora tells them it is the fire she holds in her hand, beautifully expressing its value for them in these words:

Y pues ya en este usurpado
rasgo del luciente alcázar,
en tres edades del fuego,
pasando de luz a brasa,

y desde brasa a ceniza,
su actividad aplicada
a la dispuesta materia,
tenéis quien supla la falta
del sol para los comercios
de la noche, en dignas gracias
de su doméstica lumbre,
repetid en voces varias

(Since in this flash of light usurped from the citadel of heaven, in the three ages of the life of fire as it passes from glow to burning and from burning to ash, with its activity applied to the matter in hand, you have what makes good the absence of the sun for the commerce of night-time)

(II, 434–43) [*BAE*, III, p.709b]

With the statue leading them, all begin to sing the chorus that opened this scene and so deliberately wound its way through it until it here reaches its climax: 'for he who gives knowledge gives speech to the clay and light to the soul . . .', but the chorus is broken off by the sound of drums and trumpets and the call to war, and there ensues the symbolical warfare of human life as described in chapter 23.

Pandora, or Humanity, enlightened by Minerva has discovered who she is, and the purpose of her existence. But since Palas is the reverse or other face of Minerva, the purpose of human existence is constantly belied by Discord and clash of arms. The positive purpose of existence is theoretically reiterated in Apolo's final judgement and in the marriage of Pandora to Prometeo. Perhaps it is not only the modern reader's knowledge of the history of the last two hundred years that makes the play's conclusion only an ideal to be clung to, not one to be fully realised. The twin faces of humanity, Prometeo and Epimeteo, we know to be ultimately irreconcilable. Fire will flare up and give its light and warmth, but though divine in origin and immensely beneficent in its action, it must ultimately fade to an ember and die in ashes. The apparent optimism of the play is tempered by an underlying pessimism, of which the chief symbol is the archetypal Pandora, who gropes for knowledge of the whence or the whither of human destiny.[2]

This central episode of *La estatua de Prometeo* has symbolised the emergence of Man as an intelligent being who can acquire knowledge of his destiny as he slowly overcomes the ignorance of his first cave dwelling. This is the second of what we have called the two main archetypes in Calderón's mythopoeic dramatic thought. This archetype occurs several times in the *autos sacramentales* as part of the Creation of Man, in those plays that encompass in a single allegory the doctrines of the Fall and the Atonement.

A group of *autos* among those dramatising the Creation present the transposition of Segismundo's Tower with the stage-direction 'Ábrese el peñasco, y aparece el Hombre dormido, vestido de pieles' (The rock opens, and Man appears asleep and dressed in skins). This 'imprisonment' represents the state of Non-Being: Man exists as an idea in the Divine Mind, not yet actualised. Able, in the allegorical mode, to talk in his sleep, he longs for existence as the 'eleven Segismundos' of Blanca de los Ríos longed for freedom. This, of course, is the 'freedom' that the first Segismundo longed for as he stood in his prison doorway. But is existence going to be worthwhile, if life will be so fleeting?

    que llega como fin, cuando
    se aguarda como principio?

(that it arrives at its end as one is awaiting its beginning?)

In some of these plays Man, stepping out of his rock and with Death before him, wishes to return to his prison because existence seems purposeless. Two fine examples of this are *La segunda esposa y triunfar muriendo* (The Second Spouse and Triumph by Dying) and *El Año Santo de Roma* (The Holy Year in Rome), but perhaps the most impressive is found in *El pleito matrimonial del Cuerpo y el Alma* (The Matrimonial Lawsuit Between Body and Soul). Here Body and Soul appear separately and come to life when joined in marriage. As Body awaits life in his 'prison', he soliloquises:

    Sin oír, hablar, ni ver,
    en noche continua estoy;
    si nada antes de ser soy,
    ¿qué seré después de ser?
    Mas no lo quiero saber,
    confusa naturaleza,
    ni ser quiero; que es tristeza
    a mi ser anticipada
    ver que acabe siendo nada
    ser que siendo nada empieza.
    Mas ser quiero; que es error
    no ser si en mi mano está,
    pues peor no ser será
    que siendo ser lo peor;
    y tengo ya tanto amor
    al ser que espero tener,
    que por ser tengo de hacer,
    juzgando a más pena yo
    dejar ya de ser, que no
    ser para dejar de ser.

(Without hearing, speaking, or seeing, I lie in perpetual night. If I am nothing before I have life, what shall I be when I have it? But, confused nature of mine, I do not want to know the answer, nor do I want to be; for this would be to anticipate the sadness of my life if I could see that I, who am beginning by being nothing, should be nothing when I end. Nonetheless, I want to live; for it is a mistake not to have life if having it depends on me, since it is better to have life on the lowest level than not to have life at all; and already I feel such love for the life that I hope to have, that I must strive to exist, judging it to be a greater misery to be deprived of existence now, than not to live now in order not to die.)[3]

This is a wonderful piece of Calderonian dialectic, closely knit and never losing the logic of the difficult phrasing with the contrasted phrases constructed on the two meanings of *ser*, the verb 'to be' and the noun 'being'. When the Soul descends to marry the Body, she laments having to enter a prison, and it is she who cries out for freedom. Man could not have refused life if he had been given the choice, but the choice to create or not create was God's. The question we ask, would it not have been better if Mankind had never existed?, was for God to answer in the light of the 'horoscope' he casts for Man.

For the final stage of this particular archetype, it is fitting that we return to its first occurrence, *La vida es sueño*. Calderón twice allegorised his most famous play as an *auto sacramental*, in both cases keeping the same title. The earlier version of *La vida es sueño* (*auto*) was probably written shortly after the *comedia*, but there is no record that it was ever performed and it was never published until Ángel Valbuena Prat edited it in *Revue Hispanique*, vol. 41 (1924), pp. 258–93. The second version is the definitive one, and a masterpiece of the Eucharistic *genre*. It was written near the end of the poet's life for performance in Madrid at the Corpus Christi celebrations of 1673. The plot of the *comedia* hinges on King Basilio's casting the horoscope of his newly born son and in his foreseeing the violent and rebellious temperament he will show as a young adult. This is crucial to the whole theme and cannot therefore be omitted when the allegory of the *auto* turns the problem of how to deal with Segismundo into the problem of how God will be able to deal with violent and rebellious Man if He creates him. God is represented in the *auto* by the three Persons of the Trinity, who are called by the traditional patristic attributes of the Trinity, *Poder*, *Sabiduría*, and *Amor* (Power, Wisdom, and Love). The *auto* opens with the Trinity imposing harmonious order on the warring rivalry of the four Elements by making them submissive to the voice of authority and telling them that they must serve and obey the ruler destined for them, namely Man. This submission of the world to the rule of Man is made dependent on his preserving the order of creation by his being himself submissive to the order and harmony of the Law of Nature, thus representing to the world the authority of the Creator. If Man should break the harmony of Creation through his ambition and his actions, the Elements for their part will be given the power to disobey him. It is at this point that the divine 'horoscope' is cast. Wisdom foresees the future violence and destructiveness of mankind, and puts the question: ought he to be brought to life to wreak such havoc? But Love begins to weep. The idea of the Holy Spirit weeping at the prospect of denying Life to Mankind is very moving for a Christian; even a humanist who is able to suspend disbelief by a leap of the imagination must find it moving also. Not to create Man, says Love, will be to punish him for a crime he has not yet committed (the great error of Basilio). Not to create Man would be to punish him for all eternity by confining him in the prison of non-existence. In this context of God's weeping for the man he has not yet created, the Divine Persons debate whether it is proper to create man at all. Love alleges that

> Los amenazados riesgos
> no son, Poder, tan precisos
> que hayan de ser, pues no fueran,
> coartando al nombre el arbitrio,
> ni mérito las Virtudes,
> ni demérito los Vicios.

> (The threatened risks are not, Power, so clear-cut that they must come to pass, for, by inhibiting man's free will they would make Virtue cease to be meritorious, and Vices cease to be blameworthy.)
> [*Autos*, Aguilar, p. 1391a]

In other words, absolute predestination cannot exist theoretically.[4] The 'horoscope' is thus not an impediment to the creation of Man. When Man is about to be created, the stage direction is that 'a rock is uncovered' (i.e. in one of the carts for the outdoor performance) and man is seen 'dressed in skins'. He must of course have been asleep, in accordance with Calderón's fixed convention in this context. As he lies asleep, there stands beside him a female figure with a lighted torch. In the list of characters she is called 'Light'. In the text she is called 'Grace'. Man's creation here bears an important thematic relation to Pandora's coming to life in *La estatua de Prometeo*, for the concept of Light and its imagery play the most important part in the creation of Man in this particular *auto*. His coming into existence is referred to as 'le sacas a la luz', or 'bringing him into the light', for it is actually represented by his marriage to the character called Light. On the humanistic level of *La estatua de Prometeo* Pandora's holding the lighted torch represents humanity's being given the light of intelligence and reason. On the spiritual level of the *auto*, light represents the theological concept of Grace, that quality, directly infused by God, which elevates the actions of the men who receive it to the supernatural level that 'justifies' them. There is an analogy on the level of poetic drama, if not strictly speaking on that of theology, between the 'light of reason' and the 'light of grace': it is man's destiny to allow his mind and heart to be illuminated by the supernatural light. It is the Messianic Light in the prophecy of Isaiah (ch. 9, 2): 'The people who walked in darkness have seen a great light; those who dwelt in a land of deep darkness on them has light shined'. Just as the symbolism of *La estatua de Prometeo* required Prometeo to marry Pandora (Humanity wedded to Intelligence and Reason) so in this different allegorical Creation it is necessary for Man to be wedded to Grace. While in the *comedia* the marriage of Pandora to Prometeo had been frustrated by the violence of Passion and War until the direct intervention of Apolo from Olympus; here in the *auto* Man's marriage to Light is a delicate union that can be snapped if he chooses the anarchical following of Self-Love instead of the submission to the harmony of the universe so carefully outlined in the opening section of the play. If this happens, another Divine intervention will be required to restore the marriage. It is clearly stated that Light here is man's knowledge of himself and of the purpose of his existence: Light in short is what will bind Man to the will of God in the harmony of Creation. Darkness, on the other hand, is associated with the blindness of non-being in which uncreated Man is lying – 'el ciego/vientre de su obscuro limbo' (the blind womb of his dark limbo) (*Autos*, 1391a). The concept of non-being is associated with imprisonment. The creation of Man is thus represented by his removal from the darkness of imprisonment to the light of freedom; and this illumination by the light of Grace signifies his emergence from a state of moral negativeness to the positive one of moral consciousness. As the lighted torch brings him to life, it gives him knowledge of his destiny (that he is to inherit the government of the world), knowledge of good and evil, and freedom of choice and action. These three gifts correspond on the plane of human nature to the three perfections given to all Creation by the three Persons of the Trinity. Man's destiny is determined by the fact that he is endowed with Power, has the capacity to attain to Wisdom, and is enfolded in Love. He can achieve this destiny only by being responsive to the Law of Creation. This destiny cannot be fulfilled like an arrow speeding straight to its target. On the contrary, Man has to grope his way like Calderón's Henry VIII, 'treading on the darkness of death'. Man's self-knowledge, which he acquires through the light of Grace, embraces two extremes: his nothingness and his greatness. His understanding stresses the former;

his free will stresses the latter. Urged on by vainglorious ambition, he comes to think he can control his own life. Giving way to the dream of power, he awakens in a new prison, bound hand and foot, not in the realm of light, but in that of darkness. True self-knowledge and harmony can be restored only by Love, not the love of proud self-seeking but the Love of faithful submission to the Laws that govern the Universe. This submission cannot be brought out by Man from within himself. It requires divine interpretation in the form of a Saviour who can make and teach Man the supremacy of self-sacrificing love. Thus the last section of this *auto* unfolds the mysterious drama of the Redemption as Wisdom enters Man's prison, lies down in his place and receives the deathly blow intended for the human prisoner.[5] Calderón, faithful to the inheritance of his Christian civilisation, could see no other answer than this to the riddle of existence. No humanistic philosophy has yet provided a more satisfying answer. The great religions provide answers that may satisfy the human mind if it makes the leap into the realm of faith.

Epilogue

In 1976 Manuel Durán and Roberto González Echeverría published in two volumes an anthology of Calderonian criticism entitled *Calderón y la crítica: historia y antología* (Madrid: Gredos 1976). A reviewer of this anthology stated that: 'Calderón the dramatist disappears from view under the weight of Calderón the thinker and moralist'.[1] It may be that similar criticism could be made of this book; for after all Calderón did have a philosophical cast of mind and a strong ethical sense, whereas these pages have not laid much emphasis on Calderón as a technician of the stage. But what exactly does this distinction mean? It cannot mean that the purpose of existence, the workings of human psychology, and the problems of Good and Evil are not relevant to poetic drama. It must somehow be a question of the right balance between what the reader's mind makes of human problems and the way a dramatist manipulates the human figures of a plot within the framework of a fixed stage. There are different ways of reading plays, which will differ according to the reader's temperaments and dominant interests. The reader whose interest lies primarily in plays as spectacles will, as he reads, visualise the stage action in his imagination, seeing how it would work out on the stage if he were the producer. The reader who is interested in literature as a mirror of human life with all its problems will have, in the forefront of his mind, those that arise, and will be relating them, as he reads, to human psychology, to professed and unprofessed aims, to society with problems of domination and subjection, to authority and its abuse, and so on. He will of course be visualising the settings of the dialogue as he proceeds, but not so much in terms of a stage-set as in terms of the supposed setting, indoors or out of doors, a living room, or a street, or a garden and so on. The theatre-going public is nowadays in the hands of the director or producer who, especially in the case of plays from the past, feels free to make their meaning subjective, sometimes re-interpreting them in ways that go counter to the author's intentions as revealed by the text.

This book has proceeded on the assumption that its main task has been that of facilitating the comprehension of Calderón's plays by approximating as far as possible to the meaning he wished to convey in each one of those selected. One must tread carefully here. No critic can ever recreate the mind and intentions of a poet who died 300 years ago, but he must make the effort not only to understand a play in the light of the world-view prevalent in the dramatist's own time, but to understand it in such a way that his interpretation becomes relevant to his own day. As T. S. Eliot once put it, every new work of literature alters all preceding literature. We cannot divorce from our minds everything that the last three centuries have taught humanity. The historical school of dramatic criticism that would try to recreate what a play by Calderón could have meant to an audience of the time may fail to show what he can mean to us. Calderón did not know Freud or Jung or Marx, but he had the insight into human nature and behaviour that every great dramatist must have. His characters must be analysed in terms of the universals of human nature provided this does not stretch the poet's meaning.

Comprehension of the Spanish seventeenth century for a twentieth-century English-speaking reader has therefore been the aim of this book. Whether it is really possible in literary criticism to write for the present without distorting the past is probably an unanswerable question. Another similar question that may not be easy to answer is whether it is possible to draw a clear line between 'philosophy' and 'drama' in any particular dramatist. If one were to write a 'Spanish-Habsburg World Picture', one would be able to select numberless quotations from the writers of the age, including the dramatic poets, as illustrations of the ideas on the world and on human society as they saw them, though one would run the risk of misinterpretation out of context.[2] One can do the same for particular aspects of Calderón's thought (e.g. his conception of the freedom of the Will or his definitions of the passions, etc.) but such compilations would inevitably destroy any view of him as a dramatic poet, for, except in very general terms, his 'philosophical' concepts are relevant only within the limits of individual plays and cannot be interpreted outside the particular framework of character, action and theme that each play separately presents.

The first aim of this book, therefore, was to make Calderón's ideas and the language in which they are cast comprehensible, which means expounding the text with clarity. There are those nowadays who say that this begs the whole question. In the 'deconstruction' theory of contemporary literary criticism, which is an attack on all traditional authority in these matters, it is held that a play has no final 'text', there are only 'performances'; just as with novels there are also no 'texts', only 'readers'. It is not easy to see what bearing this extreme nihilism can have on the plays discussed in this volume, most of which no English-speaking reader will ever have seen performed, or will ever be likely to see performed. Certainly, it must be readily admitted that these pages have disclosed a 'reader', and in fact only one reader. The traditional common sense of his own readers will determine whether his readings will have any validity for them or for literary criticism in general. Perhaps most of us will think that the statement 'there is no text' is at best a quibble, at worst meaningless. This book will finish as it began, with the fact that the first task of a literary critic is to comprehend a text in the light of the idea of the age that produced it, and to write a relevant and lucid commentary on it.

The implication that it is possible, indeed necessary, to excise moral philosophy from drama must result from a suspicion or fear of didacticism. It cannot be maintained that literature must never teach anything; what we are afraid of is its overt preaching. Literature should insinuate, guiding, and not forcing the reader to ideas. Intellectual content is supposedly unpopular nowadays; if this is true, it may be partly because the pressure placed on our minds by the means of mass communication is making it more and more difficult to absorb and develop thought. Properly speaking, a play is didactic when it moralises directly in the form of appendages to its plot structure. The old criterion that content is inseparable from form means that the 'moral' is intrinsic to the form (dialogue, character, action) and is not attached like a label.

It used to be thought up to about forty years ago that Calderón did preach to us in a blatant and sometimes offensive form. It used to be thought by his countrymen that he preached not only a husband's right but his *duty* to kill an innocent wife on suspicion of intended adultery. However cruel the dramatic husband acknowledged this act to be, however painful he said it was to him, nonetheless the imperative of honour transcended all else. In *El médico de su honra* it was thought that not only he, but the King and the second wife the King gives him, acknowledge this overriding sense of duty. This universal interpretation followed from taking the words spoken by the characters at their face value. This failed to make two important distinctions. The first is that a dramatist in such cases can write either 'in character' or 'in person'; he can either make his characters speak in accordance with the character and temperament that the play has already established for them, or else he can present them as his mouthpiece. The second distinction is that between straightforward or ironical communication, the former occurs when the words mean literally what they say, the latter occurs when the words mean more than they say, generally in contradiction. The analysis of *El médico de su honra* in chapter 17 showed how the plot is so structured that, if we follow it closely, it impels us to judge the characters in a way that goes counter to the way they judge themselves; further, we are impelled by the plot-structure to see their actions in a very different light from their motives. The play is thus revealed as deeply imbued with irony of a tragic, not a comic, kind. The analysis of *El príncipe constante* suggested that the traditional didactic interpretation is also wide of the mark. In both these cases 'Calderón the moralist' has been misunderstood precisely because 'Calderón the dramatist' had not been noticed. The detection of the dramatist does not necessarily imply analysing stage technique; it means analysing plot structure. It is hoped that this book will have demonstrated how often Calderón's plots have revealed the 'doubleness' of literature – the interplay of two levels of meaning, like the literal and the figurative senses of metaphors. Stage plots, like that of *King Lear*, have rightly been called 'metaphorical' if the action by its very nature leads us away from the literal;[3] that some of Calderón's plots move from the literal level to the symbolic has been amply demonstrated. There are others, however, that can be better called 'metaphorical'. Two of those analysed in this book have metaphors as their title. That the title 'Surgeon of his Honour' is as ironical as the whole action was suggested in chapter 2. That it was mistaken to take the metaphor *Life is a Dream* at its face value as an intrusion into the meaning of the drama was suggested in chapter 1. Only by taking fully into account the context in which the metaphor keeps on recurring and influencing Segismundo's conduct can we realise that the dramatic action itself is imposing on the metaphor a meaning that differs from the literal one. The principle applicable in these cases applies, *mutatis mutandis*, to the majority of Calderón plays. It must be applied to incidents and characters in any play that appear to be superfluous; their dramatic function must be sought in their conceptual relationship to the theme. An example of an apparently superfluous incident is the mule stuck in the mud at the beginning of *La devoción de la cruz*; its subsequent metaphorical transformation into a coach is an example of apparently superfluous imagery. Don Mendo in *El alcalde de Zalamea* is an apparently superfluous character, since he does nothing to further the action. Since, however, his attitude to Isabel is a contrast to Pedro Crespo's conception of honour, Don Mendo is a necessary element in the theme and is therefore properly dramatic as a foil. Examples of anecdotes that may appear nothing more than jokes have been analysed in *La cisma de Ingalaterra* and *El pintor de su deshonra*. Calderón's supreme skill as a dramatist lies in his often uncanny ability to construct a dramatic plot that moves it forward with unerring insight, while making every element of its structure subserve the ends of the theme which is what gives unity to the whole. By the same token his skill as a poetic dramatist is seen in the way he conceives images that bear the same sort of conceptual relationship to the theme, although his early plays do sometimes make use of rhetorical images for declamatory effect. Muley's speech in *El príncipe constante*, describing the arrival of the Portuguese fleet, was adduced as an example of this rhetoric; on the other hand, Rosaura's opening speech in *La vida es sueño*, which was so often condemned as high-flown rhetoric, was shown to have the intimate conceptual relationship to the theme typical of the mature Calderón.

Since his skill is of this kind, it is no denigration of his artistry to call him an *intellectual dramatist*. Rather does this bring out the fullness of his artistry as a writer for the stage. He was by nature and education a man who used his mind and could not do otherwise. That this does not mean the subservience of feeling and emotion to reason has surely been made obvious in these pages. In fact, it would be a great mistake to consider Calderón a rationalist in the eighteenth-century sense. Though close enough to the neo-classicists in time, he is poles apart in mind and spirit. The term 'intellectual' is more properly applied to his poetic style and the way he orders arguments among his characters than to the substance of the thought itself. The modern reader will no doubt consider, as readers have done in the past, that Calderón's poetic style is too formal; his stanzas, his syntax, and even words themselves too well-balanced in comparisons and contrasts, all of this at the expense of the natural. Though this formalism may at times tire the reader by being carried too far, its great virtue, if one keeps one's mind open to this as one reads, lies in the clarity and neatness of the thinking. A fine example of this was quoted on page 353 in the passage where unborn Man discusses with himself whether it would be worthwhile to be born. The verbal and syntactical structure of this passage is purely intellectual; nonetheless, it is deeply moving in its implications for all human life.

That Calderón is very far from being a pure rationalist is seen above all in the creative mythopoeic capabilities of his poetic imagination. Perhaps the main argument of this book has been to demonstrate how Calderón's mind and art moved from the questioning of his first experiences, through the questioning of human experience in general to a universality of concepts and images that find their fullest expression in symbols, archetypes and myths. In his symbolic and mythic poetic world, his intellectualism finds expression in his handling of symbolism and in the ordered construction of his mythical plots, but his imagination has moved away from any rationalist framework into a poetic world whose universality is expressed intellectually but never rationalistically.

There is a connection between the last four plays of Shakespeare and the late mythological plays of Calderón. It is not, of course, a connection of theme or of dramatic technique. It is rather a question of insight, of the connection between the way of looking at human life and the poetic imagery that expresses it; by 'imagery' is here meant both the action on the stage and the plot that this is mirroring. The movements and actions of the actors on the stage are the visible 'images' of the insight into life which is being extracted from the plot. The plots of Shakespeare's four last plays are not only markedly different from the plays that preceded them, they have a common literary mode. For all their violence and anguish, the 'dark tragedies' had a contact with 'real life' which the spectator or reader could examine rationally. They represented a plunge into the world of passion and terror that retained a lifeline with reality. In the last four plays, however, the type of plot is different. Though most of the incidents and much of the dialogue are recognisably 'real', the lynch-pins of each plot belong rather to a world of romance, fancy or magic. The common elements of the four have been thus described:

> The essential myth which runs throughout the last plays, *Pericles, Cymbeline, The Winter's Tale* and *The Tempest*, is the finding of what is lost. Pericles loses and finds Marina; Cymbeline loses and finds his sons; Leontes loses and finds Perdita; Alonso loses and finds Ferdinand. This myth, however, is complicated in certain ways. There is throughout the plays another myth, which is run into the first, namely, the bringing to life of what is dead . . . These two myths, essentially one in idea, are again fused with a third, namely, that of the recovery of a lost royalty . . . Again, there is a fourth element, namely, that of the seeking of what is lost by a royal personage . . .[4]

The theme of estrangement (expressed in Shakespeare through a storm at sea) and of reconciliation through the recovery of a lost daughter must, by its fourfold repetition, and its setting in a near-mythical world, have had for Shakespeare an archetypal significance analogous to that which the theme of the Prisoner and the longing for liberty, with the first groping steps towards it, must have had for Calderón.[5]

In Shakespeare this came at the end of his career as a dramatist and foretold his retirement from the stage and from London. In Calderón it was already given form in a mythical mode in 1635, and the theme of rupture of a close family relationship with the disappearance of a son and the estrangement from a daughter are found in dramatic plots before that date. As has been suggested in this book, the obviously intense preoccupation with this personal 'myth' was formed in Calderón's boyhood. Familiarity with classical mythology as a source of dramatic plots was early bred in him through the genre of the *auto sacramental*. Calderón had already shown himself to be a master of its symbolical and allegorical techniques by the time he wrote *La vida es sueño*, for the early masterpiece *La cena de Baltasar* (Belshazzar's Feast) was written before 1635. Furthermore, the association, begun in Italy, of classical mythology with stage spectacles and vocal music gave Calderón a second and a more fruitful medium for developing the symbolic and mythic mode appropriate to his archetypes. His cultural world was conducive from the beginning of his dramatic career to moulding his thought and imagination towards myths and symbols.

There has been no intention to suggest that the association of their respective creative imaginations in the last phases of Shakespeare and Calderón implies any equality of poetic and dramatic value. Their poetic and dramatic visions of human life remain very different. What there is in common between them in this respect is the fact that, given a suitable cultural climate, it is natural for the imagination of poets to move in this direction.

Notes

Bibliographical note

There are two general studies in English of the Spanish drama of this period: Margaret Wilson, *Spanish Drama of the Golden Age* (Pergamon Press Ltd., 1969) Edward M. Wilson and Duncan Moir, *The Golden Age: Drama 1492–1700*, in the series *A Literary History of Spain*, General Editor R. O. Jones (London, 1971) The standard work on theatres and staging is N. D. Shergold, *A History of the Spanish Stage from Medieval Times until the End of the Seventeenth Century* (Oxford, 1967).

The first biography of Calderón remains the standard one: Don Emilio Cotarelo y Mori, *Ensayo sobre la vida y obras de D. Pedro Calderón de la Barca* (Madrid, 1924).

Edward M. Wilson published a series of scholarly papers which corrected and expanded some of Cotarelo's biographical information. The following are useful supplements to the standard Life:

'Textos impresos y apenas utilizados para la biografía de Calderón', *Hispanófila*, no. 9 (1960), 1–4; 'Some unpublished works by Don Pedro Calderón de la Barca', *Homage to John M. Hill. In Memoriam* (Indiana University, 1968), 7–18; '¿Escribió Calderón el romance *Curiosísma señora?*', *Anuario de letras*, 2 (1962), 99–118; 'Calderón and the stage-censor in the seventeenth century. A provisional study', *Symposium*, 15 (1961), 165–84; Fray Hortensio Paravicino's protest against *El príncipe constante*' *Ibérida-Revista Filológica*, 6 (1961), 245–66; 'Calderón y el Patriarca', *Studia Iberica, Festschrift für Hans Flasche* (Berne-Munich, 1973), 697–703; 'Calderón's enemy: Don Antonio Sigler de Huerta', *Modern Language Notes*, 81 (1966), 225–31; 'Calderón y Fuenterrabía: El *Panegírico* al Almirante de Castilla', *Boletín de la Real Academia Española*, 49 (1969), 253–78; 'Un memorial perdido de Don Pedro Calderón', *Homenaje a William L. Fichter*, (Madrid, 1971), 801–17.

Introduction

1 For a general study of this Eucharistic Drama as handled by Calderón, see A. A. Parker, *The Allegorical Drama of Calderon. An Introduction to the autos sacramentales* (Oxford, 1943).

1 Principles of interpretation

1 The phrase 'principles of interpretation' denotes guidelines for practical understanding of the plays rather than theoretical critical postulates. Much of what will here be said will bear resemblance to a pamphlet first published by me in 1957 and often reprinted and also translated into Spanish: A. A. Parker, *The Approach to the Spanish Drama of the Golden Age, Diamante Series*, No. 6 (London, Hispanic and Luso-Brazilian Councils, 1957). A corrected, expanded, and definitive version later appeared under the title 'The Spanish drama of the Golden Age: A method of analysis and interpretation' in *The Great Playwrights: 25 Plays with Commentaries by Critics and Scholars Chosen and Introduced by Eric Bentley* (New York, 1970), 1, 679–707. The title of the original pamphlet has been criticised for implying that '*the* Approach' means that there is no other. This misunderstood my purpose, which was to show that the drama from Lope to Calderón followed certain conventions and features of construction that differentiated it from the contemporary English and French dramas. It maintained that for the plays to be understood, they had to be approached from those permanent features of their construction. To illustrate how these features could function, I gave brief critical appraisals of selected plays, but this was not intended to imply that no other critical appraisal was possible – merely that whatever appraisal emerged ought to have taken into account the characteristic structural features of the *comedia nueva*.

2 A recent book on Calderón does not follow the principle here set forth: *Reason and the Passions in the comedias of Calderón* by David Jonathan Hildner (Amsterdam, Philadelphia, 1982). He argues that the belief that the plays of Calderón demonstrate a world view is misplaced. With considerable detail Hildner maintains that the Augustinian-Thomistic world view on which Calderón's is based is not acceptable nowadays because of the numerous 'cracks' in its intellectual structure. The same is said to be true of Calderón himself, whose 'cracks' are not only intellectual defects in themselves but a failure to give consistent and coherent dramatic form to his 'ideology' in a way that can satisfy our minds today. Furthermore, his 'ideology' is limited by the fact that, together with the mental climate of Spain at that time, it does not move out towards new political, economic and social ideas. The case is well argued according to its own principles, but these are not principles of literary criticism that the present book can accept. The distinction must always be made between imaginative, poetic drama and modern expository politico-social interpretations of human life. The idea that the constructs of poetic imagination must have the logical consistency of a social science, though seemingly axiomatic to some minds today, is a vast break in the tradition of humane studies. Hildner's book is intelligently argued; not so an earlier attempt along similar lines, which shows little

understanding of Calderón's work as a whole: James E. Maraniss, *On Calderón* (Colombia, University of Missouri Press, 1978).

3 Gerald Brenan, *The Literature of the Spanish People*, (Cambridge University Press, 1953), p. 289.

4 Mircea Eliade, *Images and Symbols* (Search Book edn, New York, 1969), p. 59. This book was originally published in France (1952) by Gallimard under the title of *Images et Symboles*.

5 Eliade, p. 59.

6 Northrop Frye, *Anatomy of Criticism* (Princeton University Press, 1973).

7 T. S. Eliot, *Selected Essays* (London, 2nd edn, 1934). The quoted passage comes from his 'Essay on Ben Jonson' (1919), p. 153.

8 This is Calderón's most famous play. Basilio, king of Poland, has had the horoscope cast of a baby son about to be born. He foresees that the baby will cause the death of his mother in childbirth, and will grow up to be an unruly and violent man, waging civil war against the king his father and defeating him. To prevent the horoscope, Basilio has his son (Segismundo) brought up a prisoner from birth in a tower in the mountains, his existence known only to his jailer, Clotaldo, who looks after him and educates him through boyhood and youth. Basilio, doubting his wisdom in believing the horoscope, decides to drug Segismundo and have him wake in the palace, waited on as a prince. If he proves the horoscope to be true, he can be drugged again and returned to his prison, being told by Clotaldo that his palace experiences were only a dream. Clotaldo explains that when a nightmare becomes violent, one always wakes up. Puzzled by the intensity of his 'dream' Segismundo comes to think that all human happiness and power are dreams that violent behaviour will dispel. He decides, if he should dream again, to act warily in order not to destroy the dream.

Meanwhile, Clotaldo finds out that the 'young man' who had at the beginning of the play discovered Segismundo's prison and heard of his inexplicable fate is his illegitimate daughter, whose pregnant mother he had been compelled to abandon when he was summoned back to the king's court. He leaves his sword with her, saying that if, when the child grows up, he takes this sword to the Polish court, he will find someone there who will befriend and help him. The child is a girl, Rosaura, who is eventually seduced under promise of future marriage by Astolfo, a noble man who has a claim to the succession to the Polish throne. Astolfo decides to press his claim and abandons Rosaura. She follows him to force him to keep his word. Dressed as a man she proceeds to Poland. She finds the secluded prison and meets the mysterious prisoner. Clotaldo finds her, recognises from the sword that she is his 'son', and takes her to the court.

The people of Poland, having learned that there is a legitimate heir to the throne (Segismundo), rise up in rebellion against Basilio on Segismundo's behalf. They free him from prison and promise him his throne if they are victorious over the king. Rosaura, unable to obtain satisfaction from Clotaldo, who cannot side against Astolfo and Basilio in the civil war, offers to join Segismundo's army if he will champion her cause. Though passionately attracted to her from the first, Segismundo realises that this may all be a dream; that it is his duty as a future king to bring about justice, and to make peace rather than war. He defeats his father in battle, but does not take the vengeance the latter has expected. After blaming Basilio for his treatment of him, he restores him to the throne and restores Rosaura's honour by making Astolfo marry her.

9 E. M. Wilson, '*La vida es sueño*', *Revista de la Universidad de Buenos Aires*, 4 (1946), 61–78. Revised and reprinted as 'On *La vida es sueño*' in *Critical Essays on the Theatre of Calderón*, ed. Bruce W. Wardropper. Though not published till 1946, this essay had been written, and read by me, in 1937 or thereabouts. Like Brenan later Arturo Farinelli, who wrote two volumes on the play, had also failed to detect its unity and to understand it; as also in 1881, had a much greater scholar and critic, Marcelino Menéndez Pelayo.

10 'la mas honrada/Burra de toda la aldea'. *La devoción de la cruz, Comedias de Calderón*, ed. Hartzenbusch, Biblioteca de Autores Españoles (*BAE*), I, p. 54b.

11 Instances of this kind and especially the thematic relevance of humorous anecdotes are frequent in Calderón. Further examples will be given in connection with *La cisma de Ingalaterra* (The Schism of England) and *El pintor de su deshonra* (The Painter of his Dishonour).

12 This type of Calderonian imagery was analysed by E. M. Wilson, *not* as examples of Calderón's bad taste, but rather as his conformity with the aesthetics of the baroque. He analysed 'the varieties of (Calderón's) metaphorical procedure' and produced an important paper; and related the resulting impressions of violence and chaos to the baroque in general. Here I have attempted to go somewhat further, and to suggest that the metaphors themselves are linked to how the characters are going to act in their lives, thus being integrated into the theme of the play, part of its organic unity, and not only of its 'baroque' qualities. 'The four elements in the imagery of Calderón', first printed in *MLR*, 31 (1936), 34–47 and several times since. Its final form is in *Spanish and English Literature of the 16th and 17th Centuries*, by Edward M. Wilson (Cambridge University Press, 1980), pp. 1–14.

13 Miguel de Cervantes Saavedra, *Don Quijote de la Mancha*. Ed. Martín de Riquer (Barcelona, 1968), I, ch. II, p. 42. Translation by Samuel Putnam.

2 From metaphor to symbol

This essay was read at the first International Congress of Hispanists held in Oxford in 1962, and was published with the title 'Metáfora y símbolo en la interpretación de Calderón' in 1964 in the Proceedings of the Congress, *Actas del primer congreso internacional de Hispanistas*, ed. Frank

Pierce and C. A. Jones (Oxford, Dolphin, 1964), pp. 141–60. It has here been translated and revised, with some additions and a slightly altered title.

1 *Calderón y su teatro*, in *Obras completas* (Edición nacional), vol. viii (1941), page 303.

2 In using the term 'symbolism' I keep to the traditional concept, according to which a symbol is an intuition or a vision that penetrates below the surface, rather than a direct or realistic representation. For a philosophical study of symbolism that can provide a theological background for this essay, see W. M. Urban, *Language and Reality: the Philosophy of Language and the Principles of Symbolism* (London, 1939), pp. 401–502. For a corresponding use of symbol in literary criticism, see *Myth and Symbol, Critical Approaches and Applications*, 15 essays by Northrop Frye, L. C. Knights and others (Nebraska, 1963), p. v. Here a symbol is defined as an image that has 'both a literal reference and a much greater range of unwritten meaning, implication and emotion'.

3 Erich Auerbach, in the first chapter of his work *Mimésis: dargestellte Wirklichkeit in der abendländischen Literatur* (Berne, 1946), makes a comparison between two different modes of narrative technique, one in an episode from the *Odyssey*, the other in the Biblical episode of the sacrifice of Isaac. The first is only reality narrated – a detailed foreground; while the other leaves time, place, physical appearance and motivation entirely imprecise, but it has a significant background which points to a mystery: the former can be analysed but not interpreted, the latter demands to be interpreted. The latter is symbolical art; the unrealistic actions in Calderón's play are, for the most part, of this kind.

4 Doña Blanca de los Ríos, '*La vida es sueño' y los diez Segismundos de Calderón* (Madrid, 1926). In fact there are more than ten Segismundos.

5 On the relation between metaphor and symbol, cf.: 'The general law of language development is, as we have seen, from copy to analogy (metaphor) and from metaphor to symbol . . . All poetic symbols are, then, metaphors and arise out of metaphor. *The metaphor becomes a symbol when by means of it we embody an ideal content not otherwise expressible.* The difference between *mere* metaphor and metaphor become a symbol may, I think, be expressed in this way. We often speak metaphorically and figuratively when we do not speak symbolically. In the former case, we use metaphor to *illustrate* ideas or assertions which are expressible wholly in abstract or non-figurative terms. The metaphor is a symbol when it *alone* expresses or embodies our ideal meaning. In other words, it is only as the metaphor is part of the intuition itself and functions in the intuition, that it is a symbol.' (W. M. Urban, *Language and Reality*, pp. 470–1; the italics are the author's own.)

6 E. M. Wilson, '*La vida es sueño*', *Revista de la Universidad de Buenos Aires*, 4 (1946), 61–78.

7 B. W. Wardropper, 'Poetry and Drama in Calderón's *El médico de su honra*', *Romanic Review*, 49 (1958), 4–6. One must insist on the

equivalents established by Wardropper. An objection has been raised against this; that Honour, and not Mencía is the patient, and that in consequence the metaphor still applies, because the illness, Dishonour, disappears and the patient, Honour, is cured; this objection cannot be sustained. This fails to distinguish between the two levels that exist in every metaphor, the fiction and the reality. 'Surgeon of his honour' is the fiction; to give it meaning, one must find the 'objective correlative'; a surgical operation on the plane of reality needs a surgeon, a patient, and an illness; on the level of the drama these can only be Gutierre, Mencía and the dishonour which is what seems to be her ailment, marital honour being centred in the wife. 'Gutierre heals the dishonour of Mencía' has, in consequence, a real meaning; while 'Gutíerre heals the dishonour of his honour' has none; if this has any meaning at all, it is still only metaphorical.

8 *Obras de Lope de Vega*, ed. M. Menéndez Pelayo, vol. ix (Madrid, 1899), pp. 436a and 439b.

9 Calderón de la Barca, *El médico de su honra*, ed. C. A. Jones (Oxford, 1961), Act II, 223 [*BAE*, i, p. 355a]. Subsequent references are given after quotations in the text.

10 [*BAE*, iii, p. 107c]. Compare also 'cúrese en salud quíen teme,/quien se turba y desalienta,/y dé en fin satisfacción/la que necesita della;/porque no ha menester darla/quien no ha menester tenerla'. (Let the woman who is afraid, who is anxious and discouraged cure herself while in health, and let that woman justify herself who needs justification; because she who has not done anything to need justification does not need to justify herself'). (*Apolo y Climene, Obras Completas*, ed. Aguilar, i, p. 1870b) [*BAE*, iv, p. 154a].

11 Notice that Leonor does not say 'cura mi vida en *siendo* mala' (cure my life if it does wrong). This is really what she is wanting to say, but she, like Gutierre, is brought to a state of confusion by the metaphor which demands '*estando mala*'. 'Cure my life' means 'cure my honour', but this is still a metaphor which has to be given a literal meaning; it could be given the meaning of 'kill me', but it is not the metaphor which Leonor uses. 'Cure my life', with the literal meaning of 'kill me', is a very revealing *lapsus linguae* or, rather, a *lapsus mentis*.

12 B. W. Wardropper, 'Poetry and drama in Calderón's *El médico de su honra*, pp. 10–11; A. E. Sloman, *The Dramatic Craftsmanship of Calderón* (Oxford, 1958), pp. 52–4; P. N. Dunn, 'Honour and the Christian background in Calderón', *Bulletin of Hispanic Studies*, 27 (1960), 85–7.

13 P. N. Dunn, 'Honour and the Christian background in Calderón'. According to Dunn, the imagery of darkness is not in itself a symbol, that of Night, but rather means the destruction of the symbol of the Sun; I believe that it comes to the same thing.

14 *BAE*, i, p. 358c.

15 *La estatua de Prometeo* (The Statue of Prometheus) (Paris, 1961) and *Eco y*

Narciso (Echo and Narcissus) (Chefs d'Oeuvre des Lettres Hispaniques I, Flers 1961), ed. Charles V. Aubrun.

16 I have altered one paragraph of the original lecture (p. 152). I had accepted too readily the traditional view that Calderón did present, as in the case of Segismundo, a man or woman reversing the fate forecast for him or her by the exercise of free will, thus exemplifying the concept of moral responsibility governing, whether positively or negatively, all human actions. Closer consideration of this question showed me that this traditional view was mistaken. I set out the different types of Calderonian prophecies in a later public lecture, which is reprinted here as chapter 7.

17 *Obras*, Aguilar, I, *Dramas*, p. 1045a; [*BAE*, III, p. 43c].

18 'Tan sagrado es el preceto/tuyo, que humilde y postrada,/vivir del sol ignorada,/y aun de mí misma prometo' ('Your ruling is so sacred, that I promise, humbly bowing, to live hidden from the sun, and even from myself.' (Aguilar, p. 1022a) [*BAE*, III, p. 29b].

19 *Metamorphoses*, Book I, line 747, Book II, line 328.

20 'Fábula de Faetón' (Story of Phaethon), in *Obras de Don Juan de Tarsis, Conde de Villamediana* (Zaragoza, 1629), p. 231.

21 *Rimas Humanas*, Sonnet LXXV in *Obras sueltas* (Madrid, 1776), vol. IV, p. 226.

22 Ovid, *Metamorphoses*, Book I, ll. 438–47. Fray Baltasar de Vitoria calls him *Pytón*; the form *Fitón* (Phiton) is found in the *Philosophia secreta* (1585) of Juan Pérez de Moya, Book II ch. XIX, art. 1.

23 Sátiro, the *gracioso*, says: 'El magro Fitón es ermitaño del demonio' (Python the magician is the Devil's hermit) (p. 1898b) [*BAE*, IV, p. 169a]; then he calls him 'un diablo de un pastor' (a devilish shepherd) (1904a) [p. 172a], and says of him 'me deja sin señal, con ser diablo' (Although he is the Devil, he leaves me without the sign) (1904b) [p. 172a]. The reference here is to the sign of the cross drawn with ashes on the foreheads of the faithful in the Ash Wednesday service, there having been a joking reference in connection with Sátiro to the words used ('dust thou art, and unto dust thou shalt return'). The sign is not put on Sátiro. Compare with this what Fray Baltasar de Vitoria says about the Delphic Sibyl: 'inside there was an extremely precious three-legged table made of gold, under which nestled the serpent Python or, to give him his proper name, the devil, to give the answers' (*Teatro de los dioses de la Gentilidad*, (Theatre of the Pagan Gods). (Madrid, 1620), 1st Part, Book V, ch. IV).

24 This 'paradox' is the main theme of my book *The Philosophy of Love in Spanish Literature, 1480–1680* (Edinburgh, 1985), where *Apolo y Climene* is discussed from this point of view on pp. 199–207.

25 In addition to Fitón's intervention in the plot and the contrast between the Temples of Diana and Venus, Calderón makes use of the metaphor of a 'mina' or 'tunnel' to indicate the sexuality of this love, as explained fully in the *Philosophy of Love*.

26 'Más fácil es de argüir/que hay en el humano ser/tropiezo para caer/que escalón para subir./Dígalo yo, pues el día/que como humano viví,/me dio sima en que caí/la trémula noche fría,/y ni ella ni el día me dan/el mismo despeño; pero/¡qué mucho, si considero/cuánto distantes están/el bien y el mal para quien,/en la porción de mortal,/ve el bien convertirse en mal/más veces que el mal en bien!' (It is easier to argue that in human nature there is a stumbling-block for falling, rather than a step for ascending. I am witness to this, because on the day when I lived like a human being, tremulous cold night gave me a tunnel into which I fell; but now neither day nor night hurl me down in the same fashion. But this is not surprising, when I think how remote good and evil are from each other, in the one who, on the human side sees good turn to evil more often than evil to good.) (p. 1888b) [BAE, IV, p. 163b], Apolo calls himself an 'enigma' (1900b) [BAE, IV, p. 170a] insisting that he does not know who he is, because 'I have denied all the knowledge that proved my divinity'. His divine nature being thus destroyed, Júpiter 'has reduced me to the life of a human monster'.

27 At the end of El hijo del Sol Epafo, Faetón's rival, marries Tetis, whom Faetón loved but could not win. Related with this is one of the many changes, which are always significant, which Calderón made in the myths: he has Epaphus recognised as the king's long-lost son, whose name is changed to Peleus. Thetis is the Nereid who married Peleus; this being possible because Peleus was a mortal and not a god. In Calderón's play Epafo, in order to court Tetis, is favoured by the dryads; he, therefore, represents the earth. Tetis always appears on stage accompanied by the naiads. The two of them can marry because the union of earth and water is a natural one. On the other hand, a union between Tetis and Faetón, son of the Sun – a union between fire and water – is against nature and is impossible. In this way, too, Calderón symbolises Faetón's refusal to accept life's limitations. Compare this: 'Thetis and Peleus' marriage signifies that all bodies are naturally engendered by the mixing of earth with water . . . That Jupiter should wish to be united with Thetis, and should leave her so that she may not conceive someone who would become greater than he himself, that he should banish her from his kingdom, means that fire, which is Jupiter, when it is only mixed with water, is put out because the two elements are made up of contrary qualities' (Pérez de Moya, Philosophia secreta, Book IV, ch. XLIII).

28 See Pierre Paris, 'La Mythologie de Calderón: Apolo y Climene – El hijo del Sol, Faetón' in Homenaje ofrecido a Menéndez Pidal (Madrid, 1925), vol. I, pp. 557–70.

3 The dramatic structure of El alcalde de Zalamea

From the third paragraph, this chapter reproduces, in translation, the essay 'La estructura dramática de El alcalde de Zalamea' (The Mayor of

Zalamea) in the *Homenaje a Casalduero*, eds. Rizel Pincus Sigele and
Gonzalo Sobejano (Madrid, 1972), pp. 411–18.

1 'Calderón de la Barca; Sentido y forma de *La vida es sueño*' in *Estudios
sobre el teatro español* (Madrid, 1967), pp. 172, 170.

2 *Ibid.* p. 180.

3 *Ibid.* p. 185; *La vida es sueño*, ed. A. E. Sloman (Manchester Spanish Texts,
1961). The numbering of the lines in Sloman's edition needs to be
corrected at this point: line 2030 should be line 2031; and the numbers of
the lines that follow are displaced accordingly.

4 Casalduero: 'Sentido y forma', pp. 170, 172.

5 *Ibid.* pp. 189–190.

6 *Ibid.* p. 170.

7 'La correlación en la estructura del teatro calderoniano' in *Seis calas en la
expresión literaria española* (Madrid, 1951), pp.159, 178, 165, 177.

8 Edition of *El alcalde de Zalamea* by Peter N. Dunn (Pergamon Oxford
Spanish Series, 1966), pp. 7–10.

9 A. E. Sloman, 'Scene division in Calderón's *El Alcalde de Zalamea*' in
Hispanic Review, 19, 1951, 66–71.

10 This is the division in the editions of Hartzenbusch (*Biblioteca de Autores
Españoles*), Krenkel (Klassische Bühnendichtungen der Spanier, III) and
Augusto Cortina (Clásicos castellanos). Ángel Valbuena Briones discards
the division into scenes, but retains the changes of place; thus, when the
editor assumes that the change from 'countryside' to 'street' has taken
place, he gives the stage direction 'Exeunt all', which includes the
Captain and the Sergeant, followed immediately by 'Enter the Captain
and the Sergeant', who actually have remained on the stage without
ceasing to speak; the same thing happens with the change from 'street' to
'courtyard', because Crespo, Juan and the Sergeant should 'leave' and
'return' immediately afterwards (*Obras completas*, Aguilar, 4th edn,
Madrid, 1959, I, pp. 854a, 857b). Only Dunn's edition, already mentioned,
follows the original text faithfully, without scene division or changes of
place.

11 The 1651 edition has the stage direction, which is not retained by all
later editions, 'Enter Mendo, a nobleman, *de figura* and Nuño'. A *figura*
meant a pretentious ill-looking man of ridiculous appearance.

12 In numbering the lines I follow Dunn's edition. The edition in *Clásicos
castellanos* has an error: line 793 should be 794, and the numbering
remains misplaced up to 875.

13 There is once again an error in the numbering of the lines in *Clásicos
castellanos*: line 405 should be 406. This error is not corrected, and the
Act finished with line 979, which should be 980.

14 Dámaso Alonso, 'La correlación en la estructura del teatro calderoniano',
p. 183. The italics are mine.

4 'Poetic truth' in the shaping of plots

Parts of this chapter are reproduced from 'The Spanish drama of the Golden Age: a method of analysis and interpretation' (see above, p. 366)

1 *Calderón y su teatro* (1881) in *Obras Completas*, Edición Nacional, vol. VIII (1941), p. 283.

2 *Poetics*, cap. XIII in Ingram Bywater's translation reproduced in W. Hamilton Fyfe, *Aristotle's 'Art of Poetry'* (Oxford, 1940) p. 34. The phrase put in square brackets is Fyfe's footnote.

3 Thus Isabel in Calderón's *El alcalde de Zalamea* is the innocent victim of rape. The manner in which the perpetrator is to be punished constitutes the problem with which the play deals.

4 The voluntary death of martyrdom in religious plays is not of course 'punishment'. In the spiritual context of the action poetic justice does not apply.

5 For a full discussion of this and the rest of the play see E. M. Wilson, 'La discreción de don Lope de Almeida', *Clavileño*, 2 (1951), 1–10. The indication of Don Lope's coming death is also stressed by T. E. May, 'The folly and the wit of secret vengeance: Calderón's *A secreto agravio secreta venganza*', *Forum for Modern Language Studies*, 2 (1966), 114–22.

6 *Parte treynta una de las mejores comedias que hasta oy han salido* (Barcelona, 1638). This popular play was frequently published up to *Biblioteca de autores españoles*, vol. XLV. It is found with alternative titles, *Dar la vida por su dama* and *La tragedia más lastimosa de amor*. For particulars about the authorship and performance see E. Cotarelo y Mori, 'Dramáticos del siglo XVII: Don Antonio Coello y Ochoa', *Boletín de la Real Academia Española*, 5 (1918), 574–84. Lessing greatly admired this play (*Hamburgische Dramaturgie*, lx–lxviii, 27 November–25 December 1767).

7 Francisco Bances Candamo, *Theatro de los theatros de los passados y presentes siglos*, ed. Duncan W. Moir (London, Tamesis Books Ltd., 1970), p. 35. First version, written 1689–90. The full context is very interesting, but too long to quote.

The same principle of decorum must have been one of the reasons why Calderón 'emended' history in *La cisma de Ingalaterra* by refraining from presenting Henry VIII as the lustful monster he read about in his source; there were also, however, more important and more 'poetic' reasons, which will be later discussed in the chapter on this play. For a modern study of Elizabeth's role in this play, see D. Rogers, 'Los monólogos femeninos en *El conde de Sex* de Antonio Coello' in *Estudios dedicados a James Leslie Brooks* (Barcelona & Durham, 1984), pp. 175–90; and for its possible relationship to Calderón's *El médico de su honra*, see the same author's 'El médico de su honra de Calderón y El conde de Sex de Coello' in *Hacia Calderón. Séptimo Coloquio Anglogermano, Cambridge 1984* (Wiesbaden, 1985), pp. 175–82.

8 Joaquín Casalduero, *Sentido y forma de las Novelas ejemplares* (Buenos Aires, 1943), pp. 145–53.

9 *El pensamiento de Cervantes* (Madrid, 1925), pp. 242–4.

10 See especially the difference of detail pointed out by Casalduero between the death of Loaisa (in the first version) and that of Lotario (pp. 147–9). The most remarkable example of Cervantes' preoccupation with poetic justice is that in the second version of *El celoso extremeño* Loaisa no longer dies but 'despechado y casi corrido, se pasó a las Indias' ('chastened and almost shame-faced, he left for the New World'), because as Casalduero says, he was not now guilty of adultery but only of housebreaking (pp. 150–1).

11 'For Cervantes' aesthetic sensitivity, adultery would have besmirched his character; not because adultery could not be portrayed, but because Leonora did not deserve to incur it. The moral fault would have been accompanied by an aesthetic fault.' (Casalduero, *Sentido y forma de las Novelas ejemplares*, p. 150).

12 *An Introduction to Dramatic Theory* (London, 1923), p. 83.

13 In *La vida es sueño* the guilty king is indeed defeated in an insurrection, but only to be pardoned and restored to his throne. It is perhaps significant that he is King of Poland, not of any Spanish kingdom. We may remember that in Italy even as late as 1859 the censorship insisted that the king assassinated in Verdi's opera *Un ballo in maschera* should be changed from Gustavus III of Sweden to an English 'Governor of Boston'.

5 The Coriolanus theme: *Las armas de la hermosura*

This chapter reproduces, with extra introduction and a modified conclusion, the essay 'History and poetry: the Coriolanus theme in Calderón' published in *Hispanic Studies in Honour of I, González Llubera* (Oxford, Dolphin Book Company, 1959), 211–24. The first four pages of the essay, however, have been reprinted in part of the preceding chapter.

1 *The Dramatic Craftsmanship of Calderón: His Use of Earlier Plays* (Oxford, Dolphin Book Company, 1958).

2 *Decades*, II, xxxii–xl.

3 *Roman Antiquities*, VI, xcii–xciv; VII, xxi–lxix; VIII.i–lx. Calderón could have had access to Latin translations of this history, but it is most unlikely that he derived his knowledge of the Coriolanus legend from this source, since Livy and Plutarch were of course much more widely read.

4 *Parallel Lives*, VI, Alcibiades and Coriolanus.

5 It could be argued that the kind of dramatic inconsistency that will here be alleged may account to some extent for the dissatisfaction which so many critics have felt with Shakespeare's *Coriolanus* and for the lack of any agreement in its interpretation, since this is largely due to uncertainty whether, and to what extent, our sympathies are intended to be aroused or repelled by the hero's character and conduct. Compare, for instance, three divergent views on his tragic death in M. W. MacCallum, *Shakespeare's Roman Plays and their Background* (London, 1910),

pp. 598–627; G. Wilson Knight, *The Imperial Theme* (London, 1931), pp. 154–98; D. A. Traversi, 'Coriolanus', *Scrutiny*, 6 (1937), 43–8.

6 This is one interpretation of Shakespeare's *Coriolanus*: the hero's death is 'sacrificial'.

7 The Comendador of Fuenteovejuna is guilty of a political crime, but only against the crown; his crimes against his serfs are moral ones.

8 It should be noted that there is also historical justification for this, since Livy after reporting Coriolanus's murder by the Volscians also mentions a second tradition according to which Coriolanus lived in exile until old age. (*Decades*, ii, xl).

9 *Decades*, ii, xl.

10 *Plutarch's Lives*, Loeb Classical Library, vol. iv, pp. 203, 211.

11 This episode from Roman legend is the theme of another play, *El robo de las sabinas*, which is connected with *El privilegio de las mujeres* both chronologically and through its authorship; it was performed in the court theatre in 1637, and Antonio Coello collaborated with his brother Juan and with Rojas Zorrilla in writing it. (See E. Cotarelo y Mori, 'Dramáticos del siglo xvii: Don Antonio Coello y Ochoa', *Boletín de la Real Academia Española*, 5 (1918), 558–60, 594). Calderón may have had this play in mind when writing *Las armas de la hermosura*, since the *gracioso* (Pasquín), the *criada* (Livia) and two other characters have the same names in each. In *El robo de las sabinas* there is a suggestion (scarcely developed) that the Romans are fierce barbarians until civilised by the love of women, which provides a parallel between it and the two Coriolanus plays; but unlike the latter it attempts to extract no significance from its historical theme, using it only as a background to a fictitious and conventional story of constancy in love. The much more intelligent interest in 'history' shown by *El privilegio de las mujeres* is unlikely, therefore, to be due to Antonio Coello: this strengthens the assumption that Calderón conceived and planned the plot. *El robo de las sabinas* was published in *Comedias nueuas escogidas de los mejores ingenios de España. Onzena Parte.* (Madrid, 1658) and attributed only to Juan Coello.

12 *Plutarch's Lives*, vol. iv, pp. 201–3.

13 The association is implicit in the original story, but the emphasis Calderón gives it may have been influenced by Plutarch's introduction to his biography: 'Verily, among all the benefits which men derive from the favour of the Muses, no other is so great as that softening of the nature which is produced by culture and discipline, the nature being induced by culture to take on moderation and cast off excess. It is perfectly true, however, that in those days Rome held in highest honour that phase of virtue which concerns itself with warlike and military achievements, and evidence of this may be found in the only Latin word for virtue, which signifies really *manly valour*; they made valour, a specific form of virtue, stand for virtue in general' (*Plutarch's Lives*, p. 121).

14 *Las armas de la hermosura* (*Obras completas*, vol. i, *Dramas*, Aguilar, ed. Ángel Valbuena Briones (Madrid, 1959), p. 1313a) (*BAE*, iii, p.209c). This passage is copied practically unchanged from *El privilegio de las mujeres*, where it continues with four lines omitted in the later version. In the earliest edition I have seen these are: 'Y que ellas puedan, sin el/ matarle, atarle y prenderle,/ por que han de ser absolutos / dueños de la honra siempre' (So that without destroying men's honour, they may hold it and bind it, because women are to be absolute rulers over honour, always). (*Comedias Parte Treinta compuestas por diferentes Autores*, Sevilla, 1638, p. 383b.) Later editions (eg. Hartzenbusch, *BAE*, iv, p.412c) omit the first two of these lines, perhaps because of their obscurity.

15 *El privilegio de la mujeres*, *BAE*, iv, p.412c.

6 The father–son conflict

This chapter, after the short Introduction, reproduces the major part of the paper 'The father–son conflict in the drama of Calderón', *Forum for Modern Language Studies*, vol. 2, no. 2 (1966), 99–113. The subject of this paper was later redeveloped in 'Segismundo's tower: a Calderonian myth', *Bulletin of Hispanic Studies*, 59 (1982), 247–56, and much of this version is here preferred to the original. The ending of this chapter is reproduced from the first of these papers.

1 The will was published by Narciso Alonso Cortés, 'Algunos datos relativos a D. Pedro Calderón', *Revista de Filología Española*, 2 (1915), 41–51; see p. 48.

2 Emilio Cotarelo y Mori, *Ensayo sobre la vida y obras de D. Pedro Calderón de la Barca* (Madrid, 1924), pp. 65, 74–5. An uncle of Don Diego Senior had apparently emigrated to the New World (p. 75n).

3 Alonso Cortés, p. 48. 'I order and request Pedro on no account to abandon his studies, but to continue and complete them, and become a very good chaplain of the one who with such generosity left him the means to become one.' He was destined for a living endowed by his maternal grandmother which was to remain within the family.

4 In Narciso Alonso Cortés, 'Algunos datos relativos a D. Pedro Calderón', p. 50.

5 Cristóbal Pérez Pastor, *Documentos para la biografía de D. Pedro Calderón de la Barca* (Madrid, 1905), p. 35.

6 Pérez Pastor, p. 235.

7 Pérez Pastor, pp. 7–10.

8 Cotarelo, pp. 74–5.

9 As we have seen, Calderón himself had an illegitimate son, whom he first called a nephew and then made legitimate by publicly acknowledging him after the mother's death. This public acknowledgement contrasts the situation of this boy with that of Francisco González Calderón: see pp. 9 and 172.

10 See Dorothy Schons, 'A Calderón document', *Romanic Review*, 19 (1928), 157.

11 See Anton Constandse, *Le Baroque espagnol et Calderón de la Barca* (Amsterdam, 1951).

12 See Pedro de Ribadeneyra, *Flos Sanctorum* (1599–1601), under October 25.

13 *Obras completas*, ed. Ángel Valbuena Briones (Madrid, Aguilar, 1959), I, 800b. [*BAE*, III, p.251c]. This quotation follows the text in the *Verdadera quinta parte de comedias* of Vera Tassis (1682). Lines 9 to 11 and line 13 of the above quotation are not easy to construe; the translation is an interpretation of the general sense.

14 *Alimentos* is a legal term denoting the provision that must be made for the adequate maintenance of a person who is legally entitled to it by testamentary right, or contract of any kind.

7 Segismundo's tower: a Calderonian myth

This chapter reproduces, with some alterations, the major part of the paper published with the same title in the *Bulletin of Hispanic Studies*, 59 (1982) 247–56. The closing section of the original paper is reproduced as part of the final section of this book.

1 Lectures given at the *Centro de Intercambio Intelectual Germano-Español* (Madrid, 1926).

2 Doña Blanca's nine Segismundos occur in the following eight *comedias*: *La vida es sueño, El monstruo de los jardines, La hija del aire, Apolo y Climene, Eco y Narciso, En la vida todo es verdad y todo mentira* (a play containing two 'Segismundos', Heraclio and Leonido), *Hado y divisa* and *Las cadenas del Demonio*. I would reject this last-named play as apocryphal: it is a very poor one and does not appear on the list Calderón himself compiled of his plays. It contains some other Calderonian motifs besides 'Segismundo's tower' and Calderón may therefore have collaborated in its composition. The question of its authenticity deserves a full examination. The two *comedias* omitted by Doña Blanca are *Los tres afectos del amor* and *Andrómeda y Perseo*.

3 *La vida es sueño*, edited by Albert E. Sloman (Manchester Spanish Texts, 1961), Act I, ll.111–12. [*BAE*, I, p.1c]

4 A contemporary tendency may restrict the meaning of a traditional myth to what an anthropologist sees in it. The myth of Orpheus and Eurydice may therefore be taken as marking the winter and summer solstices, the death and rebirth of nature. But through the centuries of its transmission the myth has conveyed the idea that art, especially music, is a civilising force that tames the harshness of nature; the idea also that death is not an end, that love can conquer everything. With the coming of Christianity Eurydice suggested Humanity contaminated by the bite of the Satanic serpent, plunged into the darkness of sin and restored to the light by the redemptive power of Christ's sacrificial love, who thus become the

historical actualisation of the archetypal Orpheus. For Calderón this was the primary reference of the myth as he dramatised it in his *auto El divino Orfeo*. Only myth can encompass such a range of feeling and inner significance.

5 Modern staging is required to give the tower the required visual dominance. Best of all, it needs a modern spectacular film-production of the play – a fortress-like tower in a rocky mountain setting, out of which a chained youth, dressed in skins, emerges to make his impassioned plea for freedom; how impressive this could be on a cinema screen.

6 For instance: 'The astrologer's prediction is falsified' (Gerald Brenan, *The Literature of the Spanish People*, 2nd edn (Cambridge, 1953), p.288); 'What happens in Calderón's work is that Segismundo, by being convinced of the brevity and inconstancy of human glory, oversets the evil forecast by the prophecy; and that the magnanimous spirit which grows in him, after he returns to the tower, contradicts the horoscope, which seemed about to be fulfilled during his first emergence from the tower.' (Introduction by Martín de Riquer to his edition of the play in 'Colección Para Todos', 2nd edn (Barcelona, 1954), p.24); 'On analysing the play, it can be seen how, at the end, the horoscope is invalidated' (Introduction by Augusto Cortina to his edition of the play in *Clásicos castellanos* (Madrid, 1955), p.xxx).

7 He gives this as his excuse for bringing Segismundo up in confinement: 'que yo, Polonia, os estimo/tanto, que os quiero librar/de la opresión y servicio/de un rey tirano . . .' ('for I, Poland, love you so much that I wish to free you from the oppression and service of a tyrant king') (ll.761–4). [*BAE*, I, p.3a] After the battle, as he goes forward to surrender to his son, he says: 'Si está de Dios que yo muera,/o si la muerte me aguarda,/aquí, hoy la quiero buscar,/esperando cara a cara' ('If it is God's wish that I die, or if death waits for me here, I wish today to seek it, and wait for it face to face') (ll.3132–5) [*BAE*, I, p.18a].

8 This equation of what is astrologically foreseeable and unforeseeable with the results of Basilio's and Segismundo's free actions respectively, is the only point I would add to the excellent paper by Peter N. Dunn, 'The horoscope motif in *La vida es sueño*', *Atlante*, 1 (1953), 187–201. A warning must be issued against the criticism that denies any condemnation by Calderón of Basilio and his astrologising, because he is later turned into the Trinity in the *auto sacramental* also entitled *La vida es sueño* (see Micheline Sauvage, *Calderón dramaturge* (Paris, 1959, pp.140 et seq.). This approach is fallacious. The *comedia* provides the *auto* with its allegory, not with its theme; the two plays are quite different in meaning, and each provides the complete context for its own interpretation.

9 For the various forms of the Semiramis legend and for Calderón's treatment, see the Introduction to Gwynne Edwards' edition of the play (London, Tamesis Books, 1970).

10 See A. A. Parker, *The Philosophy of Love in Spanish Literature, 1480–1680* (Edinburgh, 1985), pp.174–214, where the full meaning of the plays here chosen as illustrations of the prison myth are analysed.

8 Horoscopes and their fulfillment

Much of this chapter repeats, with alterations, the paper entitled '*El monstruo de los jardines y* el concepto calderoniano del destino', *Hacia Calderón. Cuarto Coloquio Anglogermano, Wolfenbüttel, 1975* (Berlin and New York, 1979), pp. 92–101.

1 *La vida es sueño*, edited A. E. Sloman (Manchester Spanish Texts, 1961), ll. 3089–3168, [*BAE*, I, pp. 17c–18b].

2 Calderón, *Obras completas*, I, *Dramas*, ed. Ángel Valbuena Briones, 4th edn (Madrid, 1959), p. 1321b, [*BAE*, III, p. 334c].

3 Peter Berens, 'Calderóns Schicksalstragödien', *Romanische Forschungen*, 39 (1926), 47.

4 Calderón, *Obras completas*, II, ed. Ángel Valbuena Briones, 1st edn (1956), pp. 2149b–50a. [*BAE*, IV, p. 392b].

5 Covarrubias, *Tratado de la verdadera y falsa prophecía* (1588) (fol. 44v).

6 See Robert Graves, *The Greek Myths* (1955), chapters 81 and 160.

7 The interpretation of this theme has been given elsewhere. See A. A. Parker, *The Philosophy of Love in Spanish Literature: 1480–1680* (Edinburgh, 1985), pp. 193–8. In the two main characters the play presents a similar type of abnormality in the rejection of sexual rôles. Deidamia is a young woman who totally rejects marriage and scorns men. She is the type of 'feminist' not uncommon in the Golden Age drama who rejects the thought of love and marriage because she cannot contemplate losing her freedom. The abnormality of Achilles is the monstrosity he represents when dressed as a girl and living solely among women. Gardens in Calderón symbolise the sphere of women and Achilles is a 'monster' in the gardens of the palace. Dressed as a girl, he can seduce the 'feminist' Deidamia, and this experience of love makes him want to live for ever in the 'gardens' and shun the world of men. Deidamia, having come to know love, wants to keep this experience within her own private world. The horoscope shatters this delusion of self-containment.

9 Fate and human responsibility (1): the problem

This chapter reproduces, with some alterations and additions, pages 173–8 of the paper 'Prediction and its dramatic function in *El mayor monstruo los celos*', published in *Studies in Spanish Literature of the Golden Age Presented to Edward M. Wilson*, ed. R. O. Jones (London, Tamesis Books Ltd., 1973).

1 Helen L. Sears finds 'contradictions in Lope's practice and attitudes (between fatalism and free will, for example, or between Fortune as a servant of God and Fortune as an irrational independent co- or counter-divinity)'. ('The concepts of fortune and fate in the *comedia* of Lope de Vega', abstract of Doctoral Dissertation at the University of California at Los Angeles, in *Bulletin of the Comediantes*, 2 (1950), 1–3.)

2 Peter Berens, 'Calderóns Schicksalstragödien', *Romanische Forschungen*, 39 (1926), 1–66.

3 Charles V. Aubrun, 'Le Déterminisme naturel et la causalité surnaturelle chez Calderón' in *Le Théâtre tragique*, ed. Jean Jacquot (Paris, 1962), 199–209. The essay by Ángel Valbuena Briones, 'El concepto del hado' in *Perspectiva crítica de los dramas de Calderón* (Madrid, 1965), pp. 9–17, is superficial.

4 Don Cameron Allen, *The Star-Crossed Renaissance* (New York, 1966), 47–8.

5 'The mere matter of stumbling and falling appears as one of the commonest of all accidental occurrences to which was given an ominous meaning . . . when the consul Titus Manlius, who had just entered Etruria as his province in 299 BC, was drilling the cavalry, he was thrown from his horse and died three days later; an incident which the Etruscans embraced as a sign that the gods were fighting at their side, since they had thus disposed of the Roman general. Again when the haughty Flaminius, after chiding his men for their lack of courage against Hannibal, was thrown from his horse, the soldiers were dismayed by what they considered an evil omen at the outset of their campaign' (Franklin B. Krauss, *An Interpretation of the Omens, Portents and Prodigies recorded by Livy, Tacitus and Suetonius* (Philadelphia, 1930) 173–4). The two instances quoted are from Livy, 10.11.1–2 and 22.3.11–14.

6 For what follows I am indebted to the Introduction to A. Bouché-Leclercq, *Histoire de la divination dans l'Antiquité* (Paris, 1879).

7 *Ibid.*, I, 10–16.

8 *Ibid.*, p. 23.

9 *Ibid.*, p. 24–5.

10 *Ibid.*, p. 25–6.

11 *Ibid.*, p. 58–9.

12 *Ibid.*, p. 59–61.

13 The concept and treatment of fate in medieval scholasticism has less relevance to Calderón than the period of the Reformation. For a survey of what is here omitted, see Vincenzo Cioffari, *Fortune and Fate from Democritus to St. Thomas Aquinas* (New York, 1935).

14 This account of the doctrines of Báñez and Molina is an over-simplification, perhaps grossly so, which does no justice to the subtlety of their arguments. It is hoped that this over-simplification may help to make the matter sufficiently intelligible to the non-theologian. A modern statement of the various doctrinal points at issue may be found in the entries on Fate, Predestination, Predetermination, Freedom and Grace in the *Theological Dictionary* by Karl Rahner and Herbert Vorgrimler, ed. Cornelius Ernst, OP, trans. Richard Strachan (New York, Herder & Herder, 3rd imp., 1968). This work was first published in Germany by Herder & Herder in 1965. The *New Catholic Encyclopaedia* can also be profitably consulted. For a much fuller treatment of the whole problem, see *Dictionnaire de théologie catholique* under the relevant headings.

10 Fate and human responsibility (2): a dramatic presentation: *El mayor monstruo los celos*

This chapter reproduces, with additions, pages 179–92 of 'Prediction and its dramatic function in *El mayor monstruo los celos*'. The play is now placed in a more clearly defined context.

1 Tirso de Molina, *Obras dramáticas completas*, ed. Blanca de los Rios (Madrid, 1946), I, 1573b.

2 See Edward M. Wilson, 'Seven "Aprobaciones" by Don Pedro Calderón de la Barca' in *Homenaje a Dámaso Alonso* (Madrid, 1963), III, 605–18. The *aprobación* for Tirso is dated 16 July 1635.

3 I use the edition of the revised version: *El mayor monstruo los celos. A Critical and Annotated Edition from the Partly Holographic Manuscript of D. Pedro Calderón de la Barca*, ed. Everett W. Hesse (Madison, Wisconsin, 1955). The passage quoted is lines 3629–32. The first version was entitled *El mayor monstruo del mundo*. The passages deleted for revision are reproduced by Hesse. The deletions do not affect the argument of this chapter. [See also *BAE*, I, p. 501c.] Not all the passages referred to in the text are in *BAE*.

4 I have used *The Works of Flavius Josephus*, trans. William Whiston (Philadelphia, 1851). The relevant sections are: *The Jewish War* (Book I, ch. 22), II, 209–11; *Antiquities* (Book XV, ch. 3, 6, 7), I, 517–18, 525–31. There was a Spanish translation, *Los siete libros de Flavio, Josepho de Bello Judaico*, trans. Juan Martín Cordero (Perpignan, 1608).

5 *Calderón y su teatro (Estudios y discursos de crítica histórica y literaria)* (Madrid, Edición Nacional, 1941), III, 252, 253, 260.

6 Peter Berens, 'Calderóns Schicksalstragödien', *Romanische Forschungen*, 39 (1926), 1–66; 56–8.

7 Charles V. Aubrun, 'Le Déterminisme naturel et la causalité surnaturelle chez Calderón' in *Le Théâtre tragique*, ed. Jean Jacquot (Paris, 1962), 199–209; p. 204.

8 *Ibid.*, 202–5.

9 *Ibid.*, 206.

10 *Ibid.*, 207–8.

11 *Ibid.*, 204.

12 Cf. this modern definition of Fate: 'Fate exists for the Christian insofar as the free conscious activity of his life always takes shape against a prior and permanent exposure to the otherness of the world, to the incalculable and uncontrollable (since God himself remains essentially mysterious), so that the course of his life is governed less by his own plans than by what happens to him from without. Besides this, death reduces man to impotence, and his greatest, most comprehensive, final act is to accept this utter impotence in the obedience of faith. But for the believer this fate is no impersonal force before which he can only hold his peace, or, if it be such a force, at least Christ has dethroned it (Rom. 8:31–39). For the very Spirit of that God whom the Christian calls Father,

has stripped the uncontrollable event, the inescapable burden, of their power. God is indeed mystery, yet he knows himself, he communicates himself and therefore also the meaning of all he "sends" to man; he is wise Love, who reverences his creature and by the Incarnation has made fate his own destiny. Because it happens in grace and as revelation, obedient acceptance of fate, which transfigures it, is already faith and, where it reaches its perfection, love; it is already anonymous Christianity, acceptance which is conquest, the redemption of fate' (Karl Rahner and Herbert Vorgrimler, *Theological Dictionary* (New York, 1968), pp. 170–1; a translation of *Kleines theologisches Wörterbuch*, 1965).

13 Ed. Hesse, p. 222. This phrase disappeared when this passage was expanded in the revised version, where it corresponds to lines 2908–36 [*BAE*, i, p. 497c].

14 Cf. *El médico de su honra* (Act II, lines 890–1) [*BAE*, i, p. 359a], where the jealous Don Gutierre, spying on his wife, puts out the light (i.e. the light of reason) and says 'Mato la luz y llego/sin luz y sin razón, dos veces ciego' (I quench the light and arrive twice blind; without light and without reason). That Mariene should also extinguish the light has the same significance – Herod attacks 'in the dark' – but it also contributes to the tragic irony of the ending: she thinks to save the two men, and does save them, but at the cost of her own life.

15 See the Introduction to this *auto* in Manchester Spanish Texts, edited by A. A. Parker (2nd edn, 1962).

11 The functions of comedy

1 Francisco Bances Candamo, *Theatro de los theatros de los passados y presentes siglos*, ed. with Prologue and notes Duncan W. Moir (London, Tamesis Books Ltd., 1970).

2 *Ibid.*, p. 33.

3 Juan Pablo de Mártir Rizo. *Poetica de Aristoteles, traducida de Latin. Illustrada y comentada por Juan Pablo Martir Rizo* (1623) fol. 50; quoted in Margarete Newels, *Die Dramatischen Gattungen in den Poetikens des Siglo de Oro. Eine Einleitende Studie zum Thema der Dramentheorie in Goldenen Zeitalter* (Wiesbaden 1959). See p. 37.

4 Madius, *De Ridiculis* (1550); see Marvin T. Herrick, *Comic Theory in the Sixteenth Century* (Illinois, 1950), p. 44.

5 Both works have been edited together under the title *Comedy . . . with an Introduction and Appendix: "The Meanings of Comedy" by Wylie Sypher* (Anchor Books, New York 1956).

6 *Ibid.*, p. 15.

7 See R. O. Jones, '*El perro del hortelano* y la visión de Lope', *Filologia*, 10 Buenos Aires, 135–42.

8 His cloak-and-sword plays enjoyed much greater popularity outside Spain than did the tragi-comedies or tragedies by which he is now best known. For instance, the number of translations and adaptations, within the

seventeenth century alone, of the three comedies studied in the next two chapters were: *La dama duende*, four French and (via these) one English and two Flemish; *El galán fantasma*, one French, one Flemish and one German; and *El astrólogo fingido*, two French, one Italian and one English, by Dryden, called *An Evening's Love or the Mock Astrologer*, adapted from a French translation.

9 Sypher, *Comedy* . . ., p. 147.
10 Sypher, *Comedy* . . ., p. 117.

12 The vicissitudes of secrecy (1): *La dama duende, El galán fantasma*

1 Bergson, *Laughter*, Sypher, *Comedy* . . ., p. 123. Cf. '. . . the equivocal situation is indeed one which permits of two different meanings at the same time, the one merely plausible, which is put forward by the actors; the other a real one, which is given by the public. We see the real meaning of the situation, because care has been taken to show us every aspect of it, but each of the actors knows only one of these aspects; hence the mistakes they make and the erroneous judgements they pass both on what is going on around them and on what they are doing themselves. We proceed from this erroneous judgement to the correct one, we waver between the possible meaning and the real, and it is this mental see-saw between two contrary interpretations which is at first apparent in the enjoyment we derive from an equivocal situation.'

2 In a paper published in the *Tulane Drama Review*, 6 (1962), 69–105, with the title 'Flickers of incest on the face of Honor: Calderón's *Phantom Lady*', and reprinted as chapter 7 of *Calderón and the Seizures of Honor* (Cambridge, Mass., 1972) with the slightly altered title 'Flickers of incest on the face of Honor: *The Phantom Lady*'.

3 See A. A. Parker, *The Philosophy of Love in Spanish Literature 1480–1680* (Edinburgh, 1985), pp. 200–1.

13 The vicissitudes of secrecy (2): *El astrólogo fingido*

1 *Parte veinte y cinco de comedias recopiladas de diferentes autores e ilustres poetas de España* (Zaragoza, 1632).

2 *El astrólogo fingido*, in *Obras completas*, Aguilar edition, vol. II (*comedias*), p. 130a [*BAE*, I, p. 574b]. Subsequent references will be given in brackets in the text.

3 The relationship of these two Pimentels is not known. Don Vicente could have been engaged in a recruiting drive in Spain. There are records of shipments of troops to Flanders from ports in the north of Spain in 1631 and 1633, but the records do not contain lists of officers embarking. The manuscript of *El sitio de Bredá* on which the edition by Johanna Schreck (1957) is based, and which is the play in which Vicente Pimentel appears as a character, bears the title *La gran comedia del sitio de Bredá de Don Pedro Calderón. Año de 1632*. It is more likely that the date in this position

refers to a performance date rather than to the year when the manuscript was copied. Don Juan's departure could therefore refer to troop movements in 1631. (I am greatly indebted to Professor Geoffrey Parker and Dr Patrick Williams for this information.)

4 The arguments in favour of connecting the play with the victory celebrations are set out in the paper by Shirley B. Whitaker, 'The first performance of Calderón's *El sitio de Bredá*', *Renaissance Quarterly*, 31 (1978), 515–31. A later study of *El sitio de Bredá* maintains that Calderón's source was a *Descripcion de la villa y sitio de Bredá y entrada que hizo en ella S.A.S. la señora infanta Doña Isabel Clara Eugenia* (Antwerp, 1628) (S. A. Vosters, 'Again the first performance of Calderón's *El sitio de Bredá, Revista Canadiense de Estudios Hispánicos* (1982), 117–34). The author concludes that 1628 was the date of the play's composition. This is plausible but not conclusive, since there could have been an earlier edition of the *Descripción*. This conjecture does, however, bring the possible date of composition closer to the date given on the manuscript of the play, which may have been the date of performance.

5 These descriptions are referred to in the text as *pintura* (paintings). Set pieces of this kind are conventional in the Spanish drama, when setting plot and mood. in *El príncipe constante* (1629), when Muley, the Moorish king's confidant and general, reports the approach of the Portuguese invading fleet, he gives an elaborately poetic description, in which the white foam makes the sea a 'garden of flowers', which turns the sky into a 'sea of stars'. This rhetorical speech combines narración with *pintura*. In comedy these set pieces are shorter and generally more straightforward in imagery.

6 Chirinos was a loose-living character in folk literature.

7 Max Oppenheimer, 'The *burla* in Calderón's *El astrólogo fingido*', *Philological Quarterly*, 27, 3, July 1948, 241–63; see pp. 244–5.

8 e.g. 'Let us now study in detail the mechanism of the *burla* in *El astrólogo fingido*. We immediately notice that whenever and wherever a *burla* takes place, we have on one side the *burlador* and on the other side the *persona burlada*. The *burlador* knows about the *burla* since he originated it, and is thus cognizant of what is real and what is *burla*. If he did not know the difference, he would be the dupe of his own *burla* and would automatically become a *burlador burlado* (*ibid.*, p. 248).

14 Secret betrothals and secret marriages: *El postrer duelo de España*

This chapter is a translation and an expansion of the essay entitled 'Los amores y noviazgos clandestinos en el mundo dramático-social de Calderón', published in *Hacia Calderón. Segundo Coloquio Anglogermano, Hamburg, 1970*, ed. Hans Flasche (Berlin and New York, 1973), pp. 79–87.

1 I rely for what follows on the *Dictionnaire de théologie catholique*, article on *Mariage* (vol. IX, col. 2162–2255); especially on the section dealing with

the 'classical doctrine' before and after the Council of Trent. For a study of this subject in earlier Spanish literature, see Justina Ruiz de Conde, *El amor y el matrimonio secreto en los libros de caballerías* (Madrid, 1948).

2 It was possible for a woman to defraud the man even when a signed promise of marriage existed. *Guzmán de Alfarache* (1599 and 1604), the picaresque novel by Mateo Alemán, relates the story of a woman who had received the promise of marriage from a man with whom she proceeded to cohabit. Later, she affirmed that she wanted to marry another man and claimed compensation for breach of promise which was duly paid her. She repeated this fraud several times before being found out. Whereupon Guzmán realised how wise the Council of Trent had been in prohibiting secret marriages. Following on this, he continues, measures were taken to make secret entry into women's homes more difficult. If only, he concludes, the civil authorities followed the ecclesiastical in such prohibitions, there would be a great reduction in the number of 'lost' women now leading immoral lives (Part II, Book iii, ch. 2).

3 Don Cristóbal Pérez Pastor, *Documentos para la biografía de don Pedro Calderón de la Barca* (Madrid, 1905); see Document no. 130, p. 225.

4 Pérez Pastor, Document no. 132, p. 231.

5 Pérez Pastor, Document no. 133, p. 237.

6 Pérez Pastor, Document no. 147, p. 246.

7 See Pérez Pastor, p. 246.

8 See A. Paz y Melia, *Catálogo de las piezas de teatro que se conservan en el Departamento de Manuscritos de la Biblioteca Nacional*, 2nd edn, Madrid, 1934, vol. II, p. 411.

9 Fray Prudencio de Sandoval, *Vida y hechos del Emperador Carlos V*, Book XI, ch. ix (Madrid, *Biblioteca de autores españoles*, 1935, II, 15–18).

10 Quoted from the edition of Ángel Valbuena Briones in the Aguilar edition of *Obras completas*, 4th edn) (Madrid, 1959), vol. I, p. 1594b [*BAE*, IV, p. 150c]. Paul III (1534–49) was the Pope who convoked the Council, not the one who was reigning in 1522.

11 The popular revolt of many cities and towns in Castile against the coming to the throne of a foreign king with a number of Flemish noblemen, ministers and advisors who would take offices of profit under the crown. This was not a democratic insurrection, as used to be thought, but rather a gesture of medieval Spain against the new monarchy and its European involvements.

12 Because the play is set in pre-tridentine times, Calderón could have presented this cohabitation as a *real* secret marriage; he did not do so because it was not his intention to criticise what had been already condemned, but to point to a custom prevailing at the time of writing.

15 From comedy to tragedy: *No hay cosa como callar*

1 The edition here used is the *Clásicos castellanos* edition, ed. Ángel Valbuena Briones (Madrid, 1962) [See als *BAE*, I, p. 549 et seq.).

2 The commander of the Spanish forces was Don Juan Alonso Enríquez, Admiral of Castile. A letter purporting to be the account he gave of the victory to his wife has survived, but has not been authenticated. It reads: My love: since you do not understand warfare, I shall only tell you that the enemy forces were divided into four sections: one fled, we killed another, we captured another, and the other was drowned. May God keep you, I am now going to dine in Fuenterrabía.' See Emilio Cotarelo y Mori, *Ensayo sobre la vida y obras de D. Pedro Calderón de la Barca* (Madrid, 1924), p. 192.

3 (III, ll. 466–76) [*BAE*, I, p. 567b]. In the phrases placed in inverted commas Calderón is recalling the poem *Las fortunas de Diana* by Lope de Vega. Earlier in this dialogue Don Juan had mentioned 'Spain's Phoenix', i.e. Lope de Vega, as the source of remarks he was making about lovers (E. M. Wilson and Jack Sage, *Poesias líricas en las obras dramáticas de Calderón* (London, Tamesis Books Ltd., 1964), pp. 100–1).

4 (Act III, ll. 860–72) [*BAE*, I, p. 570 b–c]. It is worth noting that in this soliloquy, as well as in the one previously quoted, Leonor is apostrophising her honour as if this were another person outside herself, an independent party to whom she owes allegiance. This may well strike a modern reader as very strange, but it is a manner of speaking that does highlight the special importance that honour had in the Spain of that time. It *was* something outside a person in that, since it was his reputation, it lived outside that person's own life, in the idea that other people had formed of him.

5 II, ll. 767–70 [*BAE*, I, p. 562a]. *Cortina*, exactly like 'curtain', is the plain wall of a fortress between the bastions.

16 A Calderonian conception of tragedy: *El pintor de su deshonra*

This chapter reproduces, with some abbreviations and omissions, the paper 'Towards a definition of Calderonian tragedy', *BHS* 39 (1962), pp. 222–37. The abbreviations, for the most part, cover the introductory account of theories of tragedy. This section is now shortened because the 'definition' of tragedy is probably no longer the debatable point it was when this paper was written. This chapter follows the plan of the whole book in not introducing or referring the works published after this particular paper was printed (attention is called to two exceptions to this rule). When this chapter refers to 'modern theories of tragedy', this means only theories published before 1962.

1 See, for instance, the original version of this essay, pp. 222–6, where representative examples of this common contention were given. It is scarcely necessary to quote them now.

2 An introduction to this subject, very useful for the student of literature, is the collection of essays edited by J. S. Peristiany under the title *Honour and Shame: The Values of Mediterranean Society* (London, 1965). The apparent defence of wife-murder on the Spanish stage went counter to the condemnation of murder and of acts of private vengeance uttered by

all theologians and moralists. *Honour and Shame* shows that the disparity between religious teaching and human practice in both literature and life is equally apparent in modern Greece, for example. What have to be looked for in the case of Calderón are signs of a condemnation of wife-murder despite the approbation of the characters concerned. What social anthropologists show us is the enormous strength of traditional attitudes in certain societies despite the acceptance of religious standards.

3 See 'Towards a definition of Calderonian tragedy', pp. 223–5.

4 *The Approach to the Spanish Drama of the Golden Age*, pp. 17–22.

5 But poetic justice is of course present in the play. Neither Eusebio nor Curcio is innocent; both suffer; Curcio by 'frustration'. The fact that Eusebio suffers death does not mean that he 'deserves' the supreme penalty as an exact retribution: on the legal plane death is of course the appropriate penalty, but on the deeper level of the play – the human and the moral level (i.e. *poetic* as against *legal* justice) – he is far from being the reprobate from whose punishment we are tempted to withhold our pity. That is why the play, unrealistically, reveals his salvation.

6 All references are to the *Clásicos castellanos* edition instead of the *Aguilar* edition as in the original article. *El pintor de su deshonra*, ed. Ángel Valbuena Briones (Madrid, *Clásicos castellanos*, 1956), p. 129 [see also *BAE*, IV, p. 66b] Subsequent references will be given in brackets after the text.

7 The causal structure of this play is of crucial importance. I was first made aware of this by Edward M. Wilson in an essay whose first draft I saw and profited from around 1950; 'Towards an appreciation of *El pintor de su deshonra*', published posthumously in Edward M. Wilson, *Spanish and English Literature of the Sixteenth and Seventeenth Centuries* (Cambridge, 1980), pp. 65–89; this is the definitive version. This essay appeared earlier in a Spanish translation in *Abaco, Estudios sobre literatura española*, no. 3 (Madrid, 1970), pp. 49–85.

8 The fact that Serafina is loved and will be abducted constitutes, of course, the 'unreality' of the painter's marriage. E. R. Curtius, in 'Calderón und die Malerei', *Romanische Forschungen*, 50 (1936), 89–136, discusses this scene where Don Juan cannot paint Serafina's portrait, but he is interested in it only in connection with the technique of painting, confirming from Pacheco's *Arte de la pintura* Don Juan's statement that it is easier to paint an ugly face than a beautiful one (pp. 129–30). It is now realised that Calderón is not the sort of dramatist who would introduce a scene of this kind merely to display an irrelevant knowledge of another art.

9 R. R. MacCurdy, *Francisco de Rojas Zorrilla and the Tragedy* (Albuquerque, 1958), p. 21.

10 Clifford Leech, *Shakespeare's Tragedies and other Studies in Seventeenth-Century Drama* (London, 1950), p. 216. The quotation continues: 'Thus plays like Calderón's *The Painter of Dishonour* are only technically tragedies: their effect on us is generally tiresome, because we have not the passionate Spanish concern with family relationships.'

11 e.g. Micheline Sauvage, *Calderón, dramaturge* (Collection des Grands Dramaturges, 18) (Paris, 1959), p. 140.

12 Calderón, *Obras completas*, vol. III, *Autos sacramentales* (Madrid, Aguilar, 1952), p. 840b.

13 See A. A. Parker, 'La cronología de los autos sacramentales de Calderón de la Barca', trans. Salvador Oliva and included in *Los autos sacramentales de Calderón de la Barca*, trans. Francisco García Sarriá (Barcelona, 1983), pp. 221–52.

17 The tragedy of honour: *El médico de su honra*

This chapter reproduces, with some additions, the paper entitled '*El médico de su honra* as tragedy', *Hispanófila Especial*, no. 2 (1975), 1–23. This paper was based on a contribution to a Symposium on Tragedy in the Spanish Drama of the Golden Age held at the University of North Carolina. Since the audience was familiar with *El médico de su honra*, all the action of the play and previous interpretations could be taken for granted and the paper could concentrate on the point at issue: whether this play should or should not be classed as a tragedy. In reproducing it here, fairly extensive additions have had to be made in order to clarify the action of the play and the context of the main points discussed.

1 Edward M. Wilson showed that there was little difference in the theory of honour between Englishmen and Spaniards in our period. An essay entitled 'Family honour in the plays of Shakespeare's predecessors and contemporaries' in *Essays and Studies*, vol. VI (London, 1953), pp. 19–41 gives a very clear and concise outline of the Spanish theory and analyses a number of English plays. Though the theory is similar in both countries, differences of nuance in the treatment reveal different expectations in the respective audiences. On the matters dealt with in the last and present chapters, Wilson's conclusions as regards England are these: 'The idea that the husband can restore his honour by the murder of his unchaste wife also exists but is seldom or never depicted with approval . . . To restore lost honour, an English husband might murder the lover and spare the wife. In Spain the murder of both was considered dramatically necessary (unless the lover was of royal blood) . . . The idea that public dishonour was final and ineradicable occurs in both theatres. In Spain it gives rise to the theory of secret vengeance; in England there seems little trace of this idea . . .' (pp. 39–40).

2 This was recorded in a manuscript volume entitled *Libro de casos notables que han sucedido en la ciudad de Córdoba y a sus hijos en diversos tiempos*, compiled early in the seventeenth century. (See Agustín González de Amezúa y Mayo, 'Un dato para las fuentes de *El médico de su honra*', first published in *Revue Hispanique*, 21 (1909), pp. 395–411, and reprinted in his *Opúsculos histórico-literarios*, vol. I (Madrid, 1951), pp. 3–18.)

3 Calderón's *El alcalde de Zalamea* is another example of his recasting an entire play and retaining the title. It would seem that if a play had had some success on the stage but was poorly constructed, the director of one

of the actors' companies would commission one of the leading dramatists to rework the plot. Such re-working is not infrequent.

4 A detailed comparison of both plays is the subject of chapter 2 of A. E. Sloman's *The Dramatic Craftsmanship of Calderón* (Oxford, 1958). The conclusion is 'that *El médico de su honra*, despite its closeness to the source, has at every stage considered and significant changes which, taken together, make it a new and original play' (p. 58).

5 Act II, lines 363–8. I quote from and refer to the edition by C. A. Jones (Oxford, 1961). With the exception of Act II, where one edition makes a slight addition to the text, the line numbering corresponds to that of Ángel Valbuena Briones in *Clásicos castellanos* (Madrid, 1956) [*BAE*, I, p. 356a].

6 That of Enrique is self-evident; that of Mencía has been adequately analysed by Sloman, *The Dramatic Craftsmanship of Calderón*, pp. 38–41.

7 'lograré mi esperanza/Si recibe mi agravio la venganza' [*BAE*, I, p. 350c]. Jones's text here repeats an error from the first edition: 'Si repite a mi agravio la venganza' (I, 577–8).

8 Ludovico is the 'barber-surgeon' who bleeds Mencía. He reports to the king that she had whispered during this operation 'I die innocent; may heaven not visit my death upon you.' (III, 640–2) [*BAE*, I, p. 364a]. The point is important. In protesting her innocence she must have been telling the truth, for no Catholic would perjure his or her salvation at the point of death.

9 When the revaluation of Calderón's honour plays began in the 1940s it was necessary to react against the traditional concept of *el honor calderoniano*. The cruelty attributed to Calderón was shown to be attributable instead to his dramatic characters, with whom Calderón could be shown not to sympathise. Believing that reaction had gone too far, A. I. Watson offered a corrective by endeavouring to prove that Calderón intended to present an entirely exemplary monarch ('Peter the Cruel or Peter the Just? A reappraisal of the role played by King Peter in Calderón's *El médico de su honra*', *Romanistisches Jahrbuch*, 14 (1963), 322–46). This paper made some valuable points but was submitted to severe criticism by D. W. Cruickshank, who found no exemplarism in the way Calderón presents his King ('Calderón's King Pedro: just or unjust?', *Gesammelte Aufsätze zur Kulturgeschichte Spaniens*, 25 (1970), 113–32). Watson's resistance to too outright a condemnation remains valid up to a point, and the argument here presented will lie between these two views, inclining somewhat more towards Cruickshank's. It will develop some aspects of Don Pedro's attempts to administer justice which Cruickshank was the first to call attention to.

10 She thus apostrophises him at the end of Act I: ' ¡venganza me dé/el cielo! El mismo dolor/sientas que siento, y a ver/llegues, bañado en tu sangre,/deshonras tuyas, porque/mueras con las mismas armas/que matas, amén, amén!' (May heaven concede me vengeance! May you suffer in the same way as I am suffering, and may you come to see,

bathed in your own blood, your own dishonour, so that you may die by
the same weapons with which you kill, so be it! so be it!) (I, 1012–18)
[*BAE*, I, p. 353b].

11 We have been prepared for this correlation by the fact that the same
dagger that kills Mencía will kill the king, and by the parallel incidents
mentioned above, in which each is horror-struck at the dagger in the
hand of the future assailant.

12 This translates the general sense. Literally it would be 'let fall on me a
hundred well-beaten carrier-baskets woven with backstitches because of
vagabondage'. The baskets referred to were used by urchins whose
livelihood consisted in carrying home the goods for shoppers.

13 In 1635 the debate within the Roman Church between the 'rigorist' and
the 'probabilist' schools of moral theologians was approaching its height.
The issue was: how is one bound in conscience to act if there is serious
doubt whether the moral law applies in a particular case? The 'rigorists'
maintained that one must always obey the law as long as there is any
doubt at all about one's right to disobey it. The 'probabilists' argued that
one must decide for freedom to break the law as long as there is serious
doubt about the law's applicability. Eventually the principle of rigorism
was rejected by Rome and that of probabilism was approved. In the
particular moral issue here presented by Coquín, he is the probabilist and
Gutierre the rigorist. These debates were part of the general movement in
the seventeenth century making for a less inflexible, more practical and
humane, system of ethics. One aspect of this movement – whether a
political ruler must always be guided by an absolute standard of right, or
whether he may in practice compromise with principle for the sake of
expediency – has been studied by Monroe A. Hafter in *Gracián and
Perfection: Spanish Moralists of the Seventeenth Century* (Cambridge, Mass.,
1966).

14 In his paper entitled 'Peter the Cruel or Peter the Just', cited above, A. I.
Watson disagreed with this interpretation of this scene, principally on the
grounds that buffoons and jesters were despised and ridiculed even to the
extent of having their teeth pulled out for the amusement of their
masters. He documented this, and Calderón must have been referring to
this kind of sport, but what is there in the context of this scene and in
the whole tone of the play that warrants us in assuming that Calderón
would have approved of such an action by a Peter the Just? For further
answers to Watson's objections, see the original version of '*El médico de
su honra* as tragedy', p. 21.

15 By 'official supremacy of honour' I mean its acceptance by the people and
the power it possessed to move the emotions and passions of a theatrical
audience. Lope de Vega, in his short treatise on the art of writing plays,
stated that questions of honour were the most suitable for dramatic
treatment 'porque mueven con fuerça a toda gente' ('because they move
everybody very powerfully'). I do not mean by 'official supremacy' that it
won the acceptance of theologians, philosophers and jurists. As

E. M. Wilson put it: 'some Spanish moral writers approved of honour in so far as it approximated to virtue, but they were less sure about the cult of reputation (a worldly thing) and wholly opposed to vengeance'. (Edward M. Wilson, 'A hispanist looks at Othello', *Spanish and English Literature of the Sixteenth and Seventeenth Centuries* (Cambridge, 1980), pp. 201–19, see p. 201.

16 See 'A hispanist looks at Othello'.

17 Cf. '. . . it may be asked whether tragedy is possible without recognition . . . in some established tragedies the recognition is apparently dispensed with. More generally, in life outside drama, it is quite possible to find tragic an event in which the protagonists at least never realise their true plight. There might still be a recognition, but only by the "spectators"' (Geoffrey Brereton, *Principles of Tragedy. A Rational Examination of the Tragic Concept in Life and Literature* (Coral Gables, Florida, 1968), pp. 36–7).

18 Clifford Leech, *Tragedy* (London, 1969). This is No. 1 in the series *The Critical Idiom*, edited by John D. Jump.

19 This is a summary, with quotations, of Leech, *Tragedy*, pp. 16, 22–5.

20 Walter Kerr, *Tragedy and Comedy* (London, 1967), pp. 87–8.

21 Geoffrey Brereton, *Principles of Tragedy*, pp. 19–20.

18 The king as centre of political life

1 The title of this play strikes one as strange. One would expect it to be 'To Know Good and Evil' in accordance with the origin of the phrase, namely with the serpent's temptation of Adam and Eve. N. D. Shergold and J. E. Varey ('Some early Calderonian dates', *Bulletin of Hispanic Studies*, 38 (1961), 274–86), note that 'in the document [i.e. of payment to the theatre company which first performed the play] the title appears as *Saber del bien y del mal*' (p. 284). In fact the end of each act refers to the developing theme and every time the title of the play is quoted or referred to with Good and Evil in their traditional order. The play was included by José Calderón in the first volume of Calderón's *comedias*, which he published in 1636. The title there appears with 'good and evil' inverted. If this was a slip, it established itself.

2 *BAE*, I, p. 30c.

3 *Teatro de los teatros* (2nd version 1692–4); ed. Duncan W. Moir (London, 1970), p. 57. For an account of the way Bances Candamo developed his own 'art of speaking without telling', see Edward M. Wilson and Duncan Moir, *The Golden Age: Drama 1492–1700* (London, 1971), pp. 140–2. This is part of the series *A Literary History of Spain*, chief editor R. O. Jones. Cf. especially: 'Careful study of his works shows techniques of allusion and persuasion which can illuminate the study of the popular and court drama of the seventeenth century as a whole (for there is reason to suggest political intent in the dramas long before Bances's time)' (p. 142). See also Moir's edition of *El esclavo en grillos de oro* in *Clásicos castellanos*.

4 Anthony Watson, *Juan de la Cueva and the Portuguese Succession* (London, Tamesis Books Ltd., 1971).

5 For the drama's implicit attack on the new aristocracy, see Julio Caro
Baroja's 'Honour and shame: a historical account of several conflicts', in
Honour and Shame. The Values of Mediterranean Society, ed. J. G. Peristiany
(London, 1965), pp. 81–137. For the identification of the man holding the
office of Comendador de Ocaña when *Peribáñez* was written, see Noël
Salomon, 'Toujours la date de *Peribáñez y el comendador de Ocaña*.
"Tragicomedia" de Lope de Vega' in *Mélanges offerts à Marcel Bataillon par
les hispanistes français* (Bordeaux, 1962: vol. 64 bis of *Bulletin Hispanique*),
613–43.

19 Religion and the state: *La cisma de Ingalaterra*

This essay was first published with the title 'Henry VIII in Shakespeare
and Calderón: An appreciation of *La cisma de Ingalaterra*' (*Modern
Language Review*, 43 (1948), 327–57; republished in *Critical Studies of
Calderón's comedias*, ed. J. E. Varey (London, 1973), pp. 47–83. The
comparison and contrast of the play with *Henry VIII*, in the writing of
which Fletcher is generally thought to have had a large share, was
intended not so much as a study in comparative literature but as an
attempt to bring Calderón to the attention of English-speaking scholars.
In 1948 Calderón had scarcely advanced much in favour in Spain, and
hardly at all in other Spanish-speaking countries; in England he was
virtually unknown among non-Hispanists. As far as I am aware, only two
students of English literature discussed this comparison of the two plays
from the other angle: Anthony Herbold, in 'Shakespeare, Calderón, and
Henry the Eighth', *East-West Review*, 2 (1965), 17–32, and John Loftis, in
'Henry VIII and Calderón's *La cisma de Inglaterra*', *Comparative Literature*,
34 (1982), 208–22. The comparison with Shakespeare–Fletcher is here
dropped, there being no point in retaining it for this particular volume.
Readers interested in the discussion this raised are referred to the above
papers. Apart from this, the only substantial change made to the original
essay concerns the ending, which deals with the possible reason why
Calderón should have taken up this theme of English history. Several
years later a document was discovered which gave the date of a private
performance of this play in the royal palace. This meant, surprisingly,
that the play was written much earlier than had generally been thought,
and this earlier date raises the possibility of a quite different connection
with contemporary events, which is developed in chapter 20. This
connection gives a much more satisfactory explanation of the freedom
Calderón takes with history.

1 The title of *La cisma de Ingalaterra* should retain the old spelling of
'Inglaterra'. With it the title is an octosyllabic line, and where it occurs in
the text the modern spelling would ruin the metre, as for example in
'depóngala Ingalaterra'. More often than not the titles of Spanish plays
are octosyllabic because the title was generally mentioned at the end of
the play when one of the characters stepped forward to address the
audience on behalf of the dramatist and ask their pardon for the play's

shortcomings. *La cisma de Ingalaterra* is an exception to this particular convention. The ending of the play suggested a possible alternative title 'Y aquí acaba la comedia/del docto ignorante Enrique/y muerte de Ana Bolena' (Here ends the story which tells of the learned ignoramus Henry and of the death of Anne Boleyn). It is fortunate that this much weaker title did not prevail.

2 e.g. Chamberlain   It seems the marriage with his brother's wife
Has crept too near his conscience.
Suffolk   No, his conscience
has crept too near another lady.   (II, ii, 17–19)
And, later,
2nd Gentleman Sir, as I have a soul, she is an angel;
Our king has all the Indies in his arms,
And more and richer, when he strains that lady:
I cannot blame his conscience.   (IV, i, 44–7)
from *The Famous History of the Life of King Henry the Eighth.*

3 It is really immaterial which work he handled, since Ribadeneyra's First Part is an adaptation of the second, or Rome, edition of Sander's work, which besides the continuation by Edward Rishton contains the numerous additions made by a second editor, who may have been Robert Persons (or Parsons). Ribadeneyra translates long portions of this work, but he alters other parts freely and makes additions of his own. The common assumption that the whole work is a translation is erroneous. As Ribadeneyra enters into Edward's reign he becomes much more independent of Rishton's continuation to Sander and draws freely on other sources, bringing his material up to date by relating the imprisonment and execution of Mary Queen of Scots. His Second Part (Book III), which covers the years 1588–92 and which was published in 1593, is entirely original, and was added as a Fourth Book to the 1610 and subsequent editions of Sander's History. Though omitted from Conyers Read's Bibliography of the Tudor period of English history, Ribadeneyra's work still deserves to be read – not because it is full of impassioned invective, but because it is so eloquent a witness both to the intensity of anti-English feeling among the Spaniards of the time and to their ignorance of the nature of the English Reformation. It reads like an account of the excesses of the Anabaptists; and this ignorance fanned legimate hostility to a quite unwholesome pitch of indignation. Ribadeneyra's language is much more violent than Sander's, even where he is following the latter's text closely.

4 *(BAE)*, LX, p. 190b; all references are to this edition.

5 *BAE*, II, p. 226c; all references are to page and column of this text.

6 *Volseo*: Pienso que Dios me castiga/sólo porque la hice bien. *Reina*: Hiciéraste tu a quien fuera/agradecida. *Volseo*: Sospecho/que si bien hubiera hecho/a otra persona, tuviera/en pena fiera/el sentimiento doblado;/pues en la suerte que sigo,/advierto y digo/que a tener otro

obligado,/ya tuviera otro enemigo. /*Reina*: ¿Que a tal extremo has
llegado?
(*Wolsey*: I think God is punishing me only because I furthered her
interests. *Queen*: You should have done that to a woman who would
have thanked you for it. *Wolsey*: I suspect that if I had furthered the
interests of anyone else, I would now have my regrets doubled in the way
I would be suffering now by regretting it twice over; for in the lot that is
now mine, I affirm that if I had earned the gratitude of somebody else, I
would now have an additional enemy. *Queen*: Have you sunk to such
depths?) (228c).

7 Ribadeneyra p. 203b. In the grading of dramatic 'punishments' the
severest that a Spanish dramatist of the Golden Age could mete out was
suicide, for it was generally believed that this act would leave no time for
repentance before the actual moment of dying, and that the soul would
be damned. Suicides are for this reason rare on the Spanish stage.
Calderón is therefore seeing no redeeming spark in Wolsey.

8 As Ludwig Pfandl in 'Ausdrucksformen des archaischen Denkens und des
Unbewussten bei Calderón' in *Gesammelte Aufsätze zur Kulturgeschichte
Spaniens*, ed. H. Finke, First series (1937), vol. VI) reminds us, the
ceremonial gesture of placing something on one's head was a sign of
reverence or acceptance of authority. He explains the shuffling of the
letters as 'ein Meisterstück psychologischer Dramaturgie' (a masterstroke
of psychological dramatic technique), since it is a clear example of
Fehlleistung – an unwilled action by which the unconscious is made
conscious. Henry becomes aware of what he had formerly repressed –
through an 'informative dream', of a desire for a younger wife; through
the *Fehlleistung*, of a desire to perfect his kingship by being pope in his
own country. The real importance of the incident lies in the imagery it
gives rise to. In any case the *Fehlleistung* is Wolsey's, not Henry's. Two
other examples of these 'Freudian slips' introducing important
developments in the action were noted: Anne tripping and falling at
Henry's feet – her unconscious desire to be queen asserting itself against
her conscious dislike of kneeling before the king; and the 'slip of the
tongue' by which Wolsey addresses Anne as 'Your Majesty'. But the first
of these is required to illustrate the imagery in action; and it is perfectly
clear from the context that the second is an *intentional* ruse to test how
far Wolsey can go with Anne. Pfandl's general conclusion was that
Calderón's importance as a poet is enhanced by his presenting a synthesis
of the three attitudes to the world that have been epochs in the
development of mankind: he stands in the middle of the 'religious age',
but he has roots in the 'primitive', and branches that reach up to
'rationalism'.

9 This is probably an echo of an anecdote related of Diogenes, the Cynic
philosopher, who was said to have gone out with a lighted torch in broad
daylight to find a human being in a square crowded with people.

(Recorded by Diogenes Laertius, VI, ii, 60). This is mentioned by Baltasar Gracián in his treatise on Wit. He lists this in the section dealing with 'Wit in action, significant for its inventiveness', *Agudeza y arte de ingenio*, Huesca, 1648, ed. Evaristo Correa Calderón, *Clásicos Castalia* (Madrid, 1969), vol. II, Discurso XLVII, p. 141.

10 Task of uncovering pretension and hypocrisy.

11 Calderón was to make consistent use of his ascent–descent imagery shortly afterwards, in *La cena de Baltasar*, an *auto sacramental* allegorising the theme of Belshazzar's feast (before 1635). He did not there link it with light–darkness. The symbolical nature of the Eucharistic stage enabled him to use upward and downward movements with great effect. See A. A. Parker, *The Allegorical Drama of Calderón* (Oxford and London, 1943), pp. 169–72.

12 221c–222a. This incident expresses the inevitability of Henry's future fall. It is impossible for him not to help Anne to rise; but through the imagery stage movement is connected with moral action.

13 Note the irony of Anne's remark to him as she resists his passionate wooing. On the grounds that his position is too exalted, she says: 'Mira a lo que has llegado,/que para ti es desmérito el estado' (See what you have come to, that for you your station is demeritorious) (223b).

14 (225b). Henry's reliance on the unscrupulous use of his political power is derived from Ribadeneyra: 'Henry saw that his divorce was not as well received in the kingdom as he had wished, and that all the pious, prudent and serious-minded persons spoke about it with great regret; and wishing to forestall and cut short this obstacle at the outset, he took advice that was foolish and beyond all bounds: he determined no longer to deal with this matter by way of personal command, but through the public authority and decision of the whole kingdom; and realising that he could achieve his end (as is usually the case with kings), he summoned parliament on 3 November 1534. He knew that the Church leaders were on his side, and that some other bishops would not oppose him, and that Episcopus Roffensis [John Fisher, Bishop of Rochester] was imprisoned, and that as regards the others who might oppose him, it would be easy either to banish them from parliament, or to force them to his will by promises, threats and persuasion; he already had on his side a large number of the nobles and the gentry, because he had created many of them, and he was certain that these and all who were infected with the Lutheran heresy (and there were many) would not do or wish other than as he commanded . . . Through these ministers and by such dishonest means Henry arranged that parliament should decide everything as he wished' (210b–11a).

15 '. . . the punishment of Hell, which his wretched soul is now suffering, and which, after the Day of Judgement, in union with his miserable body, it will suffer for all eternity . . . will last for ever, as long as God is God' (233a).

16 A. P. Rossiter, in the preface to his edition of *Woodstock* (1946), deals

with the play's free presentation of history. The liberties taken are 'most particularly in making Tresilian responsible for iniquities which happened nine or ten years after he was hanged, and in presenting Thomas of Woodstock as he certainly never was' (pp. 20–1). 'If this is merely careless handling of history . . . it is a curiously constructive carelessness . . . In other words, events are arranged in a coherent plot with a distinguishable argument, and this is the play's aim – not an accurate historical account of Richard II and his parasites' (p. 20). Rossiter also gives a summary of the great liberties Shakespeare allowed himself with history in *Henry VI* (pp. 69–70). W. D. Briggs, in the preface to his edition of Marlowe's *Edward II* (1914), remarks on the 'condensations of chronology . . . universally practised in the Elizabethan period' (p. lxxi). That 'condensations' is here used in a wide sense approaching Calderón's repudiation of fact is apparent from at least one of the examples quoted. The hero of *Sir John Oldcastle* (by Drayton and others) is represented as loyal to Henry V when in actual fact he was executed as a traitor.

20 The issue of religious freedom

1 Ribadeneyra, *Historia ecclesiastica del scisma del reynu de Inglaterra*, p. 317b. This quotation is from the Second Part, published in 1593.
2 The above is summarised from Martin Hume, *The Court of Philip IV* (London, 1907), pp. 67–123. Full account was taken by Hume of Spanish sources.
3 Godfrey Davies, *The Early Stuarts 1603–1660* (Oxford, 1937), p. 52.
4 Davies, *ibid.*, p. 27.

21 Religion and war: *El príncipe constante*

This chapter reproduces, with some alterations and additions, the paper entitled 'Christian values and drama: *El príncipe constante*' in *Studia Iberica, Festschrift für Hans Flasche*, ed. Karl-Hermann Körner and Klaus Rühl (Berne/Munich, Franke Verlag, 1973), pp. 441–58.

1 There is an excellent study of the origins and development of the martyr plays in Europe, with analyses of representative examples, in Elida Maria Szarota, *Künstler, Grübler und Rebellen. Studien zum europäischen Martyrerdrama des 17. Jahrhunderts* (Berne/Munich, 1967).
2 For a study of this play, see the edition and commentary by Melveena McKendrick and A. A. Parker (not yet published).
3 This play was edited by A. E. Sloman, who gave a full account of the historical episode and the stages in the development of the legend in *The Sources of Calderón's El Príncipe Constante* (Oxford, 1950). In a later book, Sloman made a structural comparison of this play and *El príncipe constante*: see *The Dramatic Craftsmanship of Calderón* (Oxford, 1958), ch. VII, pp. 188–216.
4 See Szarota, *Künstler, Grübler und Rebellen*. This has been so far the only

work to place *El príncipe constante* within the European dramatic tradition to which it properly belongs.

5 G. Steiner, *The Death of Tragedy* (London, 1963), pp. 331–3.

6 M. Jarrett-Kerr, 'Calderón and the imperialism of belief' in *Studies in Literature and Belief* (London, 1954), p. 62.

7 A. G. Reichenberger, 'Calderón's *El príncipe constante*, a tragedy?' in *Critical Essays on the Theatre of Calderón*, ed. B. W. Wardropper (New York 1965), p. 163. Similar arguments are put forward in Y. Gulsoy and J. H. Parker, '*El príncipe constante*: Drama barroco de la contrarreforma', *Hispanófila*, 3/9 (1960), 15–23. A more interesting argument from the point of view of dramatic structure is given by W. Kayser, 'Zur Struktur des *Standhaften Prinzen* von Calderón' in W. Kayser, *Die Vortragsreise. Studien zur Literatur*, Berne, 1958, pp. 254–6.

8 Szarota, *Künstler, Grübler and Rebellen*, pp. 131, 137.

9 M. Jarret-Kerr, p. 46, maintains that in *El príncipe constante* 'the religious motive is too mixed up with the political for clarity'. This is quite mistaken.

10 Notably by E. M. Wilson, in his and W. J. Entwistle's 'Calderón's *Príncipe constante*: two appreciations', *Modern Language Review*, 34 (1939), 207–22; and by B. W. Wardropper, 'Christian and Moor in Calderón's *El príncipe constante*', *Modern Language Review*, 53 (1958) 512–20.

11 *El príncipe constante*, ed. A. A. Parker (Cambridge, 1938 and 1957, reissued 1968) (Cambridge Plain Texts) p. 45; [*BAE*, I, p. 252c]. All references to the text are to the pages of these editions in this order.

12 Not here ignorance of geography: 'Caucasus' was used metaphorically of a lofty mountain.

13 'The new conception of Fernando necessarily affected Enrique who had to take second place. But Calderón saw in Enrique the means of setting Fernando into relief by contrast, and the renowned Henry the Navigator, whose very recklessness was probably the primary cause of the Tangier disaster, is converted into one who is diffident and defeatist . . . Historical truth was incompatible with what was dramatically appropriate only to the extent that Enrique should be subordinate to Fernando' (Sloman, *The Dramatic Craftsmanship of Calderón*, pp. 203–4).

14 This is the reading of the *Primera Parte* in the first edition 1636 (QCL) and in the two editions of 1640 (VSL, VS). (For this nomenclature see E. M. Wilson, 'The two editions of Calderón's *Primera Parte* of 1640' in *The Transactions of the Bibliographical Society: The Library* (September 1959), pp. 175–91.) Vera Tassis emended the second *mía* to *suya* and this has been followed by later editors, including Valbuena Briones (p. 243a) and Hartzenbusch [*BAE*, I, p. 260b]. In my edition (p. 88) I was rash enough not just to accept this emendation but even to alter the first *mío* to *tuyo*, on the grounds that to retain even it alone gave Alfonso an arrogance out of keeping with his rôle as a second Fernando. I take this opportunity of recanting this juvenile rashness. Where the earliest texts are

unanimous, a reading must not be altered to suit what appears the likeliest interpretation; an interpretation must be found that suits the text.

15 The fact that the battle is won at night by the light of the ghost's torch is perhaps also significant, since no battles are, or at least were, won at night. The night may signify the uncertainty and confusion of human life in this world – the Fortune so often mentioned in the play, who capriciously assigns victory or defeat. Beyond this darkness there is only one goal, not political honour but salvation, to reach which there is only one light to follow, not arrogant aggression but faith.

16 Fernando's prayer is not a claim to canonisation as a reward for his services to God, but the hope that his bones may rest in a chantry chapel where masses may be offered for his soul: '[espero que] rescatado he de gozar/el sufragio del altar' ([I hope that] when ransomed I shall receive the suffrage of the church.) (86) [260a].

17 Despite this, to quote this scene in translation as well as in the original would add inordinately to the length of this chapter: with great reluctance, the Spanish is sacrificed.

18 When a refrain of this type occurs in a Calderón play, Calderón is often quoting a song that many of his readers would recognise. These quoted songs have been identified and studied by E. M. Wilson and Jack Sage in *Poesías líricas en las obras dramáticas de Calderón. Citas y glosas* (London, 1964). The only parallel they found to this one (pp. 6–7) is 'Al peso de los años/se rinde lo excelente/que a su imperio inconstante/no hay valor eminente' (All excellence succumbs to the weight of the years; for all excellence submits to its inconstant rule). This is a poem by Padre Pedro de Quirós; since he died in 1667, thirty-eight years after *El príncipe constante* was written, it is likely that it is he who was the imitator.

19 The 'I' of Fernando answering the question that Fénix directs to herself is an accidental coincidence and not Fernando's conscious reply to a question, for he does not hear it. Accidental omens of this kind are not infrequent in Calderón. Fénix, who takes the 'I' to be a direct answer, is astonished that the prince should be the ominous danger, and at his assuming the function of a servant. Leo Spitzer, however, took it to be the conscious answer to a heard question, and expressed surprise that no critic had analysed why Fernando should make himself the 'dead man' haunting Fénix's mind. ('Die Figur der Fénix in Calderóns *Standhaften Prinzen*', *Romanistisches Jahrbuch*, 10 (1959), pp. 305–53; translated into English, and abbreviated, in *Critical Essays on the Theatre of Calderón*, pp. 137–60. There are other misrepresentations of Calderón's text and some mistranslations in this essay.

20 'Maravilla' means 'marvel', 'wonder', and 'surprise'. The flower denoted by this name is in modern Spanish the marigold (calendula officinalis) and this is how Spitzer and Max Krenkel in his edition of the play identified it. The *Diccionario de autoridades* (1726), however, describes it as having blue, bell-shaped flowers striped with red, which open at

daybreak but close immediately the sun strikes them. This is not, of course, a description of the marigold, which is daisy-shaped, orange and one of the longest lasting of all flowers. The Espasa-Calpe encyclopaedia lists twelve flowering plants called 'maravilla' throughout the Spanish-speaking world. The *Enciclopedia argentina* gives only one of these under the name *Mirabilis Jalapa*, known in English as the Marvel of Peru, stating that it is very widespread in the Americas. On the strength of this and of the generic name (*mirabilis*) I chose this flower in the paper on which this chapter is based (see footnote 15 of that paper). I wish to withdraw this identification in favour of the genus *Ipomoea*, which belongs to the convolvulus family, with flowers that are more 'bell-shaped' than those of the Marvel of Peru, and whose species are natives of tropical America. The genus was first introduced in 1597. There are several species which among themselves vary between blue and red-purple. *Ipomoea rubra-caerulea* is a likely candidate. The popular name of 'Morning Glory' for the genus points to the flowers being 'fleeting marvels'.

21 Leo Spitzer, 'Die Figur der Fénix in Calderóns *Standhaften Prinzen*', misunderstood 'lo fácil del tiempo', when he took it to refer to the youthful beauty of Fénix, for whom every conquest is easy (of Muley, of Tarudante, and – perhaps – of Fernando). The phrase means simply the irresistible ease with which time conquers everything (pp. 305–53/pp. 137–60 of English translation).

22 Szarota, *Künstler, Grübler und Rebellen* (p. 138), for example, maintained that Calderón presented the Portuguese, or at least their government, in a false historical light. It is inconceivable that a country that was making such great efforts to expand overseas should have been willing to hand over a fortress as militarily and economically important as Ceuta in exchange for a single prisoner, no matter how exalted in status. It could be objected, she continued, that the action of the play takes place as early as 1437, but Portugal, which came to develop so far-flung an empire, could never have proved untrue to her politico-religious mission by accepting such a proposal; in the play the Portuguese rulers do not understand what the honour of their country demands, only Fernando does. Behind this impression that the play gives, there is concealed the fact that Calderón, the Spaniard, is criticising Portugal for failing to defend her empire against the Dutch and the English; Spain, he implies, would have performed better. In actual fact, it is Szarota's conception of the Portuguese in 1437 that is unhistorical. They could not bring themselves to ransom Fernando for the price demanded, and the later expedition was organised to rescue him.

23 In the same volume in which the above essay was published in its original form, there appeared another on the same play by Jack Sage, 'The constant phoenix. Text and performance of Calderón's *El príncipe constante*' in *Studia Iberica. Festschrift für Hans Flasche*, ed. Körner and Rühl (Berne, 1973), pp. 561–74. Quite independently, this essay offered a revaluation of the play from the same basic standpoint as mine.

22 The drama as commentary on public affairs

1 Emilio Cotarelo y Mori, *Ensayo sobre la vida y obras de D. Pedro Calderón de la Barca* (Madrid, 1924), p.177, quotes from a manuscript collection of news items for 1636, in which the promulgation of the decree is given as hearsay. The courtiers would obviously have had advance information and the play would have been written quickly, by three dramatists, and rushed into print.

2 *Obras completas*, Aguilar (Madrid, 1959), ed. Ángel Valbuena Briones, vol. I, p.1313b. [*BAE*, III, p.209c].

3 For a study of this play, see Margaret Wilson, '"Si Africa llora, España no ríe": A study of Calderón's *Amar después de la muerte* in relation to its source', *BHS*, 51, 3 (July 1984), *Golden Age Studies in Honour of A. A. Parker*, ed. Melveena McKendrick, pp.419–25.

4 *Obras completas*, Aguilar, I, *Dramas* (p.347b) [*BAE*, III, p.695c].

5 The nautical sense of 'berja' or 'verja' has long been obsolete. Corominas (*Diccionario crítico etimológico*) defines this former meaning as one of the hooks for fastening sails.

6 *Imperial Spain, 1469–1716* (1963), p.303.

7 Cotarelo (p.149) states that the periodical *El Averiguador* had given 1633 as the date of a palace performance of *Más puede amor que la muerte*, and supposes that this was in fact *Amar después de la muerte*. In fact, that was a play by Pérez de Montalbán. The bibliographical details of this play given in the bibliography of Montalbán's plays by M. G. Profeti show that this is not Calderón's play.

8 The New Christians in Portugal had lived in a less restricted and secretive way than those in Castile, due to a number of general pardons which, over the years, they had negotiated in order to counter persecution. These general pardons dated from the 1530s. The most far-reaching was granted by the young King Sebastian in exchange for a very large sum of money promised him by the Jewish community. This particular pardon gave them ten years' freedom from confiscation of property and freedom to leave the country. (See Julio Caro Baroja, *Los judíos en la España moderna y contemporánea* (Madrid, 1961), vol. I, pp.342–9.)

9 The document is one of a series of Inquisition papers published by Elkan N. Adler in *Revue des Études Juives*, and then serialised as follows: 48 (1904), 1–28; 49 (1904), 51–73; 50 (1905), 53–75; 51 (1906), 97–120 and 251–64. The document summarised above is in 51, 115–20, 251–64.

10 During the economic crisis of 1627–9, Olivares sought the help of financiers and businessmen, but this did not prevent the Inquisition taking an anti-Jewish line. In fact, according to Caro Baroja (*Los judios*, vol. II, pp.40, 42–6) an anti-Jewish faction arose which constituted the real opposition to Olivares. Quevedo in *La hora de todos* (1635) has a bitterly sarcastic attack on Olivares and his alleged pro-Jewish policy. The influx of Portuguese New Christians into Spain continued; in fact, 'Portuguese' and 'Jew' became synonymous.

11 Max Krenkel, *Klassische Bühnendichtungen der Spanier*, vol. III (Leipzig, 1887), p. 69.

12 The best-known example is in *Guzmán de Alfarache*, the picaresque novel by Mateo Alemán, whose first part was published in 1599. Pedro Crespo is mentioned near the beginning of chapter I (ed. *Clásicos castellanos*, 1968, vol. I, p. 66); see the note on p. 66. See also Francisco Rico's edition in *La novela picaresca española* (Barcelona, 1967), p. 120, n. 63.

13 These news items are known as the *Avisos de Pellicer* (José Pellicer de Tovar) and were published in the eighteenth century in a miscellany entitled *Semanario erudito*, vol. XXXI (1780). The ones summarised above occur on pp. 73, 124 and 140. There is an interesting slip in Hartzenbusch's transcription of the *Aviso* for 20 September 1639. He calls the executed nobleman Don Álvaro instead of Don Alonso, thus linking him directly with the dramatic character.

14 For the dating of the play, independently of the *Avisos*, see Peter N. Dunn's edition of *El alcalde de Zalamea* (Oxford, 1966), p. 7.

15 *Iberoromania*, 14 (1981), 42–59.

16 For these comparisons and other details, see García Gómez, *ibid.*, 55–6.

17 See García Gómez, *ibid.*, 58–9.

23 The court drama

1 On Calderón's music dramas, see Jack Sage, 'The function of music in the theatre of Calderón' in *Critical Studies of Calderón's Comedias*, ed. J. E. Varey, *Pedro Calderón de la Barca, Comedias: A Facsimile Edition*, vol. 19 (London, 1973), pp. 209–30; Sage, 'Nouvelles lumières sur la genèse de l'opéra et la zarzuela en Espagne', *Baroque*, 5 (1972), 107–14; Sage, 'Texto y realización de *La estatua de Prometeo* y otros dramas musicales de Calderón' in *Hacia Calderón*, ed. Hans Flasche, Coloquio Anglogermano, Exeter, 1969 (Berlin, Walter de Gruyter, 1970), pp. 37–52. On the music of *La estatua de Prometeo*, see also chapter 2, by Louise K. Stein, in the edition of the play by Margaret Rich Greer, in the series *Teatro del siglo de oro*, Ediciones Críticas, 7 (Kassel edn, Reichenberger, 1986). This chapter covers the rise of music drama in Spain and publishes parts of the musical score.

2 N. D. Shergold, *A History of the Spanish Stage* (Oxford, 1967), chs. 9–12.

3 See *A Palace for a King. The Buen Retiro and the Court of Philip IV* (New Haven, Yale University Press, 1980), by Jonathan Brown and J. H. Elliott. For the Coliseo, see pp. 31–54.

4 J. E. Varey, 'The audience and the play at court spectacles: the role of the king' in *Golden-Age Studies in Honour of A. A. Parker, Bulletin of Hispanic Studies*, 61, no. 3 (July 1984), edited by Melveena McKendrick, pp. 399–409; see pages 402 and 405. This paper is a concise but substantial account of the purpose and nature of these Royal entertainments in the seventeenth century.

5 For an analysis of this play based on the text, see A. A. Parker, *The Philosophy of Love in Spanish Literature 1480–1680* (Edinburgh, 1985), pp. 176–83.

6 Sebastian Neumeister, *Mythos und Repräsentation. Die mythologischen Festspiele Calderóns* (Munich, 1978). This is the only attempt so far made to interpret Calderón's mythological *comedias* within the totality of the court theatrical festivities. He attaches so much importance to every aspect of the productions that he coins a word to denote the special quality given to a Calderonian court play by the nature of the festival for which it was written – *Occasionalität*. The book is very erudite, but is unfortunately so over-crowded with interpretations of every aspect of the 'Occasion' that it is very difficult to follow, and indeed impossible to summarise adequately. Perhaps one may hazard the statement that it attempts to interpret the plays and the 'Occasion' in the light of modern sociological and psychological theories, and modern Marxist ideas on politics and history. Although several plays are studied in great detail, it is, from at least one reader's point of view, impossible to accept the results as justifiable interpretations of Calderón's thought and artistry, there is so much unresolved confusion of critical ideas and methodology, and much irrelevant and misguided scholarship.

7 The play closes with the wedding of Pandora and Prometeo. In the last scene, Discord flees, and the eyes of Prometeo and Epimeteo, who have been in hostile rivalry, are suddenly opened to its meaninglessness, and they become reconciled. Cotarelo (p. 323) conjectured that this referred to the formal ending of the war with Portugal in 1669 with a peace treaty. On the death of Philip IV in 1665, the court theatres were closed and did not re-open until January 1670. A production of Calderón's Hercules play, *Fieras afemina amor* (Wild Beasts are Tamed by Love) had been planned to celebrate the queen's birthday on 22 December 1669, and this performance took place in January. Margaret Greer discusses at length all possible conjectures about the date of the first performance of *La estatua de Prometeo* and concludes authoritatively that it was 1670 (her edition, pp. 93–5).

8 For the various forms of the myth and their development, as well as a study of Calderón's possible sources, see the admirable study by Margaret Rich Greer of *La estatua de Prometeo*, pp. 105–32. She concludes that 'the original shape and dramatic power of *La estatua de Prometeo* derive not from any previous renderings of the myth, but from Calderón's unique dramatic genius' (p. 132).

9 *La estatua de Prometeo*, p. 237 [*BAE*, III, p. 706]. The text follows the old spelling, but it is here modernised to fit into the framework of the book.

10 e.g. *La hija del aire*, Primera Parte, the opening stage directions of the first Act are as follows: 'Mountain . . . a door on the left hand side, and the sound of knocking, and Semíramis within, shouting . . . [Tiresias] opens the door and Semíramis emerges dressed in skins.'

11 Dangerous wild beasts in the pastoral settings of Calderón's court plays
are not uncommon. They of course symbolise evil of some kind. A
striking case can be found in *Eco y Narciso*. Liríope, the mother of
Narciso, had been raped by a son of the Wind; overcome with horror and
shame, she fled from men into self-imposed confinement. She hunts for
food for Narciso and herself, and, never distinctly discerned by the
shepherds, she is thought to be a dangerous wild beast. See A. A. Parker,
The Philosophy of Love in Spanish Literature 1480–1680, pp. 189–93.

12 It is the main theme of the final section on Calderón in A. A. Parker, *ibid.*

24 Mythology and humanism

1 *Divinae Institutiones, Patrologia Latina*, VI, c. 535.

2 Marcelino Menéndez Pelayo, *Calderón y su teatro, estudios y discursos de
crítica histórica y literaria*, III, Edición nacional de las obras completas de
Menéndez Pelayo (Santander, 1941), p. 145.

3 *El laberinto del mundo, Obras completas*, Aguilar, III, p. 1558a. This is a
paraphrase of the Pauline text. Calderón of course knew the Vulgate, but
there is no real difference between this text and the modern translation of
the Revised Standard Version, which runs as follows: 'Ever since the
creation of the world, his invisible nature, namely, his eternal power and
deity, has been clearly perceived in the things that have been made. So
they [the Gentiles] are without excuse; for although they knew God they
did not honour him as God or give thanks to him, but they became futile
in their thinking and their senseless minds were darkened. Claiming to be
wise, they became fools, and exchanged the glory of the immortal God for
images resembling mortal man or birds or animals or reptiles.'

4 Judges, ch. VI, 36–40. As the first sign of the promise of victory, Gideon
spreads a fleece on the ground and asks that the dew should fall on it
alone, leaving the surrounding ground dry; for the second sign Gideon
asks that the dew should fall on the ground, leaving the fleece dry. This
is one of Calderón's favourite Messianic symbols. Many of the fathers and
later commentators saw in these two signs a prophecy of the future, the
simplest interpretation being that the dew on the fleece and not on the
ground represents the Messiah sent first to the Jews, the dew on the
ground and not on the fleece means that, when the Messiah was rejected
by the Jews, the message of salvation went to the Gentiles. Calderón
develops this symbolism in an *auto* entitled *La piel de Gedeón*, where the
signs of the dew and the fleece are presented spectacularly, with very
beautiful poetry.

5 The Golden Fleece carried off to Colchis and guarded by monsters
symbolises Fallen Humanity in the power of the Devil; its recovery by
Jason symbolises humanity's restoration to grace by Christ. *El divino Jasón*
is the title of an *auto* published in 1664 under Calderón's name. It is a
very poor *auto*, and there are no other grounds for considering it
authentic. Ángel Valbuena Prat, its editor, thought it could be a very

early work by Calderón, while conceding that its structure was characteristic of the earlier generation of dramatists.

6 Calderón here associates this prophecy with Gideon's fleece when he says that the dew will fall on finer mother-of-pearl (when Mary conceives Jesus).

7 *El laberinto del mundo, Obras completas*, iii, p. 1847b.

8 This is a frequent flaw in Sebastian Neumeister's *Mythos und Repräsentation. Die mythologischen Festspiele Calderóns* (Munich, 1978), (referred to above): where myths or sections of myths have a similar 'structure', he tends to associate them ideologically even though Calderón makes no such association.

9 The reason for this pairing was Calderón's realisation that in his allegorisations of Satan's temptation of Adam and Eve in the Garden, he would be exposing himself to the accusation of Manichaeism (the belief that Evil was a Power in its own right, independent of God). Calderón's avoidance of this is ingenious and subtle. See A. A. Parker, 'The theology of the Devil in the drama of Calderón', The Aquinas Society of London: Aquinas Paper 32 (Blackfriars Publications, 1958), pp. 6–11.

25 The destiny of man

1 *La estatua de Prometeo*, edited by Margaret Rich Greer, in the series *Teatro del siglo de oro*, Ediciones Críticas, 7 (Kassel, edn, Reichenberger, 1986), Act II, ll. 236–8. The text follows the old spelling, but it is here modernised to fit into the framework of the book. [*BAE*, iii, 708a]

2 The excellent edition and study of *La estatua de Prometeo* by Margaret Rich Greer, referred to above, has a much longer and more complex analysis of the theme than the two-part analysis offered in chapter 23 and in the present one. She covers every detail of this difficult play, while my interpretation is an attempt to select the essential elements of the crowded theme. Greer's analysis is 'philosophical', but based on the characters as human beings with their passions and rivalries, rewards and punishments. My analysis on the other hand has attempted to circumscribe the symbolism and so give a more conceptual interpretation of the characters. Greer's interpretation comes under the heading of the 'universal myth' (144–69), which she defines as 'both a glorification of human reason *and* a recognition of reason's limitations', But she sees this as one of three 'texts' or 'systems of meaning', the other two being 'the myth of royal power' (pp. 135–52), and 'the political myth' (169–72). By the first she understands the belief emphasised by the production and by the setting that peace in human society depends on the beneficent rule of the monarchy. Greer says that Calderón equates his mythological deities with the royal family. There is actually no equation; it is left to the audience to make the assumption, and while the play does maintain that social harmony depends on respect for authority, the theme of the play is much closer to suggesting the authority of God than that of the Habsburg

monarchy. Basing herself on Stephen Orgel's *The Illusion of Power: Political Theatre in the English Renaissance* (University of California Press, 1975), she suggests that part of the purpose of *La estatua de Prometeo* was to suggest to king and ministers that they and their exercise of power were by no means perfect. In other words that this play may be an example of 'speaking without telling'. Charles Aubrun had suggested in his edition of *La estatua de Prometeo* (Paris, 1965) that the rivalry of Prometeo and Epimeteo reflected the struggle between rival factions at court. Greer offers much fuller and more interesting evidence in support of this theory and for identifying Prometeo with Philip IV's illegitimate son, Don Juan José de Austria (173–87).

3 Calderón, *Obras completas*, III. *Autos sacramentales*, ed. Ángel Valbuena Prat (Madrid, 1952), 78a–b. The Spanish text quoted above is supported by the critical edition of Manfred Engelbert in the series *Calderoniana*, vol. 2 (Hamburg, 1969). All the texts, manuscript or published, have 'que por ser tengo de hacer'. It would seem, however, that *nacer* instead of *hacer* would make better sense: 'que por ser tengo de nacer'; 'that in order to exist, I must be born'.

4 This passage, incidentally, is the only clear indication known to me in the whole of Calderón's theological drama of Molinism in its proper context, that of Salvation (see pp. 111–12 above).

5 A full analysis of the *auto* of *La vida es sueño* can be found in A. A. Parker, *The Allegorical Drama of Calderón. An Introduction to the Autos Sacramentales* (Oxford, Dolphin, 1943), pp. 202–29.

Epilogue

1 *Revista Canadiense de Estudios Hispánicos*, 6 (1982), p. 285.

2 A valiant attempt at such a Spanish World-Picture was made by Otis H. Green, in *Spain and the Western Tradition*, 4 volumes (Madison, University of Wisconsin Press, vol. I, 1963; vol. II, 1964; vol. III, 1965; vol. IV, 1966). It is a useful compilation, but not a substitute for critical studies of the literature of the period.

3 See, for example, the essay by L. C. Knights, '*King Lear* as metaphor' in *Myth and Symbol, Critical Approaches and Applications* by Northrop Frye, L. C. Knights and others (University of Nebraska Press, Bison Books, 1963). References to other 'metaphorical' interpretations of Shakespeare plays are referred to in this essay.

4 *Scepticism and Poetry, An Essay on the Poetic Imagination*, by D. G. James (London, 1937), pp. 214–15. See this whole passage in its context for a fuller description of these four Shakespearean myths.

5 Much of the symbolism in these last plays of Shakespeare is obviously religious, though Shakespeare strives to disguise this. For D. G. James this is a weakness, since there is a clash between the symbolism and the 'realistic' form in which it is presented, which makes much of the

symbolism 'tawdry' and 'trivial'. One might object that the 'clash' is in James's failure to make the leap of imagination from verisimilitude to myth. See also the last chapter of *The Dream of Prospero* (Oxford, 1967) by the same author. For a fuller and totally sympathetic analysis of Shakespeare's myth, see Derek Traversi, *Shakespeare: The Last Phase* (London, 1954).

Index

Achilles, 102, 105
action, 24, 26, 28, 181, 202, 215, 252,
    255, 279, 280, 304, 320, 333, 335, 339,
    344, 345, 360, 361, 363, 365;
    definition, 17; unity of, 3, 18, 44
acts, scenic structure of, 44–5
Adler, Elkan N., 403n
admiratio, 135
Alcalá, University of, 8
El alcalde de Zalamea (by Lope), 322, 323
Alcázar (in Madrid), 5, 25, 214, 329, 330
Alemán, Mateo (1547–1620), 388n, 404n
allegory, 1, 15, 34, 87, 211, 212, 288,
    339, 340–5, 349, 354, 355, 356, 358,
    365
Alonso, Dámaso, 44, 49, 375n
Amezúa y Mayo, A. González de, 391n
Andromeda, 345, 346
anthropology, 15, 197, 340
Apollo, 35, 36, 37, 82, 93, 110, 337, 341
Aquinas, St Thomas, 85, 112
archetype, 16, 86, 87, 88, 94, 102, 339,
    345, 346, 348, 349, 354, 356, 364, 365,
    366
Aristotle, Aristotelianism, 51, 54, 134,
    135, 197, 210, 251, 336, 376n
arrogance, 297–301, 302, 303, 347
astrology, 108, 110, 122, 162
Aubrun, Charles, 34, 107, 117–18, 119,
    126, 373n, 383n, 384n, 408n
Auerbach, Erich, 86, 371n
Augustine, St, 78, 85, 111
Austria, Don John of, 316, 317, 408n
auto sacramental, 1, 6, 10, 42, 69, 82, 87,
    107, 112, 127, 211, 281, 288, 301, 334,
    339, 340–5, 349, 354, 355–9, 365

Bances Candamo, Francisco, 54, 134,
    145, 245–6, 312, 376n, 385n, 394n
Báñez, Domingo, 108, 109, 111–12, 127,
    128
baroque 13, 42, 43, 129, 348, 370n

Berens, Peter, 98, 107, 116–17, 382n,
    383n, 384n
Bergson, Henri, 135, 141, 146, 386n
body (contrasted with soul), 38, 39, 336,
    338, 350, 352, 355, 358
Boleyn, Anne, 25, 108, 250, 252, 285
Bouché-Leclercq, A., 383n
Brenan, Gerald, 15, 369n, 370n, 381n
Brereton, Geoffrey, 236, 394n
Briggs, W.D., 399n
Brown, Jonathan, 404n
El burlador de Sevilla, 4, 171, 183
Bywater, Ingram, 376n

Las cadenas del demonio, 96, 101
Calderón de la Barca, Pedro (1600–81)
    ART 195, 259, 260, 270, 331, 348, 360–3
    Christian dramatist, 198–9
    court dramatist, 9, 314, 320
    mathematical precision, 42–4, 255, 364
    output, 6
    treatment of history, 254–5, 273, 274,
        275, 280–2, 286, 292, 317, 325, 338
    LIFE 7–10, 42, 171–3, 313, 324, 365
    death, 10
    his association with actors, 8
    his 'secret marriage' 9, 171–3
    Knight of Santiago, 9, 313
    military service, 9, 42, 313, 324
    ordination to the priesthood, 9, 10, 173
    public scandal, 8
    social position & education, 8
    RELATIVES & FAMILY LIFE
    his brother Diego, 70–8 passim, 172
    his brother José, 70, 71, 147, 171, 172,
        182
    his father, Don Diego, 8, 10, 70, 71, 77,
        83, 172; (his will), 71, 72
    his illegitimate half-brother Francisco
        González, 72–9, passim, 83, 84, 172
    his nephew José 72, 172
    his mother, Doña Ana María de Henao,
        70, 73

his sister Dorotea, 70, 73, 74, 77, 78, 84, 93

his son Pedro José, 9, 10, 172–3

WORKS

El alcalde de Zalamea, 7, 42–50, 51, 55, 59, 74, 143, 149, 214, 320–5, 363

Los alimentos del hombre, 82–3

Amar despues de la muerte, 315–20

Amigo, amante y leal, 44

Andrómeda y Perseo, las fortunas de, 332, 339, 345–7, 349

Andrómeda y Perseo (auto), 345, 347

El año santo de Roma, 355

Apolo y Climene, 35, 36–40, 92, 93–4, 101, 150, 372n

Las armas de la hermosura, 57–65, 81, 312–15, 324

A secreto agravio, secreta venganza, 53, 194, 214

El astrólogo fingido, 150, 153–68, 183

Basta callar, 179

Los cabellos de Absalón, 74, 101

Casa con dos puertas mala es de guardar, 26, 143, 181

Celos aun del aire matan, 9

La cena de Baltasar, 366

La cisma de Ingalaterra, 25–6, 27, 35, 52, 100, 108, 250–82, 283, 285, 287, 363, 370n

La dama duende, 137, 141, 143–7, 148, 181

La devoción de la cruz, 19–21, 26, 73–4, 75–6, 77, 79, 82, 91, 177, 199–201, 348, 349, 363

El divino Orfeo, 342

Los dos amantes del cielo, 79

Eco y Narciso, 92–3, 101, 372–3n, 406n

En la vida, todo es verdad y todo mentira, 81–2

La estatua de Prometeo, 333–9, 344, 349, 350–4, 357, 358, 372n

El galán fantasma, 147–52, 214

La gran Cenobia, 100, 104, 108

Hado y divisa de Leonido y Marfisa, 98–9, 101, 104

La hija del aire, 35, 92, 93, 101, 113, 198, 405n

El hijo del sol Faetón, 17, 35–6, 82, 101, 347

Los hijos de la fortuna, 30

El jardín de Falerina, 9

El laberinto del mundo, 341, 342

El mágico prodigioso, 289, 293

El mayor encanto, Amor, 9

El mayor monstruo los celos, 101, 107, 108, 113, 114–29, 198, 208

El médico de su honra, 5, 7, 19, 27, 28–34, 53, 108, 175, 194, 214–35, 237, 241, 362

El monstruo de los jardines, 101–5

Nadie fíe su secreto, 179

Ni amor se libra de amor, 332–3

No hay cosa como callar, 179, 181–95, 199, 206, 214

No hay más fortuna que Dios, 127

La piel de Gedeón, 406n

El pintor de su deshonra, 27–8, 194, 202–12, 213, 237, 363, 370n

El pintor de su deshonra (auto), 211–12

El pleito matrimonial del Cuerpo y el Alma, 355

El postrer duelo de España, 173–80, 181, 214

El príncipe constante, 7, 8, 23, 59, 100, 108, 287, 288–311, 363, 364

La púrpura de la rosa, 9

Saber del mal y del bien, 242–6, 248, 288

El Sacro Parnaso, 341, 344

La segunda esposa y triunfar muriendo, 355

El sitio de Bredá, 154

Los tres afectos de amor, 97, 101

Las tres justicias en una, 17, 74, 75, 76–7, 79, 91, 201–2

Los tres mayores prodigios, 9

La vida es sueño, 4, 7, 15, 18–19, 21–2, 27, 29, 34, 42–4, 45, 52, 79, 81, 82, 84, 86, 88–91, 92, 96, 99, 101, 105, 107, 108, 109, 118–19, 128, 148, 169, 170, 188, 201, 346, 348, 349, 356, 363, 364, 365

La vida es sueño (auto), 87, 211, 349, 356–9

Calderón, Rodrigo, (Duke of Lerma's favourite), 246, 248

Calvinism, 111, 286, 287

Cameron Allen, Don, 383n

Campbell, Lily, 247

Caro Baroja, Julio, 395n, 403n

Casalduero, Joaquín, 42, 43, 54, 375n, 376n, 377n

El castigo sin venganza, 213–14

Castro, Américo, 54

catachresis, 135

Catalonia, Revolt of, 9, 42, 312–14, 324

catharsis, 78, 202, 210

Catherine of Aragon, 249, 250, 252

causality, 202, 216–18

cave setting, 334, 357

Cervantes Saavedra, Miguel de (1547–1616), 3, 23, 54, 290, 370n

Chance, 109, 113, 123–8 passim, 208, 223

characterisation, 16, 17, 24

characters, 3, 16, 344, 361, 362, 363;
  (rounded/type), 3, 16
Charles I of England, 283, 284–5, 286
Charles V, Emperor (1519–58), 173, 174,
  316
chivalry (*courtoisie*), 64, 138, 145–6, 147,
  183, 186, 304
Christian Dogma, 340–7 *passim*
Christianity, 83, 110, 209, 293, 295, 303,
  311, 315, 319, 357, 359
Cioffari, Vincenzo, 383n
civil war, 176, 214, 215, 229, 247, 324
civilization and barbarism, contrast
  between, 333, 334, 337, 347, 349
cloak-and-sword plays, 133, 138, 141,
  152, 153, 179, 181, 182, 186
Clymene, 36, 93, 94
Coello, Antonio, 54, 57, 64, 65, 314
Coliseo, 5, 6, 25, 330
comedia, 2, 3, 6, 69, 107, 211, 338, 344;
  de capa y espada, 133, 138, 141, 152,
  153, 179, 181, 182, 186; *de figurón*,
  133–4; *nueva*, 4, 7, 8, 23, 134; *de santo*,
  6, 69, 199, 288–9; *palaciega*, 6, 7,
  329–39, 344, 348; structure of, 2
comedy, 2, 105, 157, 181, 182, 183, 186,
  195; of humours, 133; of intrigue, 133,
  181, 336; of manners, 133, 185
Comparative Religion, 15, 340–7
conceit, 22, 23, 28, 129, 135, 159, 268,
  344
El conde de Sex, 54
Conde, Justina Ruiz de, 388n
confusión, 261, 268, 318
Constandse, Anton, 74, 78, 380n
conversos (Converted Jews), 319–20
Coriolanus, 57, 58
Corpus Christi, 1, 342, 344, 345, 349, 356
corral, 4–7, 64, 242, 329, 330
Cortés, Narciso Alonso, 379n
Cortina, Augusto, 375n, 381n
Cotarelo y Mori, Emilio, 71, 73, 172, 314,
  367n, 376n, 379n, 389n, 403n, 405n
court, 5, 241, 245, 314, 318, 320, 329,
  330, 332
courtly love, 38
Covarrubias, *see* Horozco y Covarrubias,
Crespo, Pedro, 321–2
Cruickshank, D.W., 392n
crusading wars, 69, 287, 289–90, 295,
  310
Cueva, Juan de la (1543–1610), 247
culteranismo, 13
Cupid (or Eros), 332, 333, 338, 346
Curtius, E.R., 390n

dama, 3, 335
Danaë, 91, 342, 345, 346
Davies, Godfrey, 399n
decir sin decir (to speak without telling),
  246, 248, 287, 312, 314, 315
decorum, 51, 53, 55, 135, 141, 143
dénouement, 2, 18, 29, 101, 181, 188, 217,
  246, 252, 254, 255, 275, 293, 333
desengaño (disillusionment), 10, 25, 107,
  118
destiny (*see also* fate) 34, 40, 82, 88, 94,
  96–106 *passim*, 107–13 *passim*, 117,
  118, 125, 127, 198, 305, 306, 310, 339,
  340, 347, 348, 349, 352, 354, 358
determinism (*see also* predestination), 107
Dionysius of Halicarnassus, 57, 58
Discord, 336, 342, 345, 350, 354
dishonour, 75, 77, 149, 167, 170, 176,
  177, 187–195 *passim*, 200, 206, 208,
  209, 211, 213, 215, 223, 226, 229, 232,
  233, 244, 245, 255, 277, 306
divination (*see also* prophecy), 27, 108,
  110
Don Quixote, 3, 23, 133, 134, 135, 141,
  169, 171
Dunn, P.N., 32, 44, 372n, 375n, 381n,
  404n
Durán, Manuel, 360

Echeverría, Roberto González, 360
Edwards, Gwynne, 381n
Eliade, Mircea, 15, 369n
Eliot, T.S., 16, 361, 369n
Elizabeth I, of England, 54, 250, 251, 252,
  281, 285, 286
Elliott, J.H., 318, 319, 404n
Engelbert, Manfred, 408n
entremés, 2, 6
Entwhistle, W.J., 400n
Epimetheus, 333
existence, purpose of, 95, 349, 354, 356,
  359, 360

Farinelli, Arturo, 370
fate (*see also* destiny), 82, 85, 88, 95,
  96–106 *passim*, 107–13, 114–29, 186,
  198, 202, 203, 208, 210, 222–3, 226,
  243, 262, 305, 306
fatherless son, 20, 69–85 *passim*, 86, 339,
  348, 349
favouritism, 242, 245, 246, 248
feminism, 63, 65, 136–7
Ferdinand, Prince of Portugal (1402–43),
  289, 290, 291, 292
Figueroa, Don Lope de, 320, 321

Fortune, 107, 127, 243, 245, 246, 294, 306, 346
free will, 75, 78, 79, 85, 99, 100, 105, 107, 109, 116, 117, 118, 119, 127, 198, 358, 359
Frye, Northrop, 16, 86, 369n, 371n, 408n
Fuenterrabía, siege of (1638), 182, 194

galán, 3
García Gómez, Ángel, 323, 324, 404n
Góngora, Luis de, 13, 348
Grace, 112, 117, 118, 345, 357, 358
gracioso, 4, 175, 178, 182, 203, 230, 245, 293, 307
Graves, Robert, 382n
Greek drama, 2, 197
Greek religion, 109, 340
Green, Otis H., 408n
Greer, Margaret Rich, 338, 404n, 405n, 407n
guilt, 52, 88, 89, 109, 128, 201, 202, 205, 208, 209, 210, 211, 212, 214, 222, 223, 253, 340, 345, 349, 350
Gulsoy, Y., 400n
Guzmán de Alfarache, 137

Hafter, Monroe A., 393n
Hamilton Fyfe, W., 376n
'happy ending', 52, 55, 101, 105, 140, 181–2, 183, 195, 245, 337, 338
Hartzenbusch, Juan, 33, 153, 322, 370n, 375n, 400n, 404n
Hegel, Georg, 235
Henry II of Castile (1369–79), 175, 215
Henry VIII (of England), 25, 108, 171, 249, 250–1, 279, 280, 281, 283, 285
Henry the Navigator, 290, 291
Herbold, Anthony, 395n
Hero, myth of, 345–7
Herrick, Marvin T., 385n
Herod, 114–29 *passim*
Hesse, Everett W., 384n
Hidalgo, Juan, 9
Hildner, David Jonathan, 368n
historical drama, 251–2, 312–25
history, as treated by Calderón, *see* Calderón, art; contemporary, 282, 290, 311, 320, 324–5, 332
Honig, Edwin, 147
honor calderoniano, 65, 197
honour, 20, 21, 30, 31, 32, 33, 36, 46, 59, 61, 62, 63, 64, 75, 76, 81, 82, 138, 141, 147, 149, 153–68, 173, 174, 175, 180, 181, 186, 188, 191, 195, 196, 209,

210, 213–37, 245, 248, 254, 276, 297–311, 315, 318, 321, 346, 363;
personal honour, 62, 176–9, 226;
public honour, 62, 176–9, 226, 233, 234
honour plays, 63, 194, 210, 237
Horozco y Covarrubias, Juan de, 99, 108, 382n
horoscope, 18, 27, 79, 84, 86–95 *passim*, 96–106 *passim*, 109, 113, 118, 124, 356, 357
Humanism, 329, 337, 338, 340–7, 357
Hume, Martin, 399n

imagery, 21–4, 26, 88, 94, 159, 194, 197, 202, 206, 243, 260, 262, 263, 265–8, 269, 274, 357, 363, 364, 365
imperfection (of life, of love, of world), 39–40, 94
irony, 128, 176–7, 203, 209, 219, 222, 223, 225, 259, 261, 263, 265, 267, 268, 271, 273, 299, 362, 363

James I of England, 284–5
James, D.G., 408–9n
Jarrett-Kerr, M., 400n
jealousy, 115–25, 143, 176, 181, 202, 206, 234
Jesuit drama, 288–9
Jones, C.A., 372n, 392n
Jones, R.O., 385n
judicial duel (trial by combat), 173–4, 176, 177, 180
Jung, Carl G., 345, 361
Jupiter (*see also* Zeus), 92, 332, 333, 342, 345, 346
justice, 196–212 *passim*, 244, 245, 278, 279, 318, 321, 323

Kayser, Wolfgang, 303, 400n
Kerr, Walter, 236, 237, 394n
Kierkegaard, Søren, 235
Knights, L.C., 371n, 408n
Krenkel, Max, 320, 321–2, 375n, 401n, 404n

Leech, Clifford, 235, 390n, 394n
Lerma, Duke of, 246, 247, 248
libretti (*see also* opera) 42, 69, 329, 331
lieto fine (*see* 'happy ending')
Lisbon, 42, 291, 295, 321, 324
literary criticism, principles of, 13–16, 24, 51, 54–5, 134, 361, 362
Livy, 57, 58, 60, 61

loa, 6, 331, 341, 342
Loftis, John, 395n
Lope de Vega, *see under* Vega Carpio,
    Lope Félix de,
love (spiritual or sensual) 38, 332, 336,
    346, 356, 358, 359
Luther, Martin, 25, 111

MacCallum, M.W., 377n
MacCurdy, R.R., 390n
Madrid, 5, 10, 154, 182, 241, 313, 314,
    316, 322, 330, 331
Maraniss, James E., 369n
María, Infanta of Spain, 283–6 *passim*
Mariamne, 114, 115
Mártir Rizo, Juan Pablo de, 385n
Mary I of England, 250, 251, 286
May, T.E., 376n
Medusa, 342, 345, 346
Menéndez Pelayo, Marcelino, 14, 25, 51,
    65, 116, 119, 340, 370n, 372n, 406n
Meredith, George, 135, 136, 141
metaphor, 22, 23, 25–41 *passim*, 51, 87,
    129, 207, 211, 259, 260, 363
metaphysics, 336, 344
metres, 2, 3
Los milagros del desprecio, 137
Minerva, 334, 335, 338, 346, 350
Mira de Amescua, Antonio
    (1574/7–1644), 246
Moir, Duncan, 134, 367n, 394n
Molina, Luis de, 108, 109, 111–12, 127
Molinism, 112, 128, 408n
monarch, role of, 224–9, 241–9, 250–82
    passim, 308, 330, 331
Moreto y Cabaña, Agustín (1618–69), 6,
    137
moriscos, 315–20
mothers (role of), 16, 17, 138
Münster, Treaty of, 287, 313
music dramas, *see* opera,
myth, mythology, 15, 16, 34, 35, 51, 69,
    70, 79, 84, 86, 87, 89, 91, 92, 94, 95,
    102, 133, 329–39 *passim*, 340–7,
    348–50, 364–6
mythological plays, 34, 69, 88, 199, 329,
    332, 333, 336, 338, 339, 344, 345, 349,
    354

Narcissus, 92
Netherlands, Revolt of the, 286–7
neo-Aristotelianism, 2, 126, 135, 181,
    197, 234
neo-classicism, 2, 13, 51, 364
Neoplatonism, 38, 336, 337

Neumeister, Sebastian, 332, 333, 405n,
    407n
Nicoll, Allardyce, 54
Nietzsche, Friedrich, 235

Oedipus, 91
Oedipus complex, 72, 78
Olivares, Count-Duke, 246, 247, 284, 313,
    314, 316, 403n
omen, 27, 100, 108, 110, 116, 117, 216,
    217, 259
opera, 6, 9, 10, 69, 329, 330, 331, 366
Oppenheimer, Max, 167, 168, 387n
oracles, 108, 110, 345
Orgel, Stephen, 408n
Original Sin, 211, 212, 345
Orpheus, 329, 340, 342
Ovid, 35, 36, 37, 102, 341, 373n

Palacio del Retiro, 5, 9, 330, 331
Pallas, 337, 338
Pandora, 333, 350
Paravicino, Fray Hortensio, 8
Paris, Pierre, 40, 374n
Parker, J.H., 400n
patent of nobility (*ejecutoria*), 46, 70
patricians, 61, 62, 63
Paul, St, 111, 341
Paz y Melia, A., 388n
Pellicer de Tovar, José, 404n
Pérez de Montalbán, Juan, 57, 314,
    403n
Pérez de Moya, Juan, 373n, 374n
Pérez Pastor, Cristóbal, 379n, 388n
Peribáñez, 59, 149, 248
Peristiany, J.S., 389n
Perseus, 92, 342, 345, 346, 347
Persons (or Parsons), Robert, 396n
Peter I of Castile (1350–69), 175, 214,
    215, 227, 241
Petrarch, 268
Pfandl, Ludwig, 259, 397n
Phaethon, 93, 341
Philip II (1556–98), 42, 214, 241, 246,
    247, 286, 287, 316, 320, 321, 322, 325
Philip III (1598–1621), 246, 248, 284
Philip IV (1621–65), 5, 9, 54, 214, 246,
    247, 283, 284, 313, 329, 405n, 408n
philosophy, 38, 79, 94, 95, 245, 289, 336,
    339, 344, 348, 359, 361, 362;
    Scholastic, 49, 197
plot, 3, 17, 18, 24, 124, 125, 126, 181,
    187, 195, 197, 198, 204, 222, 254, 312,
    320, 348, 365; definition, 17; sub-plot,
    3, 18, 167; unity of, 3, 124

plot-construction, 193, 216–17, 295, 362–3, 364
Plutarch, 57, 58, 60
poetic justice, 51–5 *passim*, 58, 109, 146, 167, 201, 205, 209, 251
politics, 15, 69, 70, 241–311, 312, 332, 334
Portuguese Succession, Wars of the, 42, 214, 247, 320, 324–5
predestination, predetermination, 78, 79, 85, 100, 108, 111, 117, 357
pride (*see also* arrogance), 109, 262–5, 300
prisoner, 38, 346, 348, 359, 365
prisoners of war, 290, 296, 307
El privilegio de las mujeres, 57, 64, 65, 312, 313–14
Profeti, M.G., 403n
Prometheus, 333, 336, 339, 347, 349, 350
prophecies, fulfilment of, 34, 90, 92, 96–106, 118–19, 123
prophecy (*see also* divination), 27, 34, 39, 91, 93, 95, 96–106 *passim*, 107, 109, 110, 112, 116, 123, 252–3, 262, 263, 270, 344–5, 349
Providence, 105, 109, 110, 111, 127, 275
Psyche, 332, 333
psychology, 15, 16
pundonor (code of honour), *see* honour,

Quevedo, Francisco de, 20, 38, 403n
Quirós, Padre Pedro de, 401n

Rahner, Karl, 383n, 385n
rationalism, 15, 364
Read, Conyers, 396n
realism, 13, 26, 44, 49, 86, 365
reality (material & artistic) 40, 95, 159, 168, 207, 209, 247, 329, 344, 348
reason & passion, conflict between, 254, 256, 258–9, 260, 270, 281, 334, 336, 338, 350, 351
rebellious son/tyrannical father (father–son conflict), 69–85 *passim*, 90–1, 95, 201, 348, 349, 356
Reconquest, 289, 290
Reichenberger, A.G., 400n
Reformation, 1, 111, 250, 251, 285, 290
refundición, 6, 7, 323, 325
religion, 69, 70, 198, 250–82 *passim*, 288–31, 312, 319, 334, 339, 341, 359
religious freedom, 283–7, 292
religious plays (*see also comedias de santo*), 288–9

Renaissance, 1, 51, 135, 197, 329, 336, 337, 338, 339, 340, 347
responsibility, 78, 82, 107–13 *passim*, 114–29 *passim*, 198, 200, 201, 202, 203, 206, 253, 260, 270, 281, 308; diffused, 201, 209, 222
Ribadeneyra, Pedro de, 252–4, 275, 280, 281, 283, 380n, 396n, 397n, 398n, 399n
Rico, Francisco, 404n
Ríos, Blanca de los, 27, 86, 87, 95, 114, 355, 371n, 380n
Riquer, Martín de, 370n, 381n
Rishton, Edward, 252, 396n
Rogers, D., 376n
Rojas Zorrilla, Francisco, 55
Rome, 2, 57, 58, 60, 61, 62, 63, 81, 112
Rossiter, A.P., 398n

Sage, Jack, 389n, 401n, 402n, 404n
Salamanca, University of, 8, 112
Salomon, Noel, 395n
Sanders, Nicholas, 252, 254, 396n
Sandoval, Fray Prudencio de, 173–4, 388n
Saturn, 334, 335
Sauvage, Micheline, 381n, 391n
scenes, division into, 44–5
schism from Rome, English, 250–4 *passim*, 280, 285, 286
scholasticism, 256, 336
Schons, Dorothy, 380n
Schreck, Johanna, 386n
scientia media, 112, 128
Scripture, 6, 340–4
Sears, Helen L., 382n
Sebastian, King, of Portugal, 53, 214, 247, 403n
secrecy, 138, 143, 147, 152, 153–95 *passim*, 204, 213, 214, 224
secret marriages, 9, 10, 169–80
Semiramis, 35, 93
Shakespeare, William, 16, 58, 59, 105, 247, 251, 273, 364–6 *passim*
Shergold, N.D., 367n, 394n, 404n
Sidney, Sir Philip, 235, 280
Sixtus V, 99, 108
Sloman, A.E., 32, 45, 57, 59, 62, 372n, 375n, 392n, 399n, 400n
social classes, 5, 19, 20, 44, 45, 46, 48, 59, 60, 62, 149, 183, 248, 307, 316, 321, 329, 330
social conflict, 46, 214
social relationships, 63, 133, 169, 193, 332

social status, 176
sociology, 16, 197
Sotomayor, Fray Antonio de, 318
soul (spirit), 16, 38, 39, 336, 338, 350,
   351, 352, 355
spirit (*see also* soul), 40, 336, 350, 351
Spitzer Leo, 303, 401n, 402n
Stein, Louise K., 404n
Steiner, G., 400n
Stoics, 110, 118
structure (artistic/mathematical), 42–4,
   49, 122–3, 133, 202, 216–17, 230, 237,
   242–3, 255, 292, 297, 339, 363
styles, high, 23, 159; Three, 53
suspension of disbelief, 14, 252
symbol, symbolism, 1, 15, 16, 25–41
   passim, 51, 79, 86, 87, 88, 95, 124,
   133, 143, 193, 194, 200, 202, 206–7,
   211, 226, 259, 281, 288, 289, 295, 302,
   306, 310, 334–66 *passim*; fire, 193–4,
   206; light, 348–59 *passim*; prison, 27,
   29, 34–5, 37, 43, 84, 86–95, 96, 102,
   336, 339, 348–59 *passim*; sun, 34,
   35–40 *passim*, 263, 265, 268, 269, 335,
   352; tower, 37, 43, 86–95, 102, 349,
   350
symmetry, 42, 88, 129, 245, 269
Sypher, Wylie, 385n, 386n
Szarota, Elida Maria, 294, 399n, 400n,
   402n

Tarsis, Juan de, *see* Villamediana
Téllez, Fray Gabriel (Tirso de Molina)
   (1580?–1648) 4, 6, 19, 44, 69, 74, 114,
   135, 136, 138, 139–40, 141, 171, 182,
   183, 241, 384n
theatres, palace, 5, 64, 242, 283, 329,
   330; Coliseo, 5, 6, 25, 330; *salón de
   teatro*, 5, 25, 329, 330
theatres, public (*corrales*), 4–7, 64, 242,
   329, 330
theme, 21, 22, 24, 168, 171, 179, 195,
   242, 243, 245, 252, 276, 279, 289, 303,
   304, 320, 325, 329, 337, 338, 339, 341,
   342, 344, 348, 350, 353, 356, 357, 361,
   363, 364, 365; definition, 17; primacy
   of, 17; unity of, 3, 19, 21
Theologians, Council of, 286–7
theology, 95, 198, 252, 334, 343, 344,
   345
Thirty Years War, 182, 287, 290, 313
Tirso de Molina, *see* Téllez, Fray Gabriel
tone, 183, 251, 303
Torres y Sandoval, Don Alonso de, 322
tragedy, 2, 52, 58, 59, 78, 105–6, 125,

126, 157, 181, 182, 183, 194, 195,
   196–212 *passim*, ch 17, 244, 245, 255,
   269, 270, 273, 280, 281, 292–3, 316,
   363, 365; theory, 198–9, 200, 201, 205,
   210, 235–7
tragicomedy, 2, 105
Traversi, Derek, 409n
Trent, Council of, 111, 118, 170, 173,
   174, 286, 287, 344
Trojan War, 102–5 *passim*
truth, historical, 51–2, 251, 252, 312, 322
truth, poetic, 51–2, 54, 251, 280, 312

unity, 3, 18, 19, 21, 44, 51, 124, 251; of
   action, 3, 18, 44; of construction, 18,
   51; of place, 3, 44; of plot, 3, 124; of
   theme, 3, 18, 19, 21; of time, 3; of
   tone, 251
universality, 14, 35, 40, 79, 87, 88, 89,
   95, 245, 251, 288, 331, 339, 349, 361,
   364
unrealism, 16, 86, 87, 256, 348
Urban, W.M., 371n

Valbuena Briones, Ángel, 375n, 383n,
   400n
Valbuena Prat, Ángel, 13, 74, 348, 356,
   406n
Valladolid, 112, 173
Varey, John, 330–2, 394n, 404n
Vega Carpio, Lope Félix de (1562–1635),
   2–9 *passim*, 19, 35, 44, 55, 69, 107,
   134, 137, 138–9, 141, 149, 182, 213,
   241, 247, 248, 292, 322, 323, 325,
   393n
vengeance, 59, 62, 63, 78, 81, 188,
   189–90, 191, 209, 213, 214, 219, 220,
   224, 226, 308, 312, 315, 317, 318,
   346
verisimilitude, 13, 54, 55
victim (of fate), 39, 104, 203
Villamediana, Conde de, 35, 373n
Vitoria, Fray Baltasar de, 340, 342, 373n
vocation, 101–5 *passim*
Vorgrimler, Herbert, 383n, 385n
Vosters, S.A., 387n

Wardropper, Bruce, 28, 32, 370n, 371n,
   372n, 400n
Watson, Anthony, 247, 392n, 393n,
   394n
Whitaker, Shirley B., 387n
wife-murder, 53, 65, 75, 76, 157, 176,
   194, 202, 204, 209, 213, 223, 229, 234,
   362

Will, 128, 258, 261, 338
Wilson, E.M., 19, 28, 234, 367n, 370n, 371n, 376n, 384n, 389n, 390n, 391n, 393–4n, 400n, 401n
Wilson, Margaret, 318, 367n, 403n
Wit, 135; of the unexpected, 138
Wolsey, Cardinal, 52, 171, 250
women, rôle in drama, 59, 63, 138, 155, 185, 304, 314, 345–6; social position, 59, 62, 63, 64, 136–8, 155, 179–80, 185; special status, 63, 64, 314; victory over vengeance, 65

Xavier, St Francis, 323, 324

Zeus (*see also* Jupiter), 109, 110, 333